T0354347

The Journey of
Little Hans

Rejected by His Mother, Subjugated by His Family

JOHN FRIESEN

THE JOURNEY OF LITTLE HANS
REJECTED BY HIS MOTHER, SUBJUGATED BY HIS FAMILY

iUniverse books may be ordered through booksellers or by contacting:

iUniverse
1663 Liberty Drive
Bloomington, IN 47403
www.iuniverse.com
1-800-Authors (1-800-288-4677)

ISBN: 978-1-5320-5658-1 (sc)
ISBN: 978-1-5320-5659-8 (e)

Print information available on the last page.

iUniverse rev. date: 12/19/2018

CHAPTER 1

The Prussian German Exodus East

July 22, 1763. Following the conclusion of the Seven Years War and the death of her husband Peter III, German-born Russian Empress Catherine the Great openly proclaims that all Mennonite farmers and tradesmen, along with their families living in Germany are graciously welcome to settle within her newly expanding Russian Empire. Her declaration initiated a new chapter in history. Thereafter, German Mennonites from the old country began immigrating in flocks to the southern part of modern-day Ukraine, where the land was not only fruitful, but also free from conflict, religious persecution, military conscription, and other hardships that persisted in their native Prussia (Germany) during the 1700's. The Mennonites' faith alone prohibited them from bearing arms, something that played a significant role in their exodus east in search of their own "Lebensraum" (living space).

Convinced that agriculture was the pillar of the Russian economy, Catherine the Great necessitated diligent and skilled farmers to settle the region. Mennonites from abroad perfectly met all of these requirements. In 1789, the "1st Wave" of Mennonites arrived to colonize and prosperously cultivate the land at Chortitza, Molotschna within Catherine the Great's newly annexed region of the Russian Empire. The barren soil bore fruits, barley, wheat and various other crops. Hungry mouths became nourished. It was then only a matter of time before this ambitious, diligent, closely knit, and family-oriented Mennonite community flourished. Despite

1

living in reclusion and peace, these settlers, along with the "2nd wave" of Prussian Germans, some non-Mennonite, amassed great wealth, at times through reaping the benefits of trade with their old country. Finally possessing a region to themselves afforded these Germans the privilege of living in placated villages where homes and picket fences were freshly christened every spring with an immaculate new coating of white wash that was extracted from lime pits.

Another wave of Mennonite and non-Mennonite Prussian Germans, many of much greater opulence than those who came to the initial settlement, eventually migrated east, settling within modern day Zaporozhe Oblast (province), Ukraine, a region located east of the Molochnaya River. By 1835, it is believed that as many as 1,200 families in total settled along the Molochnaya river - Mennonites on the east bank, and non-Mennonite Germans, including a family called Tzitzer, on the west bank. This Tzitzer family of great wealth migrated east a few decades following Catherine the Great's invitation. During the ensuing century, this industrious family's mass of riches, comprised of numerous enterprises and estates, which included vast hectares of land, a successful glass factory, and a mansion with servants, grew. The acquired veneration from their and surrounding communities complimented the Tzitzer's lavish lifestyle. Over a hundred years of prosperity followed before the Communists ultimately succeeded in overthrowing the old guard in 1917.

As a part of Tzitzer (little Hans' paternal lineage) tradition, every girl in the family was entitled to an endowment of 20,000 golden rubles - valued to be worth approximately two million dollars during the 1800's - when a girl reached the age of 17. During this time in Russia, people worked for 5 cents or "kopeks" a day, so a mere ten golden rubles equated to a year's worth of salary. 20,000 golden rubles could have sustained generation upon generation upon generation.... Louise Tzitzer (little Hans' paternal grandmother), the oldest of 8 siblings, turned 17 before the outbreak of the Russian Revolution of 1917, a revolt that led the Reds to ultimately confiscate all of the Tzitzer family's wealth, including their lands, estates, businesses, and mansion. But despite all of these "expropriations", Louise concealed and retained her 20,000-golden ruble endowment.

Fortunately, Louise received her dowry before the revolution, unlike the rest of her siblings who had to flee with relatively nothing to their names as the Tzitzer family's lives slowly capsized into chaos. Them, along with countless others, were forced to flee further south with nothing more than whatever they could load onto their horse-drawn buggies. During the revolution, the Tzitzer family became completely torn apart in their search for refuge and security. Whatever happened to the remainder of the family's heirloom of golden rubles remained a mystery. If they were buried for safe-keeping or carried along with the rest of the family's belongings, or even seized by the Communists, no one knows for sure.

CHAPTER 2

The Red Revolution & German Invasion

By the time the Red October Revolution of 1917 completely plagued most of the Russian Empire, not much of the Czar's dynasty remained. The entire nation fell into despair, anarchy, and hunger. Despite the empire's tribulation, Louise Tzitzer, a noble woman of non-Mennonite descent, for the time being, managed to live a life of luxury with her Mennonite husband, Cornelius "Corny" Friesen Sr. At this juncture in history, the Whites still controlled the majority of south-western Russia (modern-day Ukraine), where Louise and Corny Sr. safe-guarded her 20,000-golden Russian ruble endowment.

Some ancestors believe that these rubles, now estimated to be worth over tens of millions of dollars, were ultimately buried, and may possibly still be buried to this day. Yet, others believe that Louise passed along her chest of rubles onto her first-born son, **Cornelius** (Jr.) Friesen. A few years following the birth of Cornelius, a Mennonite couple named Gossen, with Gerhard and Maria (little Hans' maternal grandmother), brought **Maria** (and eventually Gerhard Jr.) into the world. By the time the 2nd World War broke out, the young, beautiful, brown-haired **Maria** (Jr.) Gossen, 17, and the stout, broad-chested **Cornelius** (Jr.) Friesen, 19, conceived a boy named Johannes Friesen, or "little Hans", during the initial stages of the Second World War. To this day, no one is certain whether Maria and

Cornelius were married at the time of the possibly undesired pregnancy, but nevertheless, time showed that Hans was just as unwanted as the war that completely tore the family and Russian Empire apart and to pieces.

Prior to WWI and the Red Revolution, the Goosen's, were a well to do family; however, once the first breed of Bolsheviks and non-aligned brigands marauded and plundered the country during the revolution, the Goosen's became hunted. Bandit-like Bolsheviks ultimately stormed their residence, lining the entire family up against a wall prepared to execute them all - women and children included – yet only until, one of the bandits stepped directly in front of the executioner armed with a rifle and declared to his gang of vigilantes,

"You'll have to kill me first, before you kill them!"

This heroic Red Bolshevik bandit once worked for the Goosen family and had fond memories of serving them. The Goosen's hired help not only worked for the family, but also ate at the family table, making each and every servant feel like a valued member of the Goosen family - an actuality that ultimately led the Goosen's to be spared and survive the Red Revolution and WWI.

Decades later, in 1941, Germans from the old country once again reasserted their dominance over this very same, yet communist-controlled region. However, by 1944, the tides turned when the Russians re-imposed their reign. A brutal and merciless conflict ultimately forced the then, 4-year-old Mennonite boy "little" Hans, along with his family and neighbours, to stave off death amongst the floundering eastern meadows of carnage by travelling westward in the direction of the old country, along side not only fellow "easternized" Germans, or self-named "Russaki", but also the retreating German army.

CHAPTER 3

Little Hans

Johannes, "little Hans", Friesen was born to Cornelius and Maria in 1940 in Fürstenwerder, a village made up of approximately twenty farms located about 100 Km south of the initial Chortitza colony. When the 2nd World War commenced, Hans' father, "Corny", was conscripted into the Russian forces after the long-standing Mennonites' "special status" exemption from military service was repealed. Hans' father was initially deployed to the front in Finland, even though he could barely speak much Russian at the time. Consequently, Hans and his mother were left behind with her family as Maria refused support from Cornelius' family. As WWII progressed, and Nazi Germany initiated "Operation Barbarossa", Hans' father Cornelius was deployed into the heart of Russia against his very own German brethren after the Deutsche Wehrmacht-led Nazi forces viciously sought to conquer Soviet soil.

Cornelius ultimately ended up in the captivity of the German Army during a horrendous battle. Upon discovery of Cornelius' Germanic heritage, the Nazi army compelled him to switch sides and join the Deutsche Wehrmacht (army), the hated adversary of the Red Army, with whom Cornelius finished out the war in Germany as a truck driver. Yet, before Cornelius switched sides and joined the Germans, he was granted furlough, affording him the opportunity to visit his son and Hans' mother, Maria. On this occasion, Cornelius pleaded with Maria, his "wife",

"Please take Hans and go live with my family. That's where he belongs. Both of our families want this and you know that it's the right thing to do."

The young, snappy, and somewhat enigmatic Maria furiously responded,

"No!! He'll stay with me and my family! I don't care what you, your family, or even my own family wants!! Nobody cares that I didn't even want this little brat in the first place!! You forced him upon me!! I don't give a damn about what someone like you has to say!!!"

It was customary amongst the "Russian"-German community for child and mother to reside with the father's family. But Maria had no interest in upholding old traditions; however, little Hans' 13-year-old "traditionist", Uncle Jacob had other ideas. So, one day, allegedly under the directive of Hans' father, Cornelius' younger brother Jacob snuck into Maria's family home and kidnapped the eight-month-old little Hans, before bringing him to Cornelius' family home where little Hans "belonged". Maria was left with no other choice but to begrudgingly move in with Cornelius' and Uncle Jacob's family, even though she resented not only them, but also her very own son even more so because of it. Feisty Maria's anger, though, didn't stop with them. She even harboured bitterness towards her very own family, especially her mother, who told her daughter Maria,

"You may not like this, but you and Hansi belong at Cornelius' home with his family. It's for your own good."

Such a "bold" statement left young Maria absolutely infuriated. Hans, resultantly, became the one punished during the next four years of his life, a period in which Mother mercilessly beat and emotionally tormented poor little Hans without an ounce of remorse. Acts of enraged and incensed brutality towards him was seemingly Maria's only means to release all of her vent-up antipathy and fury, and find "salvation", almost as if she were evoking revenge upon little Hans for her very own circumstances. Merely longing for love and acceptance, little Hans constantly sought out Maria's cherished parents' home, little Hans' first home, a place, not so coincidently where his mother no longer resided. So, in an act of desperation and defiance, little Hans constantly ventured out in search of his loving maternal grandparents and Uncle Gerhard, Maria's compassionate and warm brother whose life took a tragic turn for the worst in Poland years later when he was burned alive in a barn by partisans near the conclusion of WWII while predominantly Mennonite Germans made their exodus west out of the USSR, attempting to evade reprisals from the advancing Russian Red Army.

Yet, before the war hit home, little Hans began fleeing to his maternal grandparents' house almost every morning after Mother left for work. Hans embarked on a daily journey to his comforting safe haven, all alone - a regular adventure that brought him to his place of solitude. His maternal grandparents' home was not only little Hans' birth house, but also a place where he felt protected from his wicked mother while pleasantly removed from his apathetic and seemingly unresponsive paternal family.

Such a sense of protection, however, only lasted until Mother stopped by her parents' in the evenings, following her shift as a town clerk at the office of the magistrate, to bring little Hans to Corny's family home, sometimes even when he was already fast asleep. Though, Mother's intentions had little to do with motherly intuition, or the fact that she missed and loved little Hans, but rather more to do with venting her frustration and misery by punishing him. Maria (Mother) evidently felt necessity to take out her wrath on little Hans, perhaps as a result of the fact that she was forced into not only living at Corny's family house with his family, but also seemingly having little Hans in the first place.

As Maria walked into the kitchen of her family home, Uncle Gerhard, Maria's younger brother, out of love for his treasured nephew, said to his sister,

"Let me carry Hansi home. The little guy is already peacefully sleeping away in your bedroom."

However, Mother had other ideas, along with no compassion.

"No! This doesn't concern you!"

Correspondingly, she forcibly woke up the tranquilly sleeping little Hans with a wack across the head, marching him back "home" in his bare feet while she beat him from behind with a stick that she broke off from a bush along the way. Wherever the stick happened to smack down upon little Hans was of no concern to Mother, just as long as she caught her "target", which at times was little Hans' head, and anywhere else that the stick happened to land. Uncle Gerhard attempted to compassionately intervene, yet to no avail. To this day, Hans can still feel the pain that his mother's animosity and vengeance inflicted upon him. Her justification for such inhumane treatment was always,

"He must learn to stay at home."

Mother had the mentality of a hardened-up war veteran, something that she conveyed through her merciless behaviour. Not even little Hans' paternal grandfather could protect little Hans, as he was unfortunately taken away by the authorities before Hans was even born, just to never return again. If he were immediately executed or lived out the rest of his days toiling away in a Russian work camp (Gulag) in Siberia – the family will never know. Little Hans' maternal grandfather also wasn't spared. One night, Soviet officials stopped by the family home and led him away; though unlike Hans' paternal grandfather, Little Hans' maternal grandfather was ultimately released. When Hans' maternal grandfather came back home after a year away from the homestead, Grandfather's loyal cow and dog just couldn't stop lovingly licking him upon his return. The cow immensely missed her best friend so much after the dreaded NKVD took her master away that the two of them became inseparable for days. Ethnic Germans were familiar targets and foes of the Soviet government, who seemingly took pleasure in sending Russian Germans to brutal work camps for suspected collaboration with their brethren to the west, or in most cases, as a pre-emptive measure to deter any subversive activities prior to the anticipated German invasion in 1941.

Even though little Hans' paternal grandmother, Louise Friesen (Tzitzer), was never escorted away, a true bond between her and little Hans never formed. To Hans' recollection, she was too busy caring for Hans' little sister Wanda, who was born in 1943, three years after little Hans came into the world. As far as Hans can recall, Louise, Cornelius' mother, showed little interest in him. And perhaps it was this neglect that led little Hans to become not only so determined and daring, but also so stubborn and obstinate. Nothing dissuaded him from partaking in his daily adventure of travelling by foot across town to his maternal grandparents' beloved home.

During these little escapades, every now and then, little Hans stumbled his way into a rabbit's hole. Little Hans absolutely loved entering the trenches in which rabbits were bred by slipping his way in underneath a fence. But fence or no fence, playing with and cuddling these rabbits was always a foregone conclusion and divine necessity for little Hans. Whenever his ensuing attempts to leave the rabbits' quarters failed, little Hans made the best of the situation by lulling himself to sleep inside of the rabbit hole. When the owners eventually came outside to offer the rabbits twigs to gnaw on and grass as forage, the rabbits' breeders discovered nothing other than a boy sleeping amongst their rabbits, sometimes right on top of their food. The rabbits though were very accepting of their guest, and happily welcomed him into their humble and confined abode within their fenced-in 2 X 2 X 1-metre-deep, manually dug out by the rabbits' owners "rabbit "hole". But they weren't the only ones digging up the ground.

The mother rabbits also burrowed holes within the confines of their protective captivity nest in order to have a place to hide their babies from predators, just to subsequently create a small mound over these babies' nest to mark exactly where their offspring were buried. From feeding to feeding, the mother rabbits uncovered and reburied their young. Whenever little Hans bore witness to such loving acts of kindness, he discovered that the animals were being better fostered by their mothers than he was. And perhaps that explains why he stopped in at foreign houses along the way to his maternal grandparents' place, even if there weren't a child there to play with, just looking for love, affection, and attention – simply whatever others could offer that little Hans' mother couldn't. The entire village eventually became quite acquainted with him, especially whenever they offered the curly, blond-haired, blue-eyed little Hans a little food before he continued along on his way. Many even began treating him as if he were one of their own.

Little Hans' curiosity well complimented his outgoing and extroverted ways. No matter if he were alone, or with fellow Germans, or even amongst a group of complete strangers, little Hans never showed signs of bashfulness. Not even the "gypsies" could scare him away. He simply had absolutely no qualms about approaching these darker complexioned, foreign wanderers from travelling caravans. Once a year, processions of nomadic, "homeless" gypsies appeared in town on their wooden wagons in search of food and whatever else could keep them sustained and engaged. These nomadic gypsies merely desired the daily necessities of life while appreciating whatever they received. Surviving as drifting vagabonds, they were in constant search of something to earn, or perhaps, on the rare occasion, even steal or pillage. Such a lifestyle was apparently "engrained in their blood". But neither little Hans nor the Germans living in the villages were bothered by that or them one bit for that matter. These gypsies brought the "spice of life" to town and were more than capable of shedding sweat along with their derogatory reputation by earning an honest living by repairing wagons, shoeing horses, telling fortunes, entertaining people by playing instruments such as guitars, harmonicas, accordions, trumpets…, or even carrying out the duties of a blacksmith. And despite what the locals or uncles said about them, they were definitely not lazy. These "gypsies" (Sinti and Roma) were simply after some nourishment and work to keep them occupied. They laboured and toiled in order to keep a roof over their head, just like everybody else.

During the war, these visiting gypsies were graciously welcomed by the remaining towns' people since most of the able-bodied men were off fighting in combat. Hence, women, young and old, had to take on many of the "masculine chores" in order to feed not only themselves, but also the children and the elderly. So, whenever the gypsies reared their exotic heads into town, these women were very appreciative, especially whenever they were offered a helping hand and pleasant distraction. Fortunes were told for a loaf of bread, a few eggs, or a quart of milk, items which theses gypsies sometimes secured by spitting on just so no one would feel too enticed to take a "delicious" bite or swig out of their wages. But some gypsies had a darker side. This sort occasionally abducted healthy babies with the intent of offloading them unto desperate couples who either couldn't have children or lost a child during birth.

Hence, when little Hans suddenly went missing one day, thoughts of such barters seeped into the Friesen and Goosen families' heads. Uncle Jacob, Uncle Henry, and Oma, the noble Louise, immediately went storming from house to house throughout the night enquiring,

"Have you seen little Hans!?!? We can't find him anywhere!!! We've looked everywhere!"

The residents at a few of the brick with a stuccoed faced Fürstenwerder homes informed them,

"We saw little Hans playing with the gypsies!"

Yet, when the Friesens and Goosens approached the site of the gypsies' caravan, they noticed that the caravan had fled town! Uncle Jacob immediately hollered,

"They must have kidnapped Hansi!!"

Oma Louise lamented,

"Ohhhh nein!!!! They're gonna sell him off!!! Henry, grab the horse and go get'em!! Go catch those gypsies and poor little Hans!!!"

Hans' Uncle Henry, the blond, handsome and "Aryan-like" younger teenage brother of Hans' father immediately mounted onto his horse and followed the gypsies' wagon wheel tracks into the next town. Twelve kilometres later, he located little Hans surrounded by a horde of gypsies in the distance! Storming on his horse in the direction of his little nephew, Uncle Henry knew that he had to save him before it was too late! Though, when Uncle Henry zoned in on little Hans and the gypsies' caravan, he realized that it was nothing more than a false alarm, or at least to little Hans, who was there happily playing with a pack of gypsy kids without a care in the world.

CHAPTER 4

Tide Turns - War Hits Home

Between 1941 and 1944, life in Hans' German Army-occupied village proceeded peacefully as the grunt of war and fighting remained further east, or at least for the time being. Hans' father, after joining the German Army, made sporadic visits west, one in which he helped conceive little Hans' aforementioned sister Wanda. Little Wanda, luckily enough, experienced a more sheltered life as a baby than little Hans did. Because in 1941, before Wanda's birth, when little Hans was still unable to even walk, he first-hand experienced the German Nazi military machine-led onslaught on the Soviet Empire when "Operation Barbarossa" commenced, forcing the Russians to start evacuating all of their Germanic civilians by train in an attempt to transport them to Siberia, away from their invading brethren. Yet, when the initial German air raid on Fürstenwerder was launched, little Hans and his mother had yet to board the train, leaving them directly in arms' and harms' way! As little Hans lied on the ground upon a blanket, his mother made a run for it, along with the rest of her Mennonite compatriots! As bombs cascaded down along the railway lines, blasts of artillery roared across the village! Earth trembled and soared as the German Army shelled the railroad tracks in an attempt to cut off the Russians' lines of transportation. The citizens of Fürstenwerder panicked and scattered, seeking safety and refuge from and amongst the utter chaos!

When the dust, soil, and dirt finally settled, the German army had taken occupation of the village. Families immediately set out in search of their loved ones, assuming the worst. Everyone scoured the bombarded area, but little Hans was nowhere to be seen. Townspeople began digging through upheaved soil that was sent skywards by the exploding shells in hope of discovering a body, or perhaps merely body parts. Citizens of the village openly wondered in bewilderment,

"Just how could Germans attack their own brothers!?! Even women and babies!! Their own blood!!"

But Uncle Henry remained positive when it came to finding his nephew, telling everyone,

"Just keep digging and digging away! We'll find him! We'll find the little guy!"

Thoughts of anger, despair, and even revenge initially pervaded the family's minds, until all of sudden a frantic, yet slightly somber voice bellowed,

"We found Hansi under a pile of dirt within a crater!! He's wrapped in a blanket! He's not moving!! Come quickly!! Come now!!"

Little Hans lied there, completely at peace, and luckily enough, still in one piece. Looking down at little Hans while a few townspeople entered the crater to lift him out, Uncle Henry somberly pondered to himself,

"Is he dead?"

Thoughts of "we're too late" loomed in everyone's head. Though, after a second glance, Uncle Gerhart happily realized and announced,

"He's just sleeping!! He's fast asleep!!"

Uncle Henry, who sadly died in '45 in Prague, while serving in the German SS during the concluding days of WWII, joyously whispered to himself,

"That's definitely, typical little Hans!!"

He apparently slept through the entire ordeal and knew nothing of the chaos and bombings that surrounded him. Little Hans could essentially sleep through just about everything and anything, including thunderous and ear-splitting shelling, a trait that stayed with him throughout his entire life. Afterwards, the families headed home, while the vast majority of the German Wehrmacht army stationed on the eastern front rapidly proceeded into the heartland of Russia. In only a matter of hours, the entire 150-year-old German Mennonite settlement fell under complete control of their German brethren from the west.

Yet, by 1944, the tide turned. German Wehrmacht infantry were left with no other conceivable alternative but to initiate its retreat. However, this time around, nearly every resident of Fürstenwerder and the Molotschna, Zaporozhe colony, along with thousands upon thousands of other fellow ethnic Germans saw no other choice but to side with their brothers from the old country and initiate a complete evacuation of the area by travelling west, along side the German Army, in the direction of the Fatherland. Very few took their chances by remaining at their homesteads in Zaporozhe, leading to a single-file German Mennonite refugee "wagon train" that spanned numerous kilometres to form, at times lined up directly along side the German Wehrmacht, right in the line of enemy fire. These fleeing residents of the Mennonite towns and villages, who were predominantly women, children, and non-able-bodied elderly, loaded themselves onto wagons and headed west along a treacherous and unfathomable arduous journey that took them through swampy bogs and rivers, amongst other testing terrains in an attempt to avoid Russian reprisals. Because this time around, the Mennonites were no longer welcome in Russia. The days and legacy of Catherine the Great were far removed. This generation of Mennonites belonged to a German history that was being written by deranged dictators who regarded peace as vindication to divide, conquer, and slaughter Europe, while splitting families and the continent into pieces in the process.

CHAPTER 5

Wagons West

As little Hans' wagon crossed a pontoon along a vast river, or least vast through his tiny eyes, he saw the panic of a horse, wearing short blinders, cause it to splash crashing down into the river. At that moment, four-year old little Hans witnessed his destiny, which was being written as he rode along in a wagon with his mother, paternal grandmother, and younger sister. His loving maternal grandparents, along with Uncle Gerhard, were in another wagon not far off behind. They were all attempting to merely survive during a trek that offered very few explanations, but rather, only overwhelming hardships and merciless perdition. Germans from different settlements in the USSR bonded together, after loading as many of their possessions as possible onto their wagons, forming a wagon train that was heading in the direction of modern day Germany. Along the way, these Mennonites found themselves caught in the cross fire during battles between the German and Russian armies, and sometimes even partisans, especially in modern day Poland. Hence, the Russians were not their only predator in their quest for survival.

Following many weeks of travel, little Hans and most of his family safely crossed into what was German territory for the time being – though with the Soviet Army sharply on their heels, raping and killing along the way, the Mennonites remained in a state of flux and tribulation. However, the same couldn't be said for Hans' maternal grandmother's sister, who along with little Hans' loving Uncle Gerhart, didn't share the same fate as the rest of the family. Their destiny was sealed in a Polish town, where partisans unexpectedly appeared, ultimately encircling and rounding them up, along with others, and locking them all in a barn. But instead of merely capturing their innocent "foes", these Polish partisans sought retribution by setting the barn ablaze, before watching it and the German Mennonites locked inside burn to ashes. Luckily though, all of Grandmother's sister's children miraculously staved off the attack. It would later be discovered that the three of them all safely arrived in Paraguay, where Grandfather, despite having no blood relations, raised the three children of his deceased sister-in-law as children of his own.

Though, prior to Grandfather's disappearance, he, little Hans, and the rest of the immediate family made their way to Warthegau, Germany, ending up at a refugee camp in the spring of 1945 during the concluding months of WWII. Uncle Jacob, the little brother of Hans' father, however, met another fate. He ended up in Siberia around this same time while serving in the German army, which the dark-haired Uncle Jacob attempted to enlist in as a soldier years earlier when he was only 13 years old. Yet, he was too young to be officially drafted, leaving him only permitted to accompany the German cause as a translator. Being able to speak both German and Russian was Uncle Jacob's direct ticket into the deadly, horrid, and bloody conflict. He was ultimately deployed with a regiment in the Caucasus Region, whereas his older brother - the tall, handsome, and physically fit Uncle Henry - was drafted into the German SS at the age of 17. Himmler, head of the German SS, initially set strict stringent requirements for Waffen-SS recruits, which Henry virtually perfectly met. Initially, draftees were mandated to be unmarried German nationals without a criminal record. Members were required to prove their Aryan ancestry as far back as 1800. Recruits had to be between the ages of 17 and 23 and be at least 5 ft. 9 inches tall. Unlike his brothers, Uncle Henry wasn't initially deployed to the warfront, but rather to Germany, where he enrolled in medical school. Regardless of the fact that he was relegated to a civilian status at the time, Uncle Henry ultimately ended up living out his final days in Prague where he was tragically killed in combat during the concluding hours of WWII on European soil.

Little Hans' father, Cornelius, kept in touch with Uncle Henry throughout the war while Henry attended medical school. Cornelius and Henry were quite well connected and informed, constantly keeping each other apprised of everyone's whereabouts within their torn apart and scattered family. So even though Father was away on military duty, he was able to learn of little Hans' and his family's arrival in Warthegau, Germany in 1945. Cornelius instantly instructed his brother Henry to visit the family. When Uncle Henry suddenly appeared out of the blue in Warthegau, prior to being deployed to Prague, little, 4-year-old Hans was ecstatically filled with glee! He was so excited to see his uncle who he hadn't seen in years! Though, the memory of Uncle Henry bringing him home on a horse after little Hans' rendezvous with the gypsies remained engraved in little Hans' recollection for an eternity.

During their time together in Wartegau, little Hans and Uncle Henry played together for almost the entire time. Uncle Henry even taught little Hans how to swim within the pool of the makeshift Warthegau refugee camp. So, all in all, little Hans was having a blast during Uncle Henry's furlough trip to Warthegau as the world was being blown to smithereens tens of kilometres away. Little Hans became completely oblivious to hardships whenever Uncle Henry was by his side. He never felt so loved by anyone on his paternal side of the family before that time. It was almost as if Uncle Henry were little Hans' true, biological father.

The two of them happily swam together almost every time that they had a chance. So, one morning, after little Hans arose from his slumber in the camp, he immediately hunted down Uncle Henry just like always. However, on this specific morning, Uncle Henry was nowhere to be found until little Hans entered the laundry room and discovered Uncle Henry on the floor in the arms of little Hans' very own mother! At the time, little Hans didn't see any harm in their lack of discretion and Mother's infidelity, so without giving it a second thought, little Hans joyfully and innocently approached Uncle Henry, who was still on the floor next to Mother amongst laundry, and said,

"Let's play Uncle Henry! Let's go swimming!"

Mother, on the other hand, wasn't in a playful mood whatsoever – well, at least until little Hans entered the room! Mother, in a fit full of rage and fury, immediately stormed in Hans' direction before whacking him while screaming at the top of her lungs,

"I'm going to kill you, you little brat!"

With her laundry still lying on the floor, yet to be washed, Mother furiously chased little Hans up the stairs out of the laundry room, right up into the open communal area within the camp, striking him with her bare hands along the way. In an act of desperation, little Hans sprinted to the side of his maternal grandparents who were outside attempting to find refuge in the shade. Mother stayed on little Hans' heels the entire way for everyone to see, until he positioned himself right in between Grandfather's knees, where he found refuge at last. As usual, Grandfather protected the innocent little Hans from his less than amicable mother. Fully aware that he had seriously crossed the line with Mother, little Hans elected to spend the entire day and night with his maternal grandparents, hoping that all would be forgotten by the next day.

The following morning, little Hans woke up full of joy, once again eagerly awaiting to play with Uncle Henry. Though, after searching the camp from top to bottom, Uncle Henry just couldn't be found. Little Hans quickly approached his grandparents, and enquired with concern,

"Do you know where Uncle Henry is? I can't seem to find him anywhere! I just don't know where he is! I want to go swimming with him!"

Grandfather soberly informed little Hans,

"Uncle Henry had to immediately return to school, so he had to hastily depart Warthegau without saying goodbye. I'm so sorry Hansi."

A feeling of utter disappointment engulfed little Hans. The fact that Uncle Henry left without even saying goodbye was neither comprehensible nor excusable. But as it just so happens, little did Hans know that this was only the beginning of a lot more "misunderstandings" and bitter suffering.

CHAPTER 6

Separation

That evening, the Mennonite wagon train was compelled, without delay, to get on the road once again. The Russian Red Army was progressively marching into the heart of Germany from the east, steadily closing in on Warthegau. Little Hans assumed his customary seat and climbed into Mother's wagon. Yet, this time around, Mother wanted no part of him!

"Go to your grandmother's wagon! Go! Get lost! Now!"

Before Hans knew it, he left himself smash to the ground before Mother was coarsely and aggressively dragged him by his button up shirt along the ground, hauling him towards her mother's wagon.

"Here, you take care this little brat! I don't want him! I didn't ever want him!!"

Grandmother despondently responded to her daughter, *"No. He belongs with you. He's your son."*

The older, and relatively decrepit grandmother of little Hans, who fell off a wagon at the ripe age of 7 and broke her hip, which never properly healed, also didn't want any part of the vigorous young child. Grandmother was convinced that she wouldn't be able to take care of the lively, and at times squirmy little Hans, so she repeatedly pleaded,

"Hansi belongs with you Maria, his mother!"

An aggressive shove-a-war between ultimately ensued! Frail, exhausted, and weak, Grandmother couldn't resist her persistent and viciously obstinate daughter. Already depleted, devastated, and barely coping due the horrible disappearance of her very own son, Uncle Gerhard (who they later learned was burned alive in a barn along with Grandmother's very own sister!), Grandmother was in no condition to partake in seemingly petty quarrels with her daughter, leading her to finally give in and "accept" little Hans into her arms. Exactly like Mother desired, little Hans took a seat in his grandparents' wagon, "separated" from his mother for the very first time after months of travelling next to her in the same wagon. Incidentally, Mother became free from the one who witnessed her perfidious deed of disloyalty to Hans' father – a wife's betrayal that Corny would've never excused – especially with his very own brother!

As the wagons travelled throughout the night, little Hans eventually closed his tiny little eyes and quietly dozed off with his head on Grandmother's lap. When the bright sun rose the next spring morning, Hans groggily woke up, expecting to look up into his mother's callous eyes. Though, when Hans opened up his little eyes, he saw neither a trace of Mother nor his sister Wanda, who were travelling in another wagon. Hans' maternal grandmother and grandfather, who little Hans was travelling with at the time, had no idea about what had happened to their daughter's wagon throughout the night. It simply vanished, almost into thin air in the darkness. The rest of the family couldn't fathom just how the wagon could disappear, especially considering that they had been absolutely certain that they had been following Hans' mother's wagon throughout the night. When Grandfather approached other members of the Mennonite community, they were speechless. They simply couldn't explain just how the wagon of Hans' mother could have seemingly evaporated without a trace. Normally one wagon followed the next within the single file wagon train, so how could this possibly happen? Hers was the only wagon not accounted for that morning.

Mother's wagon must have veered off route and headed in another direction. But why? Hans' paternal grandmother had the address of a brother who lived in Hannover, Germany at the time. But, why would they venture

24

off on their own without little Hans and Mother's very own parents? The original plan was for the entire family to reach Hannover together. So, just why would Mother impetuously and dangerously deviate off course? Unlike Mother's, little Hans' and his maternal grandparents' wagon followed the rest of the hundreds upon hundreds of other canvass-covered wagons as they continued along on their arduous and at times deadly exodus, which made its way northwest. Hans, strangely enough though, felt safe. He was in the hands of the one who loved him the most, so he felt protected amongst the chaos that he couldn't fully comprehend while the adventure alone pacified him into taking the journey fully in stride.

But Grandmother couldn't. If losing her sister, son, and daughter weren't bad enough, Grandmother eventually found herself without her beloved husband by her side either after he went off in search of food along the trek to Rostock, just to never return. Unable to bear the unfathomable losses that she had already suffered, Grandmother became consumed by a deep, heavy, and penetrating sense of desolation while she sunk into an abyss of nearly irreversible despair. Grandmother's hope was fledging, but it was still present. In wake of her husband's mysterious disappearance, Grandmother wondered to herself,

"Did the Red Army get a hold of him, and condemn Gerhart (her husband) for treason? Or was he captured and killed by partisans, possibly just like Gerhart Jr? So, did he stray too far off from the wagon train? But just what if he found my nieces and nephews following the partisan raid? Though, just what if he found Maria (her daughter)? And perhaps even our Gerhart Jr?"

People on the wagon train were required to go out and scour the cities, towns, woods and country sides for food, as these "passengers" were neither able to carry all of the essential provisions on their wagons, nor find enough along the routes of their treacherous journey. When Grandfather went missing, Grandmother desired to wait for her husband to hopefully return, but the rest of the people on the wagon train insisted that everybody must move on.

"Whoever falls behind has to catch up!"

John Friesen

Amongst the battles, marshland, gunfire, marauding partisans and bandits, not to mention flooding rivers, survival was as merciless as the cruel conditions. With the Russian Red Army right on their tail, their gruelling, and at times fatal journey inconceivably came to another stop. This time they were compelled to halt at the Baltic Sea port of Rostock, where the Mennonites frantically awaited to board a boat bound, for the time being, Nazi-controlled Copenhagen, Denmark in an attempt to evade the oncoming Red Army before it was too late! Soviet soldiers were brutally raping German women at will with each passing city, town, and village that they seized. They were bound to attain revenge at any means possible. When the Red Army finally arrived in Rostock, they discovered horses, cows, and wagons belonging to the Mennonites, yet not a Mennonite soul to be seen. They had boarded numerous boats before the Russians could encircle them.

Little Hans and Grandmother were the only two from the rest of the family on the "wagon train" to arrive in Copenhagen after a four-hour boat ride from Rostock that passed through the Baltic Sea and Oresund Strait. Hans' maternal grandparents, along with little Hans, intended to travel to Hannover, even following the disappearance of their daughter's wagon, to the residence of Hans' paternal grandmother's brother, who owned a home in Germany. However, Grandmother's missing husband, who disappeared without a trace on the way to Rostock was the only one on their wagon who had the Hannover address. Hence, Grandmother didn't know not only exactly where in Hannover to head, but also if she should wait for her husband. At this juncture of their voyage, the Mennonite refugees were quartered at a school in Copenhagen, a Danish city still occupied by the Germans at the time of their arrival. However, by May 1945, the war concluded with the British taking occupation and administrative control over Denmark. Terrified to travel alone, without the aid and accompaniment of her husband and fellow Mennonite group of travellers, Grandmother elected to remain in Copenhagen with little Hans, instead of immediately heading to Hannover on their own after the armistice between the German Army and the Allies was reached. Grandmother hoped and waited for someone from their family to come and get them. She waited and waited. But no one ever came.

After over three months of waiting, the British authorities instructed the Mennonite refugees to head back to where they originated from prior to the onset of the war, unless they had an address of somebody in Germany. In such case, they were free to travel to that destination in hope of taking up residence there. Unfortunately, for nobody's sake, Hans' ailing and frail grandmother had neither the German Hannover address, nor a husband or daughter to turn to – but only a 4-year-old boy to protect. At this point, Grandmother felt crushed by the pressure and stress surrounding their dire situation, especially after such a brutal and arduous journey that costed numerous lives, including her very own son's and sister's. If she would have known the Hannover address, her and little Hans would've travelled directly to Hannover, and in all likelihood, reunited with their family. However, since Grandmother was unable to furnish a German address of relatives to the British authorities, the British ordered the displaced little Hans and Grandmother to return "home" to the Soviet Union. Grandmother could have elected to remain a few more days in Copenhagen, in hope that someone from their family, perhaps her husband or possibly even Hans' father would locate them and arrive. Though, instead, Grandmother heeded the word of a woman from the Mennonite community, who played on Grandmother's fear-filled state to convincingly persuade her.

"The Brits are sending us back home to Zaporozhe. There's nothing to worry about! We're going home! Come! Come! Don't even think about staying behind! The British and Russians are friends! They'll be good to us! Just wait and see!! Now come!"

After contemplating all of their options, Grandmother elected to follow the Mennonite herd, and make the long and enduring train ride back "home" into the dreaded USSR.

CHAPTER 7

Journey East

Grandmother, ultimately, yet reluctantly boarded the train with little Hans, along with a horde of other supplanted Mennonite refugees. Her stomach told her to stay in Copenhagen, yet her fear directed her to hop on the train. Her state of angst overcame her, or perhaps it was merely the unbridled optimism of the Mennonite flock that motivated her to follow the pack. Most passengers envisioned returning by train to their beloved homes and villages within their Mennonite colonies in the Zaporozhe Oblast of modern day Ukraine.

Made up of numerous thin sheet-metal freight box cars that were being hauled by a black locomotive, their train was clearly not designed and in no condition to comfortably transport people across the continent. The train carts didn't even meet the accommodation level of steerage. Nevertheless, the passengers could only rejoice at the sight of the train, or at least initially, as the locomotive pulled into the Copenhagen Main Train Station. The train's arrival signified that the war was finally over and that these Mennonites were not required to treacherously travel by wagon under the summer's heat. Pleasant thoughts of returning to their beloved homeland flooded their minds, even though, deep down, many sensed that it could never be as it was prior to the outbreak of the 2nd World War, assuming of course that they would even be able to withstand the deplorable conditions and harsh elements encompassing the upcoming 3,500 Km train journey east.

John Friesen

These Mennonite "passengers" were packed into box cars like sardines. There was neither proper seating, a comfortable place to sleep, nor washrooms, unless one considered a bucket on the floor as a unisex restroom. Furthermore, their train had the lowest priority of rail, which meant that every other train that was still in existence after the war had precedence when it came to accessing the main tracks. At times, their train was relegated to the side tracks, without moving for days on end. To compound their deplorable circumstances, no food, not even complimentary peanuts, was provided to any of the passengers. Their dire situation compelled these Mennonites to constantly search for food or the means to acquire nourishment. Locals occasionally approached the train with cabbage, potatoes, beets, and other foodstuffs, with the intent of bartering these provisions with the Mennonites for whatever possessions that the passengers had aboard the train. Unfortunately, a majority of their belongings, including their horses, cows, and wagons had to be left behind during the emergency boat evacuation at Rostock. The people were permitted to only bring along whatever they could carry, so many had few items to exchange for food.

Each train wagon contained a fired-up steel drum equipped with a chimney that acted as a wood stove for heating and cooking. Situated in the middle of each box car, every passenger had access to the fire to heat up their meals. Though, a person was lucky if he or she were able to consume a warm bowl of soup per day. Families consisting of stronger, younger, and healthier individuals were able to pack more of their belongings onto the boat and train, leaving them in a better position to obtain or barter for more food. But this sort of family was few and far between, a family with fitter and stronger travellers could venture further into towns and villages whenever the train halted, affording them a greater chance to acquire the necessities that they all so desperately required. Little Hans and Grandmother, on the other hand, were either too young or too weak and frail to be able to carry a large portion of their possessions, let alone scour the countryside for barterable items of worth in order to acquire nourishment. All what little Hans and Grandmother had was whatever they were able to wrap in a blanket and carry aboard a freight box car that was more designed for cattle than humans.

Each box car was made out of a giant, yet thin metal sliding door along with three steel walls and a metal floor and roof. Benches, laid in rows a foot off the floor, spared the passengers from standing the entire time. Along the sides, there were "bunk beds" that were only equipped with a little hay for comfort; yet, when the train departed from Copenhagen, the Mennonites couldn't quite differentiate the "beds" from the shelves within the chockfull box car. The top shelf, for all intensive purposes, was used for storage, unless of course your name was Hans. He was little enough to fit onto the top shelf, right below the ceiling. And since little Hans was rather "expendable", the other passengers had no problem at all with tossing him up there, where he usually simply lulled himself to sleep.

Whenever little Hans got stowed away on the top shelf, he remained out of everyone's and harm's way, so it didn't bother him or the others for that matter one bit. Taking up this elevated residence kerbed little Hans from landing under anyone's feet and becoming trampled on or kicked, and for that he was grateful. There was no room for an active, lively, and mischievous little soul within the crammed confines of the box car amongst the peckish, depleted, and easily agitated passengers who regarded little Hans as more of a nuisance than anything. And without having any parents to protect him, like the rest of the kids, other passengers never hesitated to take out their frustration on little Hans, sometimes in quite the similar fashion of how the same mother who abandoned him did. Whenever little Hans got a slap across the back of the neck and heard, *"Verschwinde Du Rotzlöffel! Geh zu deine Eltern!"* (*"Get lost you little brat! Go to your parents!"*), these hideous comments became engrained within him, not only because his parents were nowhere around to protect him amongst such abhorrence and despair, but also due to the fact that little Hans feared that he may never see his "beloved" parents ever again. And even though Mother wasn't loving and compassionate whenever they were together, a young child has the fortitude to forgive his parents and only remember the pleasant moments – or at the very least, is convinced that parents are his only source of love and protection.

Despite the presence of such wishful thoughts, feelings of resentment and neglect gradually and subconsciously were becoming deeply embedded within the innocence of little Hans' psyche. It would only be a matter of time before his subliminal sediments would surface and touch him, before ultimately being unleashed. Yet, for the time being, little Hans took all of his circumstances in stride. He simply and graciously accepted everything that was thrown his way for the time being. As a free soul, little Hans didn't demand or search out any type of attention, besides whatever his boisterous sensations provided him. The excitement of the journey alone kept him curious, thankful, and energetic. But the same, however, couldn't be said for the rest. Other passengers were hungry, frightened, and under tremendous stress. Uncertainty and fear fueled the air. Even a mild sense of irritation set off other passengers, leading them to viciously erupt and react. Little Hans often found himself being hit, kicked, and more often than not, hurled up onto the top shelf, where ironically, he felt safe and sound until the train came to a halt.

Whenever the train was relegated to the secondary, sedentary tracks, where their wagon sometimes sat for days on end, little Hans, and almost everyone else for that matter joyously sprung out of the box car to savour and rejoice in the fresh air and freedom. Being "relegated" and regarded as a "non-priority" amongst the war-torn, scorched, smoking, and ravaged countryside was truly a blessing in disguise for the folks on the train. It was during these lengthy periods that every passenger got the chance to vacate the stinky and unsanitary confines of the stale-aired train wagon, and relish in the gusting air blowing against their face; stretching their legs; and feeling liberated from not only being locked in their cage on wheels, but also the stench from a bucket for a toilet within their train carriage. Possessed with a volatile aura of anxiety and bitter dread, the inside of the train wagon overtly exposed everyone's feebleness and fragility, leaving many convinced that they had already entered the confines of purgatory.

So, every time that the passengers were freed from the box cars, it not only opened a release valve within the noxious and sullied wagon, but also offered everyone the opportunity to delight in the sight and touch of daylight that brightened all of their battered spirits, at least for the time being. The liberty of inhaling fresh air was not afforded to them within the train since the wagons were not even equipped with any windows to let in the breeze, let alone rays of sunshine. The train wagons were dark and gloomy. There were no showers or sinks. No running water for that matter. So, when the human livestock could exit the wagon, and enter the countryside, or even a town if they were lucky, these Mennonite passengers had the chance to freshen themselves up with cool water from a stream or pond, or perhaps even a running faucet. Hans loved the water. Yet, he even more so cherished the moments whenever he could run around; discover the land; and collect firewood from the forest for heat and cooking in their box car when their journey re-commenced. However, little Hans made sure not to venture out too far from the vicinity of train because he could have easily been left behind if he were to stray out of sight, exactly like how Grandfather did back in Germany along the wagon train voyage in the direction of Rostock.

When the passengers escaped the train, the air and sun were no longer taken for granted, but rather prised as a luxury that was bestowed upon them. During these "breaks", the Mennonite passengers basked in the crisp air, bright sunlight, and presence and scent of pine, birch, and linden trees as if they were experiencing these splendours of the earth for the first time. Nature's harmony never felt so tranquil. Nothing is ever taken for granted when you're deprived of almost everything. Their "didactic" journey epitomized this paradigm as their story played out like a real-life bildungsroman that the protagonists had no interest in reading, a journey that began on little Hans' mothers' horse drawn wagon less than a year earlier.

CHAPTER 8

The Urals

Whenever the train got "promoted" to the main tracks, the passengers reluctantly stepped back into their dungeon on wheels that was being pulled by a locomotive that could drag them to any corner of the Soviet Union. Hours after the passengers once again soberly boarded the train following their latest halt, Grandmother felt the motion of a gradual incline as the locomotive slowly ascended into foothills. As the slope became steeper, Grandmother wondered just why they were elevating if they were approaching their intended destination, the flat steppe of the Ukraine. The weather became progressively colder. The elements played even more of a factor than ever in their survival. Some passengers were on the verge of freezing to death. Frozen corpses were simply placed upon the icy ground on the side of the railroad tracks. Hopefully theses bodies eventually received a proper burial, if they were ever discovered amongst the desolate and barren region, but nobody will know for sure. But if people never found these bodies, then the starving wolves certainly did. Sights of destroyed and bombed-out building remains became sporadic, but that was still less than a comforting sign for these Mennonites.

The effects of the conditions were only compounded by the fact that people were starving and dehydrated. The responsibility of finding provisions lied solely upon the passengers' weakening shoulders, along with their battered and depleted spirits. Scouting for water, food, wood, and other provisions became more challenging than ever. Panic, pain, and despondency suffocated the mood and air of the train wagon more than ever. Little Hans' survival also began to fall into question. Sub-zero Celsius temperatures surrounding the train were not only felt on the outside, but also within the awful confines of the box cars. Excessive moisture built up within the carts as a result of all of the condensation developing from the exhaled air exiting the crowd of passengers sealed inside of the icicled metal freight train. Droplets of water eventually froze on and around the top shelves, exactly where little Hans slept away. Frigid winds gusting against the walls of the box cars exasperated the problem by transforming the moisture into layers of ice. Poor little Hans was fully exposed to these conditions as he peacefully slept on the top shelf of the train wagon through a sub-zero night. When morning finally arrived, Grandmother bellowed out as usual,

"Hansi, come on down. It's morning!"

But little Hans didn't respond. Conscious and awake, he was able to hear Grandmother, yet so frozen stiff that he couldn't answer. After patiently waiting a few seconds without reply, Grandmother frantically asked a group of people,

"Could you please climb up to the top shelf and check on Hansi!?! He's not responding!"

When a few men stepped up onto the bench in their boots and looked upon the top shelf, there they saw little Hans lying there motionless. Initially, the men attempted to pick little Hans up, but he was so stuck onto the shelf right against the wall that they couldn't cause him to budge. If the men forcefully tried to remove little Hans, they could've removed an arm. Terror overcame Grandmother. Though, the men didn't give up. After slowly, meticulously, and carefully loosening every inch of little Hans' thin frame and fabric of his clothing that was icicled against the shelf, wall, and ceiling of the train wagon, the men ultimately brought little Hans' body downwards. As he felt his completely numb body levitate off of the top shelf, little Hans heard Grandmother gratefully repeating,

"Danke! Danke! Danke!"

But little Hans was far from out of the woods. His body was immediately laid in front of the stove in order to thaw him out. He had acquired a life-threatening bout of pneumonia. The depressed, depleted, and worn-out passengers dampened the mood by repeatedly proclaiming,

"That's it for him. He's not going to make it."

Grandmother felt despondent and hopeless. But little Hans had too much life and spirit in him to ever resign himself to the conditions, negativity, and despair. He simply refused to give up. And slowly, signs of vitality and strength aroused within him. Much to everyone's surprise, little Hans survived to live out a few more hours. Then a few more days. Nevertheless, Grandmother still heard,

"He may get well, but he'll never fully recover. The damage is done. That's how it is with pneumonia for the young and old."

But Grandmother felt hope overrun her veins. Little Hans sensed it too, and within a few days, he miraculously fully recovered. He eventually returned to his energetic self. Following this dramatic and traumatic scare, the other people on the train displayed the outmost compassion, and actually allowed little Hans to remain on the bottom bench below, next to his weak and suffering grandma. Yet, Grandmother still didn't feel assured that they were both going to be safe and survive as she could sense, with each passing bend and bone-chilling night, that the train was definitely not travelling back home. She realized that they were, without a doubt, not returning to the Ukraine. She consequently wondered to herself,

"Just where are we all being shipped? To a Gulag work camp like so many other Mennonites? Even a death camp? Or will they just leave us for dead right here? So how will I ever reunite little Hans with his mother? My very own daughter, who I have no clue where she is?"

As the weather gradually harshened, and became even more unbearable, Grandmother's prior suspicions that the train wasn't heading to her homeland were confirmed. She had never experienced a climate like this in her entire life. In the Ukraine, fruit trees blossomed amongst the sparse woodlands. Yet, this landscape was much different. The region before her eyes, only visible through a gap in the train wagon doorway, was vastly covered in dense forest and extremely heavy snowfall. And autumn had just begun. Furthermore, she could tell by the frequent jerking, upward movements of the train that they were amongst mountains, and not within the flatlands of her treasured lifelong homestead.

But Grandmother wasn't the only one cognizant of these peculiarities. A silent sense of hopeless fright consumed the confines of the passenger-hauling freight train. The people on board simply desired to feel the comforts of home. They had been on the road for months – first by horse and buggy, and now on a train – destination unknown. Whenever they inquired about where they were being taken, pure silence fell. That was their only answer. All what these Mennonites knew was that they had no clue about where their voyage was going to halt. The train was elevating in unison with the passenger's level of fear and distress. The uncertainty frightened the passengers as they nostalgically relished in the times before war battered their pacifistic communities, in between the moments that they pondered or murmured,

"Just where are these bloody Russians going to unloaded us?!? Will we step out alive or all roll out dead?"

These German passengers had no control over their destiny and fate - that lied in the hands of Russians who were still full of resentment and hatred towards ethnic Germans after the Nazi military machine terrorized and slaughtered their beloved mother Russia. Grandmother, on the other hand, was beginning to resent herself. She felt upset for ever listening to that woman in Copenhagen who convinced her to board the train that was apparently heading "home." In hindsight, Grandmother wondered just what would have been if she would've stuck around for a few more days in Copenhagen and waited for her husband or other family members to possibly arrive. She became convinced that if she and little Hans would have alternatively gone to Germany, they both wouldn't be in their current ghastly predicament of experiencing such scarcity, trauma, uncertainty, and terror. Severe guilt engulfed Grandmother. She felt blameworthy for subjecting poor little Hans to the hardships and adversity of this train journey east, even though she sensed resiliency in little Hans' disposition and youthful vigour. Nonetheless, Grandmother told herself, like a skipping record player,

"I should have never taken Hansi into my wagon after Maria, Hans' very own mother, incessantly refused him into her arms and wagon! What kind of mother does that?!? Just what kind of person is she really?! What kind of daughter did I raise?!? So, what kind of mother does that make me?"

As tears of self-pity and sorrow filled Grandmother's eyes, a perturbed feeling of helplessness and hopelessness accompanied the voices of the ones who she should have ignored – her own daughter and the Mennonite woman in Copenhagen. Grandmother always knew well enough to follow her own gut feeling, the feeling that God bestowed upon her, the one that penetrated her soul. Yet, for some reason, the wicked or overly and overtly convincing people of her world always got the best of her.

CHAPTER 9

Jug

Their long and arduous journey on the train from Denmark to the base of the Urals, the mountains that separate Europe and Asia, carried on for well over a month. Then one morning, the ride finally concluded when they pulled into a very foreign train station. As Grandmother peered outside through a tiny space within the train wagon, she wondered,

"Just what kind of journey awaits us now?"

Suddenly, the thin metal door of the train wagon roared open. Two burly Russian soldiers, in long and bulky black coats, appeared before them outside of the train. With weathered eyes and blank expressions on their faces, both of the men clenched their black glove-covered fists, and then wham! Then again, wham! And again and again! After a few more punches, the glass-like sheet of ice that developed within and encapsulated the doorway of the train wagon completely cracked before the ice finally shattered, creating shards of glass-like ice that fell into the snow or onto the train wagon floor below. Everyone in the train wagon became speechless. The temperatures were so cold and frigid during the trek that the uninsulated door frame, which was merely protected by a thin sheet of metal that the ice developed upon as a result of the condensation created by the exhalation of the passengers, became sealed by a massive, thick sheet of ice. In due course, the serious-looking Russian soldiers in black ushanka-ear-flap hats subsequently ordered the Mennonites in Russian to,

John Friesen

"Get off the train!"

Little Hans didn't comprehend a word, yet he definitely understood what these stern men in black winter boots desired of them. When Grandmother stepped down out of the train wagon, her loafer touched down upon snow. As the sun ascended in the distance, seemingly just levitating in space, she looked up and saw the word "*Юг*", Jug, painted on a rusting and pealing metal sign positioned on the facing of a wooden hut that appeared to once be a train station. Upon the horizon, snowed covered hills of the Urals cascaded amongst the clouds. A soldier in his 20's in a black, Russian winter coat with a collar covering the back of his neck eventually directed Grandmother and little Hans, along with their fellow Mennonites to sleighs parked metres away. Other Russian soldiers had already began loading numerous other Mennonite travellers onto one-horse drawn, open sleighs designed for transporting timber. Once everyone, along with their meagre possessions were loaded onto all of the sleighs, these Mennonites embarked on a cold two-hour, 12 km sleigh ride through a heavily wooded and snow-covered forest until a few timber buildings appeared on the horizon in the distance. Before they knew it, the sleigh entered the main square, right in the centre of Jug, which was situated approximately 45 km south of Perm, right off of the Kama River.

As they pulled into the snow-covered main square, government officials gruffly and authoritatively approached the sleighs in a manner that exuded their superiority. These were the Mennonites' new rulers. It must have been early afternoon, though the sun was already setting. The passengers were ordered to step out of the sleighs and move into the centre of the snow-covered cobblestone town square. Decked in white ushanka winter hats that shielded their ears from the frosty elements, and navy-blue winter coats with eight plastic buttons along the front, the Russian officials aggressively lined up the relatively cladly dressed Germans in a single file. The time seemingly came to determine just where each family was going to be placed based on their means and ability to assist in the "winter effort", assuming that they weren't all going to be marched into the forest and executed. Looking around the square, little Hans saw numerous one-storey timber buildings, along with the odd red-bricked or brown stuccoed edifice, which strikingly complimented the weathered and harden-up appearance of the Russian officials who survived a concluded war that was still taking its toll on its survivors.

The Russian officials huddled and talked amongst themselves before one Russian official in his 50's who could speak broken German eventually approached the families and directed the German Mennonites to follow their "designated Russian representative". An hour passed before almost everyone was led by the Russians out of the square. It became completely empty, except for the presence of little Hans and his feeble grandma. They were left standing there in the snow and cold, right in the middle of the square, waiting for their turn to be placed somewhere or anywhere, just as long as it provided them with shelter from the blistering snow and frigid wind. Yet, like in Copenhagen, nobody came for them. With the moon glimmering in the distance, heavens' sky and eyes fell down upon their shivering bodies as they stood there all alone, seemingly just waiting for death to collect them. Grandmother was left at complete odds. Terror overcame her as she couldn't grasp not only what had just transpired, but also what was going to happen to her and little Hans. Grandmother wondered to herself,

"Do we scream for help? But just why did I take little Hans from his mother!?!? So, do we search out our fellow Mennonites? Though, through a town that we know absolutely nothing about where we can't even speak the language while our language could get us spit on or worse!"

The fact that Grandmother could merely speak a few basic sentences of Russian only compounded their problems. They could communicate with neither an indigenous soul within this mysterious Russian town, nor their fellow German Mennonites who accompanied them along a multi-month journey through Germany and Russia as they remained nowhere to be seen. As the night became darker, colder, and bleaker with each falling snowflake, Grandmother knew that they had to find shelter for the night if they expected to see another morning sunrise. However, before Grandmother could conjure up another thought, a pleasant looking woman in here mid-40's, wearing a grey winter coat with rabbit fur trim around the collar suddenly approached them. She attempted to communicate to Grandmother and little Hans in Russian, but they couldn't understand a word. Grandmother was certain that they were doomed, but not this more than amicable woman. She was persistent and cordial. In an attempt to attract little Hans and Grandmother to follow her, she began making hand gestures, which little Hans and Grandmother comprehensibly deciphered.

At this point, they were both with nothing left to lose – everything had already been taken from them – the form and flesh merely became a burden to their soul. As they apprehensively tracked behind the woman to the front of a timber building in which a bakery was situated on the first floor, faint smells of bread entranced little Hans and Grandmother. Yet, before they could take another lungful of the whimsical and hypnotic scent, the Russian woman pointed in the direction of the second floor of the timber building that looked abandoned. She clearly desired that little Hans and Grandmother find refuge in order to survive another day. When she opened a squeaking wooden door of the timber building, a stairwell to the second floor appeared. After walking up the creaking steps through a narrow wooden stairwell possessing a gentle musky odour, the woman led little Hans and Grandmother into a vacant room possessing weathered, wooden walls and a few broken windows. The north window faced the town square.

Feeling content with herself for doing a great deed, the Russian woman graced little Hans and Grandmother with one final smile before departing down the steps, each thud indicating her gradual departure until the light wooden door below gently slammed shut. Utter silence fell until a gust of wind whistled through the cracked glass window blowing a few shards onto the floor. As little Hans and Grandmother timidly entered the room, they fully sensed the stiff breeze entering through the broken window while it brushed their red and rosy faces. Their accommodations were less than optimal, but they were still gracious over the fact that they had a roof over their heads and walls to shield them from unforgiving elements. Yet, they were still both freezing. A water heater sat in the corner of the room, but it emitted absolutely no heat. To generate some warmth, little Hans and Grandmother nestled together on the cold wooden floor in a "protected" corner of the room in order to feed off of each other's heat and stay shielded from the wind.

Their eyes closed in an attempt to get some sleep. Though, it was too cold to enter the dreamland of the sandman as their minds became filled with endless worries while intermittent flurries fluttered through the shattered window, touching their covered, yet battered bodies and exposed faces. Grandmother wondered to herself,

"Will we both survive this night, let alone find any refuge tomorrow? So why were only we abandoned once again? Do we really deserve this, especially now? What did we do God? Is it because I took little Hans from his mother? Yet, does anyone warrant to be subjected to such deplorable conditions? Why??"

Grandmother and little Hans both felt dejected, rejected, and abandoned. There was seemingly not a soul in the world that existed who cared less about them, besides the woman from the square. Grandmother was aware that both of them were quite incapable of doing hard, laborious work, and hence, nobody could exploit their means of their efforts. In the eyes of eyes, they were both of no use. In such dire straits, the religiously spiritual and faith-filled Grandmother couldn't help but to question God by wondering,

"Are you not a God of mercy and compassion? How far do You go with your tests? How hard can we be kicked while our heads are already down? Or was the woman, who appeared out of nowhere, amongst an empty square on a freezing and blustery Russian night, our guardian angel? Do you punish us for our deeds or reward us through Yours?"

A thousand upon thousand more thoughts and questions ran through Grandmother's head on that very night in between the moments that she intermittently dozed off. As they pondered over their fate – a fate consisting of dying from pneumonia, or a destiny in which they would both starve to death? At that point, they only had a blanket, a towel, a bowl, and each other, yet nothing more. Weariness eventually got the best of them, leaving them easily able to close their eyes and get some sleep until rays of sunshine and the pattering of snow sprinkled through the broken window the following morning.

CHAPTER 10

Communal Family

When morning finally arrived, they both realized that were still alive, leaving Grandmother and little Hans feeling relieved, yet still petrified. They survived a night; however, darkness was still apart of their beautiful dawn. And even though Grandmother and little Hans saw their survival as a miraculous revelation, and anticipated that today could be a better day, they acknowledged that daunting times stood before them. Standing up next to the window in hope that someone would see them and come to their rescue, they perilously wondered if their prayers would be answered while blankness ran through them. The main square was still bare. A picturesque blanket of snow covered the cobblestones. The odd person meandered through the centre, most likely heading off to work at one of the shops within or around the square. The clopping of horse shoes against stone echoed from the distance. Another woman strolled by, just as Grandmother's mind began wandering and wondering,

"Just what will become of us?"

Glancing down at the freezing, exhausted, and hungry little Hans, whose teeth were incessantly chattering, Grandmother watched him peer up at her with his piercing blue eyes. A strand of his blond, wavy locks brushed his eyebrow. Grandmother felt her fragility as little Hans brushed her dress with his soft, innocent hand and sensed her faith. Hans faintly said, *"Mir ist kalt (I'm cold)."* Grandmother replied with the hope that she relied upon.

John Friesen

"Someone will come get us soon."

They then both re-set their sights back on the snowy backdrop before them. Voices echoing in the town's square stirred a little more life into them and Jug. Earlier, only the odd person appeared on the streets, or within the pedestrian zone; but now, the shops were slowly starting to open. Patrons made their way into the bakery for a coffee and perhaps a loaf of bread. Little Hans' and Grandmother's hearts began warming up to the notion that just maybe, someone may look up and ultimately come to their aid. Yet, even if they were to be discovered and approached, that didn't necessarily mean that the locals would help them. Hatred for ethnic Germans understandably still flowed within the battered Russian hearts and souls. Many Russians harboured the same sort of vehement and insurmountable animosity that the Germans had for the world right after the Treaty of Versailles and WWI; perhaps the same sort of resentment that led them and the world into WWII. And even if Grandmother and little Hans did come across another amiable Russian face looking to offer a helping hand, how could they properly converse with them?

The Russians in this distant town, deep within the heart of Russian probably couldn't speak a word of German, and in all likelihood, never would. Grandmother's and little Hans' vernacular, names, clothing, and Germanic appearances made it nearly impossible for them to conceal their identity, ethnicity, and heritage, even though they were both born within the Russian Empire and USSR, respectively. Nonetheless, the chances that any Russian in this town would help them out were extremely slim. If a Russian were ever caught assisting a German, they could get admonished or even worse.

Yet, much to little Hans' and Grandmother's surprise, as they both gazed out through the broken window of "their" second floor run-down flat, two seemingly familiar faces approached the square in the direction of the exact timber building in which little Hans and Grandmother bewilderingly stood. The ladies walking through the town centre passed a restaurant that sat on a corner next to a clothing store that faced the main street of town. Their brown boots sashayed through the white, cotton-like snow that was becoming less pristine with each passing footprint. As the two women got even closer to the 2-storey timber building, little Hans and Grandmother waited in high anticipation. They became cognizant and then eventually certain that they recognized these women, which meant that they were definitely not Russian! Because as it just so happens, these ladies were in the same box car that little Hans and Grandmother travelled in during the entire trip from Copenhagen to Jug! They without a doubt belonged to their German-Mennonite group! A jolt of ecstasy stormed through little Hans' and Grandmother's bodies!

Without hesitation, Hans and Grandmother both stormed down the narrow wooden staircase and bolted into the main square. Grandmother didn't realize that she could still move her feet like that. Perhaps brutal suffering is the perquisite to be able to flow with the lightest of ease. The two women then instantly saw little Hans and Grandmother joyously enter the main square. Within a few moments, the four of them found themselves rejoicing in the square, emotionally embracing even though they had only been separated for a night. Little Hans and Grandmother felt relieved that their prayers had been answered. They were no longer alone, even though the whereabouts of the rest of their biological family was still unknown. But at least they were united with their wagon train and Copenhagen-Jug group or "family" once again – people who could understand German and empathize with their hardships. Although the journey tested them all, which resultantly made them testy towards each other at times, their comradery strengthened through their ordeals and tribulations. The two women immediately let little Hans and Grandmother know,

"We are so sorry! We were all exhausted! Through all the commotion in the square, we didn't even realize that the two of you were not a part of our group! They led us to and placed us in a house, but like I said, we were exhausted and scared. We didn't notice that you guys weren't there till we woke up! We're so sorry!! Come with us! My gosh! Please forgive us! What a rough night it must have been for you two! Most of the people in our boxcar, about 10 families – they all ended up in our house. When the sun shined through our window this morning, we both immediately realized, hey! - where are Hansi and Maria (Grandmother)?? They're missing! We have to go look for them!"

Little Hans and Grandmother, empathetic to the women's remorse, followed the two women out of the main square down a road leading towards the woodlands. After about ten minutes, they all arrived at a fairly-sized one storey log cabin that had been converted into a one-room, communal residence amongst the forest. As they walked into the house, little Hans gazed at a large metal woodstove right in the middle of the room. A window overlooked the main street. The only entrance was situated on the east wing of the house close to a veranda where wood for the stove was piled up. The only room in the house was 30 X 30 feet, with round timber log walls. Beds and belongings were scattered everywhere. These living quarters reminded little Hans of the box car that they all travelled in for over a month, except for the fact that this house had windows and couldn't roll along on a track. The beds, occupying the majority of the living space, were merely made out of a few flat metal bars and springs, without any mattresses. Little Hans and Grandmother were assigned to the bed right next to the entrance, where it was extremely drafty, especially whenever someone opened the door to enter or exit the building. If they wouldn't have been the last ones to move into the house, they may have obtained a better spot. But at this point, they had no other choice but to accept the less than desirable bed and placement that everyone else refused inside of the single room communal house that they were all compelled to pack into.

Families tried to partition off their areas from the rest for a little privacy by hanging up white blankets that separated their section of the room. Little Hans and Grandmother, on the other hand, only had one blanket at their disposal, which they used to protect themselves from the frigid draft while they tried to sleep within the un-isolated and uninsulated section of the house. Their worn-out blanket perfectly complimented their bed that was made out of rusty metal bars, protruding wires, and broken springs. Little Hans could barely sit on the bed without falling through the gaps between the springs.

Witnessing such conditions actually led little Hans and Grandmother to miss the confines of the cramped box car, because at least there they had a wooden board to sleep on, instead of a few old, very cold, stiff metal wires and springs that dug into the skin of their skinny and malnourished bodies whenever they tried to catch some shuteye. Little Hans and Grandmother attempted to bend the sharp points of the wires downwards, yet to no avail. For the entire first night at their new "home", they slept sitting up, huddled together while shivering, seemingly just waiting for death to offer them some condolences and comfort. The bed was not suitable to sleep on, exactly like the cold, dirty, and at times rat-trampled wooden floor, which was their only indoor sleeping alternative.

As Hans looked around the house during his first night there, it reminded him of their time in the overcrowded box car of the train, as the house too was merely lit by one kerosene lantern. There were neither facilities nor running water inside the house, just like on the train. Behind the house, close to a barn used for storing firewood, there was an old and rickety wooden outhouse in which not only the conditions were absolutely deplorable, but also the odour. Water was brought in from the river since there was no accessible well in the area, let alone a place to bathe.

Despite their difficult first night, Grandmother was forced to head off to work the very next morning with the other women in the house. They were all led to an underground storage cellar about two kilometres away. After walking into the bunker-like facility, the women were forced to sort through potatoes, beets, carrots, and various other vegetables. Their task was to remove the rotten vegetables from the ones that were still edible. Even though Grandmother was inside, she found little no refuge within the damp and cold underground cellar that was dug into an embankment, which prevented it from flooding during a downpour. Wooden logs were used for the ceiling and walls, but the floor was merely dirt. Electricity was rare in this part of the world during this time in history, so kerosene lanterns were used to hold the light. The women's misery was only incensed by being present within the extremely cold, damp, stinky, and poorly ventilated "facility". Luckily enough though, they were provided with a few boiled potatoes and a warm tea for lunch.

Grandmother worked there into the evenings, before she arrived home with a few frozen potatoes as remuneration for her 12-hour shift. Little Hans assumed that the potatoes were Grandmother's wages, or perhaps the means of energy to keep her sustained while she carried out her vegetable sorting duties in the storage facility six days a week. Since the other women had husbands, capable children, or young adults by their side who were able-bodied enough to work and provide for the family, they didn't necessarily need the potatoes. Grandmother, on the other hand, had to be resourceful. She even managed to scrounge up a few potato sacks from the sorting cellar, which she spread across their old and rusty metal bed. The potato sacks acted as a makeshift protective "mattress", making "sleeping" on their bed "tolerable", sleep that seemingly spared them for the harsh reality of their lives.

CHAPTER 11

A German Boy in Jug

Grandmother and little Hans were completely broke and in utter shambles. So, one day, someone from the house suggested that they should try their luck at the local chapter of the Red Cross. Little Hans had already outgrown his worn-out shoes that were beyond repair and winter was on the horizon even though autumn had already brought a hoard of snow. Hans was clearly in desperate need of a pair of decent footwear to protect his little feet from the cold, Russian elements.

Hence, the next morning, Grandmother and little Hans headed down to the Red Cross office to enquire about getting a pair of decent footwear. Grandmother couldn't even afford to buy a used pair from someone else. Twenty minutes after leaving home, they discovered a small wooden hut marked with a Swiss red cross upon a slightly torn brown canvass. When they stepped into the Red Cross Office, little Hans' feet were wrapped in rags. His toes protruded out of shoes that he had completely outgrown months ago. Grandmother envisioned him walking away in something more "practical", so she apprehensively approached the woman behind a make-shift wooden counter and pleaded their case in broken Russian as she pointed at little Hans' feet.

"My grandson. Feet too big, shoes too small."

The Red Cross worker patiently and pompously listened to Grandmother, until this woman, in her mid-40's with flailing nostrils and bulging eyes, commenced with her own enquiry.

"What are you doing for the Motherland, and where do you live?!? Where are you from?!? Who sent you here!?? Where are his parents?!?!?"

Grandmother was left absolutely speechless, but the woman behind the counter wasn't quite yet finished. As she not-so-compassionately assessed the situation, the less than cordial woman re-opened her mouth, incidentally revealing her crooked and chipped teeth, before condescendingly informing Grandmother and little Hans in a belittling and irritated manner.

"I have absolutely nothing for you!! I want to provide for people who are in need <u>and</u> contribute to society!!! What can two Germans contribute to society!?! What have Germans ever contributed to society! What have you personally ever contributed to society!?! You are both worthless!!!"

The Red Cross worker continued to heartlessly censure them in a sub-humanly manner until Grandmother broke down and started crying. She pleaded her case, in a mix of German, and extremely broken Russian.

"I am unable to take care of this innocent child all by myself! Why don't you want to help us?!? My grandson is innocent! If you don't want to help me, then at least help him!! How can you be so heartless??"

Eventually little Hans intervened and took Grandmother by the hand and said,

"Let's go. I'd rather freeze to death than beg for something, especially from such an angry woman."

Before walking out, little Hans glanced back at a pair of children's boots that had been sitting in a box on the floor next to the infuriated woman for everyone to see the entire time. In Russia, and perhaps in every part of the world, the ones in power distribute everything as they see "fit and fair".

This experience taught little Hans a valuable lesson which was – never ask or beg anyone for anything, since they'll know that they have power over you. When you beg, it just fuels them even more, fuels their thirst to seek out power over you since they're only cognizant of their own hideous plan. Perhaps this woman learned this fundamental basic premise from Stalin's regime, or even Hitler's - the opposing German regime that inadvertently solidified Stalin's reign and control over the USSR just that much more.

Little Hans was too proud to be degraded by their situation in life. He and Grandmother had absolutely no control over their conditions, but only their attitude. As little Hans saw it, begging was unacceptable. Whenever he was in need of food, he always proudly made sure that he earned it, as opposed to assuming the role of the victim and desperately seeking out a helping hand. Eventually, certain people recognized this trait in little Hans, and were kind enough to offer him a chore, just so he could earn his ration for the day. Even when it came to trick or treating, Hans stopped seeking a "helping hand" following a few mortifying experiences.

Years after visiting the Red Cross, little Hans occasionally joined the other kids in the Russian or Jug equivalent of Halloween or All Saint's Day. The boys would cover their faces in soot, and go door to door, in hope of a treat. Though, when little Hans reached the door to receive his "treat" of the customary piece of bread or a few Russian kopeks (pennies), the people of the homes instead handed little Hans, or "The German Boy", a wack, and sometimes even a shove right off the porch. After a hoard of abuse little Hans ultimately refused to walk up to the front doors in order to obtain a "treat" ever again, and alternatively remained behind on the road. These circumstances strengthened not only Hans' scorn for begging, but also his resolve to be as self-sufficient as possible, which slowly solidified his standing as a lone wolf within Russian society, or at least in the town of Jug.

Despite his lack of fond memories during this Jug tradition, Hans will never forget what happened to his friend Sasha when he returned home with a face decorated in black soot after the boys grabbed a few sauna stones and smeared the black residue across their faces for the occasion.

After opening the front door of his home, Sasha's mother, out of panic, instantly grabbed him by the shoulder and tossed him right out of the house! It was not until she was about to slam the door in his face that Sasha sobbingly pleaded to his mother, *"It's me mom! Sasha!!"* The next day Sasha told the boys in the neighbourhood his tale.

"Mom didn't recognize me when I got home last night. She thought that I was some sort of black vagrant! She grabbed me and threw me right out of the house!"

Little Hans didn't have it easy, but he couldn't help but to merrily laugh his face off at little Sasha's and his mom's scare.

CHAPTER 12

School Time

In the past, Mennonites had their own schools within Russia. But those days were far removed. At this point, Grandmother's only option was to enroll little Hans into a Soviet version of full-day pre-kindergarten. Little Hans' acceptance was the exception as schooling wasn't available for many German Mennonite children, especially due to their inability to speak much Russian, just like their parents. Going to daycare was a great respite for little Hans from his life of starvation, privation, and tribulations. At the school, little Hans had the chance to obtain a little warmth, not to mention some much needed warm soup and fresh bread.

However, when lunchtime arrived during little Hans' first day at daycare, the boy next to him had another idea as he quickly lunged over and snatched little Hans' bread. The little Russian then laughed away, adding insult to injury. When little Hans appealed to the teachers, they simply shrugged their shoulders and laughed the incident off. Seemingly, no harm, no foul. Hans wasn't totally impressed, but he thought,

"Fair enough. At least I have my soup."

Then, when the second lunchtime of kindergarten arrived, little Hans thought, *"Fair enough"*, and lunged over and snatched the bread from the same boy who stole little Hans' piece a lunchtime earlier. It was now little Hans' turn to laugh and ham it up. Though, he was the only one. The little brown-haired Russian boy with the tiny nose next to him didn't seem to share in little Hans' sense of humour. And before little Hans knew it, this Russian boy exploded into a fit of wailing and pouting. He immediately appealed to the teachers about the "injustice" that he was just served. When a teacher arrived at the round table shared by four children, she immediately attempted to pry the bread out of little Hans hands, yet to no avail. She then asked the victim of Hans' theft, *"So why are you crying?"* He responded, while pointing at little Hans,

"He stole my bread!!"

Another teacher inquired,

"But didn't you steal Vana's (Hans') bread yesterday?? So, what are you crying about? All's fair that ends fair, right?"

Little Hans left his final mark on the kindergarten, because the next day he was thrown out. Was it in response to the bread stealing incident from the prior day – who knows. But since little Hans, or "Vana", as the Russians referred to him, didn't have any parents contributing to Soviet society, he apparently wasn't eligible for the daycare from the start. Evidently, the whole day pre-school was only provided to Russian children whose parents both worked. Though, Grandmother was certain that regardless of Hans' family situation, if he would've been Russian, he could've stayed, instead of staying at home alone for the entire day. Little Hans' expulsion was hard on Grandmother to accept. She wanted her 4-year-old grandson to be properly nourished and looked after, especially while she worked. A major burden would've been lifted off of her shoulders if he could've attended, as she could've rest assured that little Hans was being fed and tended to at the kindergarten while she toiled away at the vegetable sorting facility. The revoking of little Hans' enrollment was as repulsing as it was inhumane and unjust, considering the fact that all of Grandmother's drudgeries were, according the Russian government, not contributing to society. She was later informed that she could have also put little Hans up for adoption, and make him the responsibility of the state, but she refused to contemplate such an unacceptable "solution". The day of re-unification between little

Hans and his mother was perpetually captured within Grandmother's visions.

Little Hans' treatment was a far cry from what she had experienced while growing up in Russia. During Grandmother's youth, prior to the Red Revolution and WWI, the majority of ethnic Germans living within the colonies scattered throughout modern day Ukraine and Kazakhstan had access to their own German schools, churches, businesses, and administrative offices. Prior to 1917, Russia was ruled by the Czar, whose family possessed Germanic roots. Under his and preceding reigns ethnic Germans were allowed to live according to their own culture, language, and traditions, without being compelled to integrate into Russian society. These German colonies were totally self-sufficient and -sustaining, so their need and desire to associate with Russians or learn the Russian language, let alone, assimilate within the confines of Russian society was minimal.

The odd exception occurred whenever a few ethnic Germans elected to go off to school in larger cities, where it was a necessity to learn Russian in order to integrate and obtain a higher Russian education, as opposed to the "Plautdietsch" (Low-German), German-Mennonite administered education and schooling of their settlements. From generation to generation, the ethnic Germans in that part of the Russian Empire only carried on and furthered their own culture, language, education, trades, and traditions while remaining quite isolated from Russian culture and way of life. In many instances, indigenous Russians only had "worth" to these Russian Germans if these industrious Germanic settlements were in need of unskilled, cheap labour.

These Germanic colonies' standard of living was not only leaps and bounds beyond many of their Russian compatriots' regions', but even higher than many states' within their old Fatherland of Germany and western societies' abroad. Accordingly, numerous Russians sought and reaped the benefits of employment within these German settlements. Since many Russians relied on these Mennonites for their sustenance, it was in their best interests to learn at least a little German. However, when Lenin arrived back in Russia after being exiled, with the aid of Germany of all countries, and the Reds seized power and overthrew the Czar, everything changed. Under the communist regime, the lands of the Russian Germans were confiscated or expropriated, and converted into collective, communal farms called "Kolkhozes".

The inauguration of the Communist Regime in the 1920's brought great famine, depression, and turmoil to the region. Government interventions brought an end to the Mennonites' prosperity within the Russian Empire. It no longer mattered how hard these ethnic Germans attempted to work and prosper, the reaps and benefits of their toil and advancements became consumed, stolen, and harvested by the new Bolshevik regime. Mennonite Germans became compelled to learn Russian, which was being introduced into these German settlements that dated back to the 18th century reign of Catherine the Great. Hans' parents' generation were taught some Russian, but German, or an old form of "Platt Deutsche", still remained the language of choice amongst the Mennonite and ethnic Prussian community.

Following the conclusion of WWII under Stalin, conditions significantly worsened for the Mennonites, especially for people like little Hans and Grandmother, who lost their homes and properties. A drastic upheaval had many shipped off to various remote villages in the heart of the USSR. But if it were any consolation, it was probably better than being sent to a Russian Gulag.

Nonetheless, from being well fed and nourished, little Hans and Grandmother became resigned to surviving on boiled potatoes, if they were lucky. Potatoes became their sole food ration and essentially the only staple of little Hans' and Grandmother's diet. Their portions came in small and limited mouthfuls, small portions that were insufficient for little Hans and his frail, weak, and handicapped grandma who broke her hip when she fell off of a moving wagon, just to have the wheel subsequently roll over her at the age of 7. Her hip never properly healed. Over the ensuing decades, arthritis slowly developed within Grandmother's body.

In Jug, extreme devastation and disillusionment consumed Grandmother. Her existence felt like a complete affliction. Taking any pleasure in her daily activities became extremely difficult, if not impossible. Grandmother merely existed in Jug with a sense of hopelessness that she never knew a human being could feel. It was as if the Holy Spirit completely exited her soul, leaving her with the blankness of agonizing sorrow. Every task felt like a burden carried out within the deepest of burrows. The only time that a mild sense of appreciation entered her was when she savoured her boiled potato and tea, during lunch at the vegetable storage-sorting facility, or at home for breakfast and perhaps dinner, if she were fortunate, with little Hans.

During their first two weeks in Jug, Grandmother slaved away in the damp bunker that epitomized what she felt inside as she drowned in a suffocating sense of capitulation. She didn't receive one cent during her first two weeks of work – only a few potatoes for lunch, which she savoured with her co-workers before resuming her duties. Resultantly, the only item that she could "afford" was the potatoes that she snuck out of the vegetable sorting bunker at the end of her shift. After her and little Hans consumed the potatoes that she stole from work, potatoes that were usually completely frozen, little Hans' very religious grandma prayed to God, and begged Him for forgiveness for her "crime." And even though she really had no other choice but to help herself to a few frozen potatoes if she and little Hans expected to survive, she, nevertheless, felt guilt-ridden for her deeds. Accordingly, she always attempted to make amends with God each and every day to lessen her guilt and clear her conscious.

During the days, while she was at work, Hans was left on his own to fend for himself. Since he didn't qualify for Russian pre-kindergarten, he instead started venturing out and about, just like he did in his birthplace of Fürstenwerder, in hope of finding adventures, and perhaps even some food God-willing. It was during these rendezvouses that little, almost 5-year-old Hans learned that he was quite the easy prey and pickings for the locals, especially the 10, 11, and 12-year-old girls. They were all too aware that little Hans didn't have any parents; couldn't speak a word of Russian, and was of Germanic bloodlines, or rather simply a "nemec", a term that he became accustomed to hearing in Jug, yet not fully understanding what it meant. When little Hans enquired with Grandmother one evening,

"In the kindergarten and around town I hear the adults and children calling me "nemec". Why?" Grandmother compassionately reassured little Hans,

"Don't worry. They're Russians and we're "nemec". It means German. We're German and they're Russians. People will see beyond that one day."

But that day had yet to come. Those older girls knew that they could torment little Hans in any way that they deemed fit and get away with it since he wasn't able to tattle on them to their parents, or anyone in town for that matter. And even if little Hans could, the parents probably wouldn't have cared less, not only because little Hans was parentless and a German, but also due to the fact that most Russians were struggling to survive as well. They too had their own torments and bitterness in life to repulsively consume them all by themselves.

Little Hans' disadvantage against these girls was only exasperated by the actuality that he couldn't understand their plans and schemes relating to their imminent attack, even when they were discussed (in Russian) right in front of his face. So, little Hans wasn't necessarily always prepared to flee, or possibly even fight these girls who were sometimes three times his age and twice his height, not to mention fully equipped in warm winter coats and cotton snow pants. Yet, the language barrier was rendered irrelevant whenever these girls instantaneously appeared out of nowhere. As many as ten of them, at times, would literally come out of the woodwork and ambush little Hans. These girls knew the terrain. They appeared out of bushes, or even homes and doorways, just to subsequently jump or tackle the sockless little Hans down to the ground like a pack of wolves. Kicking and pushing him to the snow before dragging him to a bridge and tossing him into a creek were their torment of choice. Little Hans was still relatively small, so whenever he got tossed into a frozen or freezing creek or river, his task of scaling his way up the snowy and icy banks in order to reach the top and safety was extremely ominous. Hence, he always searched out shorter banks that were manageable for him to claw his way up and out with his bare hands that bled while his ears felt like falling off from the blistery cold along the way. The girls found torturing little Hans to be absolutely hilarious, especially whenever they continuously dunked his head into the frozen stream through a hole in the ice. When little Hans returned home in the evenings with bloody hands, Grandmother immediately inquired,

"Was zum Henker ist passiert!! (What happened to you!?!?)"

Though, her concerns didn't prevent the attacks from continuing. One day, while little Hans was enjoying a "leisurely" afternoon stroll, he suddenly felt a tug on the back of his coat. His body was then hurled onto the frozen ground. Snow smothered his face as a multitude of boots hammered against his back and legs. Sounds of incoherent mutter and jeering entered his ears as little Hans closed his eyes and tucked his head away. Moments later, he felt himself become elevated off the ground, right before the girls hurled him into a wooden culvert that was ten feet long and two feet high and wide. Lying face down, little Hans felt snow being kicked inwards in his direction, some landing right on top of him. When little Hans finally opened his eyes once again, he saw nothing but darkness. Both sides of the culvert were sealed shut. Being completely entrenched by a hoard of packed snow, however, didn't prevent little Hans from hearing the pack of girls congregating on the outside of the culvert, just waiting for him to suffocate. There was seemingly no way out. As little Hans heard a multitude of boots packing and compactly patting down the snow at both ends of the culvert, he thought to himself,

"How will I ever escape this?!? Because man are these girls ambitious when it comes smothering me to death. Maybe Mother hired them."

Despite his precarious situation, little Hans somehow found the humour in his predicament. Perhaps just like little Hans' aggressive and diligent feminine assailants who were fully motivated when it came to their goal of eliminating little Hans. Compounding little Hans' concerns was the fact that he wasn't properly dressed for the conditions. He didn't even have any gloves to protect his tiny hands that were quickly becoming absolutely frozen under a layer of snow. The rags, covering his toes that were dangling out of his undersized boots, were completely soaked as he laid on his chest within the culvert. Under such dark, cold, and restricted conditions, his bodily movements were severely limited, which petrified him a bit. However, little Hans didn't panic. He always sensed that he could survive just about anything and everything. He reassured himself, in these instances, that he could escape by either moving forwards or backwards; it was just a matter of time and how.

The sight of his assailants' eyes filled with fury and pain pranced through little Hans' mind as he wondered just what makes people act out with so much hate and such little compassion. Yet, little Hans had neither time to contemplate the ills of the world, nor lose hope if he expected to escape alive. His first instinct was to rollover onto his back, and with all of his might and fury, kick away at the snow at his feet, but, to no avail.

Dumbfounded but not defeated, little Hans' next move was to attempt to crawl through the barrage of snow, so he barrel-rolled back onto his belly. Clawing at the snow, he gradually scraped his way through the 10-foot-long culvert with his bare hands, leaving them bloody and little Hans in excruciatingly pain. The snow was so jammed packed within the culvert that little Hans had no other choice but to push the loosened snow under his belly, to the sides, or anywhere else that he could find empty space to place the snow. And after an hour, his persistence paid off. Little Hans finally reached the end of the culvert! Breaking through the engulfing snow-walled entrance became his final challenge. The snow was so tightly packed at the bottom of the ditch, around the base of the culvert, that little Hans was unable to push it out, so he attempted to kick out the snow. Rolling back onto his back, he pounded at the white wall in front of him with his rag-covered feet. He kicked once. Twice. Three times. But nothing. Yet, by about his 30th kick at the snow-wall, the barrier finally showed signs of crumbling. Luckily, the snow that the "playful" girls packed near the top of the culvert wasn't as thick as the snow piled up at the bottom base of the ditch, so little Hans directed his onslaught at the top portion of the wall, and by around his 40th kick, little Hans saw daylight! Moments later, he finally broke through and out.

Such incidents constantly occurred throughout the winter. Little Hans sometimes struggled for over an hour to eventually flee the snow-sealed culverts, but destiny was always on his side. When the girls saw little Hans the following day, they immediately, seemingly joyfully said, or least Hans interpreted them to say,

"He escaped! Let's try to suffocate him in the ditch again!"

It was almost as if little Hans purposely and conspicuously revealed his face to his feminine foes, just to show them, *"I'm indestructible! I'm not afraid of you! I always win!"*

It was almost as if he enjoyed battling his fair-skinned rivals. As weeks passed, the mob of girls eventually learned, following numerous escapes, that little Hans was able to break out relatively quickly, so they began waiting for him to claw his way out before shoving him right back into the culvert and casing the exit with snow once again in hope that fatigue would get the best of him. It ultimately became a game for the girls, who were perhaps merely looking to appease notions instilled in them by warmongers and aggressors like Stalin, and maybe even Sir Winston Churchill for all what little Hans knew or didn't know - or perhaps at the very least, to punish a German by transferring their and their parents' hateful rancour in little Hans' direction.

But little Hans became craftier and keener, and started waiting until he could no longer hear the girls before making his escape. As soon as he got out, he always stormed home, where Grandmother was waiting for him after her shift at the vegetable sorting storage facility. She always wondered, upon her arrival at home,

"Just where is Hansi, and why isn't he anywhere around to be seen?"

When little Hans finally scampered through the front door with wet feet and bloody hands, he immediately scurried over to the woodstove to warm himself up, while mending and tending to his wounds. Every time Grandmother saw his bloody hands, she always emphatically questioned,

"Where have you been and what happened!?!

Little Hans, as usual, calmly explained, or rather declared,

"I was attacked. Ten girls came storming out from behind a house and dragged me to the culvert. After kicking me, they tossed me into a little tunnel and filled it in with snow. But I always escape! They're no match for me! They even once dunked my head into a barrel of water! But I'm indestructible ("nicht vernichtbar")! I always win!"

Grandmother thought to herself,

"I like his confidence, but where does a 5-year old learn the word "indestructible" ("nicht vernichtbar")? Probably from the older kids in the house."

Grandmother responded in her usual, casual manner.

"You should stay out of trouble because I'm unable to protect you. Every burden and risk lies squarely on your and God's shoulders, and nobody else's."

At this point in the journey, Grandmother was wearied and worn out. She just couldn't outwardly express her concerns, and how much anguish these occurrences were causing her on the inside. Completely numbed by what had already transpired in her life, which included losing her husband, and two children (son killed and her daughter's whereabouts still unknown). At times, Grandmother seemed to have already reached wit's end and the end of her line. Nevertheless, she constantly and strongly sensed that she could somehow reunite little Hans with his parents, even though she had absolutely no clue where they were, assuming that they even survived the war. Yet, whenever Grandmother reflected back on where they were a few years ago, and how nice they had it in their village of Fürstenwerder, she wondered,

"Just why couldn't it be like it was back then again?? When times were good!"

Grandmother was merely clinging to life and her sanity, causing her to blame herself for their deplorable situation. She told little Hans,

"Why did I give in to your mother?!? My very own daughter!! You should be with her! You belong with her. I'm too weak. I'm so sorry! But I will reunite

you two, that I promise you! Then I can tell God that my job is done and that all of my prayers have been answered!"

Even though she no longer desired to live, Grandmother never blamed God for their dreadful predicament. She constantly prayed to Him for the strength and sustenance to maintain her faith to stay alive for little Hans' sake. The fact that this innocent and loving child had to go through such atrocious circumstances and live under such depleting and brutal conditions tormented her. She continuously reiterated,

"You don't deserve this! You deserve to be with your family."

In an attempt to find salvation, she kept asking God,

"Help reunite poor little Hans with his parents before I pass away!"

A reassuring thought then came to Grandmother.

"Accept and praise and little Hans will be raised!"

CHAPTER 13

Little Hans Makes a Friend

After the latest snow-burial incident at the culvert, Grandmother instructed little Hans,

"Stay at home for a couple of days. Just until the dust settles and your adorable, but battered hands heal."

However, as usual, little Hans got bored of the monotonous, safe, and secure way of life quite quickly. Nonetheless, he spent the grey morning, drearily staring out of the window. Though, before he knew it, little Hans' curiosity instantaneously heightened when an intriguing display of a man along with two oxen pulling a sleigh slowly passed by on the slag snow-covered street. Such a scene wonderfully sparked little Hans' senses. His first instinct was to storm out of the house and track down the man draped in a long brown wool coat, along with his oxen, after they gradually strolled by the window, disappearing into the horizon out of little Hans' line of sight. But instead, little Hans heeded Grandmother's words by staying behind, nestled inside. Yet, by noon, on that very same day, little Hans' devilish impetus began to stir within him again as if he had a little red Satan on his shoulder. Despite being spurred on by his inner voice directing him to chase down the man and oxen with the sleigh as they sashayed by the communal house, little Hans once again elected to innocently watch the procession from the comforts of the inside while Grandmother's voice ran through his head; though, this time around little

Hans noticed something different - some "silo," a form of animal feed that consisted mainly of corn and a type of grass domestic to Jug, piled up in the sleigh. Gazing at the oxen in awe until they vanished into the horizon, little Hans wondered to himself,

"Will they return tomorrow?! I really, really hope so! I love horses more, but those oxen are awesomely powerful!"

The following morning, after devouring his customary boiled 1/2 potato for breakfast, little Hans immediately rushed to the window, where he simply waited, stared, and hoped. And he wasn't disappointed. Once again, two massive oxen approached in the distance. Just itching to storm outside and tail behind the wagging tails of the oxen, little Hans instead, observed Grandmother's word by remaining inside. The stout and shorter man, with long and straight black hair sheltered under his Russian winter cap slowly meandered along side the oxen. As he gazed through the communal house window, little Hans knew that they were on their way to pick up some more of that "silo" feed, and haul it back with them before the early, late autumn sunset.

By the third morning of little Hans' "quarantine," his devilish inquisitiveness completely engulfed him. So, at the first sight of the oxen and the man approaching amongst the cold morning mist, little Hans bolted out from the confines of the communal house and sprinted to the side of the road to fastidiously witness the march up close. Attentively staring in bewilderment from the roadside at the man and his oxen as they slowly cavorted by, little Hans felt euphoric. The man too was reciprocally quite intrigued by little Hans and his curiosity. He constantly kept turning his head back at little Hans, speculatively wondering,

"Just why is this kid with rags on his feet just so mesmerized by me and these oxen? Am I truly that alluring and handsome?"

The both of them, or perhaps all four of them, including the oxen, were awestruck by each other. Immediately sensing that this man emitted the energy of a friendly soul with a welcoming heart, little Hans was certain that this man wouldn't harm him, so he pursued after him and his oxen in full force, closely trailing behind making up the rear. Little Hans absolutely adored the sight of the swifter and more majestic horses of prowess, but the size and power of the oxen happily whelmed him.

Back in Fürstenwerder, young little Hans was already enthusiastically drawn to horses, especially the ones that were strong enough to draw wagons. He was utterly magnetised by their presence whenever he caught a glimpse of a horse-drawn wagon. Bravely, yet brashly and without caution, little Hans had no problem with standing right in the middle of roads, forcing drivers to halt wagons in their tracks. The driver usually cursed at little Hans under his breath until finally picking little Hans up and sitting him in the wagon, before resuming along his way. People complained to Grandmother,

"Someone will drive him over one day!! He has not only absolutely no fear, but also no intention of ever backing down to the horses and our wagon!"

But little Hans was not discriminant when it came to animals. He absolutely loved animals of every kind, so the oxen did just fine. Their affinity for little Hans matched his level of admiration for them, and the oxen loved him for it! So, it was no wonder that little Hans ultimately followed the man with the oxen right to the other end of town. During the entire walk, the man constantly kept incredulously peering back. He just couldn't imagine what this mysterious child was seeking as his feet pattered through the snow along the slag and dirt snow-covered road. Eventually, they all reached a road that was more of a path leading through fields belonging to the Kolkhoz, the Russian state-run farm. This frosty, hardened-up dirt path ran into the forest, towards some high river banks. But instead of marching into the woods, the man and the oxen stopped next to a high pile of feed, which was the food of choice for the man's, or rather Kolkhoz's cattle during the winter.

The upper layer on one end of the feed pile had frozen up, forming an organic crust that was covered by snow. This organic cocoon resembled a large hay igloo. An opening, that was roofed by straw that prevented the feed and the hole that provided access to the cattle food from freezing up, was on the south end of the heap. The air within the cocoon containing the fermenting feed was above the freezing point. Whenever the warm air escaped outside of the cocoon and collided with cold air, condensation and frost formed. Ultimately, a heavy layer of ice, or bio-organic-frost developed, encapsulating the entire mound except for the straw-covered portion on the south end where the opening was situated. As the man removed the straw, little Hans curiously looked on, and meticulously observed each and every single one of the man's movements as he entered the heap and carried out some feed with a pitch fork before loading it onto the sleigh.

Little Hans also couldn't help but notice a bag hanging from the side of the sleigh. His completely undernourished body could easily sense exactly where the food required to maintain his sustenance could be tucked away. When noon finally arrived, the man stopped loading the feed and reached for the mysterious dangling bag hung over a wooden shaft on the side of the sleigh before opening the sack. Looking on with enormous anticipation, little Hans' mouth instantly watered. He tried not to make it obvious of what he so deeply yearned for; yet, when the man pulled out some boiled potatoes, turnips, carrots, and bread, and then subsequently glanced into little Hans' eyes, the man sensed what little Hans longed for and sought. Without hesitation, he handed little Hans a piece of bread and a potato.

"Eat up boy."

Little Hans graciously clutched the food and instantaneously scoffed down the man's offerings as if he had never learned how to properly chew a morsel of food. The man was left absolutely flabbergasted! He was not only blown away by just how quickly little Hans consumed the food, but also a bit concerned. Gesturing to him, the man attempted to articulate to little Hans that he should slowly and properly chew the food, and not simply devour it all in one massive gulp like a duck would. Though, little Hans couldn't understand one word. He only sensed that without sufficient food, he would starve to death. Food, and how to get it was the only thing on little Hans' mind. As the man stared deep into little Hans' innocent eyes, he once again attempted to convey his message through gesticulations and motions as he could clearly see that little Hans couldn't understand one word of Russian.

Following their midday meal, little Hans decided that he too wanted to explore the confines of the hay igloo, so he climbed right in. Upon entry, he inhaled an unpleasant, suffocating gas that resided amongst a sharp darkness. However, within a few minutes, little Hans felt quite at home within his new place of work where he began to earn his lunch by throwing out feed with a pitch fork that the generous man handed him. In return, the man graciously smiled back at little Hans. He was more than grateful to have a little helper and some exuberant company by his side. When the sleighs were finally fully loaded up with the cattle feed, they began their journey back across town. Little Hans' pants immediately froze upon his goose-bump covered skin right after exiting the hay cocoon, so he was happy to be on the move and get the blood flowing, preventing him from transforming into a human icicle. As they walked side-by-side behind the oxen-drawn sleighs, little Hans and the man realized that a bond had been formed. And though little Hans' clothes were soaked from kneeling on the slimy feed, he savoured his time as a right hand 5-year-old man to the man with the oxen. When they finally reached little Hans' house, Hans ran inside, but not before waving good-bye to the man as he and the oxen continued down the main street before crossing a bridge and making a turn onto a road that led to the Kolkhoz's barns at the south end of town.

A couple of the women and other co-inhabitants were arriving home after a long day of work. When they walked inside, they found little Hans standing by the wood stove, drying off his pants while warming up his shivering body. After inhaling a strong whiff of manure within the house, the women immediately inquired about just what or who was emitting such an objectionable odour. The other children immediately pointed in little Hans' direction and said, *"It's him!"* Out of utter irritation, the women interrogated little Hans.

"What have you been up to Du Mistkerl (you "macurehead")"

73

However, everyone calmed down when the men, who had been working in the barns the entire day, arrived home all possessing the same scent of manure that was embedded within their and Hans' clothing. All of the neighbours within the town had pigs, chickens, cows, and sheep, so the pungent odour wasn't as foreign to the communal house as the women made it out to be when little Hans brought home something unpleasant to inhale. Nevertheless, being uncomfortably jammed packed within a single-room-house with numerous families in chockfull quarters constantly led the inhabitants to become quickly frantic, and consequently, to fly off the handle. Though, in this case, negative emotions metamorphosed into astonishment over the fact that a 5-year boy could possess the same stench as men who were working hard for the entire day. The women recognized that little Hans too needed to survive, or at the very least, find activities to keep himself occupied throughout the day. So, when Little Hans mentioned, *"I was helping the man with the oxen. He provided me with some food."* – his roommates within the communal house became rather empathetic and understanding.

The following morning, little Hans once again joined the man with the oxen, who slowly befriended him. Their connection solidified over the ensuing weeks that came and went. Every morning, the man not only eagerly awaited little Hans' company, but also appreciated his eagerness and determination in assisting him with all of his daily tasks. For his entire first winter in Jug, little Hans made it a routine to work with the man with the oxen almost each and every day. On those rare mornings when little Hans wasn't waiting along the roadside for the man and his oxen, the man constantly peered back, hopefully anticipating that little Hans would miraculously appear. And more times than not, little Hans didn't disappoint. Whenever he came charging out of the house, it instantaneously brought a huge smile to the man's face. During the 2-km trek from little Hans' home to the feed pile, little Hans picked up the frozen horse droppings that contained vital nourishment such as undigested oats.

After arriving home from "work", little Hans let the collected horse droppings thaw out, before eventually plucking out and washing the oats with a bucket of water from the river, prior to boiling them in hot water over the stove. When Grandmother returned home from work and saw Hans cooking up a hand-full of oats, a massive smile overtook her face as she ruffled little Hans' golden locks.

"Richtig gut gemacht Hansi! (Really well done!)"

Afterwards, little Hans and Grandmother happily ate their oats. They considered such a meal to be quite the delicious and nutritious treat. Whenever they could muster out a handful of "manured" oats from a few droppings to consume, they were more than gracious. Horse droppings were deemed to be quite "the delicacy", making them surprisingly difficult to find in Jug during the winter months. Everyone was looking for the droppings in order to survive by any means, so Grandmother was tremendously enthralled with her 5-year-old's hard work and resourcefulness.

The man with the oxen worked for the Kolkhoz, the national farm also responsible for processing dairy products such as cheese, milk, and yogurt at a production facility. The Kolkhoz was also in possession of a cistern truck, and one day the oxen man opened up the tank on the truck and instructed little Hans,

"Take this stick and fish out some curds and whey, boy."

Little Hans was so excited; it was the equivalent to offering a hungry boy an entire box of chocolate bars and instructing him to eat away. The man knew well enough that little Hans was starving, so he was fully aware of just what a delight the curds and whey would be for him. And luckily enough, from time to time, whenever Grandmother saved up enough money, she treated herself and little Hans to another delicacy. On these very special occasions, little Hans woke up before sunrise and headed down to the local bakery. Despite being the first to arrive, little Hans had to battle for a place in line once other patrons arrived. It sometimes took him as long as two hours just to purchase a loaf of bread. And even though he was the first one to arrive - sometimes even before employees of the bakery - Russian women had no problem whatsoever with grabbing little Hans by the hair and dragging him to the end of the line.

John Friesen

"That's where German boys belong!"

In the face of this abuse, little Hans remained dogged undiscouraged, so ultimately, he almost always bought himself a loaf of bread, occasionally by sneaking back to the front of the line by crawling between the legs of the ones who dragged him to the back. Yet, little and sneaky Hans seemingly could never acquire a loaf before a certain pregnant woman who had long brown hair and pants four sizes too big for her thin short legs. The other ladies in line bitterly and sarcastically joked,

"She's been pregnant for ten years!"

Nevertheless, the less than amicable women's behaviour never dampened the mood one bit when little Hans walked through the door at home with a firm and hearty loaf of dark brown bread. Delighting in every morsel of that loaf, Grandmother and little Hans swore during those brief moments that they had already died and gone to heaven. Words just couldn't express how it felt for fresh bread to touch a starving tongue.

But this was a rarity. Grandmother wasn't earning enough money to feed them both, which meant that they had to constantly settle for the precious scraps that were tough to come by. Even potatoes were too expensive to purchase. And since Grandmother felt too guilty to keep stealing them from work, attempting to buy potato peels from their Russian neighbours became her last option. Though, when she approached the neighbours across the way, they bluntly informed her,

"We'll feed the peels to the pigs before giving them to Germans!"

But like little Hans, Grandmother was determined and never gave up. She relentlessly kept approaching other Russians, enquiring if she could purchase their potato peels until ultimately, she came across a few compassionate Russians who simply gave her some potato peels, free of charge.

CHAPTER 14

Tough Times Become Tougher

Possessing more than one day's worth of food was not an option for Grandmother and little Hans, because if the other children in the house ever discovered that there were "leftovers", they would consume them while little Hans and Grandmother were not around. So, whenever little Hans and Grandmother had anything extra, they stuck it in their pockets and took it with them for safekeeping when they left the house.

A Russian-Ural region winter was inconceivably cold, harsh, and at times, seemingly without an end in sight. Spring couldn't come soon enough for little Hans and Grandmother. Once the snow melted, little Hans could scour the lands for food. And regardless of the fact that little Hans wasn't acquiring a sufficient amount of nutrition, he was nonetheless outgrowing his clothes, the ones that he wore day-in, day-out. Little Hans' coat was getting tighter on him at the same rate that his shoes were becoming so small for his feet that his shoes were splitting in half.

With the arrival of spring, little Hans would no longer require not only his winter coat, but also his shoes, since he could simply walk around bare foot during the warmer weather. But the long and harsh winter was far from over, driving Grandmother into absolute despair. She felt utterly depleted, leading her to reckon with suicide. Grandmother simply felt no other viable solution. On numerous occasions, she took little Hans down to the frozen river, where they both stood right in front of a hole in the ice of the river from which people gathered water. As water from the opening in the frozen river intermittently splashed onto the ice, Grandmother looked at the hole and then peered into Hans' piercing blue eyes lit up by the moonlight, while his little body shivered and jaw clattered. Grandmother contemplated whether they should both jump in and put an end to their relentless misery. One leap would have provided them both with eternal relief from the earth's unwavering elements – leaving them one spring away from "salvation". Pondering and contemplating in front of the hole as their knees shook while their teeth chattered, Grandmother eventually faintly whispered into little Hans' ear,

"I'll push you into the water and jump in after you."

Little Hans nervously awaited a force that would propel him into the water, but such a timely thrust of fate never came. Grandmother just couldn't do it. After a long pause, she turned to little Hans, with vapour expelling from her mouth with each breathe.

"Well, let's leave it till tomorrow. Tomorrow is another day. Maybe it will bring something better. God has sustained us to this day, so He's proven that He can sustain us to the next."

As a result of living under such horrifically brutal and testing conditions, and already experiencing circumstances that were worse than death itself, it didn't matter to little Hans what Grandmother thought was best and chose to carry out (with them). He was freezing and starving, so he could've easily jumped in alongside Grandmother in (her) hope of and hop for "greener pastures". The thought alone of living without Grandmother shattered little Hans just as much as the notion of him not living out his destiny crushed Grandmother. And perhaps that was, for some known or unknown reason, her justification for changing her mind every time that they walked to the hole in the frozen river.

Despite the hardships, Grandmother's decision left little Hans feeling content and relieved. It meant that he could live out another day to experience another adventure. Grandmother's suicidal U-turns also gave little Hans hope, because if she could seemingly still see a light at the end of a perilous tunnel within her morbid state of mind, it meant that it was only a matter of time before their luck would change for the best. Nonetheless, Grandmother constantly spoke of suicide to little Hans inside of the house, yet nobody else cared since their housemates too were enduring their own hardships. They could fully empathize with just why Grandmother would revert to such drastic and dramatic measures. Many believed that if she were strong enough to take her and little Hans' life, it would be a blessing in disguise since it would bring an end to their bitter anguish.

Poor Grandmother still had to carry the burden of not knowing where her daughter and husband were while knowing that her very own son and sister were both rounded up into a barn in Poland by partisans and burned alive during their "Great Trek" in the direction of Germany. Every night, Grandmother thought about her dead son and sister, along with her husband's and missing daughter's whereabouts. Grandmother felt apathetically sullen and listlessly empty on the inside. Not knowing whether her daughter and husband were alive compounded her unbearable misery. Past agony exasperated her current distress, which was further incensed by the long and arduous journey to Jug. The trials alone drove her to her condition and vindicated her desolation. Grandmother simply lost all hope and her will to live. She didn't even know where her murdered sister's three children were. It was just another affliction that worsened her feeble state of wretchedness. Grandmother's existence became more unbearable than ever.

During the 1st World War, Grandmother lost all five of her brothers, who were male nurses or medics, while serving under the Czar. They were all travelling on a Red Cross train, when all of a sudden, it got shelled. All of them were killed. To further her privation, following the Red Revolution, near the conclusion of WWI, the family lost a significant portion of their possessions, estates. and most of their wealth to the Communists and bandits. Lose is what Grandmother became accustomed to. It's all what she now knew.

CHAPTER 15

Spring 1946

Melting snow, dripping icicles, and blooming buds were the first indication that springtime in Jug was finally on the horizon. Little Hans and Grandmother outlasted their first Russian-Ural winter. The sun fading slower on the horizon with each passing sunset brightened their days. However, spring also meant that the man with the oxen would soon no longer necessitate to travel by little Hans' house every day since his cows could soon graze amongst the meadows in the mild temperatures.

Ice in the river began to crack and split before floating down the river in the direction of Perm, confirming that another Russian winter was losing wind and winding down. Thawing amongst blossoming incited the boys' curiosity and youthful exuberance. Little Hans' neighbour and this friend began joining little Hans on his adventures of venturing down a path leading to the river where they all watched ice float down stream while imagining just what kind of fun could possibly be created amongst the rejuvenating landscape. Ideas flowed through their minds as their invigoration and new-found vitality streamed through their veins. Witnessing pieces of dislodged soil from the banks splashing into the swift current of the brown river water only sparked the boys' senses, stimulation, and imagination just that much more. So, it was only a matter of time before the three youths searched out the 10-foot-high river banks for cracks in the ground, which manifested from the thaw in combination with the frost and moisture saturating the dirt. Resultantly, large pieces of soil along the river became unstable before ultimately breaking off from the bank and falling into the water. The end result – an enormous splash! Deciding to help nature along, the boys began jumping on or kicking at cracked portions of soil until the clefts and split pieces of earth turned into severed land that plopped right into the river. Every splash brought a massive smile to the boys' faces, leaving them in heaven and yearning and searching for more!

Whenever it became clear that a chunk of land was ready to tumble or soar into the river, the boys halted their bouncing and pouncing, and simply waited for the fruits of their toils to make a majestic splash. Or otherwise, they could have fallen right into the fast-flowing river along side the dislodged lump of earth. Eventually, the boys came across a portly, cracked piece of earth along the river bank. Sparked by the challenge, the boys were motivated more than ever to bounce all over the massive portion of loosened soil, before continuously leaping back onto solid ground, just waiting to see if the chunk of earth was ready to crash down into the river. After battling the earth for half an hour, the boys happily cheered as an enormous splash ensued. They were left absolutely euphoric and insatiably craving for more.

After about a week of dislodging small and larger pieces of soil, the boys discovered an absolutely mammoth section of ground that was roughly 10 feet long X 5 feet wide X 4 feet thick. Only a narrow crevice between this massive block of soil and solid ground existed, but the boys were ambitious and optimistic that if they exerted enough youthful force through a powerful pounding of bombarding pounces down upon that chunk of earth, the crack would gradually lengthen and widen. From there, it would only be a matter of time before the entire mass would come smashing down into the river and create a splash of biblical proportions.

Yet, after toiling away throughout a good portion of the afternoon, the chunk of land just wouldn't budge. The determined and boisterous boys were left exhausted and demoralized, and eventually gave up and sought out smaller, cracked chunks of earth. Even though they were once again successful after focussing their efforts on hoofing away more manageable pieces of dirt into the river, the "mother", behemoth chunk just couldn't escape their aspirations, remaining in their sights. So, once again, the boys reverted their onslaught back to the largest cracked piece of soil that they'd ever seen. They were absolutely relentless as they insatiably converged and concentrated on the challenge at hand because they knew the prize, even though it drove them to sweat and exhaustion. Though, after thirty more attempts, the boys once again conceded defeat as the sun slowly set. Eventually, little Hans turned to the boys and said,

"Let's go home! We can always pick up tomorrow where we left off."

Vladimir responded, *"Go and get a head start Vana (Hans)! We'll catch up with you!"*

Little Hans subsequently sprung off of the large piece of soil and headed up the hill. When he reached the halfway point, he turned around and glanced back at the shaggy-haired boys continuing their battle against the enormous piece of soil. Yelling to them to call it quits fell on deaf ears. Little Hans then proceeded further up the hill. When he reached the top, he turned around one last time and saw the boys still labouring away at detaching the massive cracked piece of land from the river bank. But instead of succumbing to his instinctive, or perhaps rather instinctual drift, and sprinting back down the hill to help his resolute friends "in need", little Hans continued along his way home to greet Grandmother when she returned home from her shift at the vegetable sorting storage cellar.

When little Hans arrived home, Grandmother was already back from work. She was boiling a potato on the communal stove that they shared with ten families. The entire evening, little Hans fantasized over dismantling that piece of earth from the bank with his friends the next day. He was definitive that they couldn't have achieved success without him. An enormous grin overhauled his face as a thirst for destruction occupied his head as a morsel of potato entered his mouth. After finishing dinner and heading off to bed, Grandmother and little Hans both fell fast asleep.

Yet, not long afterwards, they were suddenly awakened by voices originating from outside in the dark. A few hefty knocks thumped against the main door. Little Hans and Grandmother were startled upright in their bed that was positioned right next to the entrance. A black hole of fear engulfed little Hans as he thought,

"Who would come bother us at this hour? The police? The same ones who took (paternal) Grandfather away forever. Or are these people here to tell me that they know where my parents are?"

When Grandmother opened the door with little Hans by her side, they saw no one other than the parents of the two boys who little Hans had played with throughout the day. Looks of distress loomed over their demeanours as their faces were covered in dread. The parents swiftly marched into the house and immediately approached little Hans.

"Have you seen Vladimir and Boris?!? They didn't come home this evening."

Little Hans responded with concern, and even a bit of guilt, perhaps as a result of the insinuating nature that the parents approached him.

"I was playing with them down by the river bank. But I went home before they did. Where are they?? They didn't come home at all!?!?"

A horrible feeling overcame little Hans. The parents vehemently requested,

"Vana (Hans), take us down to the river bank! The place where you kids where playing today!"

Little Hans quickly leaped out of the doorway and said, *"Follow me!!"* A million thoughts scampered through his head, but the vision of that lump of land stuck against the bank remained like a ceaseless portrait within his head. Refraining from talking to the parents along the way, little Hans could sense their anxiousness as if it were running right through the depths of his soul. Faint rays of light shone down from the half moon. Hovering fog draped the air. They all eventually arrived at the spot where little Hans last saw the boys. But Boris and Vladimir, along with the huge piece of dislodged soil that they were ceaselessly and ecstatically jumping on all afternoon were nowhere to be found. Little Hans fearfully surmised,

"It must have fallen into the water."

It was almost pitch black in the valley along the river as the moon momentarily hid behind the hill and clouds, making it difficult to determine if that truly were the correct spot. Nevertheless, a vile chill seeped into Hans' veins. He hoped and prayed the entire time afterwards that he had brought the parents to the wrong location as it truly was too difficult to ascertain against Nature's black backdrop and mist. Little Hans then returned home and went to bed, yet couldn't sleep throughout the entire night while a search party of town's folk banded together. People from the Russian community returned to the valley with kerosene lanterns on that very same night and scoured along the high river banks that encapsulated the fast flowing, freezing cold river water. The search party combed through the forest deep into the night till dawn and beyond, incessantly bellowing, *"Vladimir!! Boris!!"*, in hope that boys' sweet little voices would answer. But they never did. The only reply that the search party ever heard was the echoing of their very own voices amongst the wooded valley. When the sun rose the following morning, there was still no sign of the two boys, so the parents went to little Hans once again, and asked him in a frenzied panic,

"Where exactly were you all playing yesterday?!?!"

Hans responded, *"I'll show you! Let's go!"*

He felt a horrible surge of toxic energy consume his body. His legs became weak, his stomach nauseous. But little Hans still felt a glimmer of hope simmer through him. When they arrived back at the exact same spot where the boys were playing the prior day, little Hans was certain this time that the huge piece of soil had, without a doubt, tumbled down the bank into the river. He consequently wondered to himself,

"Did the boys not jump off in time?? Did the chunk actually tumble into the water with them still on it?!?"

He just couldn't bearably fathom, let alone presumptuously infer aloud that they had conceivably fallen into the ice-cold water. He didn't want to think it. The current of the river was extremely strong, and Boris and Vladimir couldn't swim. Hans felt crushed and helpless, as there was nothing that he could do but wait – yet wait for what? The search party, though, refused to give up. Their search continued. The concerned community scoured the entire area in hope that the two missing boys would finally appear, yet, sadly to no avail. Boris and Vladimir were never seen again. It was concluded that the boys must have drowned in the river. They were declared dead. The parents, however, couldn't accept this conclusion. They continued their search for the ensuing three weeks before despondently accepting the reality that they would never see their precious boys ever again, despite the fact that they had vehemently hoped to at least discover their bodies. Seeing them one last time would have brought the parents resolution and closure. But their devastation never lessened.

The parents of Hans' neighbour, Vladimir, were especially deeply affected and afflicted, since he was their only child. In due course, they searched for someone to blame – that someone was no one other than little Hans. They burdened the complete blame on his shoulders. When Vladimir's mother, a slender woman with black as black hair in her 30's saw little Hans sadly meandering through the neighbourhood, she approached him.

"It's all your fault you little German!! I told Vladimir not to play with you! A German! You brought him and Boris to the river! You made'em play there! I explicitly forbad him from playing with you, and now look what happened!! Look what happens when you're friends with a bloody German! I hate you Germans! I hate you all! I hate you Vana (Hans)!!!"

Before the incident, whenever Vladimir's mom caught her boy playing with little Hans, she came storming outside screaming, *"Don't play with that German kid!"* Vladimir's father diplomatically murmured,

"Leave the boys alone. They're just kids. They don't know anything of your fury."

Even before the drownings, Vladimir's mother showed tremendous animosity, and very little remorse not only towards little Hans, but also Grandmother. She even refused to sell Grandmother potato peels that were discarded and lying in a basket, ready to be tossed to the pigs. Regardless of their circumstances and dire straights, she unconditionally refused to help out any German. However, luckily enough, the parents of the other deceased boy, Boris, neither put any blame on little Hans nor displayed an ounce of resentment towards him, whereas Vladimir's parents, or at least his mother, on the contrary, openly expressed her acrimony to Grandmother.

"Just why did this happen to our son and not to Vana!!! He doesn't even have any parents!! Nobody would grieve his death!! He's only a burden to you and nothing more!!"

After seeing Vladimir's parents' frustration and anger come to the surface, Grandmother became quite concerned for little Hans' safety. Under such a fragile and spiteful state of mind, Grandmother didn't know how far Vladimir's parents could possibly go to exact revenge against him in order to alleviate their pain. The parents of Boris ultimately intervened and attempted to convince Vladimir's parents to back off, by insisting that the two boys' deaths were the result of the fact that the 5-year-olds were merely behaving exactly like any curious 5-year-old boys do. Nothing more. But their pleas fell on deaf ears.

Despite being guilty of nothing, Vladimir's deeply hurting parents couldn't accept what happened to their son, so they re-directed their guilt for their perceived short-comings and failure as parents onto little Hans to maintain the lie. Accepting such a devastating truth is difficult for even the most rational of human beings, let alone for parents who were bitter, heart-broken, and completely shattered.

Yet, as weeks passed, and the shock of the loss of their son dissipated in unison to the heightening of their suppressed denial, the tormented parents "came to terms" with Vladimir's death, and actually began displaying signs of affection and cordiality to little Hans and his fallen sick grandmother, whose health was slowly deteriorating day by day.

CHAPTER 16

Grandmother Falls Seriously Ill

Signs of the Grandmother's diminishing health magnified. She was on the verge of death. If Grandmother didn't drink a sufficient amount of water, her stomach wall lining could collapse. If that were to happen, it would spell the end of her. But that wasn't her only motivation to gulp copious amounts of water. Due to a lack of food and nutrition, Grandmother forced herself to flood her stomach with litres upon litres of water in order to convince her body and mind that she wasn't hungry. However, drinking excessive amounts of water caused her to became water-logged. Her body became so bloated that she ballooned out to twice her normal size. Reaching such a state usually spells the end for the victim, especially a woman of her poor health and physical and psychological condition. But not attending work while she tried to recover from her near to incurable illness was not an option. She remained strong, though the same couldn't necessarily be said for little Hans. Initially diverting from his overt worries by obsessing over his cold feet, little Hans eventually faced reality and pondered,

"Who will take care of me if Grandmother doesn't make it? Who will be there to love me?"

Grandmother was the only person that little Hans had, and he was her only reason to live. That's what was keeping her strong and alive. After the loss of Vladimir and Boris, Grandmother realized just how precious life can be, especially for a child who still has decades upon decades of his best years ahead of him. She unrelentingly prayed to God to save and spare her. Even at her weakest points, Grandmother stayed unfathomably strong-willed, faith-filled, determined and faithful to God while understanding her mission – return little Hans to his mother, regardless of how fairy-tale-like and impossible that dream appeared to be with each passing day. At times, Grandmother was bed ridden and in no medical condition to perform or experience miracles. Everyone in the communal house awaited the worst. All of the families were tormented by their living conditions, so pessimism loomed over Grandmother's presence, and in all likelihood, death bed. Whispers of,

"What will we do with him when she dies? She only has a few days tops. We can't feed him! We'll have to send Hans to an orphanage."

However, in a miraculous turn of events, Grandmother defied all laws of science, and overcame her illness! She actually survived, unlike many of her roommates who were unable to overcome the very same sickness - possibly Kwashiorkor or edema - but who knows with no doctor present to diagnose Grandmother's case. Though, during that very same spring, a few weeks later, when the ordeal was seemingly over, another bout of deadly bloating plagued Grandmother. Yet, little Hans' indestructible ("nicht vernichtbar") Grandmother ultimately escaped death again and again. After two more cases of extremely excessive bloating, resulting from severe malnutrition, Grandmother still somehow pulled through. In most cases, a person of her age usually dies after her first bout with the lethal illness.

Little Hans always became worried, yet never lost hope. Whenever he looked at Grandmother while she lied in bed in excruciating pain with grotesque bloating, he saw a fragile, withered woman in her 50's who appeared as if she were approaching 80. Though, when he looked deep into her eyes, he saw a spirit full of hope, something he couldn't explain. The world had trampled her, yet her strong faith sustained her while she remained certain that God's proliferating presence proved and validated an enduring and burning spirit that refused to vacate her soul. Little Hans sensed a manifestation that can only come when you have complete belief in something that no mere human will ever be able to explain with words invented to propagate negativity.

Witnessing such drama in little Hans' life even led the parents of the deceased Vladimir to contemplate adopting little Hans. Since he was of the same age of their deceased son, while even possessing similar physical traits of Vladimir, the parents felt that little Hans could possibly compensate them for their loss, regardless of the fact that he was a loathed German. In fact, adopting little Hans would've definitely eased a heavy burden off of Hans' ailing grandma, who gradually seemed to be counting her last days as her luck was finally about to run out. If she were to perish, she would at least know that little Hans would have a family to provided for him. Before informing little Hans and Grandmother of their intentions, Vladimir's parents started bringing food and clothing to them, partially in an attempt to not only gain little Hans' trust, but also make him feel dependent upon them. Hans, on the other hand, despite constantly wondering why his parents weren't around and when they would return, oddly enough, savoured his freedom and didn't necessary completely see the need to have parents to overlook him. Such a thought was a far cry from how Hans would perceive life years later.

During this juncture, Vladimir's parents realized that little Hans had also suffered a loss when Vladimir drowned in that river. Little Hans absolutely cherished playing with Vladimir and Boris. Their time together instilled him with a feeling of brotherhood, bringing a sense of normalcy to his life. Their little adventures helped Hans forget, at least for a little while, about the hunger, cold, and not having parents – parents about whom little Hans wondered.

"Where are my mommy and daddy and why did they abandon me? Why was I not good enough for them? What makes me so inferior to the rest?"

When Vladimir's parents became aware that little Hans still went looking for the boys down by the river every morning, even after they were declared dead, in hope that the boys would miraculously reappear so that they could all play together once again - just so everything could be normal again - Vladimir's parents understood that their loss was little Hans' as well. Vladimir's parents finally saw little Hans as a victim in all of these tragedies, rather than as a seditious product of German hate and Russian sediments of resentment. After Grandmother wondrously recovered from the illness for a 5th time, the "neighbourly" parents of the deceased Vladimir, in an attempt to mildly alleviate everyone's pain and suffering finally approached Grandmother and enquired about adopting little Hans. They expressed to Grandmother, quite emphatically with the help of a translator from the communal house,

"It would be a lot better for Vana if he had a nice home. Some stability, and parents. Something that you're unable to offer him."

Despite the parents' change of heart, Grandmother simply didn't trust them. Locked in a topsy-turvy fragile state, Grandmother deeply feared their illusion of temperance, even after they extended the olive branch. Witnessing their true character when they had potato peals to offer to the starving Grandmother, but refused to offer anything fully captured the behaviours of the people, who this time around, selfishly sought something that Grandmother had to offer. Growing up amongst a family of benevolence, Grandmother learned about forgiveness and showing mercy, but she was also taught,

"One's character is revealed during times of tribulation. A rainbow of colours only comes whenever the storm ebbs."

Grandmother also never lost sight of her mission. She was determined to never give in again, give in like she did with her very own daughter back on that wagon during the "Great Trek". Grandmother's resolve fortified her faith in personally reuniting little Hans with his parents. Her convictions radiated to and ran through little Hans' veins. Words of compassion were not going to deviate her from little Hans' unwavering destiny. However, nature and the elements had seemingly other plans.

Little Hans and Grandmother "survived" their first harsh Russian winter and spring was in the air, but nevertheless, little Hans and Grandmother were far from out of the woods. They were both skin and bones. Out of desperation, Little Hans scoured the fields in search of potatoes that were overlooked during the fall harvest. The "best" pickings that he discovered were a couple of rotten potatoes that felt like eggs with a soft shell. When little Hans brought them home, Grandmother fried them up like eggs on a pan, even though they smelled atrocious and tasted much worse. Though, when you're starving, you'll eat just about anything to survive, even if the "food" leads you to vomit. Afterwards, both of them became violently ill, forcing them to try their luck with wheat, a perfect supplement that didn't necessarily have to be cooked, so it could be chewed raw if so desired.

Providing the much-needed nutrition that little Hans and Grandmother so desperately lacked, they believed that they had discovered a perfect solution to their pain-staking predicament. However, after sinking his teeth into some rye grains that consisted of course fibres and happily chewing away, a bunch of the non-dissolvable hairs got stuck right in little Hans' throat! As he hacked and violently gagged away on the fibres, little Hans felt like he was going to choke to death! But Grandmother didn't panic. Instead, she simply forced her fingers down his little throat and nonchalantly yanked out the piece of rye wheat by the stem. Grandmother though, took this occurrence as a clear sign that things had to change for her and little Hans if they expected to survive.

CHAPTER 17

Farm Work

Spring ultimately brought along not only warmer temperatures and brighter dispositions, but also a lot of change within their timber communal home. By June 1946, almost everyone had moved out. Most of the families relocated to places of their own. At this juncture, little Hans and Grandmother moved into a sewing shop where Grandmother was hired on to sew during the day and act as the building's caretaker at night. And even though little Hans was required to carry out numerous chores at the sewing shop on her behalf, he was absolutely ecstatic when the man with the oxen approached him and asked,

"Vana, you want to help me out on the farm and work the fields for a few weeks?"

Little Hans' Russian improved throughout the winter, so he fully understood the man's request, an invitation that was too good to be true. The man with the oxen required a helping hand to plow the fields of the Kolkhoz. Or perhaps he simply missed little Hans' company, so he offered him a "work placement" to keep him by his side, but either way, Hans was ecstatic over the opportunity! All of the plow work at the Kolkhoz was done by horses. Little Hans' first assignment was to ride on top of and direct the horse while a man stood on a plow being dragged behind. When it came to "disking" a field, little Hans could carry out the task at hand on his own by riding and steering the four horses. Despite not having a saddle, and resultantly, ending

95

up with blisters all over his thighs and butt that both eventually bleed, little Hans was absolutely in heaven! His deep affection for horses only paled in comparison to the joy that filled him while he rode them, which made any consequential suffered affliction more than bearable.

But all of the bliss in the world couldn't prevent little Hans' skin from blistering and falling off. After puss was released, it eventually dried up and became crusty, causing little Hans' pants to stick to his bottom and thighs. Although in excruciating pain, little Hans remained resilient, and continued on with the task at hand without a fuss. He knew that it came down either to working or possibly dying of starvation since Grandmother's wages at the sewing shop couldn't properly sustain her and Hans' little, yet growing and healing body. And begging was never an option – Grandmother enforced this notion dearly and deeply by vehemently stating,

"Rather death over begging! There's no need to degrade yourself! Helping yourself is the precursor to helping others."

Luckily enough, after about a week of continuously riding the horses, not only did little Hans' skin regenerate, but it actually toughened, or rather callused up to the point that he no longer suffered from open sores for the rest of the summer. If he were using the horses to cut grass for cattle feed or bank up the young potatoes with soil – it didn't matter to little Hans - just as long as he was working with his trusty summer horse he was experiencing moments worth cherishing.

But unfortunately, not every one of little Hans' tasks, such as weeding wheat or rye fields when the grains reached approximately one foot high required a horse of course. Nonetheless, little Hans' endless curiosity and determination spurred on his grace and ethic to lead him to happily and willing do just about anything and everything in order to not only help out the nice man with the oxen, but also earn a little food and money while he was at it. Loading grass and clover onto the wagons; picking weeds with the women; and even cleaning the stables not only proved his worth and earned his keep, but also aided him in learning new trades and skills.

And whenever lunch arrived, all of little Hans' endured sweat and pain was heavily rewarded. At the Kolkhoz, the employees were relatively well taken care of and provided for, especially compared to the rest. And little Hans definitely belonged to the rest. But in this case, he felt like a part of the privileged best. What his co-workers deemed as a typical hearty lunch, was to little Hans nothing less than a delectable feast! All of the food was cooked over an open fire and eaten out in the open air. So, little, yet sprouting Hans helped himself to his fair share of the fare and then some. Within a cast iron pot soup boiled, which sometimes even had pieces of meat thrown in for flavour and robustness. Instead of the customary boiled potatoes that little Hans was all too well accustomed to, baked potatoes over an open fire was the preparation of choice. Potatoes, the staple of little Hans' diet, prepared in such an "exotic" fashion was quite the delicious delicacy and treat for him.

After lunch, it was back to plowing, disking, and seeding until it became quite hot, at which point the workers took a Russian siesta till 5 pm. They then resumed plowing and tilling until 11 pm. At sunrise (5 am), it was back to work. Little Hans spent two weeks in the fields, at the Kolkhoz, and loved every second of it! He felt like a 5-year-old man. For once, he wasn't deemed as the repulsive German, or "nemec", a stigma that followed him throughout his entire life in the USSR, but rather, as simply like one of the guys - an intricate, yet tiny member of the team. After spending two weeks at the Kolkhoz, little Hans returned back "home" where he resumed his chores at the sewing shop. Grandmother was always extremely happy when little Hans returned home from his multi-week-long assignments at the Kolkhoz, because she not only missed him beyond belief, but also found it a lot easier to let little Hans board up the windows at the sewing shop than doing it herself.

Little Hans will always have fond memories of that summer, but more specifically, of the generous and loving man with the oxen, and even the people within the fields with whom he worked. Little Hans felt that amongst the trials, God always offered him a helping hand through the hearts of the ones who were compassionate enough to offer benevolence, altruism, and life-saving food in return for graceful drudgeries.

CHAPTER 18

Sewing Shop (1946)

Luck truly shifted for the families from the communal house when every single family got re-located to places closer to their work. These new domiciles offered every family a new sense of freedom and tranquility. They were afforded the luxury of having their own rooms, which meant everyone finally had a little privacy. Grandmother and little Hans no longer had to worry so much about someone possibly snatching their scarce food rations, or watching them bathe themselves standing up with a piece of rag. Since little Hans and Grandmother were both deemed by the state to be incapable of extensive heavy manual labour, their "deficiencies" got them assigned to the sewing shop, which afforded them more private space than the rest of the families from the communal house acquired when they too moved out on their own. The work in the vegetable sorting storage cellar ceased during the warmer months. Grandmother regarded her deployment to the sewing shop as an irrefutable promotion since she truly had a passion for the needlecraft. Grandmother was responsible for stitching together military uniforms for officers from the military base that was situated roughly 10 km away from this downtown sewing shop.

Grandmother was quite relieved and grateful by this turn of events. Her new tasks were no where near as physically exerting as her work at the sorting facility, and more importantly, she was no longer exposed to the freezing cold temperatures within the confines of the noxious-smelling vegetable storage bunker. With a renewed sense of hope, Grandmother felt bound to God once again. During the day, Grandmother joyously sewed; during the nights, her wooden sewing table converted into a "bed" where her and little Hans happily slept away. Because of the increasing crime rate in that area of town, Grandmother and little Hans, ironically enough, were also assigned to watch over the building fulltime.

Little Hans had to board up the windows by placing nailed together planks that fit perfectly into each window frame right up against the glass from the inside before going to bed next to Grandmother on the sewing table. The wooden window covers were designed precisely for each specific window. Locked into place by a piece of wood that was set across the window, the boards offered a sense of security for little Hans and Grandmother. Every sunrise, little Hans excitedly sprung up onto his feet, and carried out his first responsibility of the day - removing all the window covers so the sun could glowingly shine in and brighten up the workers' day, since otherwise, they would be left with only the unpleasant-smelling kerosene lantern to hold the light while threading and stitching. As a part of his morning chores, little Hans went down to the nearby stream to fetch pails of water used for drinking and spraying uniforms while the workers ironed the fabric. Little Hans brought two pails up in the morning, and then another two at lunch, followed by two more in the evening for their own personal use. He had to make more than ten trips a day. Little Hans possessed the spirit to haul litres upon litres of water, but suffice to say, he lacked the size and strength to carry full pails at a time. But that was still more than Grandmother could haul whenever little Hans was away at the Kolkhoz.

A large black wood-burning stove that was used for heating up solid cast irons radiated within the shop during day, which was great in the winter, but not necessarily so pleasant in the summer. Every couple of days, little Hans cleaned the ashes out of this stove. On bitterly cold nights, he and Grandmother slept as close as possible to the stove on their makeshift work table bed. The burning stove glistened, providing them heat throughout the severely freezing night. However, during the hot summer months, the heat turned the room into more of a sauna, making working and even sleeping there a lot more strenuous. The workers only ironed once a week to minimize the stove's usage during the warmer temperatures. Little Hans' responsibility was to bring in the wood and keep the stove fully loaded throughout the day.

The shop's floor was swept every night, and mopped on Sundays. Cobwebs were swiped away from the corners with brooms while the shop remained closed and free from people constantly roaming around stirring up dust. This one storey building was dark, gloomy, old, deteriorated, and somewhat dilapidated. The roof constantly leaked. Rotting wooden foundations were crumbling. In the autumn of 1946, this building sited along a ravine became condemned after being deemed too unsafe, so the sewing shop was re-located about 500 metres down the street. The "2nd sewing shop" location was also situated along a ravine, about a block from the main street, with the back entrance facing the creek. But unlike the previous one, this "new "sewing shop was located on the second floor of a building in which two German families lived below on the ground floor. Since the building sat on a slope, the "second" floor was not greatly elevated above the street below.

Little Hans carried out the same chores as at the old building, except for the fact that he now had to split the wood himself because it was no longer being delivered pre-cut or -split. Whenever the wood was brought to the new building by horse and wagon, the deliveryman simply dumped the logs into a large pile that little Hans would sort through. All the logs were delivered as 1-metre-long pieces, but the wood came in various thicknesses. Little Hans was responsible for cutting the manageable pieces in half with a saw, and then split them into smaller pieces with a splitting axe, something that was no easy task for a grown man, let alone a 5-year-old child. Although little Hans was too weak to properly hold, much less swing the axe with much force, he wasn't deterred from trying. Work "only intended for adults" only inspired little Hans. So, when the sewing shop manager provided him with a large lumberjack saw with two handles designed to be used by two full grown adults, little Hans' first instinct was to try it out.

After initially struggling away at working with all these tools, little Hans eventually somehow managed to cut a few smaller pieces of wood; however, the larger chunks were too heavy for him to even pick up, let alone split. Grandmother eventually hired a few students from the local trade school to chop the larger pieces of wood on Sundays. She was concerned that little Hans might hurt himself if he attempted to cut the larger chunks, even though he tried it anyway. The students cut as much wood as the sewing shop required for the week. Afterwards, little Hans lugged the chunks of wood inside and piled them up under a flight of stairs that led up to the sewing shop. If little Hans would have left the chopped or split wood sitting outside for too long, it would have been stolen, especially in such a seedy neighbourhood. Despite the students' help, little Hans still cut the odd piece of wood if it were necessary, or if he were in a desperate need of a challenge, which turned out to be quite regularly. He savoured pitching in and working just as much as pushing his limits and learning new methods to get the task done. Curiosity drove his desire, while patience mastered his technique.

Gradually, out of necessity, little Hans became rather inventive and ingenious when it came to splitting wood since he neither had a wooden sawhorse nor could cut the wood effectively if it were positioned on the ground. Determined to carry out the tasks at hand, little Hans wondered to himself,

"How do I raise the wood in order to cut it?"

His first idea was to take two bigger logs that were about 20 inches high and thick, and place them relatively close together. Little Hans then rolled or dragged over a smaller log or plank of wood, and attempted to cut that piece in half on top of the two 20-inch logs. However, the two bigger logs usually rolled apart and away. To prevent this from happening, little Hans placed his foot on one of the logs to keep it from wobbling. On little Hans' first attempt with this new technique, he lost his balance. On his second attempt, he was sent tumbling to the ground. On his third attempt, he made a conscious effort not to injury himself, but nonetheless, the saw's sharp teeth cut right through his pants and nicked his flesh. With his fourth attempt, little Hans applied so much force with his foot against the log that the round piece of wood rolled away on him, not only forcing him into the splits, but also causing his only pair of pants to split right down the middle. Balancing the oversized saw itself was no easy chore. The two-man saw was quite long relative to the pint-sized Hans; but ultimately, through shear determination and sweat, he more or less got the hang of splitting wood.

The initial cut always presented the greatest challenge as the log would usually sway and spin. Yet, it was only a matter of time before little Hans smartened up, and started cutting concave indentions, or notches into the placeholder logs in order to prevent them from rolling away. In essence, little Hans created his own wooden sawhorse out of logs. The manager of the sewing shop also provided him with a file to sharpen the saw. But instructions or no instructions, filing the teeth was a daunting challenge for any grown man, let alone a child pretending to be a man. Balancing the saw itself was quite the feat, let alone sharpening each individual tooth from one end to the other. Proving his ingenuity, little Hans placed the saw on a flat bench, before sitting on the long and flat dull end of the saw so it wouldn't shift. Applying his weight prevented the saw from shifting around while he meticulously filed every tooth.

Whenever the saw started jamming as little Hans sawed away, he had no other choice but to calibrate the teeth. He eventually became even more inventive with his sharpening technique by making a 4-inch-deep cut into a log, which acted as a blade holder. Little Hans then placed the saw into the groove, with the teeth facing in an upward direction. Since little Hans didn't have a chisel at his disposal, he had to use the pointed part of the axe to push the teeth apart to create the necessary gaps between the teeth.

After manicuring and calibrating the teeth, the saw was ready for smooth sawing again; however, due to all the filing and trimming, not only did the teeth became shorter, but the spread between them also became narrower. Ultimately, wear and tear led the blade to constantly jam within the wood to the point that it became impossible to cut with. Frustration and disappointment consumed little Hans. So, the next time that the delivery man came with a wagon load of wood, little Hans approached him.

"Just why isn't the wood being delivered properly split and cut, just like how it was at the old building? We can't afford to pay students!"

The driver responded curtly, *"They changed the rules and specifications!"* He then rode away, seemingly with pleasure. Little Hans instantly grumbled to himself,

"They're not splitting the wood anymore on purpose! They hate us Germans! They enjoy making life a living hell for us! Why do I gotta be a German in this backwards country!?! Just why can't I be living in Germany right now with my parents! So why didn't they want me!?! Look at how well I chop wood!! And at my age!!!"

Little Hans' right eye dispensed a tear while his heart ached and longed for a normal, functioning family, just like everyone else. The animosity towards Germans in Russia was quite high following WWII because the Russians regarded the Germans as the ones who ruined their lives and country. Some Russians sought to get even in any way that they could, sometimes at any cost. This actuality, along with the fact that little Hans' family abandoned him left him in fury and feeling inferior, and at times, like discarded refuse.

Nonetheless, little Hans and Grandmother had to do everything possible to keep a roof over their heads and have enough money to buy their bread and potatoes, which meant that they were forced into making the best out of the cards that they were dealt. To save money, little Hans continued to attempt to cut most of the wood all by himself so it wasn't necessary to hire students. And after a while, little by little, Hans kept improving on his cutting and splitting techniques at the same rate that he gradually grew and strengthened. His little muscles were developing and even slightly protruding within his scrawny and malnourished frame. To simplify the cutting process even further, little Hans created a few thick pizza-slice shaped wedges that he drove into the partially split crevices of the logs, before taking the back of the axe and pounding in the wedges to split the wood right in half. And even though he was slowly getting stronger, little, barely 6 years old Hans was still quite weak in relation to a full-grown man. But to his benefit, improvisation, patience, and creativity were his focal strengths. Little Hans applied trial, error, and failure to ultimately succeed in completing all his tasks at hand. And fortunately enough, lady luck and even Russian benevolence was occasionally on his side whenever the wood came delivered in "smaller sizes" (sometimes even pre-cut), which offered Hans a well-deserved respite.

CHAPTER 19

Gunman

Late September. Midnight's moon shines down upon Jug. Little Hans is awakened by a heavy banging on the door situated at the bottom of the stairs. A shouting man demands the occupants to,

"Open the door!!"

Little Hans, who had already fallen fast asleep on the workbench by the second-floor window, leaps up to his feet and runs to the door on the same floor, not realizing what is going on as the loud banging persists. The noisy ruckus originates from the door on the first floor. After eventually opening the second-floor door, and creeping onto the landing of the stairwell, little Hans peers down the flight of stairs that leads to the main entrance of the building. Through the gaps in between the planks of the door made out of old wooden barn boards, little Hans sees the shadow of a man. An eerie full moon draped in thin clouds illuminates the night as lunacy fills the air while butterflies enter little Hans' belly. Outside the door, sounds of a madman holding a metal object whose kicking and banging heightens little Hans' senses keeps wailing *"Open the door!!!"*, while he hammers his weapon against the wooden boards.

Suddenly, the latch on the door springs upward! With every wack up against the planks of the door, little Hans fearfully waits for the latch to fly right off of the hook and cause the door to unlock and open! Within a split second, little Hans darts down the steps of the stairwell in the direction of the first-floor door to hold down the latch so it can't pop up and out. Yet, that doesn't deter the prowler outside the entrance of the building one bit, who incessantly screams,

"Open the door or I'll kill you!!"

Little Hans calmly wonders to himself,

"Just what does he want? Does he know that me and Grandmother are staying at the shop on the second floor? He must know! He must know we're German!"

Through all the commotion, screaming, and banging, the two families on the ground floor awaken. Out of panic and fear, a voice cries out,

"Open the door and let the gentleman in!"

But their pleas fall on deaf ears as little Hans isn't budging while he calmly remains as quiet as a mouse. Grandmother eventually awakens completely startled! But she too refuses to let out a peep. Finally, everything becomes quiet. Little Hans peers through the gaps of the ground floor door, where he sees the angry intruder mount back onto his horse and ride away under the glowing moonlight on a misty Jug night. Immediately storming back upstairs to the sewing shop in the direction of the spools of thread, little Hans picks out his favourite coloured thickest thread, and rushes back down the stairs with the spool in his right hand.

When he returns to the downstairs' door, little Hans ceaselessly winds the thread around the latch until there is no thread left on the spool in order to secure the "lock", or rather hook on the door to the best of his ability. Little Hans then sprints his way back upstairs to the sewing shop where he closes the second-floor door. After barricading the entrance of the sewing shop with a table, benches, and whatever else he could humanly ram in front of the door to protect themselves just in case the foul, terrorizing man returns, little Hans hops back onto the work bench, next to Grandmother, and surprisingly falls back asleep.

But then again, Little Hans awakens. Someone lurks outside, though this time, right in front of their second storey sewing shop window. As a horse neighs, little Hans knows that the enraged man has returned! Despite the commotion, little Hans remains in a groggy state, not sure if he were dreaming or half awake, only until a gunshot rings amidst the silent night! A bullet pierces through the protective boards over the window! A revolver's shadow dances along the wall! As splinters of wood scatter throughout the room, little Hans springs up absolutely terrified in a state of trepidation! This is no dream! Little Hans was sleeping right next to the window below the wooden shutters that he had boarded up hours earlier, but the boards were no match for the bullet!

Little Hans immediately hits the deck! Grandmother and Little Hans become absolutely terrified, thinking that this is going to be the end of them! Nevertheless, the awakened, frantic families downstairs once again loudly insist,

"Open the door and let the man in!"

But little Hans isn't listening (to such ridiculous nonsense)!! Instead, he keeps his head tucked away under the bench until the moonstruck man on a horse hopefully vanishes into the foggy air, under the glow of the full moon. A few more shots fire into the air while the flailing of a cursing utter madman continues!

"Open the bloody door! Open up or I'll kill you all! Kill all you bloody Germans!"

A few minutes later, silence falls. The man on a horse seemingly finally gives up and rides away under the gleam of a full moon, and not into the sunset, as one might expect. After the coast clears, Grandmother lights a candle. Upon further inspection, she notices blood oozing out of little Hans' wounded body!! Grandmother falls into a state of shock! Large splinters of wood from the boards covering the window are lodged right within little Hans' upper arm and on one side of his back! Grandmother hurries to the drawer and grabs a pair of tweezers. One by one, she removes the splinters from little Hans' diced up body. Upon further inspection, she comes to the realization that the first shot fired narrowly missed him, and got lodged within the wall close to the ceiling, right across from the window that they were quietly sleeping next to. The workbench that little Hans and Grandmother were sleeping on was slightly higher than the window sill, leaving him not completely protected by the wall and exposed to the bullet. Luckily enough for little Hans, the bullet barely grazed him.

In the morning, when the other workers arrived at the sewing shop, little Hans and Grandmother explained to them what happened that night before. The sewing shop's manager, after hearing the story, immediately set off to the city hall to report the incident to the authorities. A man hunt for a psychopath on a horse was issued. That night, little Hans and Grandmother apprehensively went to bed, just wondering if he would return.

Though, when sunrise arrived, they realized that they survived the night. Throughout the day, every time that the door at the sewing shop opened, Grandmother clenched up, fearing that it was the man on the horse from that night, returning to carry out his deed. Her mind incessantly raced as anxiety engulfed her. Eventually, a man on a horse did enter through the doors of the sewing shop, but he turned out to be a gentleman from the authorities. The man in his 40's, with thick black hair in a crewcut came in to empathically inform Grandmother and the shop manager,

"We caught the man while he was heading out of town through the forest!"

Grandmother and little Hans were relieved and finally at ease beyond belief! Following the man's arrest, he was tossed into a jail cell at the police station. The subsequent day, the police came to the sewing shop and questioned little Hans and Grandmother about the incidents that transpired a few nights earlier. Little Hans was requested to remove his shirt.

"We'd like to take a look at where the splinters entered your body."

Following further examination, they let little Hans know,

"You were extremely lucky!! If that lunatic would've aimed his revolver a little bit lower, the bullet would've gone through your heart instead of going right in between your chest and arm! The bullet only marginally grazed you!!!"

Days later, little Hans and Grandmother were both called into court. During the courtroom cross-examination of the defendant, the assailant attempted on numerous occasions to rise up from his chair and attack little Hans! While staring at little Hans with his glossy eyes of fury, he screamed,

"You little German!! I am going to tear your head off!!"

Strangely enough, the behaviour of this madman, a drifter in his 40's with a thin narrow face, shoulder-length hair and a scruffy beard reminded little Hans quite a bit of his very own mother's; yet, still to this day, nobody knows if they were related. After witnessing such a psychopathic tirade, Grandmother became terrified about what this man could possibly do to them if he were ever released, since he knew exactly who they were; where they lived; and what they looked like. During the hearing, the police asked Grandmother and little Hans,

"Do you recognize this man?"

They both answered, as if it were exiting one mouth, *"No"*, since neither of them actually caught a glimpse of him from behind the shadows. Little Hans and Grandmother were eventually permitted to leave the court room; however, the man stayed behind for further interrogation by the authorities. He eventually confessed,

"I felt unbearably humiliated by the fact that a decrepit women and stupid little German boy were able to prevent me from breaking into the sewing shop! I simply wanted an officer's uniform to put on. I sought to heroically parade through town to acquire the admiration and veneration of all the town's folk! I merely desired to acquire their approbation and acceptance! To be regarded as an esteemed war hero by all the people of Jug has been my dream ever since I was a child! If I had access to one of the officer's uniforms from that sewing shop, I would've gained all the respect that I so deserve, if it weren't for that

little German brat!!! I'm gonna tear him to pieces!!! I went to war for this country. It's the least I deserve!!"

Ultimately, the courts determined, or at least decided that the man was suffering from post-war depression or traumatic stress syndrome, something quite common amongst soldiers returning from combat. So, instead of being regarded as a war hero, the man was deemed by the state to be a threat to society, and hence, in no state to coincide with the folk. Russian authorities took him away. He was never seen or heard from ever again. In all likelihood, he lived out his days in a Soviet Gulag work camp.

CHAPTER 20

Unjust Punishment
(from the Past)

The idea of the gunman on the horse, and his severe punishment triggered memories within Hans' head back to an instance during the autumn of 1945, not long after they all moved into the communal house. Following the long and treacherous train ride from Copenhagen to Jug that was preceded by an even more arduous five-month horse wagon trek west through WWII battle zones and perilous terrains, all the train's occupants remained under extreme duress and fully loaded with hair-triggered tempers. Many had lost numerous family members and friends, not to mention their homes and possessions. All hope was lost through all the horrific devastation. These people were resultantly constantly left on edge and tormented by fear. Hence, completely flying off the handle and going berserk became a regular occurrence amongst the families. A thick penetrating and volatile aura of irritation and despair afflicted the group crammed inside of the communal house. At the drop of a pin, pandemonium could erupt out. In order to keep their "situation" under control, the inhabitants never hesitated to resort to severe punishment.

The manifestation of such feelings proliferated like a bacterial culture within the communal home. One day, not long after moving in, while tensions, fear, uncertainty, and anxiety amongst the "roommates" were at its peak, a 12-year-old boy prompted a very minor incident that ultimately galvanized into a major outcome that will remain engrained in little Hans' thoughts for an eternity. The boy's deed led the adults in the house to overreact, and consequently, unleash their searing vexations out on the young lad. The inhabitants' uncontrollable mental states searched for a cause to vent their frustrations. Thus, sternly punishing the 12-year boy for his faux-pas in order to re-establish control over their precarious predicament seemed more than rational at the time. However, the people had no intent of delivering the gruesome conclusion that resulted from their firm stance.

On the main level of the communal house, there was a hinged door on the wooden floor that led to a cellar that was previously used for storing vegetables. As a "reasonable" punishment, a few men opened the hinged door and heaved the 12-year boy down into the cellar so that he could think about what he had "done." The 6-foot-deep, or rather high cellar, was cold, damp, drafty, and dark, with the only ray of light entering in from the main floor through a narrow opening in the door. After landing on his back on the dirt cellar floor, the boy screamed out in terror and pain. He cried feverously; yet, after a short while, all the commotion and uproar suddenly ceased to exist. All fell silent. The people upstairs were quite relieved to hear his excruciating crying come to an end and comforted to know that he had finally fallen asleep.

In due time, the adults decided that the boy had learned his lesson, and permitted him to return upstairs. Though, after unlocking and opening the hinged, wooden floor-door and calling his name, there was no response – not even a stir of movement. A few men eventually creeped down into the cellar to see just why the boy was refusing to answer. Was he still bitter and angry, or simply sleeping? Though, when they finally found him, he wasn't sleeping at all. He was just lying there, motionless on the dirt floor that was completely infested by rats! The two men quickly picked the boy up and carried him upstairs into the main and only room of the house where they discovered that their stern punishment had turned into a gruesome tragedy. The boy's body had been fatally bitten and gnawed on by rats. The residents of the house were under such a complete shock after the catastrophic incident that they refused to talk about the ghastly happening for a long time to come. Eventually, the kids started saying,

"If you don't behave, you'll be thrown into the cellar and eaten by the rats!!"

Issues with rats were not foreign to any part of Russia, including the communal house in Jug. In Russian folklore, a moving train gets halted by countless aggressive rats whose blood entirely floods the tracks.

Little Hans was the youngest in the house at the time, and still too young to fully comprehend what had transpired, even though he knew enough to sense the horror emanating from the house's occupants. He figured that their rules and forms of punishment didn't apply to him. This impression was compounded by the fact that it appeared as if he and Grandmother didn't even exist to the rest of the families within the house. But that wasn't necessarily a bad thing, since the people of the house were constantly bickering at each other, engaging in bitter quarrels and squabbles that little Hans and Grandmother had no interest in getting involved in while staying tucked away, going more or less unnoticed amongst the perpetual commotion. Both had enough frustration in life and no energy to voluntarily get entangled up in such petty, trivial nonsense.

However, all that unfortunately changed one morning in the spring of 1946, when Grandmother forgot to take her prized and precious ruble with her to work, just as she always had. Every morning, before heading off to her shift at the vegetable sorting facility, Grandmother placed the ruble that she earned from all her toil at work on the blanket on their bed. Then, right before she left for work, she placed the ruble in the pocket of her grey wool coat. However, on this very occasion, Grandmother accidently forgot her prized ruble. Little Hans, in his usual, quite carefree manner, simply went out for the day to pursue his daily dose of adventures outside of the confines of the "mundane" communal house. However, the house became a lot livelier when Grandmother returned home from work that evening. Upon arrival, she immediately searched everywhere for her ruble. But, it was nowhere to be seen. Innocently enough, Grandmother enquired with the women stationed across from her in their house,

"Did you happen to come across a ruble?"

This turned out to be a drastic mistake! Grandmother immediately wondered,

"Did she take that question as an accusation?"

The enquiry alone triggered, or rather conjured up an outburst of animosity out of the women. When little Hans arrived home, the husbands of these women, in their eyes, had no other choice but to grab and shake little Hans.

"Where is the ruble! We know you took it! What have you done with it you little thief!!!"

Before little Hans knew it, he was being tossed around from person to person, until someone grabbed him and opened the wooden door in the floor, before throwing him down into the cellar with the deadly rats. Grandmother incessantly wailed, pleading with them,

"Get him out of there! He's innocent! Why would he steal from me!?! His very own grandmother!! You're going to kill him just like the other boy you threw down there!!!"

Since this matter didn't concern any of the house residents, Grandmother knew perfectly well that they merely desired to get out their own frustration, which meant Grandmother had absolutely no clue how far they would go to make someone suffer in order to prove their point. Grandmother believed that something horrible could happen to little Hans, exactly like with the other boy who was picked alive by rats in the vegetable cellar. Though, little Hans wasn't quite as frightened as the deceased boy. Little Hans simply climbed up to the rickety top step of the ladder in the cellar, right next to the floor boards of the main floor. Perching himself up on the ladder, little Hans figured that he had a much better chance of surviving if he didn't touch the ground and come into contact with the hoard of hungry rats below. And although little Hans was terrified, he remained as quiet as a mouse. Even at a young age, little Hans had too much (senseless) pride to give the impression that people possessed power over him. Hence, he had no interest in giving his punishers, or even the rats for that matter any satisfaction. Little Hans could hear the rats congregating and crawling around down below him. Whenever one came close to him, he handed it a kick or a wack. During this entire time, Grandmother desperately and repeatedly pleaded with the people, *"Let Hansi out of the cellar!"*, until a woman finally came to her senses and unlatched and opened the door.

However, many were not satisfied with little Hans' punishment one bit. They believed that his reprimand was not severe enough. Their belief of justice could only be met if little Hans were viciously pelted with a belt. Only a savage lashing could absolve little Hans of "his crime". So, four "heroic" men instantly grabbed little Hans and laid him down on his stomach on a bench while a fifth man held onto his legs. Two men firmly grasped little Hans' arms, just so the 5-year old couldn't squirm. In the meantime, the fourth man grabbed a hold of a four-foot long black belt with a silver buckle on the end. Tightly and furiously grasping the belt that he folded in two until his veins started bugling, the man aggressively raised his arm with a motion that perfectly captured the tension in his spirit. Little Hans then felt a horrendous lash upon his back! Then another! His punisher showed little concern for where the belt happened to land. During the beating, a memory of little Hans' mother lashing him with a stick over his back, back in Fürstenwerder entered his mind. As he felt the flogging of the belt across his back and bottom, little Hans sensed a past torturing at the hands of his very own mother rush through his bones. A dark sense of abhorrence entered his veins. Nevertheless, he didn't let out a peep, at least until one of the ladies witnessing the merciless whipping whispered into little Hans' ear,

"If you scream a bit, they may let you go."

Out of compulsion, little Hans eventually gave in, and briefly let out a short-winded yelp. Alas! The men were finally satisfied by the fact that they had obtained power over little Hans, so they let him go. Following the "punishment", little Hans could barely walk, let alone comfortably sit down for the next few weeks. He remained in constant physical agony – the mental anguish would come later. Bruises plastered his body, even though his behind was apparently the only target during the entire lashing. Grandmother felt horrible, not only about the whole torturing incident, but also because she blamed herself for what transpired since she was the catalyst of what materialized.

"If I had only kept quiet and my big mouth shut about the missing ruble nothing would've happened to my poor, little, innocent grandson!"

Word of little Hans' torturing quickly spread throughout the neighbourhood. It didn't take long for a store clerk across the way to hear word of the tale. Two days following the punishment, this very same clerk entered the communal house and pointed out two little girls with matching blonde pigtails, who she claimed had come into the store and bought some candy a few days earlier. These two sisters, along with their very own mother, with passive nuances of guilt, vehemently denied all the accusations.

However, the rest of the people, many as blood-thirsty as usual, were not convinced. They were seeking justice, or at the very least some more drama in an attempt to alleviate and "ease" in their tumultuous lives. Many adults demanded that the two sisters' pockets be searched. The girls and their mother naturally refused. But the residents of the communal home were determined to find another guilty party, so a few of them resolutely drove their hands into the girls' pockets! An abundance of candy was found along with numerous empty wrappers. As their faces turned red, the girls admitted to stealing the ruble.

"We took it but we didn't know who it belonged too!! We found it on the ground and not on the bed!"

The clerk at the store knew little Hans, and simply couldn't fathom that he would ever steal anything, especially from his very own ailing grandmother. So, when the store keeper's kids, who happily played with little Hans told her about the incident, her first thought went to the two sisters who entered her shop a few days earlier. Her suspicions were confirmed when she heard that the two sisters were bragging about not only stealing the ruble (and 5 kopeks), but also getting little Hans punished for their deed; she felt that she had no other option but to intervene. This woman was fully aware about how hard little Hans and his grandmother already had it, so she knew that he neither deserved nor necessitated to experience any unfair punishment on top of his already massive pile of misery.

Grandmother became unbelievably grateful to the clerk for clearing little Hans' name as she couldn't stomach Hans being labelled as a thief. She always taught him that decency and honesty are the only ways to live by. Little Hans sensed, already at an early age, that it wasn't necessary to steal. He learned in life, that if he required food, all that he had to do was offer his services, and eventually someone would be nice and appreciative enough to reward him with a morsel.

Despite all the hardships brought on by the war and Stalin's regime, people were not necessarily always vindictive. At times, individuals exhibited the utmost compassion to one another. And even though many Russians lost family members during the war, which resultantly led them to despise the Germans, little Hans always found people who could transcend their hate, and follow their benevolent heart by graciously offering him a helping hand and nourishment - like the man with the oxen, or the man who took a chance on them by providing Grandmother and little Hans residence and jobs at the sewing shop. And Grandmother was acquainted with benevolence herself. While possessing a ruble, a beggar approached her at the communal house, asking for some spare change. The beggar had nothing until Grandmother handed the beggar her last ruble and was left with nothing herself. Little Hans was shocked by her "absurd" act of generosity. In complete disbelief, little Hans asked Grandmother,

"Why did you give him your last ruble?? Now you have nothing!!

She wittingly responded, *"True, but now he has a ruble, so we both know exactly what the other felt like."*

There was one less ruble in the communal house to steal, but nevertheless, little Hans still found grounds to be punished for one "deed" that to this day is still unknown to him. Consequently, a few of the men in the home elected to lift little Hans up and carry him outside, where he was deposited

John Friesen

into a 6 X 6 X 7-foot hole that was intended to become their future outhouse repository. Little Hans was left amongst the darkness for the entire night. He was too small to be able to escape the hole and despicable sternness of his "new" family. Eagerly awaiting sunrise like never before, little Hans nonetheless appreciated that he at least finally had his privacy and peace. When dawn finally arrived, little Hans' playing buddies came looking for him; yet, he was nowhere to be found, until Boris and Vladimir eventually discovered little Hans in a hole that served as his "bedroom" for the entire night. The boys immediately lunged for his hand, but couldn't gain a grasp in their attempt to haul little Hans out.

Alternatively, Boris and Vladimir, the boys who eventually drowned in the river weeks later, attempted to pass little Hans the end of a long stick. Boris went down right onto his stomach with the stick in hand, while Vladimir grabbed a hold of Boris' legs. Little Hans clutched a hold of the stick, and scampered his way up to the halfway point of the hole, only till he found himself tumbling back in on his behind. Boris and Vladimir simply couldn't find enough leverage and strength to fully pry little Hans out of the hole, but they were by no means prepared to give up without a tug of war.

Vladimir and Boris realized that if they wanted to play with their little buddy, they required a stronger and more robust piece of wood to haul little Hans out of the hole. Eventually they discovered a long piece of wood attached to a fence that they slid down into the hole, in hope that little Hans would be able to climb his way up to safety. And even though they were fully aware that they could be in for a severe punishment if they were ever caught dismantling the fence, they believed that if it came at the expense of rescuing their little buddy, then it was a risk worth taking. So, the two boys grabbed a hold of the long shaft of wood that was horizontally mounted onto the fence, and arduously dragged the heavy piece of lumber 20 metres over to the hole. Before they knew it, the boys found themselves sliding the shaft of wood downwards into the well dug hole in which little Hans was still hopelessly trapped within. Though, when little Hans saw the piece of wood slowly approaching him, hope filled his eyes. He optimistically grasped for the long and round shaft of wood. Yet, as little

Hans attempted to climb up the log to safety, it started rolling around, ultimately sending him tumbling to the ground. At first, the boys had difficulty holding the round piece of wood in place while little Hans toed the incline upwards on the log. However, eventually they all got the hang of it and prevented the wood from swaying and rotating. It was then only a matter of minutes before little Hans cautiously and slowly tippy-toed his way up the log until he neared the top of the hole, which was when the boys reeled him in by clamping onto his small and dirt covered hands.

Although the people in the communal house probably wouldn't have been so excited to know that little Hans had escaped, he didn't care. Boris' and Vladimir's act of comradery left little Hans feeling gratefully bonded when the boys' hands linked, bringing their adventurous play pal back into play. But their fun sadly ran out weeks later when Boris and Vladimir tragically drowned in the river. But that was unfortunately now all history, or as the Germans say, *"Snow from yesterday."*

CHAPTER 21

Down by The Creek

In late spring of 1947, Grandmother was informed that the second sewing shop was closing after it was deemed to be too small. Little Hans and Grandmother were once again rendered homeless. After gathering their pot and bowl and wrapping them up in a blanket, they headed down by the river where they set up camp between the flowing water and high bank. Floating driftwood fuelled their fire that they used to boil water for cooking, washing, and staying warm. The trusty river provided them with not only water for drinking, bathing and washing, but also fish and shellfish for eating. Little Hans also prowled after bird nests, so he could snatch eggs for cooking.

The water level of the river was fortunately quite low during the summer, so little Hans and Grandmother could settle along the bank and find shelter for the night, quite close to the water. A burning fire provided them warmth until they fell asleep. Throughout the days, the weather was usually quite pleasant. Surprisingly, they found their new living quarters rather tranquil, except for when it occasionally rained. Every night, Grandmother prayed. Prayer gave her hope that someone would eventually offer them a place to stay by the time autumn reared her chilly presence while God provided them with sustenance and serenity throughout the summer.

In the meantime, little Hans kept on looking for work throughout the days, regardless of the task. During the nights, he gazed with Grandmother into the heavens and stars and wondered about just how magically and mystically the Universe radiantly spirals within such a flawless sphere. Hans cynically wondered himself,

"How could mere dust create something so pristine and glorious? Something so immaculate and perfectly aligned? The Communists can't even explain where that dust and big bang came from. And why? Why create anything?"

He sensed that it was all too perfect and beatific to be the mere coincidence that the Communists forcefully claimed. A surreal feeling overcame little Hans and Grandmother as they sensed that they were at the hands of Heaven's grace and mercy, which oddly enough left them feeling empowered. They had nothing besides their freedom, freedom that possessed them with spirit. Worrying about someone venting rage in their direction, like in the communal house, or even at the sewing shop, like on the night of the gunman wasn't present here. Unpleasant humanly elements seemingly vanished amongst Nature's stillness. Grandmother's and little Hans' main, and perhaps sole worry was to find something to eat, while taking life moment-by-moment.

Grandmother spent her days soaking up the sounds of summer down by the river, sometimes even making sounds of her own by playing her cherished harmonica, whereas little Hans eventually resumed working with the man with the oxen. Luckily enough, little Hans remained healthy, vibrant, and vigilant, which was a blessing because not all were so lucky. Many Russian children of his age were malnourished, and resultantly, fell victim to illnesses and even spinal deformations. However, even little Hans' luck could change.

Because as fall approached, Mother Nature brought along cooler days and even brisker nights. At this point, little Hans and Grandmother were in dire need of shelter, as even the healthiest of the fittest couldn't survive the upcoming months living outside next to the river amongst the unforgiving Ural region "autumn" elements. Still, Grandmother's faith proliferated. She continuously prayed to God to help them out, in hope that something special would come their way. Frequent meditation and thoughts about her life of wealth in the past brought back pleasant memories of when food was abundantly bountiful. Sitting by the fire at night, Grandmother reminisced. She explained to little Hans how life used to be.

"I came from a wealthy family, so I never had to work until after the revolution. Our family owned lots of land and a flour mill. Back then, we hired these Russians to do our dirty work! Before the revolution, the Germans here bought fancy furniture in the States; had electricity and phones in their homes; and even had opulent glass ceilings embedded with huge fish tanks in their mansions. We were all well ahead of not only our time, but also most countries, including Germany and the United States."

With a slight sense of bitterness, she continued.

"But now look at us! All of us Germans! And even these Russians! Back in those days my life mainly consisted of socializing. I had five brothers and one sister. My five brothers were killed during the 1st World War when the Germans shelled the train that they were in."

As she choked up, tears dispelled from her eyes.

"Then my very own sister and son were murdered a few years ago when Polish partisans burned them alive in a barn. But God spared me. Well, at least my body. Perhaps to be with you. My soul is shattered, but a Spirit possesses me and lets me endure and see beyond these happenings. When I think that I'm too weak to go on, a wind from seemingly nowhere enters my soul and lets me sail."

A few more tears rolled down her right cheek as she looked down at little Hans while she brushed his sweaty blonde hair. If they were tears of pain, anguish, self-pity, or joy – little Hans wasn't sure, but nonetheless comforted. Grandmother continued.

"When I was younger, we often visited relatives and friends in nearby towns. I always enjoyed riding in a horse drawn carriage, especially when I got to dress up in fashionable clothing. And even though I fell off a carriage and broke my hip when I was seven, I always had trust in God, which led me to never

fear getting back onto a carriage. It's still a dark memory, but I believe dark memories exist for a reason.

There will be times in your life when you will be confronted by demons. It will matter neither how positive you try to think, how pompously you try to talk, nor who you try to avoid or fraternize with, you will be confronted with tests. This is a critical fundamental of life. It is our decision how we react to these circumstances. Our reactions always lie within our hands and heads."

She added, with her eyes wide open and lit up as if she were six years old again,

"I also used to love knitting, embroidery, sewing, and even going to school. I could write gothic German quite exquisitely. Well, I still can! I also loved my time in the church choir. I could play music by ear. Well, I still can!"

While she stood up to grab a piece of wood to toss onto the fire, she admitted in a somber tone,

"But after I fell off that carriage, my hip never properly healed, and that's why I still walk with a limp. Sometimes our tests come sooner than later."

Little Hans felt deep sorrow for his dear, little grandmother, but was amazed at how she was able to muster up a smile and a spark in her eyes, even during the most trying of times, especially considering that she never put the blame on anyone else besides herself. She bore all the guilt for accepting little Hans into her wagon and arms from his mother a few years earlier after their stop in Wartegau, Germany, during the concluding months of WWII.

"I will be tormented by that incident for the rest of my life. I know God forgives me, and I shouldn't feel guilty, but it doesn't matter — this burden will be sewn within me for an eternity. But I accept that."

Each time that she glanced into little Hans' piercing blue eyes, it reminded her of how she ruined his life by taking him into her wagon, or at least, that's what she convinced herself of. Though, in Hans' eyes, he was nearly certain that his parents accidently lost him, and nothing more. Or at least that's what helped him sleep at night. But regardless of what truly transpired that day years earlier, Grandmother told Hans,

"You don't deserve this type of life. I must get you back to your parents! I promise, that's what I'll do! It will come to fruition before I die, even though I neither have a clue how, nor know where your parents are! I have no idea how the Soviets will let us leave this god-forsaken land! But I sense through my veins, heart, and soul that this prophecy will be fulfilled.

All what I know and believe is that God will answer my prayers. This is the only revelation that keeps me from succumbing to the echoes of bleakness, total despondency, and self-imposed damnation. Even though I am completely worn out, hungry, stressed, and suffering from deprivation, hope still flows through me. Hope dictates and solidifies my belief. My destiny is written in gorgeous gothic calligraphy. Written before Lenin, Engels, and Marx were even born. The Communists only believe in power in hope of more power. I faithfully believe in fate stemming from God's will."

A day later, a prayer was finally answered when little Hans and Grandmother apprehensively spotted a man walking down the hill in the direction of the river bank. Though as the man got closer, their apprehensions transformed into appreciation when they realized that the man was no one other than Pavel, the manager from the sewing shop! Pavel was joyful and spirited as he was the bearer of wonderful news!

"Hello, hello, you two again! You look relaxed! Now guess what!? We're opening up another (3rd) sewing shop!! We need you two back!! I'll return and let ya know when it's all complete and formalized. Then you guys can resume your work and have a place to stay. You'll have a nice roof over ya heads as usual."

Before giving them both a hug and departing, he added,

"The new building will also be down on the main road."

Immediately afterwards, Grandmother turned to little Hans and said,

John Friesen

"See! God does answer prayers! We're saved from freezing to death! The darkest moments prove that light exists. Without darkness, you'd never recognize that light shines through."

Days later, little Hans discovered a crow with a broken wing staggering by the river. He immediately picked it up and fed it a few raspberries and a tiny piece of a Silver Bream fish. In a matter of days, the crow was fully healed and gleefully flew away. Right when Hans wondered about the large black crow a few days later, and felt sorrow that he would never see the crow again, that seemingly same crow astonishingly landed right on Hans' shoulder, as if to thank him. Experiencing such an act of love and gratitude following the crow's downfall made little Hans think about what Grandmother said.

"The darkest moments prove that light exists….. that light shines through….."

CHAPTER 22

School Time

A few days later, Pavel, the sewing shop manager happily returned.

"Come with me you two. I'm going to show you your new home! Let's go!"

He led them down a dirt road towards the new sewing shop. Walking along, Hans stared up at a red billboard that the communists displayed all over town and even in the schools. With a picture of Stalin spattered on it, it held the caption, *"Если вы не работаете, вы не едите (If you don't work, you don't eat!)"* Grandmother once told Hans that the slogan, ironically enough, was a proverb from the New Testament. This axion looped around in Hans' mind until he heard Pavel say,

"We're here! This is the new sewing shop!"

It was one storey. Falling apart. The floor and foundations were rotting. Rats appeared from time-to-time. But it was their new home sweet home! Little Hans and Grandmother had a roof over their heads for the upcoming winter; work to keep them busy; and money to buy a little food, so they were more than content. Days later, Grandmother was back to sewing, exactly like how little Hans was back to carrying out his chores and tasks. He continued to search for any other kind of work that he could find in order to get some food in his stomach. And fortunately, for their sake, it was early fall, which meant that farmers were in full harvest. Food was in abundance, making it rather affordable. Little Hans attempted to fatten up during this time, before the harsh and cruel winter reared its ugly, yet white, pristine, and snowy head – a time when food was in short supply for almost everyone. If little Hans and Grandmother would have lived by the river for another month, they both would have either frozen or starved to death.

Once autumn fully set in, little Hans was off to school every morning. But, before he left, he still had to un-board the windows and fetch two pails of water from the river. By noon, he'd return home from school and haul two more pails of water to the sewing shop. Afterwards, he cut wood for the next day. By this time, little Hans was strong enough to do all the wood cutting on his own, so hiring students to carry out this task was no longer necessary, helping Hans and Grandmother save even more money. In addition, Grandmother was able to make clothes for Hans out of discarded army uniforms. She was taking quality material out of old uniforms that the officers brought into the sewing shop to show Grandmother which sort of patterns they desired for their new uniforms. Afterwards, the soldiers simply left the old uniforms behind. "Little" Hans was quickly outgrowing his clothes. Not needing to buy new clothe for clothing for little Hans' developing body helped Grandmother save even more money.

Another ancillary benefit of this new sewing shop was that it came with a dirt backyard that could be converted into a garden. Grandmother saved up as much money as possible during the winter, so when the warmth of spring arrived, they could afford to have their backyard plowed and seeded. All winter long, they relished in knowing that they'd be able to grow their own potatoes, cabbage, carrots, cucumbers, beets, and even peas. Just the thought of harvesting their own food left them feeling blessed. A man with horses and a plow went to private homes (or a "private sewing shop house") and plowed peoples' gardens for a fee.

Money became even sparser when little Hans was required to buy his own textbooks and notebooks for school, so he and Grandmother searched out more affordable used school books. Occasionally, little Hans even made his own workbooks by cutting out edges from old newspapers.

Every child in school was mandated to wear a red kerchief or bandana around his or her neck. The obligation of buying the kerchief lied squarely on the parents' shoulders. Yet, little Hans had absolutely no desire in garnishing anything around his neck, let alone paying tribute to the Communist brethren by brandishing a costly bandana representing Soviet solidarity. So, he attended his first day of school defiantly, without wearing the compulsory red kerchief. Standing out like a blond German amongst dark haired Russians, the parties in charge at school eventually informed little Hans,

"You must wear the kerchief! "It is not optional! Even for you Germans!"

Little Hans refused to heed their word. He had no interest in wearing the bandana, which in his case, was more like a noose around his neck than an homage to proletarians. He was convinced that it was only necessary for Russian kids to bear the red kerchief, so he believed with all his conviction that once again the rules didn't apply to him. Though eventually, little Hans learned otherwise. As punishment for his insolence, his female teacher in her early 40's shamed and reprimanded little Hans right in front of the entire class by sending him to stand in the corner.

"Vana, are you too good for the kerchief?!? Are you above the rules?!? Are you too good for your comrades?!? You are not worthy of being educated!! Stand in the corner until I see a red bandana around your neck!"

Little Hans eventually informed his teacher,

"I can't afford to buy a kerchief. It's hard enough to scrounge together enough money to buy books."

But little Hans' pleas fell on deaf ears. His teacher insisted,

"You must wear the red kerchief! These are the rules for everyone! You are no exception to the rest! You are not above the rules. We will expel you if you don't comply!"

When the kids saw little Hans without the kerchief they complained.

"Why doesn't he have to wear this irritating thing, but we do!?!

For this reason alone, the teacher had to make an example of little Hans, and not an exception. But little Hans and Grandmother had nobody, and inherited absolutely nothing - not even a Communist kerchief, like the other kids. They were both left in dire straights once again. When he returned home from school, Hans told Grandmother,

"They keep insisting that I must wear that kerchief! They yelled at me and sent me to the corner. The teacher said that these are the rules and I'm not above them!"

The following day, Grandmother brought little Hans to a clothing store in the town's square to purchase the "beloved" red kerchief. Though, after a brief glance at the price, they immediately realized that there was no way that they could afford one. Their meagre savings were not nearly enough. Little Hans was "surprisingly" relieved. He simply couldn't imagine wearing the red kerchief around his neck in the presence of kids not only much older than him, but also who had no problem with imposing their dominance over little Hans. Hence, Hans was driven to rebel against being one of them.

Little Hans purposely avoided wearing the bandana for another good reason as well. He knew from past experiences that if he were to wear the kerchief, the older kids would happily grab a hold of it and drag him around the school yard. The kerchief acted more as a means for bullies to choke him than anything else. Older boys were already grabbing little Hans by the ears and lifting him up into the air, so he had no interest in learning just what they'd attempt if he were to ever wear one of those kerchiefs around his neck.

At the time, Hans was just about to turn eight, whereas some kids in his class were already 15 years old. During the WWII, the schools were closed in Russia. When they re-opened after the war, many students were still in Grade One, some with seemingly no signs of ever passing. The Russian government "attempted" to educate the kids up to a Grade Seven level.

Nevertheless, illiteracy rates in Russia were quite high, leading Hans to mockingly think to himself,

"So evidently these red kerchiefs aren't helping kids learn how to read."

Most of the students had absolutely no interest or desire to learn. Many were merely looking for mischief, instead of academic instruction. These juvenile delinquents usually dropped out and found jobs. There were two or three trade schools across from a local orphanage not far from the grade school that teenagers attended until they were summoned into the Russian Red Army. Enlisting was a mandatory duty to the Motherland when a Russian male turned 19 years of age.

Once little Hans arrived back at school the next day after shopping for a kerchief, he informed his teacher,

"My Grandmother and I went to buy a kerchief yesterday, but we don't have enough money to pay for one."

The now, somewhat sympathetic teacher responded, *"I'll try to find you a used one."* But she never did. So little Hans was ultimately permitted to enter the classroom without brandishing the Soviet red kerchief, but that was the least of his troubles.

Since little Hans was the youngest and smallest, he always sat in the front of the classroom. As soon as the teacher turned her back on the rest of the class, the other students pelted him with whatever they could get their hands on. Pens, scrunched up paper, rulers, books. It didn't matter. They even hurled ink containers that splattered all over poor little Hans. Whenever they luckily enough failed to smack him, their projectiles landed in the vicinity of the teacher, and at times, even hit her. At first, she presumed that little Hans was the one tossing all of the objects in her direction; yet, after a while, she realized that it was the older kids further back, so she placed little Hans at the back of the class with the broad-shouldered boys who deemed learning as an unnecessary evil. Such a measure was necessary, or the teacher would have had absolutely no control over the classroom. Sometimes, the kids even took the plastic or metal tubes from their pens, and used them to spit potato pieces, or even the metal writing tip of the pen in little Hans' direction. In one instance, another child lost an eye in such an incident. Little Hans, fortunately enough, kept both of his eyes, but that was seemingly his only break. One morning, upon entry into the classroom, four teens of physical stature in wool sweaters approached little Hans and hoisted him up into the air. Little Hans calmly thought, *"Oh boy, what's next?"*

Before he could think another thought, a boy a foot and a half taller than him provided an answer.

"You're going to hang around for a bit German boy!!"

Little Hans seemingly had become immune to the abuse, even though deep down the condemnation was tearing him apart while molding him on the inside. When the teacher eventually entered the classroom, she discovered nothing other than little Hans dangling from the top of the blackboard, with his feet swinging through the air. Initially, she merely gazed at him in astonishment and awe, until she, still in shock, asked,

"Just what are you doing up there Vana?!?!"

Eventually, she saw the "humour" in little Hans' unfortunate predicament, yet she consciously attempted to conceal her amusement and smirk as she neither wanted to encourage such behaviour, nor appear totally insensitive to little Hans. Glaring into the back of the class, she ordered to his class-"mates",

"Take him down immediately!"

Yet, when the bigger lunk-heads came to the front to detach little Hans, they realized that it was much simpler to get him up there than down. Little Hans was stuck on the hook by his thick wool khaki button-up shirt made from old army uniforms. The boys' persistent effort, though, eventually paid off. But the moment that little Hans was literally let off the hook was the moment when he felt himself land face first flat onto the floor! After it was all said, hung, and done, he walked away with a few bruises and some aches and pains that perfectly complimented his emotional agony. But Hans was a resilient lifer, so he kept on chugging along, even though the pain-staking toll and trauma consumed him on the inside. No human can possibly escape unscathed from such inhumane and hateful treatment. Little Hans was no exception. Luckily enough, in this instance, he didn't get punished for the incident and for what he "caused", like in many others cases when he got reprimanded, regardless of whether he deserved it or not.

But school wasn't little Hans' only concern since he still needed to eat. Therefore, he constantly searched for work, in hope of receiving at least a sandwich in return. At this point, Grandmother didn't even know where little Hans was most of the time, and was actually surprised whenever he made an appearance at home. She usually greeted him with, *"Oh, you're home again"*, on the occasion that they happened to cross paths. Grandmother had her own issues as well, so she spent much of her time despondently in her own world with her head in dreary storm clouds unable to dissipate on the horizon. But that didn't necessarily mean that other kids and families were living at the end of the rainbow. Many Russians, at least in Jug, struggled to survive. Though, in little Hans' case, he was constantly not only the victim, but also a punching bag for people who found their lives so grim that they were convinced that crushing others was their cure and route to salvation from their own personal misery.

On the way home from school every day, little Hans had to walk by an orphanage complex that resembled a massive grey concrete block army barracks, which was closed in by a 6-foot tall wooden fence. Kids whose parents died, were murdered, "displaced", or killed by the Germans during the WWII flooded the orphanage. Whenever little Hans strolled by this orphanage, older kids residing within the complex constantly brought little German Hans to a halt, and searched his pockets for any "valuables". Though, all that they ever found was dust and lint. Yet, that didn't prevent them from pushing, tossing, and kicking him around until they got bored with tormenting him, which is when they released and let him head off along his way. Their favourite form of "play" was to pick up little Hans and chuck him into a puddle of mud. Needless to say, the gratifying result was always a filthy splash of brown water that left little Hans felling dejected and covered in mud. Some of these foster kids went to the same school as little Hans, whereas others went to the high school in the vicinity. After returning from school, these orphans were again locked up within the orphanage complex.

On the bright side, one boy from the orphanage felt for and befriended little Hans. He didn't condone the behaviour of his fellow "inmates," especially because he too was a constant target of theirs. This boy, with wavy black hair, was two years older than Hans and a grade higher, but nevertheless, wasn't spared from the shenanigans and tomfoolery of his fellow orphans who took pleasure in deriding him as well. Hence, he despised living in the orphanage. However, there were a few perks to residing there, since all the orphans were provided with their own school supplies and kerchiefs, not to mention a constant supply of food. Whenever a few "extras" were to spare, little Hans' new friend Alexander, offered him whatever he could obtain – pens, paper, pencils – courtesy of the orphanage. Sometimes Alexander, who wore pants three sizes too big for his thin legs provided little Hans with some food like a lump of bread.

Yet, what made their bond even stronger was the fact that both were in search of their parents. Their common dilemma solidified their friendship, even though Alexander was Russian. But, he was quite different from the rest. The sensitive Alexander possessed an extremely peaceful demeanour, which made him a clear target for bullies in search of victims and easy prey. Being possessed by an innocent and kind presence left Alexander quite un-understandable to the rest.

To compound Alexander's concerns, his fellow orphans were not too impressed that he had befriended little "German" Hans, which just led them to intensify their abuse. The other foster kids had absolutely no qualm when it came to forcefully painting on Alexander's face; putting cotton balls between his toes, before lighting them on fire; pouring water all over him; or even tying him to his bunk bed while he slept. At the orphanage, the kids slept in wooden bunk beds within one gigantic room that were lined up in rows upon rows for as far as the eye could see. Alexander repeatedly told little Hans,

"I envy the fact that you have so much freedom. I know times are tough for you too, but I realize that freedom is the defining factor in life."

All the kids within the orphanage were not allowed to vacate the fenced-off premises of the compound, except for when they had to go to school or attend organized events. Little Hans sensed that their restrictive life just fuelled the orphans' anger, which is why, a few years later, Alexander surprisingly came joyously running towards Hans one day to let him know,

"I'm leaving the orphanage!! They've located my parents!"

Alexander could hardly wait to be re-united with his parents, even though at the same time he was a bit hesitant and concerned.

"Vana, I remember almost nothing of my family. Will they remember me? Do they truly want to see me? Or will I simply be a burden to them and nothing more? What should I do? What do ya think? Ya think that they'll be able to love me? Or will they abuse me like they all do here at the orphanage? And what if they give up on me? I want to fulfill their expectations, just like how a son should! But if I don't go, and stay in the orphanage, then I can't fail 'em!"

Little Hans, empathetic to his concerns, told Alexander,

"If you don't go, you'll never know. You'll live with regret for your entire life. Love yourself, and they'll have no other choice but to love you. Let them prove their worth to you! You've been handed an opportunity that I will likely never have."

Alexander heard a lot of demoralizing stories about other reunited parents, about how they were drunks, drug addicts, derelicts, poor, resentful, or simply unable to provide for their children, which left him wondering if leaving the orphanage were such a great idea considering that at least there he was guaranteed food and a roof over his head. Though, once all the papers were processed and the official verification check by the respective authorities regarding his future living conditions were complete, Alexander happily re-united with his parents. Upon leaving the orphanage and little Hans once and for all, Alexander bid farewell with mixed emotions, and promised little Hans,

"I'll write about how things are going! Just how it is to live with my long-lost parents. I'm gonna miss you! You were my best buddy!"

Alexander, after leaving Jug, probably never missed the orphanage; yet, the same couldn't have been said when it came to little Hans as their friendship meant a lot to both of them. Alexander used to always tell little Hans,

"I will never find a friend like you."

They were nearly inseparable. The two of them always walked to and from school together. Feeling strongly connected to him, Alexander's departure left little Hans with a void and a sense of sadness. Not only had he lost his best friend, but he knew that he was never going to see Alexander again. According to Alexander's first few letters to Hans over the ensuing years, everything seemed to be going quite well. Reuniting with his parents was a dream come true; however, after a while, his life eventually made an unexpected turn for the worst. Alexander was ultimately compelled to take care of his parents, forcing him to drop out of school and become obliged to find a full-time job in order to sustain his family. In hindsight, Alexander had a few regrets about returning to his parents, and wondered if he would have at least completed a degree at a trade school if he would have stuck it out at the orphanage. Little Hans, on the other hand, simply wondered just what could have been if he had (Russian) parents.

"Would I feel complete, instead of completely unwanted? Would I not be picked on so often by these horrific Russian kids? Will these thoughts and feelings stemming from being abandoned by my parents cease to exist? Yet, if this relentless feeling of inadequacy and being beaten with a branch by my mother while I was a few years old still haunts me, what's the value of a family really?"

At the same time, going to the orphanage was not an option. Nevertheless, Little Hans just couldn't help wondering just what could've been....

Days after Alexander's departure, little Hans found himself somberly marauding alone through the woods in search of berries with his trusty bow and arrow, which Hans made himself out of some feathers, thread, string, and sticks. Queen's Pirate and Robin Hood were playing in the theatres across the country at the time, so every boy yearned to have a bow and arrow to mimic their heroes. Though, before little Hans could think another second about Little John, and his friend Alexander, he suddenly felt a stabbing puncture penetrate his leg! When he looked down, he saw not only blood, but also an arrow stuck right in his thigh! Little Hans' first instinct was to yank it out, look up, and fire it in the direction of his assailant who fled from the bushes in which he was hiding after his well-planned ambush. The boy was accompanied by others, but none of them were neither missing an arrow, nor guiltily taking off in flight; though, Hans' assailant couldn't flee quickly enough. The hot-shot, quick-firing little Hans nipped the problem right in the butt by shooting the arrow right into little Hans' bullseye, the fleeing boy's bum! Letting out an excruciating yelp, the boy instantaneously wallowed in agony, mimicking the sounds of a squealing pig on the verge of being slaughtered, until he fell to the ground as if he had been shot beyond repair. Blood steadily crept from his behind. While approaching the boy in haughty triumph, little Hans wittingly bellowed out,

"The arrow is yours. You left it behind. You shouldn't be so forgetful. Even though you're older than me, you're too young to have Alzheimer's."

As little Hans got even closer to him, he told the boy,

"Shut up!! Shut up!! Stop screaming!! Did you see me screaming like a baby!! We're now blood brothers! My blood has contaminated yours!"

Little Hans truly enjoyed dishing it out to his enemies, but he nonetheless, while hearing the boy wail away, wondered,

"Just how is Alexander doing? Just how is it to have parents? Just how is it not to be a German living here in Russia?..........."

CHAPTER 23

Another Closure

1949. Little Hans was eight at the time. After finally settling in at the third sewing shop, Pavel, the sewing shop manager approached Grandmother to inform her that following about a year and a half at their current location, the "3rd" sewing shop was closing down. The building was in serious need of repairs from the foundation right up to the roof. A few weeks later, Hans and Grandmother found themselves homeless once again. Luckily enough though, it was early summer, so they could safely return to their "camp site" down by the 15-foot-wide river along the bank. And fortunately for their sake, the sewing shop structure was still somewhat in tact, so during nasty rain storms, Hans and Grandmother snuck into the old building from time-to-time. Yet, only at night, since the building was being renovated throughout day. The windows were torn out, but the building was jacked up so they were too high to reach and climb through, at least for a young boy and a woman in her late 50's with a bad hip. Hence, little Hans and Grandmother had to crawl underneath a wall in order to gain access to the building, where they slept on the old wooden floors, sometimes next to rats. Nevertheless, being able to take refuge in the old sewing shop building under construction brought them an extreme sense of gratitude.

Holes plagued the roof; the floor was filthy; and rodents ran throughout, but in little Hans and Grandmother eyes, it was nothing less than "sleepable" for the night. When your standard of living drops, your level of acceptance rises, or in the case of theirs, it insurmountably soars. Still having access to the garden in the back that they worked felt like an utter blessing. The garden, along with the river that bestowed them with whatever they could catch along the bank that they once again termed "home sweet home", supplied them with food. But fall was approaching, leading them both to wonder just how they were going to survive another Russian winter - well, at least until a man suddenly appeared coming down the hill that converged with the river bank.

It was Pavel, the sewing shop manager! His glowing smile and delightful charm indicated that he had some great news! Just like last time, he came right down to the pebble-laced river bank with a joyful grin on his face.

"Looks like you too had a pleasant and relaxing summer once again, but it's time to get back to work!"

After giggling at himself for more than a few seconds, he provided a few details relating to their future at the "4th" sewing shop.

"The new sewing shop is gonna be located right to the west of the main street. It's actually gonna be located in a big, old house that those Reds confiscated from a very wealthy family during their revolution back in 1917. It's 2-stories. You two are gonna love it! It's the best one so far!"

Two weeks later, Pavel personally escorted them to the exact location of their new home that appeared like some sort of mansion situated on a massive plot of land or even estate. Little Hans was excited, yet a bit puzzled by its appearance. An internal conflagration erupted within him, leading him to ask Pavel,

"Just how come there ain't any windows on the 1st floor?"

Responding with a grin, Pavel informed Hans,

"That's for security reasons. The wealthy family that lived there a long, long time ago worried that bandits might break-in and rob 'em or even worse! But

*that's not gonna happen with you living there! There ain't a soul in the world
that wants to mess with you and your grandmother!"*

With a big smile on Pavel's face, he brushed little Hans' blondish-brown
curly locks before giving him a wink. The new sewing shop resembled
more of a complex stationed within an estate. The property was a relatively
vast plot of land, sealed in by a wooden fence and a large timber gate by
the road. The main entrance to the house was secured by an expansive
and thick wooden door. A few wooden storage buildings for grain and
equipment, and a barn for a couple horses, pigs, sheep, and even cattle were
situated in the back. The entire complex was enclosed under an expansive,
brown rusting metal roof.

An exit at the side of the estate provided access for a horse and buggy to
drive straight through the grounds leading to a side lane. Conveniently,
a horse and carriage could also loop around and exit along the curved,
circular dirt driveway through the covered front entrance. Downtown Jug
was in the vicinity. A deep gulley lied to the west. Forest and meadows
to the south. The roof, rusty from neglect, not only covered the entire
complex, but interlinked all of the estate's buildings on the east and north
sides of the complex, which meant that little Hans could go from building
to building, including to the cleanest "outhouse" that he had ever seen,
without facing the elements. A large skylight that was situated in between
a buttress above the high front gate provided natural lighting for the
building. Little Hans absolutely loved his new residence and was outright
ecstatic over the fact that the delivered wood could be chopped inside. All
was not only protected from rain, wind, snow, sleet and harm's way, but
also from anyone who felt inclined to snatch a few pieces of wood during
the harsh winter months. The house was covered by unpainted wooden
siding, in comparison to most of the homes in Jug that had fully exposed
log-facings.

The new sewing shop was always quite lively. Majors and generals from
the military base based about 10 km away came in to either have their
uniforms altered, or pick up their new uniforms. One day, a distinguished
looking general with a round, yet chiselled face in his early 40's with

slicked back teenager-thick brown hair noticed little Hans toiling away at cutting some wood. After glaring away in awe and amusement for a few seconds, the general in uniform adorning numerous red stars, eventually approached little Hans.

"What's your name young man?"

Without looking up while chopping away, Hans replied, *"My friends call me Vana."*

Taking one step closer to little Hans, the general enquired,

"May I ask just why your parents let a boy your age carry out such strenuous and laborious work?"

Hans proudly responded,

"I am almost nine and quite capable, independent, and self-sufficient. And I don't have any parents. I don't know where they are. Only Grandmother is around. We live together here at the sewing shop. But I have to work for my food."

When the general returned on his next visit, he brought along a nurse with him, who carried-out a full physical assessment of little Hans. She ultimately concluded,

"You're in great shape! Your health, hearing, teeth, and eye sight are all in solid condition! And most importantly, there's absolutely no signs of any deformations or abnormalities! You're an amazingly fit little guy! I've never seen such muscles on a boy your age! Keep it up!"

Her comment brought a huge grin to Hans' face, exposing his nice white teeth. Following the examination, the general approached Grandmother and let her know,

"I would like to adopt little Vana (Hans)."

The general explained to Grandmother,

"I lost my son during the war. If he were still alive, he'd be the same age as Vana. Vana even somewhat resembles my son. The similarities are uncanny. It's like destiny brought us together."

On the general's ensuing visits, he even brought along his wife who was in her 30's with gentle blue eyes of sorrow with light, yet elegant bags under them. They both seemed like very nice, well to do affluent people who could provide little Hans with endless opportunities. Though, oddly enough, they desired to bestow Hans with their deceased son's name, Konstantin. Grandmother became quite concerned. She felt that one day they may simply take Hans away from her and easily get away with it. So, during their next visit, Grandmother attempted to explain her dilemma to the general and his wife, in her poor Russian,

"I'm sorry, but I can't give him up. He's not mine to give up. He belongs to and with his parents. I pray that one day I will reunite him with his parents. That is my dying wish! I just can't give him away. It's not my right or decision to make. I can't gift you with something that's not mine."

The general's wife immediate disappointment led her to tersely respond,

"But you don't even know where little Vana's parents are!"

Grandmother gracefully and calmly replied,

"I know, but for some unknown reason, I'm convinced that we'll locate them. I can sense through my veins that it's a part of Vana's destiny. Vana will see his mother again one day, and I'll be there to hand him back to her at that time, just like how she handed him over to me on that wagon in Germany years ago."

The general's wife was left speechless. She instantly became quite empathetic and even touched by Grandmother's hope and dedication to Hans. The general and his wife ultimately gave up on their pursuit of little Hans, simply accepting Grandmother's reasoning behind her decision; but nonetheless, they still gave Grandmother their address just in case she had a change of heart or suddenly fell ill. On their next visit, the general and his wife returned with food, material for clothing, and even a pair of shoes for Hans. Little Hans even got to go for a ride in the general's jeep. The truth of the matter was, if they would've agreed to take Grandmother with them, they both would have gone with the general's family. When Grandmother asked Hans if he wanted to go with the couple, he answered, *"No, not without you."* The general and his wife continued to subtly entice little Hans, even though deep down they had already conceded defeat. Irregardless of that actuality, they cherished the fact that they could not only help little Hans and Grandmother, but also have the opportunity to occasionally tend to a boy once again, even if he weren't their son.

Though, here at the "4th" sewing shop, little Hans never fell short of company. It was a lot livelier here than at the past three sewing shops. Not only were the military personnel constantly stopping by, but also many of Hans' friends. The sewing shop complex, was quite a playground paradise for the kids. A long rope hung from the rafters, right in between the two indoor multi-tiered building structures. The kids could happily play Tarzan by swinging from one level to another. If they weren't swaying and dangling around, then they were either playing tag or climbing up the barn walls' ladders that led to the hay loft above.

From there, the boys could run across the beams leading to the next building before taking a ladder back down to ground level, unless of course they simply leapt all the way into a pile of hay down below instead. Though, if the dangling rope were somewhere in their vicinity, they could easily swing back to wherever they desired to land. The complex itself provided year-round protection for the kids, making it quite the haven and heaven for the little rascals. Even whenever Hans was chopping wood, he'd sometimes have company if a buddy pitched in; yet, usually only until another friend showed up, at which point they'd run off and play while little Hans completed his chores.

More times than not, more kids appeared, sometimes, literally out of the woodwork. And before Hans knew it, there'd be half a dozen kids swinging around the complex. On one occasion, Hans was having a blast with his friends, only until he saw Boris, who was Hans' age and the son of a furniture factory worker, lose grasp of the rope while swinging in mid-air, causing him to lose his grip! Boris' slip sent him soaring over 10 feet to the ground! The rest of the kids hurried over to Boris' side, just to discover him motionless! All the boys, including Boris' brother Victor, were utterly terrified! The entire time Victor wailed,

"Wake up little brother!! Wake up!!!!"

Yet, to no avail. Eventually, Little Dimitri blurted out in a somber tone, *"Is Boris dead?"* Victor was frantic, yet still optimistic.

"No! My brother just picked up a concussion! He just smacked his head on the log! But he's fine!"

Boris, though, remained there lying motionless. At the exact moment that tears entered Victor's eyes, Boris' eyes instantly opened, before he uttered,

"What ya guys staring at?!?"

Victor told him, *"You hit your head and knocked yourself out!"*

Boris casually retorted, *"Is that so!!! Blah! Blah! What ya talking!?! Let's play!"*

Boris vigorously sprang up to his feet with more spirit than ever. Luckily enough, nobody ever got seriously hurt playing within the complex. And even though the boys were protected from the elements within the compound, that by no means discouraged them from savouring the outdoors. In the winter, the boys strenuously climbed up the ladders attached to the complex's wall while carrying their skis until they reached the top level where they climbed through a window that opened, providing them access to the snow-buried roof. Once they ascended to the building's summit and strapped on their skis, the boys skied down to the roof's edge until they were sent soaring directly, sometimes even head first, into a massive 10-foot high pile of snow below that was created throughout the winter by drifting. After a while, the youngsters learned how to pull off the perfect landing by creating a slope out of snow and wooden planks that elevated the boys as they approached the edge of the roof where they launched off the complex roof into the air, soaring amongst the, at times, misty Jug horizon.

Before going down, the kid set to soar always had to scream, "*прочь с дороги!*" *or* "*get out of the way!*", as there was no way to catch a glimpse of what or who was down below as the boys swiftly skied down the sloped roof. If anyone were still in the snow, right within the kids' landing pad below, he had to take cover when the next boy descended downward, or otherwise he could possibly be landed on. But despite all of their fun, this type of skiing lacked the practicality, especially when it came to reaching the roof since it was an arduous journey for the kids to climb upwards on a ladder while carrying their skis to the 40-foot high apex of the rooftop.

As an alternative, there was a ravine on the west side of the house that offered more optimal and "orthodox" skiing conditions. Skiing within the inclines of the ravine, down into the valley, was another winter daily occurrence for the boys. The ravine's slopes converged into a flat plateau at the bottom, which meant that the boys could ski downwards and then use their impetus to propel themselves back upwards in the direction of the pinnacle of the other hill on the opposite side of the ravine. After their momentum died out, the youngsters took off their skis and walked up the remainder of the way to the summit, before skiing downwards, back into the valley of the ravine.

Grandmother couldn't afford to buy little Hans his own pair of skis, unlike all of Hans' friends' parents who bought their sons skis. Yet, that didn't prevent Hans from making his own pair out of 4X4X1-inch-thick birch boards that Boris and Victor brought over for little Hans. Boris' dad worked at the local furniture factory and sawmill located northwest of the town centre where there was plenty of extra, discarded wood. Such boards were put aside for the employees who could take them home to use as firewood or for fences since they were not suitable for furniture, but to little Hans, they were perfect for converting into skis. Sticking the ends of the boards into boiling hot water till they softened, Hans gradually curved the "points" of the planks that Hans made by slicing away wood with an axe. After the tip of the board softened, little Hans placed the front end of the "ski" under a door and then pushed the other end of the board upwards as far as he could extend it without breaking it, before bracing the ski with another piece of wood and leaving it in that position overnight. The following day, little Hans performed the same procedure until he was satisfied with the degree of curvature.

However, little Hans still required bindings if he ever expected to use these furniture factory boards to ski; though, that wasn't a problem for him one bit. In order to create and mount his own bindings, Hans first took a steel rod that he heated up to an extremely high temperature inside of the sewing shop stove, before pushing the rod right through the middle of the ski until there was a hole big enough for a leather strap to be weaved through. Extra scraps of leather were provided courtesy of his friends at the blacksmith shop where harnesses were repaired. As little Hans' finishing touch, or ""coup de grace", he smoothed and grooved out the bottom of the boards with a piece of glass since he had no other tools or sandpaper at his disposal. And voila! Little Hans was ready to hit the slopes.

CHAPTER 24

Blood in Water

Despite all of Hans' new found fun and friends at this sewing shop, the latest neighbourhood still turned out to be a hostile district. A lot of the older kids in the neighbourhood took pleasure in attempting to ambush and beat up little Hans. One day following school, Hans was walking down a dirt pathway along the main road that was seamlessly lined with houses, board fences, and the odd rickety, wooden barn. Out of nowhere, Hans suddenly heard the voice of a boy bellow,

"Vana!" (Hans!).

Innocently enough, Hans turned his head in the direction of the voice, and incidentally, towards the wooden planks of a barn that were positioned four inches apart. The inside of the dilapidated cowshed was pitch black so Hans couldn't see any movement stirring from within. It was all a blur to him, but after looking to see who hollered *"Vana"*, he instantaneously felt a stabbing blow between his eyes, right where the nose meets the forehead! Little Hans' head was instantly propelled backwards! A ringing pain instantly roared between his ears. When he laid his hand upon the spot above his nose where he took the blow, fluid drenched his hand. Yet, when he checked to see if it were blood, he didn't know for sure. Hans couldn't see a thing. He could only sense what he could feel, feel blood streaming into his eyes and down his nose. The more blood that he wiped away, the more blood that flooded into his eyes and down his face.

Smear after smear, blood persistently gushed, blinding his vison. With a significantly heightened sense of sound, Hans could easily pick-up not only the taste of blood on his lips, but also his assailant bragging,

"I got him! I got him and I think I poked his eye out!"

His assaulter spoke with so much excitement that Hans swore that the boy had triumphed in the most glorious and masterful feat in his life! At this point, though, little Hans could have cared less about triumphs, as he would have been more than content if the blood would simply cease to flow before his very eyes. To compound his concerns, Hans couldn't even see who his assailants were, let alone count just how many of them were there behind the barn wall amongst the blackness of the lightless inside. Either way, Hans knew that he had to obtain space between him and his attackers. Without his vision, Hans used the fences to guide him by running his hand along the wooden boards in order to reach home. Minutes later, Hans felt his hand brush along the corner point of two walls converging. He knew that he had reached the sewing shop. A mild sense of relief possessed him. Incidentally, he turned right and used the walls of the sewing shop to lead himself to the back of the building. From that point, he felt the dirt path that led to the creek against his bare feet.

Desperately yearning to wash the blood out of his eyes to see if he still possessed his eyesight, Hans scurried along the path with more urgency than ever as he anxiously scampered to reach the stream. Little Hans knew the distance like the back of his hand. As he cautiously bustled along the path, with his eyelids down preventing the blood from seeping into his eyes, little Hans feared the entire way that he was already blind. Soothing sounds of birds chirping and the stream flowing intensified with each shallow and anxious inhalation. After reaching the bank of the creek, Hans fell to his knees before cupping water between his hands and splashing it upon his bleeding face in an attempt to wash the blood out of his eyes. Next came the moment of truth. Finally raising his eyelids, Hans noticed that everything around him was muddily visible, yet still middling blurry. He immediately rejoiced!

"Alas! I see something! I have sight. I can see! Hallelujah!"

When he touched his forehead, he felt a hump and a lump, but merely thought to himself,

"That'll be gone in a few days."

Hans then sat by the creek for a while in untranquil introspection, while his head rang like a cracked church bell as a nauseating clinging ran through his ears. Nevertheless, Hans was utterly ecstatic to have his vision back, especially after seeing his face reflect back at him in the creek once the blood subsided from fluidly streaming down into his eyes. Hans couldn't stop testing one eye at a time, just to make sure that he wasn't dreaming. Tears kept pouring down his face as a result of the pain and the wood and dirt remnants still embedded within his eyes; Hans' vison remained out of focus. However, that didn't stop him from envisioning that everything was going to be alright with his sight, and for that he felt blessed.

Hans learned valuable lesson from this incident – stay away from plank-board fences - as they only protect and conceal his ambushing enemy while they hunt down their prey. Hans became a defensively vigilant target for years to come following that happening. So, in some respects, that poke may have been the best possible hit to take early on if Hans expected to experience life later on. When he arrived home from the stream and stormed inside, Grandmother immediately questioned him.

"What happened to you? How did you get that big gash by your eye? And your forehead! It's swollen! How did you get that massive goose egg?"

Grandmother spoke in her typical, cool and calm fashion. After explaining what happened, all what Grandmother could say was,

"When you walk, stay away from fences. And never fight back. Things will only get worse since there's just too many of them, and they're bigger and older than you. You're all by yourself. I'm too old to protect you."

Little Hans simply nodded as she tended to his wounds. Ambush attempts against Hans became a regular occurrence, so he had to remain vigilant and on high alert. Constantly monitoring his surroundings and being prepared to escape, evade, and avoid any possible attack was the name of the game. Eventually, Hans got to "know" and recognize all the kids from his end of town. So, when a few of them seemingly went "missing," he knew that something was up, leading him to go on high alert.

His street was lined with 6-foot-high wooden-board fences along both sides. Hans familiarized himself with all the loose boards along each fence in which his "predators" could sneak behind by lifting the unfastened end of the wood and squeezing through in order to hide and wait for little Hans to appear. To avoid all possible confrontations, Hans always kept a safe distance from his enemies so he could escape if need be. A 20-metre-long, log bridge over the creek was situated along the main road near the sewing shop. Whenever Hans saw a gang of boys congregating near that bridge, he waited until they crossed over to the opposite side before making a dash for the sewing shop gate, since at that point Hans was out of their striking distance. Hans was quick. His speed was his proverbial shield, but sometimes he required an even greater means of protection.

On one winter day, Hans saw over half a dozen older boys suspiciously congregating near the bridge. They chatted away and overtly paid no attention to little Hans. In Hans' eyes, these were signs of an imminent ambush, so he rushed to the sewing shop gate thinking that he was home free. However, when he went to open the 6-foot-high wooden gate, he discovered that it was locked! One of attackers had snuck into the sewing shop complex and locked the gate from the inside, not leaving Hans safe and sound as anticipated! At that very moment, the group, who were "innocently" standing on the bridge advanced on, and ultimately converged upon Hans! He became surrounded and trapped with nowhere to run! Almost a dozen teenagers had created a semi-circle around Hans with his back right to the gate! Before Hans knew it, chunks of ice and pieces of iced-up snow were pelting him! Hans had no fear for the iced-up snow, so he focused on determining in which direction the chunks of ice were flying in from. Diligently paying close attention to each of his attackers, little Hans monitored exactly what each one of them was picking up. Out of the corner of his eye, Hans noticed a short, thin, and wimpy looking boy named Evgeny picking up flat pieces of ice and viciously hurling them in Hans' direction. The sight of a boy of such inferior physical stature motivated Hans into realizing,

"I gotta start firing back!"

And what better way to do it than with the enemy's weapons of choice. Following Hans' epiphany, he reached down and grabbed one "Evgeny's" chunks of ice that landed right next to Hans' boot. Standing back up, Hans chucked the chunk of ice into the air in the direction of the wall of his assailants. Moments later, a boy dramatically went down in a hustle! Hans' projectile pegged Evgeny right off in the head! Hans couldn't believe it. He simply didn't think that the piece had even the slightest of chances of striking anyone when it left his hand since he launched it so high into the air - but Hans wasn't the only one. After little Hans tossed that piece of ice up into the frosty, Russian winter air, Evgeny simply gazed at the 4-inch long white projectile float airborne; however, at the very last second, the disc of ice curved like a parabolic arch, and caught Evgeny right across the nose and lower part of his forehead! Blood instantly streamed from Evgeny's nose at the propensity and with the intensity that he screamed at the top of his lungs. The white snow around him turned Soviet-kerchief red from the spurting blood while Hans' exposed cheeks remained rosy. Evgeny's scrawny appearance and blighted spirit made him appear more like a victim than an attacker, so that's what he became. The rest of the group, including the boy behind the gate, panicked and scurried away, leaving their wounded "comrade" behind. When Hans approached Evgeny, he kept reiterating to Hans,

"Look what you've done!! Look what you've done!!"

Hans retorted gingerly telling Evgeny,

"That's the piece that you threw at me. I just returned it to you, so what are you screaming about?!?! Just put some snow on your face to stop the bleeding! But I'm not sure it's gonna stop your whining. You may need diapers for that."

Eventually, Hans picked up some snow and placed it up against his "enemy's" face to keep the gash on his nose and forehead from gushing blood. Evgeny stilly appreciated Hans' help and loving tenderness. He happily let Hans continuously apply fresh snow to his wounds until the blood subsided. In the meantime, the whole neighbourhood went into an uproar over the incident. The other kids who ambushed Hans swiftly headed home to squeal and tattle on him to the rest of the parents. The injured boy's mom and dad eventually arrived on scene in a bustle over the tussle and demanded an explanation!

"How did he get hurt!?! What did you do to him German boy?!?!?!"

Hans eventually explained everything to the parents. Evgeny didn't deny one word. Hans clarified by expressing, *"I didn't mean to hurt Evgeny. I was simply defending myself."*

After hearing the truth, Evgeny's parents scolded Evgeny.

"See what happens when you try to hurt somebody!"

In Hans' heart, the teenagers' malicious deeds were immediately nullified by Evgeny's parents' compassion. Afterwards, the group of boys not only felt a bit guilty, but also somewhat embarrassed for being defeated by a smaller, younger, and thinner kid. Hans sympathized with Evgeny since he could put himself in Evgeny's place. Hans knew exactly how it felt to get viciously struck, and bleed heavily afterwards. Yet, at the same time, Hans knew that he had to do whatever it took to protect himself and survive. And if he taught his enemy a lesson in the process – even better and so be it! Though, to this day, Hans is absolutely convinced that something else guided that piece of ice right into Evgeny's face. It was as if Nature were trying to teach Evgeny, and possibly even his cohorts a lesson while protecting Hans in the process. He still swears to this day that that piece of ice was about to fly right over Evgeny. The projectile was well wide off the mark just a fraction of the second before it strangely swirled like a boomerang right into Evgeny's face as if it were a divine twist of fate. Because as it just so happened, it was this same Evgeny who told Hans, prior to throwing this same piece of ice in Hans' direction,

"I hope it hits you right in the face!"

Hans' face was almost completely covered, just like Evgeny's, by a Russian winter cap and a high collared coat; but nonetheless, the ice that Hans hurled still found a way to catch Evgeny right in his minutely exposed portion of skin.

Following the incident, those boys left Hans alone for quite a while; yet, Hans knew that it would only be a matter time before they regrouped and retaliated. But when this gang of boys did eventually reconvene with their onslaught, they were always a bit more cautious. And fortunately for little Hans, his body was getting bigger; however, that meant he required more food, more sustenance, and therefore, more jobs...

CHAPTER 25

Lumbering Horses

Hans absolutely loved horses. Whenever he caught a glimpse of a colt, galloper, or hauler, his eyes instantaneously became magnetized to his favourite 4-legged creature. On almost a daily basis, Hans gazed at horses and sleighs cross the wooden bridge by the sewing shop day and night. But on one specific day, a few sets of horses strapped to three sleighs designed for hauling logs, sleighs that were as long and wide as a couple of combined fridge doors with two 60-inch-long runners slowly slid by on a Thursday morning. Mesmerized by such a sight, Hans' eyes became transfixed to the horses' swift struts, which meant, in Hans' eyes, that he had no other choice but to further investigate their activities by exploring their route of travel. Hans hoped that the workers, who were steering sleighs equipped with wooden suspension connectors attached to the horses' harnesses and stanchions required some assistance. So, the following day, after seeing the caravan of horses and sleighs saunter by once again, Hans stormed out of the sewing shop, pursuing the log convoy of sleighs all the way into the forest. At first, the rugged horsemen covered in thick winter clothing and beards looked at Hans suspiciously, as they couldn't quite comprehend just what this boy was up to and had in mind. The mystified men wondered just why this 9-year-old was practically glued to their sleighs.

Hans was rather calculating at times, but most importantly, knew that his curious, yet peculiar and unorthodox behaviour usually worked in his favour, just like how it did with the oxen-man a few years earlier. So, when the sleighs entered the forest and the workers began loading up the logs, Hans' first instinct was to help the men out without even asking them if they required any assistance. Hans could always sense just who was friend or foe by their demeanours, the tone of their voices, and expressions on their faces. At first, the men were quite amused by Hans' actions, which signaled that they meant him no harm; though, after a few minutes, their amusement turned into amazement as the loggers were absolutely flabbergasted at how "little" Hans could roll, pull, and pick up the logs, almost exactly like a grown adult. The men never fathomed that a child of his age and size could possess such strength, let alone the ability to perform this sort of task. After a while, they became quite curious and inquisitive about their very unique little helper. Eventually, a man in his 40's with a graying beard, thin nose, and broad neck, wearing a long black coat that extended down to his ankles asked Hans,

"Where ya from boy? Where ya live?"

Little Hans responded by telling them,

"I just moved into the home on the corner by the ravine. It just got converted into a sewing shop."

A worker started joking with Hans by saying,

"You must be a very wealthy boy to be able to afford to live in a place like that!"

Feeling the need to explain, Hans informed the men,

"My grandmother works there. She sews during the day and is responsible for the night watch. She's gotta be there all day, every day. Opened or closed. Day and night. I gotta do my part so I work. Chores, tasks and stuff. I'm responsible for chopping wood and carrying it into the house. I help Grandmother. Grandmother is in no condition to do these things. She needs me. I need her. We love living in that house."

A man in his 50's with weathered, piercing, yet wise wincing eyes that peered out between his black winter cap and high coat collar responded by

160

giving a history lesson about the house. His voice was rather sophisticated, seemingly more suitable for a professor than a log transporter.

"You know lad, the old owners there, in that house, they were quite the family with a stately touch of nobility. As it just so happens, that house had been vacant for quite a long time. However, when it was still occupied once upon a time, it belonged to a very wealthy Russian family that owned a lot of land. They possessed quite the plot that was passed down from generation to generation. Following the Red Revolution in 1917, the house and properties were confiscated and expropriated. The Reds took it all. That place became property of the state. They took the whole shebang; just like they still take everything. The old owners there were descendants of a family that was exiled to this region of the Urals in 1825 after they were accused of playing a part in an attempt to overthrow the Czar during the "Decembrist Revolt.""

Immediately afterwards, another worker in his 30's with protruding cheekbones took his turn by concluding their story.

"That family had a pile of empty land that needed working. If you was alive back then, you would've worked for them and definitely done their working, and a darn good working you would've done!"

Eventually, the workers stopped for lunch. Going into their goodie sacks, they pulled out cheese made from horse milk, along with some horsemeat, cabbage, and even strips of bacon that they cut up and tossed into a potluck cauldron that was heated up over an open fire that they all nestled around. With their potluck soup, they savoured some nice homemade "borodinsky" sourdough bread and baked potatoes that were roasted over the steaming cauldron. The loggers graciously told Hans, *"Help yourself boy!"* A humongous grin came over Hans' face while his mouth watered. He was extremely appreciative of the men's generosity, just like the men were utterly grateful for Hans' helping hand. Lunch was always Hans' favourite time of the day, even though he absolutely loved working as well. He regarded food as not only his reward, but also as the fuel to perform even more tasks.

After devouring their food, the men boiled up some tea over the open fire. When the sleighs dusted in fresh snow were finally full, the men all headed to the furniture factory, which was located on the outskirts of town. At this point, they unloaded the logs at the factory grounds, where a sawmill that was used to cut up logs into planks that were piled up for drying was also located. In one section of the yard, there was a steam generator for drying lumber. Leftover wood was used for burning. The loggers eventually also provided a little history about the factory by letting Hans know that it used to be used as a copper smelting foundry decades earlier. There was still a huge black pile of slag that was left behind. A blacksmith shop, on the other side of the river that was connected to the lumberyard by a bridge was also situated amongst the furniture factory grounds.

Eventually, little Hans became acquainted with a tooth-shy, wide-eyed Tatar in his late 50's of Mongolian-Turkish descent who originated from the "Russian" city of Kazan, the great Tatar capital in the distant past. This man worked at the furniture factory. His responsibilities included tending to the horses, sleighs, and wagons. The stables were situated on the main street that led to the copper mines, close to the sewing shop complex on the other side of the gully. This Tatar named Timir, a friendly man with a Persian-like face carrying a white goatee and thin lanky arms was also responsible for hitching the horses to the sleighs and wagons, as well as cleaning the stables. Timir resided in an old house in front of the stables on an estate similar to the sewing shops' grounds where Hans and Grandmother lived.

Little Hans slowly got to know Timir; however, it didn't take Timir long to learn that Hans was looking for chores to perform in exchange for food, experience, and a bit of know-how. So one day, Timir the Tatar asked Hans,

"Ya wanna earn a sandwich Vana? Can ya take these horses to the blacksmith shop? They need shoes."

Hans particularly enjoyed partaking in the shoeing process. Four posts and a lift with two leather straps, which were used to support the horse and keep it balanced while one of its legs was raised during the shoeing, were situated underneath a canopy outside of the blacksmith shop. The leg of the horse that was being shoed was tied up to a post, keeping the horse almost totally immobilized. But the horse was not impressed one bit to say the least. The horses didn't enjoy being shod. Hans attentively observed the entire process step for step. Caressing the elegant horse by the head, Hans stroked the auburn brown, rugged, yet gentle horse, keeping him calm until the horse overcame its fear. As it sensed that Hans loved him more than Hans loved himself, the horse instantly became calm, almost as if he were under a spell. Amazed at the tranquil aura emitted by the horse, a worker said,

"You've got a magic touch boy! A touch not of this world."

The men couldn't begin shoeing the horse till the frenzied stead became completely calm, or otherwise, the horse could be hurt during the process. The horse's fear faded in Hans' presence as if it never existed. The stud simply gazed in the distance as if he were staring into pure nothingness as serenity possessed him under little Hans' palliative spell.

Besides comforting the horses, Hans also happily helped Timir the Tatar fetch hay and straw from the fields, where it was piled up into 10-foot heaps that were let to sit until the winter months. During the colder season, when the ground was frozen, the hay could be transported out by using sleighs. Jug mainly consisted of dirt roads, so the wagons' wooden wheels sunk deep into the ground during the rainy weather that reared its muddy head in autumn. Storing hay and straw indoors wasn't feasible since barn space was limited as wheat grains always had indoor priority.

The factories' sleighs and wagons, used for hauling lumber, hay, and straw, in need of repairs were taken to the local blacksmith shop that was situated roughly half a kilometre from the stables. Through helping the Tatar, Hans eventually also got to know a few wide-eyed, pudgy nosed, dark-haired men in their 40's with Turkish appearances and hardened up hands, yet soft demeanours and features named Aydar and Anton. They both worked at the blacksmith shop. Whenever Hans had a chance, he headed over to the blacksmith shop to converse with and learn from Aydar and Anton. As Aydar attentively witnessed Hans' eagerness and curiosity as he monitored each of their movements, Aydar eventually said,

"Vana, see that forge, boy. Pull down that long metal bar so the bellows fill up with air like in an accordion, will ya? We need to heat up the metal for forging."

Anton was sceptical, but only until he saw the 9-year-old Hans leap up into the air to grasp the bar before pulling it downwards as if he were doing a chin-up. Anton's jaw dropped! Initially through irony, but ultimately in amazement!

"Where does a boy your age get such strength! You must've been working the coal mines since ya popped out of that belly of your mama!"

As Hans smiled back, he noticed that his body acted as a counterweight by exerting leverage, which caused the lever to slowly move downwards while the wooden bellows with leather "flutes" filled with air. The amount of air and its speed were controlled by the counterweights attached to the top of the bellows. Once they were full, Hans released the lever, causing them to close. During this process, the air became expelled through a pipe on the opposite side of the forge where fire heated up the metal.

Amazed at Hans' ability and keenness, Anton and Aydar eventually got Hans to cut the metal thread into nuts, bolts and even horseshoes, as everything was made from scratch at the blacksmith shop. In between these moments, Hans fetched water from the river that was used to cool off the heated metal. The men discovered their workhorse. For a sandwich a day, Hans happily carried out any task that they'd ask of him, which included going to the furniture shop and collecting scrap pieces of wood that kept the fire going within the forge. In order to transport the wood, Hans tied a rope to a wooden, wheel-less box, in which he tossed planks and pieces of logs into before dragging the crate along the ground back to the blacksmith shop. Hans' "co-workers" were quite amazed at his ingenuity, so it was only a matter of time before he became a popular little figure on the plant grounds. Some saw little Hans as a bit of a nuisance, whereas others just adored their new, pint-sized helper. Years later, as a sign of gratitude, the folks at the factory built Hans a massive chest when he and Grandmother were on the verge of leaving Jug for a move to Zajarsk.

CHAPTER 26

Cow Pasturing

Hans enjoyed exchanging work for food, but he had his eyes set on earning some money for the first time. Every spring, the pasturing of cattle, sheep, and goats commenced. Most of these animals were the property of the state; however, the government permitted each family to own a cow, a couple of sheep, a few pigs, and perhaps even a llama if they were able to afford to import one in from South America.

If a family could afford some "private" livestock, like a pig, which in due course would be slaughtered and chopped up, it was mandated that a certain percentage of the meat and the entire skin of the pig become property of the state. Whenever any "private" animals were used to produce milk, half of their output had to be brought to the state-run processing plant since the state had a legal right to that portion. The remaining private, or "personal" allotment of milk could be converted into cottage cheese, sour cream, butter, etc., and then consumed by the families themselves. Every time a sheep was sheered, the government was entitled to half of the wool. Animal owners used wool to create clothing, blankets, and warm boots called "valenkis" by boiling the wool until it became a solid lumpy mass that was pounded and moulded into the shape of a boot. Top to bottom, the entire boot, including the sole was made out of wool.

If the Russians weren't using their backyard lots for livestock, then they converted them into gardens. This precious soil was used to grow potatoes, cabbage, beets, peas, and cucumbers for the residents and to feed their livestock. Plots of land situated either along rivers or within meadows, desolately situated away from town were of no value to the Kolkhoz, which acquired the most fertile fields, meadows, and groves available following the Red Revolution. The communist government's Kolkhoz even blasphemously and degradingly converted a local Jug church into a pigsty, leading a distraught local pastor to jump out of the church's second storey window in a suicide attempt that led him to break his leg. Farming and grazing properties not expropriated by the Kolkhoz remained communal areas for animal grazing.

Individual farmers cut grass in these non-Kolkhoz grazing zones during spring and summer, and then saved the grass for winter when livestock was unable to forage in the fields. Animal owners collected whatever they could carry home from the fields and stored it in their backyards. The remaining cut was left in the field until winter, which is when farmers could pick up the feed with one-horse sleighs, rather than their rickety wagons whose wheels constantly got stuck in mud. During winters, not even "left-overs" could be wasted, and this applied to everything from cut grass, weeds, pea strings, potato peels to cabbage scraps, which were all fed to the pigs, cows, and sheep.

Non-Kolkhoz controlled fields and meadows were also used for the pasturing of cattle and sheep. The summer pasturing of the locals' cattle and sheep was privately organized, managed, and carried out by the same families from generation to generation. Within the town district of Jug, there were 5 or 6 different organized herds, totalling about 500 cows and 500 sheep, animals that were owned by town's folk within the community. One specific herd, managed by two families who had been pasturing animals on behalf of the town's folk for a fee for decades consisted of roughly 100 cows and calves, and 100 sheep and goats. At this time, only one woman from each family remained to carry out the task. Their husbands either passed away or were killed during the war, while their grown children had no interest in carrying on the family tradition, and instead chose different livelihoods for themselves.

When the spring of 1950 arrived, the two women were in desperate need of some help with maintaining the herd. Hans heard about this job from other kids who had all tried their hands at pasturing. But, after only a couple of days, the boys usually quit. The job was unpleasant, so it required someone who not only was tenacious and desperate, but also had a passion for and could be patient with animals. When Hans initially approached the two women and enquired about the job, they were rather sarcastic, sceptical, and a little bit derogatory. They cynically asked Hans,

"What makes you think that you can do this task when others couldn't??"

Hans, somewhat irritated by their demeanor, matched their moxie with his own somewhat coy, tongue-in-cheek, yet arrogant, and perplexing metaphorical response.

"I can always try, and if I'm pathetic, you can find somebody else. If I turn out to be as bad as a llama, you can always hire someone with the prowess of a Mongolian horse to carry out the task, assuming you can find one."

Needless to say, mystified was the only term to sum up their reaction to Hans' unorthodox response. But at the same time, the women were not only intrigued enough with his brash nature that they could easily empathise with, but also absolutely desperate considering that they couldn't find anybody else reliable enough to pasture the animals. The two women were simply out of options.

Hans would receive money for his services, and not just "merely" food, something that made this job extremely tempting. The women were offering 200 rubles per month, along with a loaf of bread and a pail of potatoes per week. If he were to do the pasturing job for the entire three months, based upon Hans' calculation, he'd earn enough money to be able to buy himself a pair of pants, a jacket for the winter, a used pair of boots, and some books for school. Inspired by the thought of what he could do with that sort of money, Hans was determined to see this job through to the end. Logistically, it worked out quite well for him because the women gathered the herd from the middle of town and headed westwards, meaning by 7 pm, the women, along with the herd, reached the west end of town where Hans lived. Grandmother then locked up the gate every night after Hans left. When he arrived back home at 7 am, after his 12-hour shift with the herd, Grandmother unlocked the gate so Hans could get back into the sewing shop complex.

Early on in the spring, the pasturing of all types of herds was done during the day when the grass was lush and abundant. The animals usually grazed on the outskirts of town in open areas along the river. However, when late June, July, and August came along, daytime pasturing, especially in these areas was virtually impossible due to the heat and infestation of extremely aggressive horse flies. During the daytime, these little buggers stung cows and then deposited eggs for hatching into the wounds leaving the cows restlessly wagging their tails; scratching and rubbing themselves; and occasionally running in different and diverging directions. Under these conditions, the cows were unable to produce much needed milk not only to feed their calves, but also to be sold at the market. Most of the milk was produced during the summer months, and that's exactly why it was necessary to have the cows grazing throughout night, away from the sun and pests.

On Hans' first day on the job, he finished boarding up all of the windows at the sewing shop at 6:50 pm. Ten minutes later, the two women appeared on time with over two hundred animals. Hans was nervous at such a sight, yet still brashly confident. He liked control and he knew that he would possess it over these animals. With no greeting at all, one woman with a cucumber-like nose sneered out,

"They're all yours German jung!"

Hans took the herd under his wing, while the two nervy women became burdensome and fault-finding spectators, and led the animals further outside of town. The nearby fields were slowly becoming depleted of grass, which meant that Hans had to drive the animals deeper into the rural outskirts in order to find greener pastures for the night. The women accompanying Hans were in their late 50's, but looked like they were in their 80's. They moved as if they belonged to the herd. Yet, they were nicely dressed for the occasion and conditions in long skirts, sporting kerchiefs or thin scarves over their heads, making them look like true Russian babushkas. Hans, conversely, only had shorts and occasionally a shirt on as he strolled barefoot through the meadows. The women always wore bulky and hefty rubber boots, along with their "stari bubba" scarfs, and babushka rain coats, all while carrying blankets, umbrellas, and bags full of food that they refused to share with Hans. These "stari bubbas", or old ladies, usually simply "walked", or rather waddled along on the side. They wore their misery on their faces and captured it through their demeanours, resenting the fact that they still had to pasture cows at their age.

Since the battle-axe-like women were quite immobile, the main responsibilities of preventing the herd from scattering all around lied squarely on Hans' shoulders. He had to vigilantly keep an eye on the herd. Maintaining a headcount at all times was imperative. If the herd were to scatter, it would become a nightmare for him. Shouting, running, and whistling were his means to maintain order. Here and there, Hans had to resort to whacking the animals with a long, flexible stick, but he found that whistling was his most effective tool to keep them in line. He always had a couple of long sticks by his side, along with his trusty, broken, half-bladed pocket knife, which his friends at the blacksmith shop made for him out of a broken leaf-spring from a truck. Hans used the knife to cut and sharpen sticks. The two women completely relied upon Hans to take care of the herd, so he had to be prepared for just about anything and everything as all of the responsibility relating to controlling the herd lied squarely on Hans' little shoulders.

The herd usually grazed from 7 till 11 at night. Then, at 11 pm, Hans guided the herd to a point where the river made a tiny, sharp U-shape. At this location, the pasture formed into a tiny peninsula that was boxed in on three sides by the river. This piece of land offered the herd the most protection as there were high banks on both sides of the river, making it difficult for predators to reach the pasturing area across the water. Containing the herd within this narrow strip of the meadow simplified the task of corralling the animals, something vital to the herd's existence. This specific section of land was not only big enough to accommodate the entire herd, but also became quite narrow at the open end of the U-shape in which two parts of the river ran parallel. Hans rounded up the herd behind a wooden fence and gate enclosure that was rotting after years upon years of deterioration, a fence that Hans repaired with driftwood. It would be in this exact area that Hans set up a camp fire in order to fully box in the herd while they digested their food and rested from roughly 11 pm till 3 am when the sun began to rise. Using their two stomachs – one for storing food and the other for digesting - the cows regurgitated their food from "stomach #1" and chewed on it before sending the food to "stomach #2".

One night, about a week into the job, Hans tended to a blazing fire while the cows ate or slept, when all of a sudden he heard the resonating of a howl, causing the herd to rile. The wolf's wail originated from the other side of the river, so it seemed like only a mere diversion. A quiver of angst ran through Hans' knees as Grandmother's voice ran amidst his head.

"Nothing will happen to you."

Hans' true work only began at this point. A large population of hungry wolves were in constant search of easy prey. The feeling of fear suddenly subsided from Hans' veins as a blast of blood rushed through his legs as Grandmother's voice repeatedly ensured little Hans through his thoughts and memories.

"Nothing will happen to you on this job."

A spark then entered Hans' step as his fear spurred him on to fight the wolves in hope that they'd take flight, even though there still wasn't a wolf in sight. Hans diligently prepared for this moment every night by gathering driftwood that washed up along the river in order to make his fire and collect his "tools". This night was as cool as usual, so the fire provided comfort and protection for not only the herd, but also Hans and the two old women as well. But at times like these, the fire became a weapon. A second howl resonated in the distance. At that very moment, Hans grabbed a few charred pieces of wood from the fire, and thenceforth, simply waited with his back in the direction of the howling wolf across the bank.

Concentrating on the darkness before him with lightly burning sticks in hand, Hans deeply inhaled the fresh and crisp night air until he noticed tiny yellow dots lighting up the meadow of blackness like stars in the sky floating towards him! Glowing wolves' eyes suddenly stood at Hans' and the herds' doorstep! The two old babushka women instantly wailed away while Hans headed, with his arms behind his back, in the direction of the wolves' illuminated eyes! Nearly ready to pounce, a lead wolf apprehensively observed Hans, seemingly questioning his erratic motives. Yet, once Hans revealed what he concealed behind his back as the wolf leaped in mid-air at Hans, the wolf fully understood Hans' actions! Slapping the end pieces of his charred wood together led sparks to fly right before Hans acrobatically tossed a glowing piece of wood in the direction of the soaring wolf! Instead of voracious wolves attacking the herd in a fit of tantalizing hunger-filled fury, it was a fearless 9-year-old pursuing the wolves with fierier wood!

Wolves seek to intimidate and invoke fear-breeding chaos, but in this case, they apprehensively approached an uncharacteristically brave child holding his ground after the lead wolf leaped at Hans at the exact moment that Hans revealed the fire in his hands with the intent of singing wolf fur! In mid-air, the leaping wolf attempted to retreat, leading it to tumble right onto its back. Hans' aggression terrified the other wolves as well. These gray and white predators became frenzied at the sight of the sparks floating in their direction while Hans' high pitch whistle pierced their heightened sense of hearing in the process. Conceding their superiority, the wolves fled while Hans flogged away on the still startled lead wolf with his trusty stick.

Little Hans carried the same pain of being caned across his back, which he endured at the hand of his very own mother, so the wolves learned of his pain even though they knew nothing of his past. Hans knew that his torturing would remain deeply engrained within the wolves' memory as he could empathize with their punishment. The wolves then retreated, in search of simpler, more vulnerable prey and pastures in the area.

Though, the wolves always returned. It was only a matter of time and how deeply entrenched the prior beating and assault at the hands of Hans burned in their memories. If they didn't return the next night, they were certain to reappear a few nights later. At times, the wolves were persistent and relentlessly reappeared night after night, hiding amongst the shadows of their protective and prowling darkness. But Hans got to know the behaviour of the wolves and the herd, and knew almost exactly what to do in every situation, day or night.

After every scare, the two women eventually snored the night away next to the fire like two growling lions till 3 am came along. At that point, the herd rose in unison with the sun while the wolves remained no where to be seen. The glowing rays of the sun left the wolves vulnerable, so it was the perfect time to leave the camp site and lead the herd home through greener pastures to safety. By 7 am, they reached town. The women then took control of the herd and returned the animals to their respective owners, while Hans un-boarded the windows at the sewing shop before carrying the protective shutters to the corner of the room, right next to the woodstove where he piled them up every morning. After finishing his indoor chores, just like always, Hans fetched a couple of pails of water from the well on the other side of the creek, which was about 10 minutes away by foot. Occasionally, he cut up some wood to feed the sewing shop's fire in between his trips to fetch a few more buckets of water used for ironing the clothes, brewing the worker's midday tea, and washing their hands. Quick powernaps were squeezed into Hans' busy schedule.

Then, when 7 pm rolled around again, it was back to pasturing the herd. Wasp nests sporadically lied upon the meadow ground. Stomping cows agitated the wasps' nests. The disturbed wasps resultantly stirred in search of retribution. Aware of the wasp's vindictive nature, Hans, from time to time, purposely poked his trusty stick right into a hole containing a wasps' nest in an attempt to exact revenge against his two derisive bosses for treating him so miserable. In a flurry and out of fury, a swarm of wasps instantly stormed out of their colony, right in the direction of the immobile old babushkas! A smile overtook Hans' devious face while he sped off as the swarm engulfed his employers. Attempting to evade getting stung, while erupting into a hissy fit, the stari bubba women danced a Russian pirouette to the buzzing of wasps, instead of Tchaikovsky. These stari bubbas never showed any signs of life until a swarm of wasps set them in motion.

The following day, one of the women, completely swollen up and in excruciating pain from being brutally stung, wasn't able to come to pasturing while the other woman made an appearance sporting a completely red and swelled face, with one eye half open. Her face looked as if she had suffered the effects of being knocked around and out in a boxing ring the night before. One of the women always had to be present since they were responsible for gathering up the herd and returning the animals to their respective owners afterwards. However, this woman was in no shape to work. She could barely open her eyes. The compunction-less Hans found her appearance quite humorous, even though the woman probably didn't share in his sediments. A part of Hans fully rejoiced in their suffering. He believed that the women deserved what they got for the way that they were treating him. Not only did the women refuse to help Hans gather wood for the fire at nighttime, but they showed neither appreciation nor gratitude. They expected him to do all of the work, even though they collected most of the pay.

By the end of the summer, both woman each received about 5,000 rubles, of which Hans only saw about 600 rubles in total after the three months of work. When Hans learned of this perceived inequity, he enquired shockingly,

"Why do I get such a small portion of the earnings!?! Is that fair?!?"

One woman pompously explained,

"We're responsible for the animals! If anything were to happen to any of these beasts, we would have to compensate the family out of our own pockets!!! Not you!! We do!! So, we bear all of the risk!! You don't bear any risk!!! Got it!!! How dare you even question us!?!?! You got a lot nerve you little German!! You get what you deserve!! Nothing more!!"

This is how the women nastily justified offering Hans such a disproportionate wage. Nonetheless, little Hans had a job to do, and a part of him thoroughly enjoyed having all of the (physical) responsibility for the animals on his shoulders. It made him feel like an important man. Hans savoured being in control of the animals because he felt at the mercy of man and the world; so, Hans appreciated having the tables turned in his favour.

Another part of Hans' job was to teach the animals how to obey his orders in order to keep the herd tight, compact, and intact, or otherwise, chaos would ensue and the animals would storm off. During Hans' little "boot camp," most of this training occurred under daylight during the first two weeks of pasturing season. Hans learned that communicating with the animals by whistling was the most effective way of keeping the herd together, especially without any help from the two obese women, or "alte Schachteln" – a derogatory German term that Hans constantly uttered under his breathe whenever he felt displeased with them.

Over this time, much to Hans' delight, the animals gradually became more disciplined; however, regardless of their cooperative spirit, expecting mother cows, sheep, and goats desired to run off and have their babies in peace. But unfortunately, other animals wanted to follow suit. During these episodes, Hans had to keep the herd on a short leash, figuratively speaking. He learned (from his mother of all people), that punishing the disobedient cows, similar to how his mom "disciplined" him, by giving them a wack over the back with a stick taught them to fall in line - especially to the resonating of his whistle. Hans treated the cows like his 4-legged soldiers. And with good reason, because "dishonourable conduct" could cost "soldiers" their lives to predators, the hungry and sly wolves, and consequently, cost the two stari bubbis retribution compensation to the cows' owners. At times, the cows were so persistently stubborn that Hans sometimes had to hit them so hard that they occasionally developed welts on their backs. When the cows were returned to their owners for milking, the owners occasionally saw not only the welts, but also that their precious cows (with these bumps) were unable to produce much milk. The owners eventually complained to the women, scorning them.

"Quit touching and hurting our stinking cows! They can't make any milk with those bumps!!"

The women conveyed the nasty messages onto Hans by scolding him in return.

"What the hell are you doing to the cows you little brat!! Our clients are complaining that they ain't producing any milk, or that their milk is sourer than witches' milk! You evil nazi raisbonic! Go back to Germany with your fellow savages!!"

Hans brashly responded by craftily informing the ladies,

"The cows are getting scraped while running through the bushes. Go blame them!"

Perhaps if the women would have approached Hans diplomatically, and treated him with more respect, he would've told them the truth – but only God knows how these two women would've accepted to the truth. Hans didn't enjoy punishing the cows; on the contrary - he considered himself one with all animals – he regarded them as friends, and not merely as a means to power. However, the animals could be such undisciplined, out of control misfits, especially during the first two weeks of pasturing, that Hans had to resort to any means possible. Sometimes the animals ran in every direction possible! Hans had no other choice but to apply a brutal means in order to train them to respond to his whistle. His trusty stick turned out to be quite the effective instrument of instruction and persuasion. The cows that were constantly running off and attempting to escape just had to learn!

Occasionally, cows from the herd even strayed off into a clover field away from the river, onto property that belonged to the Kolkhoz. By the time that Hans reached the cows, they had consumed so much clover that their stomachs were swelling up to the point that they could've eventually died from a build up of gas. Such an expansion of the cow's belly severely disrupts its breathing system, especially when the rumen puts extensive pressure on their lungs. In such cases, a veterinarian would normally puncture a hole in the cow's side or rumen, or administer some Glauber's salt so the gases could be released, causing the rumen to deflate. But Hans was neither a veterinarian nor had access to Glauber's salt, so instead he simply made the cows run around until they got diarrhea, causing the cows' excess gases to expel. But nothing horrible ever happened to "Hans' cows". In spite of being rough with them at times, Hans truly savoured their company and comradery, leaving him even more compelled to try to save his four-legged comrades and partners in play.

Whenever Hans felt a bit weary, he amusedly attempted to cross the river on a cow's back instead of uneventfully walking next to the herd while leading the animals through the river. Though, the cows didn't necessarily appreciate the extra load on their backs. More times than not, the ridden cow tried, normally quite successfully, to throw Hans off of her back, causing him to splash down into cold river water. At nightfall, Hans dried himself up by a warm fire and recollected on the cow's deed, appreciatively basking, with a grin across his face, in the humour of the cow's act of defiance. Ironically, Hans' clothing became dewy amongst the nighttime grass while he laid next to the fire attempting to dry off. Once Hans left the confines of the fire's glowing flames when they all headed back towards town at the dawning of sunrise, Hans learned quite quickly just how brisk the air had become throughout the night. He shivered so strongly along the way that his teeth incessantly chattered while he meandered through the damp, shoulder-high grass. Hans simply couldn't keep his jaw still while goosebumps assailed his skin as he gratefully anticipated the moment when the sun would rise high enough for him to relish in the radiating heat. By around 7 am, Hans returned home dry after soaking up the morning sun.

Week by week, summer by summer, the women became not only reliant upon Hans, but also utterly surprised that he had yet to quit, like so many of his predecessors. Hans was quite capable and extremely dependable when it came to performing his duties. The idea of him quitting always unpleasantly resided in the back of the women's minds. However, they were not concerned enough to keep their emotions in check and treat Hans with respect, even though he was becoming more irreplaceable with each passing pasturing. People who saw Hans work were extremely impressed with his abilities. The women too were flabbergasted with how well Hans handled the wolves, and trained and disciplined the herd, but nevertheless, they grudgingly refused to offer him more money for his drudgery.

During the summer of 1950, Hans fell into the routine of spending his nights with the herds in the meadow and forests, and his days at home carrying out the chores that were expected of him at the sewing shop. Though, since Hans was still only 9 years old, he wanted to get some solid playtime in with his neighbourhood buddies. So, from time to time, he "snuck" away from the house to go swimming, fishing, and horseback riding with the boys. During playtime, one day, Timir the Tatar approached Hans.

"Could you get a loose white colt back for me Vana? He headed for the pastures."

Hans' playing buddies happily joined him in his search. When the horses were put out for pasturing, their front feet were tied up so that the horses could only make small steps, or hop like a bunny, yet never gallop. Such a measure usually kept the horses within the confines of the pastures. However, the rope around the Timir's horse's feet became loose. To take advantage of the freedom, the horse immediately ventured out and about into the higher fields. After about an hour of looking for the colt, the boys spotted it grazing along a slope adjacent to the meadow. Hans, along with the boys, apprehensively approached the incompliant foal, before placing a rope around its neck with the intent of just walking the horse back to the barn.

Though, after a little while, Hans and the boys had a change of heart. They saw a chance to have a little fun and captured it. After guiding the steed to a tree stump that all of the boys used to help hop onto the animal, the white horse found itself with the weight of four playful kids right on its back. At first, the horse was rather amused and had no qualms with the extra load, happily chauffeuring the youngsters in the direction of the stables. Yet, after a while the horse became a bit wearied by the burden and decided to swiftly veer off, galloping towards the looming limb of a tree. Hans immediately thought,

"Is he actually going to try what I think he's about to try?"

Before Hans could ponder another thought, with one swift stoke of the branch, the horse swiped all of the boys right off of its back, ridding himself of the extra weight. When all four of the boys plopped onto the ground onto their back sides with bruised behinds, they couldn't help but to endlessly laugh away at the horse's antics. The hysteria from the horse's lark and ingenuity left the boys rolling around on the ground howling, absolutely impressed at the horse's "insolence" that sent them tumbling into the high grass. Once the horse weighed four boys less, he happily, meekly, yet proudly pranced straight for the stables as the four boys enthusiastically tailed behind their new friend.

After handing the horse over to Timir, Hans headed home alone, though on his way, he discovered a stray 3-foot tall, 5-foot-long pig near a tree, and knew exactly what to do. Before giving it a second thought, Hans sprinted over to the little porker and mounted himself right onto the pig's back. The pig looked displeased while it squealed away, whereas Hans, on the contrary, looked to triumphantly and regally ride the oinker through town; or at the very least, take the pig for a spin. Like the horse, the pig actually appeared to enjoy it at times, yet after a few minutes, it seemingly felt quite violated. So eventually, on its own accord, the pig headed for a run along the river bank, evidently to savour the view of the tranquilly flowing current of the water. Though, when the pig reached the perfect point along the river, it unexpectedly leaped into the water, not necessarily to cool down, but rather to lose its 9-year-old passenger! Hans was left soaked, shocked, and speechless, but needless to say, utterly amused as the pig swam ashore to the riverbank.

CHAPTER 27

Busting Broncos

Every spring, the town's folk partook in the taming and training of bucking broncos that were approximately two-and-half-years-old and had neither been ridden nor placed in a harness. Uniting Jug, this annual ritual offered springtime entertainment and festivities for the whole town to relish. Horses played a vital role in the townspeople's livelihood and even survival, being used for the transportation of goods, people, supplies, natural resources, as well as working the land until they got long in the tooth. But instead of simply being put out to pasture, veteran horses were converted into horse burgers while their skin became hides.

At the time, the furniture factory had only one truck at their disposal, and the Kolkhoz was the only one in town with tractors, which basically meant that most of the people, including commercial traders, heavily relied upon horses. Once in a while a bulldozer appeared in Jug to grade the roads; yet, once finished, the bulldozer was immediately hauled away and deployed to a new town where roads, designed for horse traffic were tended to and manicured.

Many, including Hans, regarded horses as a type of iconic figure. The annual taming of the horses took place along the main street, right in front of the sewing shop. The area where the broncos were busted was roped off. The event was quite the spectacle and ritual all-in-one. Crowds formed a large circle surrounding the performing area. Volunteers were sought out to mount the saddle-less horse with nothing to hang onto besides a rope and the mane around the horse's neck. Younger adults were the typical volunteers. Parents never let their kids participate in the busting of the broncos because the parents were concerned that their children could get hurt. However, Hans was another story. He was an easy target for the men seeking a "volunteer" because not only was little Hans light in weight, but more importantly, nobody was there to object, besides a grandmother whose favourite line was,

"Nothing will happen to you."

At the end of the day, Grandmother never got involved, except for continually telling Hans *"to be careful."* Always up for a challenge, especially when it came to his beloved horses, Hans had absolutely no qualms with Grandmother's passive stance. He gladly participated in these spectacles, attaining a sense of joy that proliferated during every ride. Because Hans absolutely adored horses, his fear was simply tossed into the wind on such invigorating occasions. Clearing seeing his eagerness to volunteer, the men at the taming exhibitions happily grabbed Hans and hurled him right on top of the bucking bronco. Hans then took the "reins" or rope as the horse was let loose, going wild. The sight of a bucking bronco attempting to hurl Hans off of its back resembled scenes of any wild west rodeo, or perhaps, more appropriate to the setting, a massive Russian drunk trying to be corralled by a squirrel. Being frequently tossed off the horse onto the dusty terrain didn't discourage Hans one bit. He was vigilantly tenacious every time that the men corralling the horse tossed him right back on top of the bronco, even whether he was or wasn't up for another try. Hans basically had no opportunity to resist or protest – though he had absolutely no desire to turn down the challenge to docile a horse by quelling its madness.

The busting process progressed until the horse tired himself out, incidentally finally resigning itself to the demands of oppressing man. It usually took about an hour to tame one horse; after the horse was broken in, one of the men jumped on the stallion's back and rode away into the sunrise or sunset, assuming that it wasn't too cloudy on that specific day.

Even though Hans was bruised after starring in these spectacles, he nonetheless savoured every second of it. Stimulating and invigorating were the only words that could be used to describe how Hans regarded the experience – the accompanying rush perfectly fit into his no risk, no fun philosophy of life. But Hans never truly considered participating as a risk, but rather as a jolt of adrenaline that confirmed that he was alive and one with his animal of choice - well, perhaps except for whenever the horse erected itself straight up onto his back legs, leading its entire body to become perpendicular to the ground. In such an upraised position, the horse could easily lose its balance and fall right onto its back, crushing Hans in the process. And though he was absolutely terrified whenever the horse elevated into such a stance, Hans was quick and nimble enough to dismount, slide off, and roll out of harm's way. Hans regarded the dangers surrounding the busting of a bronco as a fulfilling necessity. His passion for riding and calming horses afforded him the opportunity to gradually, yet drastically improve his technique while he became more intimately acquainted with his beast of choice. After a while, after fully breaking in the horse, Hans became such a self-assured rider that he began standing up on the galloping stead, just to give the audience a show while Hans mastered a feat. His bond with horses was so deep, profound, and well known, that a man once screamed out during the event,

"Vana, you'd happily trade in your grandmother for a horse!!"

Roaring laughter from the crowd ensued. Hans pondered over the comment, yet without totally grasping its meaning. Though, if it stirred on the crowd and aided the performance, Hans more than welcomed the cheers. Hans adored the attention, a trait that only proliferated throughout his life.

After triumphantly dismounting from the horse on this occasion, Hans, out of the corner of his eye, noticed that a "black" stallion was being pulled "on stage", instantly humbling Hans as butterflies fluttered through his stomach. A "black horse" went against the unwritten laws of the "game." Hans sensed that there was something very peculiar about this utterly eerie and unique "black" bronco. A blood-agitating aura surrounding this animal brought Hans to goosebumps as his mouth instantly became dry; nonetheless, Hans' adulation for the colt soared, even though something felt off. When the men hoisted Hans up onto "blackie", he sensed a form of energy running through this colt that he'd never felt before. And before Hans knew it, the horse was attempting to escape Hans and the ring by storming into the throng! Spectators scurried and scattered out of fear! Stomping through the crowd that parted like the Red Sea, the "black" horse galloped right in the direction of a log farm fence! In disbelief, Hans realized, as the horse furiously dashed like the dickens, that this colt was going to attempt to leap over the fence with Hans still on its back! Metres from the fence, Hans didn't know what to do.

"Do I make a jump for it?!?"

Instead, he elected to see the taming through to the end. A second later, the stallion's body elevated and then instantaneously hammered down upon the wooden beam while Hans remained tucked down on the back of the horse. As he felt his bronco teeter back and forth, Hans realized that the horse's torso was stuck right in the middle of the top rail of the fence. It was like being on a life-size and living rocking horse. Neither its front nor back legs could touch the ground, so in an act of desperation, the horse leaned forward in an attempt to reach the dirt with its two front hooves. As the horse leaned forward, Hans immediately slid down its neck before tumbling to the dirt ground; though, the horse came tumbling after! When Hans looked up, he saw a 1000-pound stallion crashing down upon him! Hans' only option was to barrel roll away from the plummeting horse or otherwise, he'd certainly be crushed to death! A cloud of dust mushroomed into the air exactly where Hans was lying! But luckily enough, Hans evaded the colt by the thread of his pants.

After standing up and dusting himself off, Hans gasped for air while a grin, along with a mass of dust overtook his face. Seconds later, Hans' thoughts drifted back to a time when he was pasturing horses for Timir the Tatar, and teaching them how to jump over the creek by having them gallop with a blistering pace towards the water; however, in one instance, when Hans and the horse reached the water, the horse had another idea, refusing to leap. Such an abrupt and unanticipated stop brought Hans, along with the horse, to an immediate halt, leading Hans to go soaring over the horse's head right into the water! An enormous splash ensued! When Hans looked up and back at the horse wondering, *"What just happened?!?"*, Hans swore that he saw a grin across the horse's face.

On his next attempt, Hans "cleverly" leaned backwards, so he couldn't possibly fly forwards over the horse's head just in the case the steed once again refused to jump the creek. Though, on this attempt, while Hans leaned back, the joke was on Hans as he was sent flying backwards in the opposite direction of the springing horse that soared over the creek! This manoeuvre forced Hans into performing a backwards summersault, right before carrying out a swan dive and landing on his derriere, again splashing down into the creek! Yet, on this occasion, Hans, along with the horse were left grinning; though, Hans was never left deterred. It was quite the opposite.

Days later, Hans spotted a horse grazing in the distance close to the bank. The horse was in a perfect position for easy mounting, at least in Hans' eyes, since Hans was on higher ground than the horse. Cautiously, quietly, stealthily, yet not very slyly, Hans snuck up behind the horse through some adjacent bushes. After getting within striking distance, Hans soared through the air, happily preparing to expeditiously mount the horse from behind. Yet, the horse astonishingly anticipated Hans' "counter-rook chess move", and accordingly, the colt moved forward in unison with Hans at the exact moment that Hans leaped into the air, leaving him with no chance of landing on the horse. To add further injury to the insult, the horse kicked out his hind legs, catching Hans right in the belly while Hans sailed through the air! Hans was sent flying back into the same bushes at the top of the bank that he originally snuck out from. Once again, Hans was on the ground in pain, but nonetheless, thoroughly impressed with the horse. He only saw himself and his daftness to blame, while learning a valuable lesson - never covertly and sneakily attempt to mount a horse while it peacefully grazes.

John Friesen

However, not everyone in town loved horses as much as Hans did. Some town residents found that the horses' strolling along dry, dirt, and slag covered roads stirred up too much filth for their liking during the warmer, arid months. In an attempt to discourage Hans, the residents on his street found dubious ways to deal with and "express" their dissatisfaction. On many sunny, hot summer days, Hans brought horses back from the pastures. Along the way, he travelled by peoples' homes that were directly right next to the road, since most homes didn't have any front yards. The horses, whiling walking or galloping, made a lot of noise and whirled up a hoard of dust that sailed its way through open windows right into people's homes, leading one man to angrily scream out of his window,

"Keep those bloody horses off of the road or you'll learn a new lesson in bucking, Vana!"

And even though Hans and the horses couldn't possibly help but to incidentally stir up a little dust, the constituents on Hans' street felt that he and his horses had a lesson to learn. So, a day later, a few men inconspicuously dug up a few 2 X 2-foot holes along the road in an attempt to vent their frustration, and not to mention deter Hans and his horses in the process. But Hans wasn't going to be intimidated, so on the following sunny afternoon, in typical Hans fashion, he proudly galloped and pompously paraded on his favourite beige-coloured horse in front of a few devious looking onlookers, including the man who hollered at Hans a few days earlier. Hans couldn't have felt prouder, only until all of a sudden, he felt the leg of his trusty stallion plummet deep into the ground! The horse stepped right into one of those well-dug holes! Hans and the horse were both sent crashing to the dirt and slag covered road! Excruciating pain ripped through Hans' shoulder! He tried lifting his arm but he couldn't! All what Hans could hear was the laughing and hollering of the few spectators along the roadside who must have dug up those holes. Yet, Hans didn't care about himself as all what he cared about was the health of "his" horse! Hans' first thought was,

"Oh no! Will he have to be destroyed?!?"

Crawling over to the horse on all fours, Hans took a look into the horse's innocent and sad eyes and at its left leg as blood dripped to the ground. In a state of complete panic while filled with a plethora of whirling emotions, Hans pleaded,

"You're okay boy, right?!? It's just a scratch boy! It's just a scratch, right?!?"

As if the horse understood Hans' words, the stallion stood up and took a gingerly stroll, almost showing Hans that there was no cause for concern. Hans never felt so relieved. If the horse had broken its leg, it could've led him to being destroyed. Hans, on the other hand, couldn't lift his right arm for weeks after the incident. The culprits also didn't go unscathed. People fervidly complained about the "well" dug holes after the wagons were unable to pass through them. The responsible perpetrators were forced to fill in the holes, and were prohibited from digging up the road ever again.

CHAPTER 28

Shotgun

Hans' horse-riding escapades, and the resulting repercussions for their hole-digging parents didn't necessarily make a lot of the older teenage boys from the "affected" families very happy. They figured that Hans had to learn a lesson that nobody would ever forget. A gang of older boys from the neighbourhood had gotten a hold of a sawed-off shot gun. It didn't take long for the younger brothers of these teenagers to warn Hans.

"Our older brothers are out to get you Vana! You better watch out!"

Hans' friend even showed him the shot gun and said,

"Our older brothers are trying to fix it! There's a bounty on your head! Stay on high alert Vana!"

Hans heeded their word, but still went about with his daily routine of passively fishing down by the river, which seemed innocent enough, until all of a sudden, he spotted about twenty older boys by an old linden tree! He could hear them talking, but they outwardly paid absolutely no attention to Hans as if he didn't even exist. Hans felt relieved and believed that he was in the clear. or perhaps, that's exactly what the teens wanted him to believe as it fell perfectly into their plot. After peacefully fishing unabatedly, Hans headed down the path leading back towards the sewing shop, when out of nowhere, one of his friends, Andrei approached Hans. *"I have something to show you Vana. Come with me."*

"What is it?", Hans asked.

The shorter Andrei, with his slender face and shaggy brown hair didn't say a word. He remained completely silent. As they continued along the dirt path covered with sparse patches of grass, Hans found himself fixated on a pile of discarded garden stones nestled in amongst a high sward patch in the distance. An unnerving sense of fear overcame Hans as he followed Andrei. With each step, Hans' sense of flight strengthened at the same rate that his inclination to fight declined, creating an uncomfortable sensation of cognitive dissonance as he unwantedly, yet fawningly followed Andrei. During this entire time, Hans' eyes remained absolutely locked on those old garden stones that they were slowly approaching along the path, but Hans couldn't comprehend why. He just sensed something, something just didn't feel right. Andrei carried on silent the entire way. A light wind brushed Hans' face as an eerie silence entered his ears. Then, out of nowhere, as if time halted for a split second, twenty teenage boys appeared on scene and instantly surrounded Hans! It was all a trap! Hans was circled! Andrei had deceptively guided Hans into the vicinity of the exact garden stones that Hans had constantly and puzzledly glared at.

At this point, Hans realized that this was nothing less than an extremely, well-planned, and executed ambush! And even though a throng of malicious teens surrounded him at that very second, Hans remained obsessively preoccupied with the garden stones protruding from the grass. Coming to an abrupt stop, Hans assessed the situation in search of an escape, or perhaps it wasn't necessary, because for absolutely no explainable reason, the teens were slowly, almost inconspicuously retreating. Immediately turning around, Hans saw that Andrei was also nowhere to be seen. Completely dumbfounded by this peculiar turn of events, Hans wondered in astonishment; yet, before he could conjure up another thought, he suddenly heard some boys screaming,

"Pull!!! Pull!!!"

When Hans turned around again in the direction of the garden stones, he found himself palely, starring into the face of a double-barrelled shotgun!

It was positioned one metre away, nestled in and camouflaged amongst the rocks and the grass growing right in between the exact garden stones that left Hans uneasy during the entire time that he headed down the path leading up to the ambush. The teens kept insidiously yelling,

"Pull, pull!!", until another boy hollered back, *"I am pulling!! The bloody string is tangled up in the grass!!"*

They were attempting to blow Hans' head right off! Though instead of panicking, Hans casually moved to the side, away from the barrels of the gun, but at that point it was too late! The gang had once again completely circled Hans! The gun may have not gone off, but their plan to kill Hans was still on! Hans had absolutely no conceivable way to escape!

As he peered around the converging circle, Hans realized that these were not the typical gang of boys from his neighbourhood who normally attacked him, as strangely enough, he couldn't recognize a single one of them. Hans later learned that these teenagers were from a gang from the other side of town, whom which the local older boys apparently entered into a deal with in order to get rid of the German Hans, so the "death" or murder through an "untouched" trigger attached to a string couldn't be traced back to any of Hans' common enemies. At this time in Russia, most of the youths carried knives, sticks, and on occasion, even guns, which were rather accessible following the conclusion of WWII. There were many gangs within Jug who fought each other, and sometimes evidently even formed the odd alliance. This "foreign" gang assumed that Hans was just a simple 10-year-old target who could be easily eliminated.

As the boys gradually encroached on Hans ready to beat him beyond oblivion, he knew that he had to do something drastic to escape. Out of the corner of his eye, Hans noticed that the part of the circle closer to the river wasn't as densely concentrated with teenagers as the rest, so Hans decided that that was his best escape route if he expected to elude this blood thirsty gang. Slowly edging towards the river as the teenagers closed in on him from behind, Hans suddenly pointed to the meadow across the river and hollered the first phrase that came to his mind.

John Friesen

"Hitler is coming!"

Stymied, all of the teens immediately turned their heads in that direction, giving Hans just enough time to run through the gap within the gang's circle and down into the ravine by the river. When the teenagers realized that Hans had duped them, they pursued after him in full force. But Hans was quick. Taking off like a flash, he dashed the 100 metres stretch like Jesse Owens in the '36 Berlin Games. The gang of boys never laid a hand on Hans. When he reached the 10-foot-high river bank, Hans, without hesitation, leaped into the water and swam towards the other side.

The gang eventually reached the river bank, but none of them had any interest in getting wet. So instead, they attempted to pelt Hans with whatever they could get their hands on while he swam across the river. When Hans reached the other side unscathed, he got out of the river and launched rocks and pebbles in the gang's direction while screaming,

"You damn cowards!! Hitler is a long-time dead, and you're still afraid of him!!! Still afraid of a dead man! Didn't you ever watch the movie "Fall of Berlin"?!?!"

Hans absolutely loved that movie! Fall of Berlin romanticized the Soviets' annihilation of Nazi Germany in 1945. The film played across the entire USSR year after year after year. Following the 2nd World War, vehement hatred towards the Germans consumed many Russians even more so as a result of the public being bombarded by Soviet propaganda films that elevated the status of Russians by glamourizing their superiority, while portraying the Germans as their eternal barbaric and capitalistic enemy to the west. To compound this resentment, a lot of kids lost their fathers during the war, so many didn't require an excuse to exact revenge, by any means possible, against anyone possibly deemed "responsible". Being an ethnic German didn't help Hans' cause, especially while nationalistic pro-Russian, anti-German films were being constantly broadcasted and featured throughout the country. Hans must have seen the film *Fall of Berlin* at least a dozen times. Ironically enough, Hans loved it; perhaps it was because his parents were German as well, parents who heartlessly abandoned him in his eyes. Hans and his buddies snuck into the local theatre by digging out the dirt below the bottom log of the wooden foundation before sliding through a gap. After sneaking into the theatre, the boys found a "conference area" where they could lie on the floor and inconspicuously watch films for free and hours on end. However, whenever they were spotted, they were immediately kicked out of the theatre and told to never return.

A boy in Fall of Berlin called "Vana sonzev", or sunny Ivan (Hans), had no name on his army uniform. Hans wore a lot of military looking outfits since Grandmother transformed material from old army garments into clothes for Hans, making him appear like a "nameless" soldier. Eventually, Hans got the nickname "Vana sonzev" from his friends. As for the "friend" who led Hans to the shotgun – Hans eventually approached Andrei a day after the incident, and walked right up to his face.

"Just what kind of a friend are you?!?!?"

Andrei, while fearfully backing away the entire time, timidly repeated,

"They made me do it! They threatened me! I had no clue what they wanted to do! No clue! I would've never done it! I swear! They made me do it!"

Andrei then ran away down the street, letting the guilt consume him all along the way.

CHAPTER 29

Hunted

Hans escaped his executioners after the shotgun incident, but he always stumbled across new adversaries and foes whenever he crossed into new neighbourhoods. Being a target of the Russians was just as a common occurrence for Hans as it was for the Russians to find him to be a bullseye. In Jug, it was quite a rarity to have new people move into your neighbourhood, especially of German descent, so Hans always stood out like a sore thumb, or rather, a curly blonde, blue-eyed boy amongst a horde of local, straight, black-haired Russian kids. One day, during the summer, the stable-master Timir the Tatar, saw Hans and asked,

"Vana, one of my boys broke free! Go hunt down the colt will ya?"

Hans went searching up the knoll and beyond, amongst a forested area on the other side of the river. From such a vantage point, high above the grazing meadow within the valley, Hans diligently gazed far and wide for the horse, yet to no avail. Requiring a more elevated viewing position, Hans climbed to an even higher plateau to meticulously scour the area below. But even from there, Hans was still unable to locate the missing horse. Though, what Hans did find was a bunch of absolutely drunk teenagers smoking and drinking away in a forest. Attempting to subtly and indiscreetly stay out of their sights, Hans tried to circumvent them, but it was too late! The teenagers spotted Hans! Immediately and aggressively approaching him, Hans was completely circled by them within a matter of seconds! With a cliff on one side and the boys on the other, Hans had nowhere to run this time around! Hans suddenly felt hands grasp a hold of his ankles and arms before carrying him over to the teens' camping area where a bonfire blazed. Hans tried to stay calm, and optimistically hoped that the teens would eventually just let him go, only until a few more teenagers appeared on scene and bounded Hans' hands together with a string. Hans thought,

"Are they going to throw me in their fire and burn me to death?"

But instead, they dragged him along the ground, before violently shoving Hans up against a tree. As his head smashed against the trunk, Hans felt the string being removed from his hands as another string became entangled around his bare ankles and feet. The remainder of the string tied around Hans' ankles became wrapped around the tree behind him. A massive boy, with an enormous gut and massively round head with deep set dismaying eyes then grabbed a hold of Hans' wrist, and wrestled his arms around the tree right behind Hans' back. Being completely bounded to the tree by his hands and ankles left Hans feeling helpless and doomed. To compound his concerns, another group had just brought over a bunch of twigs and set a second fire right at the bottom of the tree that Hans was fastened up against! Before long, a massive, almost 7-foot Avvim-Goliath-like monster in his late teens, early 20's with long black hair, picked up a burning stick out of their bonfire while the rest of the boys chanted in unison,

"Let's burn him!! Let's burn him!! Let this German filth burn!!"

However, the second fire wasn't strong enough, leading the teenagers to realize that they required more wood to transform Hans into ashes and dust. The group all diligently scurried off into the forest in order to collect more pieces of wood so they could finish off the job and Hans once and for all. The inebriated teens figured that Hans was captured for good, so no one even bothered to stand guard and take notice that the string around Hans' ankles had caught fire, leading his bare feet to become liberated! Moving to the other side of the tree, away from the fire, Hans attempted to get his hands free by rubbing the string bound around his wrists back and forth against the tree until the tomato twine ultimately snapped! Hans was free! Sprinting away, Hans gazed into the distance at the freedom before him as he glided towards the vast green meadow. Motoring down the hill in the direction of the grazing area within the valley below, Hans happily spotted Timir's horse. When the boys saw Hans escaping, they languidly scampered after him in dejection, but Hans was not concerned since he could outrun each and every one of them.

Hans was regarded as the "German boy without parents", so he was deemed easy prey and pickings - simply a target who could be abused, and even killed with seemingly no consequences. Hans felt like a bullseye for Russian darts. Vigilance had to be constantly practiced if Hans expected to avoid such altercations. Though, living so cautiously didn't make it easy for him to carry out a normal life and go about with his daily routines and tasks without fearing the hunt and reprisals.

And even though those older boys from the next neighbourhood over tried to kill Hans with a sawed-off shotgun on his way back from fishing only a few weeks earlier, that incident didn't deter Hans from going back down to the river to fish in order to supplement his meek food supply while savouring the outdoors. So as usual, Hans plopped himself down along the river bank, and tossed his bait into the water, just waiting for the fish to bite his "hook" as a worm dangled on the end. Hans couldn't afford a fishing rod, so he simply made one by attaching a string to his long, flexible, and trusty pasturing stick. As he fished, Hans lulled himself into a surreal zone in which he was left almost solely concentrating on snatching fish, while sporadically and solemnly wondering just why his parents abandoned him. His surroundings became blacked out amongst the invisible backdrop. Angelic sounds of birds chirping, the river flowing, and moor frogs ribbiting sent Hans into a trance, only until all of a sudden, he heard the rustling of footsteps. But it was too late!

Before Hans could turn his head backwards, he felt a heaving shove from behind! After being rammed right off the river bank, Hans found himself caught within the current of the river's water and between the crossfire of rocks and stones that the boys were tossing in his direction! Hans recognized these older kids, as they were from his neighbourhood, and not the ones from the shot gun attack. When Hans looked back at the teens while he glided down the river, he got the impression that their intentions were less than amicable and playful as they hollered,

"You will not escape this time Vana!!"

The strong current carried Hans swiftly down stream, but he remained calm while searching out something to grab onto as water filled his mouth. Becoming swept underneath a fallen tree wedged up against the bank, Hans quickly grabbed a hold of the roots of the tree in the nick of time! The trunk was quite large and partially submerged in the cold, spring river water, while the tree's branches were exposed. Most of the root network remained above the surface. Fortunately, there was enough space between the water and trunk for Hans to stick his head through in order to catch a breath of air without being spotted by the boys who Hans could hear saying,

"Where did he go? Where did he go? Can you see him? Where is he?"

After a while, Hans eventually heard a boy's voice say,

"He must've drowned. There's no trace of him. His body probably got tangled up in the branches."

It then became rather quiet. Hans could hear neither the boys' voices nor their movements anymore. But Hans cautiously waited till the coast was absolutely clear and he was certain that the boys weren't just hiding somewhere, quietly and patiently waiting to pounce. After finally letting go of the roots and timidly swimming over to the other side of the river where the bank was lower and more manageable to climb, Hans scaled the damp dirt bank. He still had to walk across the old wooden bridge in order to get back to the other side of the river. Yet, before arriving at the bridge, Hans stopped in at the blacksmith's shop and paid a visit. Upon arrival, Anton sarcastically said,

"Isn't it too cold for swimming?"

Little Hans, quick-wittedly responded, *"Yes, but somebody else thought otherwise."*

He removed his clothes and dried them off by the fire. Aydar and Anton, both in their 40's, but with amicable and boyish appearances with gapping eyes and bubble noses, gave Hans a lot of advice. But in the end, they basically told Hans,

"Avoid those boys at all costs!"

Hans always had fond memories of these men in the blacksmith shop, and Timir the Tatar from the horse stables, and even the loggers that he helped from time-to-time. When Hans' clothes fully dried up, he left the blacksmith shop and crossed over the bridge before heading back down to the river in search of his fishing rod that he ultimately found stuck in the grass. Hans was quite appreciative of the fact that the boys didn't chuck his fishing rod into the river after him.

CHAPTER 30

Water's Edge

Constantly being targeted didn't hurt Hans' sense of compassion and righteousness. Weeks after being shoved into the water, Hans strolled home along the river, when he suddenly heard the screams of an 11-year-old girl.

"Help! Help! Help me, someone!!"

She accidently swam into the deep end of the gently flowing river causing panic to set in! Hans was a strong swimmer, so he had no qualms about leaping into the pleasantly mild river water, let alone attempting to rescue the cute and petit brown-haired girl. Using the breaststroke, in his brown shorts with his chest bare, Hans quickly zoned in on the distraught girl. Seeing the absolute fright in her eyes as she unpleasantly gargled water in her mouth led Hans to increase his tempo by switching to freestyle strokes. Moments later, Hans swung his right arm around her waist, and hauled the gracious girl to the shallow base of the river and safety.

"Oh thank-you Vana! Thank you so much!!"

Hans modestly, yet proudly swam back across to the other side of the river with a massive grin across his face, not thinking much of what had just transpired, yet flooding his mind with thoughts of being a hero. It felt good saving a life, especially during a time when others were looking to take his. A day later, the girl's parents surprisingly stopped by the sewing shop and personally thanked Hans. He was not only astonished and appreciative, but also flattered to the point that his ego began to inflate. Feeling capable of carrying out any feat, while sensing unyielding belief in his abilities helped Hans survive. An insecure and fearful coward would've perished years earlier.

During that summer, Hans also enjoyed fishing at a manmade lake that only existed in the summertime, situated about 100 metres from the sewing shop complex. The lake, which separated the well that Hans fetched water from and the sewing shop, formed when the gates of the dam sprung open as spring sprang into season. The entire area became flooded. Small carps were brought in from a hatchery for fish farming. An airplane would fly over and drop the fish into the lake while still in mid-air. The fish were fed pressed 2 by 3 feet by 3 inches thick corn-, sunflower-, and rape-seeds sheets. Stored in the sewing shop's "first floor" basement, Hans had easy access to these nutrient-loaded seed-sheets. Hans occasionally broke off a few pieces with an axe and stuck them into his pocket before he snuck them out of the cellar. The pieces were extremely hard and unchewable, so a human couldn't just bite through them if he intended to keep his teeth. So, instead to biting down, Hans simply stuck a piece into his mouth and sucked on the chunk of seed-sheet until his saliva slowly broke it down, before swallowing the crushed seeds.

The seed sheets were loaded onto a wagon and taken down to the river where they were transferred onto a flat-bottom oar boat before being rowed to the designated area where the sheets were broken up into small pieces with a hammer and dumped into the water for the fish to feed on. The fellow who was in charge of the operation was also of Germanic blood. This lad's name was Thorsten. Thorsten lost one of his legs when he was only 8 years old after he fell from a train in which its wheel severed Thorsten's knee from the rest of his body. Hans sometimes assisted Thorsten, who was in his mid-30s and possessed a massively muscular left leg, with the loading of the wagon; taking the sheets to the lake; and even rowing the boat. Three or four of Hans' legs equaled the size of Thorsten's. Hans also helped Thorsten with bringing straw in from the fields to feed the horses during winter, and taking the horses to the pond for a drink. From time-to-time,

Thorsten passed Hans a little money for his work. Other times, Thorsten simply handed Hans a few cans of fish or liver paste.

Being of German descent, along with having access to food, left the one-legged and "handicapped" Thorsten prone to attacks. He walked around with a self-made crutch for decades, so he definitely knew how to use it, at times even as a weapon if need be. One afternoon, while unloading a few seed-sheets for the fish, two men jumped Thorsten from behind, believing that they had easy pickings! Thorsten landed right onto the flat bed of the wagon. Instantaneously swinging his crutch around like a Scottish claymore, Thorsten hammered the one assailant in his late 30's right in his face! As blood poured from his attacker's broken nose, Thorsten sat up on the back of the wagon and rifled the point of the crutch like a spear right into left side of the other attacker's chest! Both of Thorsten's attackers fell to the ground, slowly crawling away bloody, and full of agony, shame, and regrets. The outnumbered crippled Thorsten absolutely annihilated the two (attempted) thieves, who left with neither a seed nor a carp.

By the middle of summer, the carp grew to be 6 to 8 inches long in size. When Hans was hungry, he went down to the artificial lake and fished them out while remaining inconspicuous to horse-mounted watchman. After rolling up his worn-out and faded gray pants and placing both of his feet into the shallow and mild water, Hans waited until a carp swam right in between his legs, before he grabbed it with his bare hands. Sometimes, Hans even went fishing with his cat, which he found as an abandoned kitten. Hans loved every animal he had contact with, and this cat was no exception. He named her "Krystal" after here pristine and radiating white fur. She followed Hans like a shadow wherever he went. Eventually, Krystal started observing Hans' bare hand fishing technique, and before long, she too was snaring fish with the greatest of ease and grace with her bare paws. Krystal's hunting technique of choice was grabbing the fish behind the head, paralyzing it in the process, before carrying it out of the water and dropping it onto the grass. At the end of these fishing excursions, Hans picked up the fish and took them home to fry up.

Hans and Krystal fished almost everyday together until the security guard on horseback, Mr. Fedokovolev, who monitored the lake, caught Krystal skimming fish out of the pond all by herself. Without a blink of his eye, he took aim with his shotgun and pulled the trigger! It was the job of the security guard to prevent anything or anyone, including an innocent cat, from stealing any fish, so that's exactly what he did! Bullets entered right through Krystal's right side of the head and her front paw! As blood cascading down her chest, Krystal dragged herself home to Hans, marking her path red along the way. When Hans saw Krystal slowly limping towards him with blood all over her white and slightly beige fur, he became absolutely devastated before entering into a state of complete rage! His first instinct was to grab the shotgun out of the watchman's hands and shoot him right in the head! But instead, Hans bandaged up Krystal in old rags. Afterwards, she could only see out of one eye and hop around on three legs. It appeared as if she had lost her eyesight in one eye forever. Yet, miraculously, after only a few days, she quickly recovered and her eyesight fully came back! Krystal even went back to fishing on all fours; however, she became extremely careful, cautious, and vigilant. Every time that she saw the malicious and wicked Mr. Fedokovolev on his horse, she sprung into the high grass out of sight.

Everybody in town hated Mr. Fedokovolev. With his long sideburns, slicked back black hair, and thick and imposing handlebar moustache, he resembled a rugged, yet nasty cowboy. Though, if you were ever to look deep into his blank eyes, you'd see the demeanour of a village idiot. Even though Krystal fully healed, revenge consumed Hans. So, one day, Hans and a buddy hid in some bushes on the bank of the lake and tossed pebbles at Mr. Fedokovolev's horse. Absolutely spooked, his trusty horse didn't think twice before throwing the watchman to the ground and darting off to the stables that were located about two kilometres away. Mr. Fedokovolev was forced to walk all the way back to the stables to fetch his horse, grumbling under his breathe the entire way.

But the resentment for the watchman lied deeper than the artificial lake. Whenever the watchman caught any farmers' cows grazing amongst the Kolkhoz's fields, he took them to a holding barn, an act which left him vehemently despised by the community. The cows' owners had to pay a penalty in order to bail the cow out of the barn if they ever expected to see their prized possession ever again. A few weeks after the Krystal shooting, Mr. Fedokovolev captured a cow that belonged to one of Hans' friends, Sergei, an older boy with a clever, quick, and if need be belligerent tongue, along with the necessary solid physique to go along with it. The watchman immediately confiscated the cow and took it to a Kolkhoz holding barn, leaving Sergei frantically in a panic. He immediately tracked down Hans.

"Vana! The watchman just took the cow that I was supposed to be watching!! I'm gonna get a beating from my folks for losing her!! I should've been watching the heifer!! We have no money to bail her out!! I'm doomed!!!"

Hans calmly mollified Sergei.

"Don't worry! We'll get her back!! Let's go to the barn! Mr. Fedokovolev is by the lake as we speak."

The boys headed on over to the barn with the intention of freeing the cow, but when they got there the barn door was padlocked shut! Sergei moaned in defeat, but Hans confidently retorted,

"Not to worry!! I know another way! We just gotta pry a couple of barn boards off and we'll be in!"

Hans brushed his hand along the old, slightly dilapidated rotting barn till he found a loose board. One by one, Hans and Sergei removed a few panels in order to allot enough space for the cow to be able to walk her way out of the barn. When the boys slowly creeped their way into the dark barn, they discovered the cow, seemingly just quietly waiting for her rescuers to arrive. Hans instantly grabbed her by the ear, even though the cow eagerly knew where to go by following the daylight, clearly requiring no aid to escape the confines of the barn. Once out, Hans and Sergei meticulously reset the three removed boards in place to the point that it appeared as if they had never been tampered with. Knowing exactly where to head, the cow led Hans and his friend back to her "home sweet barn", safe and sound.

When the watchman ultimately returned to check up on the cow, he was shocked and utterly furious to discover that she had vanished! In a state of ferocity and madness, Mr. Fedokovolev stormed to Sergei's house and demanded to know,

"Just how the hell did you get that fat cow out of the barn?!?!? Tell me that much will ya!!!"

The watchman with the shotgun had no definitive proof that they had entered the barn, so he couldn't fine them for "stealing" the cow. Sergei coyly responded to the watchman,

"You must've left the doors open, and that's how the cow must've escaped. We're certain that's how it happened. Not a doubt in my mind. How 'bout yours?"

Hans and Sergei made a complete fool of Mr. Fedokovolev. He left Sergei's home absolutely livid! To make matters worse for this watchman, he actually got caught sleeping on the job on a haystack just a few days later, when one of the townspeople furtively snuck up on him in the act, and set the surrounding hay on fire. Mr. Fedokovolev was literally left blazing away in a fit of fury and angst! That disgruntled citizen of Jug tried to make it appear as if the watchman had fallen asleep on the job while smoking, or at least that's how his boss saw it. The constituents of Jug got even with Mr. Fedokovolev, and he knew it!

When autumn appeared once again, and pasturing season concluded, Hans started spending more time on the furniture factory grounds. One day after school, Hans headed over furniture factory, but rather than crossing the wooden bridge, he took a shortcut through a ravine before heading up the hill near the loggers drop off point a few 100 metres from the saw mill. Along the way, Hans savoured the sounds of the stream and the scents of fallen leaves only until he heard a loud thud and saw a 30-foot-long log from the mill tumbling down upon him! Then another! Then another! As more logs came rumbling down the hill, Hans' first reaction was to leap over each and every one of them; yet, he knew that jumping uphill and over numerous, thundering logs was a near impossible feat against gravity for anyone, especially a young boy! To compound Hans' concerns, there was no time to sidestep the long logs tumbling down along different stretches of the valley hill. Having absolutely no clue how to escape this mess, Hans began to panic as he was on course to be crushed in a gridlock of logs only until he looked to his immediate right, where he noticed a three-foot-deep, oval-shaped tiny crater that appeared as if it were freshly dug. Without hesitation, Hans sprang inside the crater and took cover knowing that this was his last hope! The first tumbling log fell within metres and split seconds of mowing Hans right over, rolling right over top of him, without even touching a hair on his head.

Hans' gamble paid off as every single one of the logs along his path went sailing over his head, so he walked away unscathed. After the logs splashed down into the river, Hans cautiously snuck his head out of the bunker, just to see a bunch of teenagers scatter to conceal their identity, even though Hans knew exactly who had been targeting him. His assailants went through all of the trouble of rolling the large logs that were stacked up against the furniture factory mill along the perimeter of the hillside to the edge of the hill and patiently waited for Hans to walk by, before pushing them over the edge in hope that the large pieces of timber would run Hans down. But once again, his assailants were left disappointed.

CHAPTER 31

Winter Wolves

In the winter, there was always a dearth of food, leaving everyone suffering, including the hungry wolves. With no exposed herds to prey on during the winter, wolves became even more aggressive and vicious. During severe cold spells, wolves even entered towns in search of food. Under these dire circumstances, wolves even attacked humans. Nobody was safe.

On one frigid winter evening, Grandmother's co-worker left the sewing shop to head home. As he strolled by a five-foot wooden farm fence while looking up at the beautifully bright full moon masked by thin clouds, he suddenly felt sharp pricks pierce into his neck as a mass of weight crashed down upon his back! The heavy burden on his torso led the man to fall right over, forcing him to drop into a mound of snow! A wolf lept off a tree stump out from behind the farm fence and ambushed the man, thrusting its jagged fangs right into the man's neck!! An extremely thick layer of clothing and a high collared winter coat prevented the wolf from gaining a complete grip and sinking its teeth through the man's skin. As the wolf feverously attempted to clench his neck, the man turned around and handed the wolf a wack right across its nose with his walking stick! Deeming the attack to be a shameful failure, the wolf immediately aborted his assault. Even though the wolf sent the man tumbling to the ground, seemingly in triumph and victory, this lone wolf ran away after failing to grasp the man on its first attempt. Lone wolves prefer not to bear any risk, especially, against people. Wolves are intoxicated by the chase, and like man, the rush from a sense of superiority; yet conversely, the wolves shy away from confrontations whenever they feel intimidated, in danger, and "inferior".

The following evening, this very same sewing shop worker encountered a similar foe when he went to feed hay to his cows outside of his barn, where he was protected by an extended overhang of the roof. On this frigid January evening, he dug his pitch fork into a pile of manure. Lifting up the fork, the man, out of the corner of his eye, noticed a massive grey blurry orb soaring down through the manure chute right before something hammered down upon the man's back! It was once again, a 130 pound, 5-foot-long wolf! The beast vehemently toiled to sink its fangs into the man's neck! A fierce struggle ensued, but luckily enough, the man was heavily dressed for the occasion in winter gear once again, so the wolf couldn't get a good grip on him and his gray, high-collared coat. The moment that the wolf fell off of the man onto it's back was when the 250-pound, 6'5-foot man in his 40's with the strength of a few men thrusted his pitchfork right through the stomach of the wolf! A deafening howling cry of agony fell when the man drove a second and third thrust of the pitchfork into the bleeding wolf before its eyes slowly closed. Fang and claw marks imprinted in the man's neck and back reminded him of Nature's forgiving cruelty as he wiped the wolf's blood off from his pitch fork and face as the man humorously wondered to himself,

"Did the same wolf come back to finish off what he failed to do the evening earlier? Was he so ashamed of not succeeding?"

Despite these lone wolf attacks, the wolves preferred to hunt as a pack. These marauding wolves kept their prey on high alert. All animals, especially dogs, were the first to sense the presence of their predators. Barking dogs indicated the insidious and ominous looming of danger, which caught the attention of the people inside the safe confines of their homes. Residents assumed the worst, and came out armed and prepared for a bitter battle on penetratingly cold and dark Russian nights. People's properties and building structures were completely closed off, so the wolves' chances of breaking indoors were slim. However, on the odd occasion, a wolf managed to sneak into a barn complex through an opening that was used for throwing out manure if it were not properly secured and sealed.

On a night of such nights, a wolf leap into and slid through a manure chute opening. The home owner's dog attempted to play hero, but the pooch was no match for his fierce and sly opponent. Hearing the bellows of his dog barking and the ensuing sounds of a vicious scuffle, the owner leapt to his feet to grab his loaded shot gun that he stored in a closet. After his dog let out faint whimpers of defeat, the night fell eerily silent until panic-stricken stirring erupted within the barn. The man inside knew exactly who had come to pay a visit as the ruckus stemming from the barn intensified - the wolf's intent was to kill every single animal in sight without hesitation.

Hollering for his son, the man awaited a hostile skirmish. As his knees nervously trembled while he courageously carried a shotgun in his shuddering right hand, and a kerosene lantern in his still as silence left hand, the man apprehensively tip-toed into the snow on a blustery cold night in the direction of the barn alongside his son. Moments later, they discovered their loyal dog lying motionless face down in the white snow possessing traces of red. The father then turned to his teenage son, whose heart palpitated at the sight of such merciless carnage that defined the wolf's superior claim. The father's eyes captured his own distress. Upon reaching the barn door, the father whispered mightily,

"Grab the pitch fork!! Let's teach this wolf a lesson on hunting, boy!"

With shuddering hands, the son cautiously opened the barn door. The father then hesitantly entered the confines of the pitch-black barn with a lantern in hand. As his right foot stepped down, the hay below his boot crutched, instantly leading glowing eyes to glance in the man's direction! Shining the kerosene lantern towards the sparkling spheres, the son and father caught the wolf with its teeth sunk right into the neck of a cow. Startled, the wolf promptly glared into the men's innocent and fearful eyes with its piercing, dilating pupils as a ferocious grin exposed its fangs! Out of sheer terror, the owner feverishly swung the lantern like a dainty woman swinging a designer purse in the direction of the wolf! Slipping out of his hands, the lantern dropped onto a pile of dry hay that instantaneously caught on fire! The wolf scurried in fright in the man and his son's direction as the confines of the barn blazed! In a state of panic, the man and his son reacted hastily by storming out of the door, "cleverly and calculatedly" leaving it open, allowing not only the wolf, but also the terrified cow and sheep to frantically escape.

When confronted within the boundaries of a building, the best solution is to just open the gate, and let the frenzied wolf out. Take flight, or fight to death is the wolf's mantra. A cornered and trapped wolf's ferociousness increases when it feels fear breeding.

As a form of Russian winter entertainment, families gathered inside of their homes in the evenings and nestled up next to the window where they watched wolves in the streets hunt down any prey. After school one day, the parents of the girl who Hans rescued from drowning in the river during the summer invited him over for dinner, and to watch the wolves in action. The sewing shop's windows were all boarded up, preventing Hans from bearing witness to the prowling exploits of wolf packs during the night, so he happily headed over the girl's house with his trusty massive whip in hand for protection in case of a wolf pack ambush. A loud and chilling crack of the whip alone could send wolves scurrying.

Following a delicious bowl of borscht soup, the family, along with Hans, gathered by the window of the girl's family's house to catch the activities of the marauding wolves. Across the street from the girl's family's house lived a little dog that had access to a small opening in the gate, which allowed the pooch to exit its owner's property at will. The hole was not big enough for a wolf to slither through, but nonetheless, probably should've been sealed shut.

Spotting this little dog outside of the hole close to the road, the wolves elected not to immediately attack, but instead, theatrically and innocently jumped and rolled around in the snow like children without a worry in the world. Playfully chasing each other through the fluffy snow 20 feet away from the small opening in the gate, these wolves gave off the impression or illusion that they were simply horsing around. The presence of the little dog appeared to the human eye to be completely outside of the spectacles of the wolves engaging in a playful spectacle. It was this calculating facade that, in fact, completely irritated the dog, leaving it feeling totally slighted and ignored. Every time that this little pooch desired to communicate with the wolves, he jumped through his hole in the gate, and barked out in the direction of the wolves before quickly scurrying back through the hole where he was protected behind the fence. The wolves constantly pretended to be scared off by his "tenacious" barking, before running a little bit further away from the dog's hole each time that the tiny mutt exited through the little hole in the gate. With each retreating scamper, the wolves moved slightly further away from the fence, at the same distance that the little dog crept further outside of his hole and barked, before promptly retreating back behind the fence. The little pooch knew to be careful, yet at the same time, wondered if these wolves truly were friendly and without a care, hunger, or hostile intention in the world.

This game of cat and mouse went on until the dog moved far enough away from the hole, while being outside of the confines of his protective fence, which is exactly when the third wolf that was hiding around the corner the entire time darted to the opening in the fence and blocked the little dog's way to safety! Shocked by the sudden appearance of the 3rd wolf, the little pooch stopped stunned in his tracks! At this point, he had no place to retreat! His hole was completely blocked off! When the dog turned in the opposite direction, in search of a way to escape, he saw the "playing" wolves storming right in his direction! Within a few seconds, the sly, calculating, and patient wolves had the pooch in their clutches, which was the wolves' plan from the onset. Even more wolves then converged upon the dog and tore it to pieces before completely devouring every part of the mutt, except for its head.

During winter, dogs' heads could be found all over town. For some strange reason, the head of a dog was regarded as some sort trophy for the kids (even though the wolves did the killing). Young boys tied a piece of wire through the dog head's nostrils, and dragged the head behind them as a sort of weapon, or perhaps trinket. During a fight or skirmish, boys swung these dogs' heads at each other through the air in an act of combat. But needless to say, possessing a dog's head wasn't enough to stave off a wolf attack. So, when people travelled to work, they always set off in groups for safety, especially those people who lived on the outskirts of town. Wolves usually wouldn't attack a group of people because in the wolves' eyes, that wasn't a risk worth taking.

Every morning, a group of German women who all worked at a pig farm in a barn on the outskirts of town set off for work. These women, who all lived in the same communal townhouse complex always went off to work together as a pack, making them less susceptible to a wolf attack. However, one day, one woman was running a little bit late, so she told the others,

"Go ahead! I'll catch up!"

After the group of women went through a gully and reached the other side of the river, they suddenly heard a loud, horrified scream of agony! Quickly looking back, the women noticed that it was the helpless yelp of their neighbour and co-worker! Yet, by the time that they stepped in her direction, she was no longer visible. A pack of wolves had already swarmed her! The other women could only hear a hysterical voice in the wind as the woman continued to scream and shout for help. Though, within a few minutes, nothing was left of her besides her rubber boots and torn clothing, which the wolves left behind. The wolf pack then dragged her corpse away to a location where they teared her to pieces and devoured her remains in peace.

A group of men immediately organized a "rescue party" that was armed with shotguns. Their aim was to hunt down the wolves responsible for her death, but the group was unable to find any trace of them and her, except for the wolves' tracks, which the men couldn't pursue, even with their horses, since the snow was too deep. A head and bones were eventually discovered in a nearby forest, but there was absolutely no sign of the wolves. After the incident, the women always travelled to work in a group that was escorted by a man holding a shotgun.

But winter wasn't a time for only the wolves to have fun. The local pond froze and converted into a skating rink, offering kids some exercise and excitement. In the winter of 1951, Hans became so overzealous at the first sight and sign of freezing that he desperately yearned to head down to the pond to go skating. So, one afternoon, following a half day of school like always, Hans got home and chopped some wood; yet, he only had one thing on his mind – the vision of the pristine and immaculate surface of the frozen pond. His craving for skating was overwhelming. As he gazed into the distance and saw a glass-like frozen pond, he knew that he had no other choice but to storm inside of the sewing shop and fetch his homemade skates. Sprinting down the hill with both skates in hand, Hans could only feel ecstasy and anticipation flowing through his veins. Once he arrived, he quickly strapped his skates onto his boots and he was off! Gliding along the fresh sheet of ice, Hans felt like he was in heaven! Wind flushed through his curly, dirty long blond hair at the same speed that the smell of brisk winter air entered his nostrils, until all of a sudden – splash!! Hans fell right through the ice! The water wasn't too deep, but frigid enough to instantly transform Hans into a human icicle.

With water up to his armpits, Hans felt as if he were being stabbed by thousands upon thousands of little forks all over his body. He was stuck and frozen with no inclination to move; but he knew otherwise if he expected to survive. Making a fist, Hans began shattering the ice. Inch-by-inch, he slowly edged through the boggy bottom of the pond on his skates towards the four-foot high bank. With each passing frozen fistful of fury, Hans was one skate closer to the massive fireplace in the sewing shop. Warm thoughts, or rather thoughts of warmth rose through his mind like the vapours coming off of the pond. Once Hans reached the shoreline, he felt utterly relieved, believing that he got himself out of this mess. However, he first had to get back onto solid, yet slippery ground by scaling the bank. But everything was frozen. The mud on his boots. His nose. His clothing. His hair. Himself. Everything. In Hans' mind, climbing up the high and slippery bank appeared like an almost impossible feat. With his first try, Hans slipped back onto his belly. With his second try, he fell back into the water. On the third try, Hans slid down the bank again onto his stomach. He subsequently wondered to himself,

"Is this the end of me? Will I ever get out?"

Though, on his eighth attempt, after getting a good grip on a protruding rock, Hans finally reached solid and flat ground! He was out! As quickly as a frozen boy could, Hans ran directly into the sewing shop and stormed to the glowing wood stove before undressing himself, and letting himself, along with the shirt and pants that were frozen to his body thaw out. Grandmother immediately brought Hans a blanket and wrapped it around him, warming up his body as she pressed her thin frame against his. Grandmother commented to Hans, quite jokingly,

"Isn't it too cold for swimming? Next time you should wait until the ice is thick enough for skating."

Hans was always forced outside whenever the people were working in the crammed sewing shop, and only allowed to return after the other workers left for the day. But luckily enough, the stove was in a separate room, so Hans wasn't under any of the workers' feet whenever he wanted to warm himself up.

In order to go skating, Hans made his own homemade pair of skates out of wood, since he was unable to afford new or used ones. First off, he chopped off and sculpted a chunk of a log into a "V" wedge shape before flattening a piece of wire with a hammer and attaching the wire to the bottom of the "V", in which a groove was carved out. Hans then hammered the bent piece of wire through the front and back ends of the wood. Strings, which were used to tie the skates around each of Hans' boots, were pulled through holes that Hans punched into the log. Despite being quite the nifty invention, the skates were actually better suited for travelling on frozen snow than ice. On a sheet of ice, Hans found it extremely slippery after he strapped his skates underneath his "valenkis", felt-like, stiff, 100% top to bottom wool boots, and glided along the frozen surface. Occasionally, Hans bought a second-hand pair of valenkis for the soles, which he stitched onto his original pair after he brutalized the boot bottoms to the point that they cracked. Hans though, had lots of thread and sewing practice at the shop to pull off his boot repairs quite easily himself. And if he couldn't manage, Grandmother certainly could.

CHAPTER 32

Bulrushes to Bullying

Spring reappears. As the ice melts, the water levels rise. Loggers are able to let the logs float down the river to the furniture factory, instead of lugging them with a horse drawn wagon when the water level is too low to be able to transport the logs along the river. Loggers take full advantage of the fast-flowing river current during springtime. Cut trees are de-branched. Tree trunks are piled up along a slope on a high river bank. Once the tree branches are removed, the logs easily roll down the hill right down into the river. Lumberjacks, who are primarily Tatars, work and live in the forest and lumber yards for two months at a time, returning home the odd weekend. Once a month, potatoes, carrots, onions, flowers, flour, beans, peas, and cream of wheat are brought in by wagon for the on-site cook, who is a lumberjack's wife; she too resides at the lumber camp, and occasionally even plays music for the men on a six-string Russian "gypsy guitar".

Along the river, by the furniture factory, there used to be a wooden dam, but the old logs gradually rotted causing the water to break through the gates. The lower part of the dam, however, still remains functional, so when spring came along, and the ice melted, this portion of the dam trapped the water. Logs were placed across the river and bound together with a steel cable in order to prevent the wooden beam-like pieces of wood from travelling further downstream past the sawmill and furniture factory. All of the lumber floated around in that part of the river for the entire month, during which the logs were hauled out of the water by horses, before the wood was piled up by the saw mill situated right on top of the dam. Since the 11-year old, usually bare-footed and shirtless Hans was light in weight, he easily moved around throughout the matrix of floating logs and directed them close to shore using a long pole with a hook at one end and his well-defined muscles. The water was still ice cold from the bitter winter, so Hans tried his best not to fall in while he earned his food for the month of May.

Once June came along, Hans found another form of food and entertainment that kept him amused for the summer. Across from the sewing shop, bulrushes grew within the shallow portion of a pond. Cranes, wild ducks, fish, and other small birds nested in the bushes situated amongst the water, making this ecosystem a hunter's haven. Accessing the nests was nearly impossible on foot, so Hans built a simple raft out of two old barn planks, which he used to navigated through the bulrushes to gain access to the bird's nests from which he snatched eggs from for his next meal. However, steering the raft was far from an easy task. Hans' contraption was quite flimsy, causing it to tilt on a whim. Hans required perfect balance to be able to navigate the raft through the pond to prevent it from toppling over. He usually gained access to the eggs from the raft, but on one occasion, he saw some tiny eggs belonging to Siberian blue robins nestled in amongst the bulrushes in a nest, not reachable by raft. Peering around, Hans saw some birds soaring around in the vicinity, but he knew, based on his level of hunger, that capturing these eggs was a risk worth taking. Before dismounting from the raft, Hans tied a rope around his waist that was attached to the raft before grabbing a hold of his trusty 6-foot long stick. He then looked down into the mucky and marshy pond water, unsure of how deep the bottom laid. Kneeling down, Hans dropped one foot into the water, and then another. The pond wasn't that deep, and Hans' feet didn't sink more than a few inches into the slimy and muddy bottom so he was able to relatively easily waddle through the water towards the bulrushes in pursuit of the nest. With his eyes on the prize that was three delicious looking eggs, the staving Hans took one final glance into the sky, just to make sure that the parents of the eggs were not ready to strike. Their ear-splitting squawks intensified so he knew that he had to proceed swiftly. Taking a quick look into the 6-inch diameter straw nest, Hans stuck his hand in and grabbed the three eggs before going underwater in the direction of the raft. When Hans reached the raft, and elevated his head out of the water, he thought that he was off scoff free until he felt a sharp pierce enter his right check! And then another into the crown of his head! But Hans didn't want to relinquish those eggs, so he grabbed his stick and stroked his way to shore until he felt another sharp pierce in the back of his neck!

Blood streamed down his head as arriving on shore with a few baby eggs in hand. Before darting off to the sewing shop to take cover and boil up his next meal, Hans discovered a crow with a broken wing, waiting to die or be saved on shore. Feeling heart-broken, while holding three mother's eggs, Hans epitomized the duality and contradictory nature of man by picking up the injured crow with his free left hand, and brought it home with him where he fed the crow seeds right before Hans devoured the three birds' eggs.

A week later, after the wing fully healed, the crow rejoined Nature once again. Hans was sad to see it fly away into the sky, but he knew that that was where the crow belonged. Though, days later, while Hans was chopping some wood, he felt a mass of weight land down upon his shoulder. When he looked to his left, he noticed that it was no one other than the injured crow stopping by, almost as if to say thank you. The crow's arrival brought tears to Hans' eyes, as he realized that the crow was grateful for being nurtured, a motherly nurturing that Hans never received.

Being at home and experiencing the beauty of Nature, though, was a far cry from the experiences that he was encountering at grade school where he usually found himself being challenged to violent wrestling matches during recesses. Summer holidays were weeks away, but a part of Hans wished they weren't, as he actually enjoyed many of the skirmishes that he partook in; they were rough though. On wooden floors or gravel-laced pavement. Inside or outside. Sometimes Hans won, and sometimes he was less successful, but he always found excitement in the challenges and battles, even if he walked away bloody, filthy, and bruised. But, at the end of the day, Hans, more times than not, found himself being picked by the bigger kids in school, just to be tossed down a steep ravine. So, whenever he was challenged to a relatively speaking civil wrestling match, he didn't shy away from the chance one bit. It provided him a fair chance to meet his enemies head on.

However, what Hans found less enjoyable, was being bullied at recess. He was a constant target of the older kids who would encroach on Hans and ultimately encircle him. As always, Hans had nowhere to escape - either take it or fight back, but no in between. Hans usually chose the latter. Two weeks before the end of the school year, Hans found himself being shoved and kicked around within a circle. Instead of simply protecting himself, Hans decided to grab a hold of the coat of one of the bullies, who was at least a couple of years older than Hans, and hauled the teenager into the circle, eventually hurling him to the ground. Like many bullies, he didn't appreciate a taste of his own medicine. The boy instantly broke into tears, weeping and wailing like a baby. When a teacher, who just so happened to be the boy's mother heard the incessant moaning and lamenting of her "innocent and precious" son, she came running in a jiffy and a tizzy to his rescue! Once she bore witness to her son on the ground in tears, she scornfully reprimanded Hans.

"Who do you think you are Vana!! Get lost and never come back!"

The fact that a German kid was getting beaten up was totally irrelevant. Her demeanour alone expressed the fact that *"He's not my kid and he's German!"* Hans was expelled for yanking a bully down to the ground, in an attempt to protect himself while enclosed within a circle of terror in which older kids tossed him around like a tetherball, but nobody cared. If you weren't a child of a communist dignitary or a school faculty member, you seemingly didn't matter. The son of a town pastor, whose father went crazy and broke a leg after attempting to commit suicide by jumping out of a church's second storey window when he saw that the communists had converted the church into a barn filled with animals, also got brutally teased. This boy with webbed hands was constantly taunted.

"Your hands are webbed so you can snatch money easier from the townspeople just like your pastor papa does!! The money won't slip between your fingers!"

Perhaps this boy wished that he got expelled as well. But he wasn't. Only Hans. Following Hans' expulsion, he simply walked to the other end of town and fished by a tranquil riverside fire for hours on end, free from any derisions. Hans made a routine of it for the next couple of days till the bully found out where Hans was, and ultimately tracked him down at the river where he approached Hans.

"Hey Vana. Man, you must love fishing. Don't you get lonely here? That's a nice rod, can I see it?"

Hans handed him the rod while remaining speechless. After the teenager, with long, straight black hair and puny eyes returned the rod to Hans, he asked,

"So, aren't you coming back? You can come back, you know. It's not right what happened. I'm sorry."

A few hours later, even Hans' teacher came by, and asked him,

"So, are you coming back? I spoke with the teacher who expelled you, and the boy who was bullying you, and they feel awful about what happened."

With justice being served, along with the fact that he felt emotionally hurt for being mistreated, Hans nearly unleashed a tear of self-sympathy. But instead, he happily grinning because he was pleased to see that even his foes were compassionate enough to apologize and sympathise with a parentless, German boy. From time-to-time, some people saw the errors in their ways and tried to mitigate their damages by making everything right. Nonetheless, this principle didn't apply to everyone. Being regarded merely as the German kid or *"nemec"* without parents meant that Hans could easily be picked on without recourse. Russian kids, on the other hand, could go home and appeal to their parents, who would intervene in search of justice, and at times, retribution. Hence, Hans had to fight for himself as he had no such luxury.

On the final day of school for the year, as Hans joyously headed home near the downtown area, he crossed paths with an absolutely imposing figure named Victor. He was 17, and almost twice the size, tall and wide as Hans, who wasn't even a teenager yet. Victor's eyes were dark brown, almost black as coal. His over-hanging -arcing forehead left him with a constant furrow over his eyelids. Full-grown adult's knees could tremble within his beast-like presence. When Victor approached Hans on this sunny and calm afternoon, he immediately grabbed Hans' head and hurled him downward to the ground. After shoving Hans into the fetal position, Victor, in a savage and intoxicating fit of rage and power, informed Hans, *"I'm gonna break your back German boy! You're gonna have to crawl home after I'm done with you!!"*, while he attempted to stretch out Hans vertebrae by pushing down upon Hans' shoulders. Many people, young and old, just looked on pedestrianly and walked by acting as if it were a playful act in a game. But it wasn't. So, if Hans expected to walk away unscathed, he had no other choice but to defend himself, so he sunk his teeth right into Victor's leg while pinching his flabby stomach in an attempt to protect himself, or otherwise, Hans' spine could've ended up split.

Victor was a daunting goliath-like monster, whereas Hans truly was as scrawny as he was undernourished. But ultimately, all of Hans' persistence paid off when Victor eventually tired himself out and gave up in his attempt to paralyze Hans after all of Hans' biting, kicking, wiggling, and scratching got the best of Victor. As rumour had it, Victor lost his father in Stalingrad fighting against the Nazis, and since then was determined to exact revenge in search of retribution anyway that he deemed appropriate.

CHAPTER 33

Greener Pastures

By the time late spring came around again, Hans got back into pasturing the cows, sheep, and any other type of animal that got thrown into the herd. Hearing of Hans' experiences, exploits, and remuneration led other kids to acquire an interest in pasturing. So, whenever Hans brought along a few of his buddies for "the ride", the two older shepherd women never objected. It was quite the contrary. The two stari bubbas were constantly concerned that Hans could quit, so they knew that it was in their best interests if Hans showed a few "apprentices" the ropes.

So, on one July night, a boy, two years older than the 11-year-old Hans tagged along for the adventure, accompanied by his parents. They too wanted to experience a night of pasturing and see if it were suitable work for their son. That evening began like every other, with the leading of the herd to pasture. After arriving at the herding site, Hans collected driftwood for a camp fire that was lit ablaze by a wooden match that one of the old women provided. A stunning full moon made it rather easy to see in the dark, especially with two campfires glowing amongst nightfall's shadows. It was only a matter of time before the two old women nestled in by the fire; the cows laid down to digest their food; and the boy and his parents fell fast asleep. Hans, on the other hand, was on full alert with a pair of charred sticks in his hands, seemingly just happily anticipating the chance to offer his guests an experience that they will never forget – a chance to witness Hans' bravery. Hans had no parents to attentively watch over him, so he loved the attention. Before everyone drifted off to sleep, Hans proudly, yet nonchalantly informed them,

"Sometimes wolves stop by and pay us a visit, just to see how we're doing."

As Hans stood on high alert while the rest slept, he thought to himself,

"Why did they tag along? They fear what could happen, yet they ironically still crave it?"

All of a sudden, much to Hans' satisfaction, the howling of a wolf resonated through the damp summer's air. The sheep and cows began to snort and yelp out of unrest and a sense of danger. They were no longer alone. Hans could see the howling wolf hovering over on the high bank on the other side of the river, so Hans steered his head in the opposite direction. Another wolf's wail then reverberated through the night. Hans' entourage quickly awakened completely startled! The howling in the distance scared the boy and his parents so much that they almost flew out of the seat of their pants right into the campfire! Hans attempted to calm them down by informing them that the howling wolf was on the other side of the river, and of no threat to anyone. As everyone stared into the distance at the wolf on the bank, Hans, somewhat coyly, yet somewhat provocatively, said rather nonchalantly,

"But you might want to watch out behind you as the howling wolf is only a red herring. Its goal is to stir the animals into panic so they'll all run in the opposite direction as a pack waits. Wolves wait where they expect their prey to run."

Hans knew that the pack of wolves had already set up camp, and were most likely patiently waiting to ambush the herd once it made it beyond the "safety point", in this case, the camp fire since there was no proper fence at this location to corral the herd or hold the wolves at bay. In order to help Hans' spectators savour the full experience as they kept staring away in the howling wolf's direction full of jitters, Hans instructed them,

"Look behind you! There's no need to look at the howling wolf. He's revealed himself for a purpose. Now turn around and say hello to his friends who are more than happy to make your acquaintance."

After the boy and his parents quickly peered in the opposite direction, while scared out of their wits, they were greeted by nothing other than a hoard of glowing eyes belonging to a pack of wolves that were hungrily anticipating the herd, or rather their next meal, to come running out in turmoil and panic! Just licking their chops expecting to finally pounce upon their prey, the wolves patiently and optimistically lingered for their plan to come to fruition. But instead, all what appeared and came running their way to greet them was a 11-year-old boy with a pair of charred pieces of wood in one hand, and a long stick in the other, just itching at a chance to get within striking distance! From the onset of Hans' pasturing career, he recognized that the wolves avoided bonfires at all costs, which was a sign of their Achilles heel and weak spot. Wolves also prefer to pursue, and conversely, become sceptical and timid when being pursued. Any act or sign of fear, and you're done, an actuality that happily spurred Hans on as he licked his chops just looking to launch his sticks at the wolves in hope of catching a few of them across their jaws just so some sparks could truly fly! As expected, the wolves kept their distance from the fearless Hans, as to them, he was nothing less than a reckless and unpredictable fire enchanter! A charred, shimmering stick suddenly soared through the air! The wolves became absolutely terrified at the sight of the "floating" and soaring flames and flickers! Dashing like the dickens, the pack fled like a bunch of chickens, some even tumbling backwards, right out their tracks!

These wolves were lucky, as on some special occasions Hans brought along his trusty bow and arrow (along with cotton balls), which in reality was merely a wire attached to a stick. Hans would dip the cotton into the flaming fire and let it fly! However, if Hans weren't careful, the dry brush could turn into a modest inferno. The wolves were left unfathomably terrified by such a sight as the flaming cotton intensified while the arrow smouldered through the air.

Hans staved off an attack once again, but the herd stirred in unrest while the horned cow was left flat out enraged and in search of blood! But the animals weren't the only ones in an uproar. When Hans rushed back to the campfire, he returned to a group of petrified, yet trembling camping mates who were almost huddled right in the fire, just searching for any protection that they could find. The tails of the accompanying dogs were so deep into the fire that the stench of burning dog's hairs masked the scent of the burning logs.

Before Hans could address his audience, out of the corner of his eye, he spotted the horned cow on the other side of the river, high up on the bank bravely attacking the howling decoy wolf! During Hans' theatrics against the wolves, the horned cow must have stormed through the river and motored up the high bank. This veteran cow, with her long, sharp horns was constantly seeking a scuffle or kerfuffle, or at the very least, an exciting endeavour. She had no fear when it came to attacking wolves, even though it could've spelled the end of her if there were ever more than two wolves present and no one around to protect her. Fearless and tempered, it was these exact traits that made her a liability to Hans, especially whenever she elected to attack even him.

But in this instance, the bullheaded cow needed Hans' help! He immediately grabbed a few pieces of charred wood out of the fire, and placed them in his mouth before swimming across the river, cautiously making sure that the glowing pieces of wood never touched the water. The river was cold, but Hans was too high on adrenaline to notice. After reaching the other side of the river, he climbed up the high and dry clay bank in the direction of the howling wolf. When Hans got to the top of the river bank, he saw the cow challenging and charging at the wolf that was vigilantly avoiding the horns of the cow as it retreated towards the bank. As Hans peaked up over the edge of the top of the bank, the backpaddling wolf eventually turned around and eventually came face to face with Hans, completely startling the wolf! Instead of retreating back down the bank, Hans' first instinct was to give the wolf a smack with the smouldering end of his hot stick right across the nose! A pile of sparks flew through the air! The wolf became so terrified at the sight of the sparks after receiving the blow to the face that it jumped backwards, making a summersault right in the air before scurrying off. Just to make sure that the wolf got the message, Hans whistled sharply. His high-pitched whistle absolutely irritated the wolves that were equipped with ultra-sensitive hearing that was usually used to their advantage, and not their handicap. Hans' ultra-sharp whistle was effectively used not only to penetrate the wolves' sensitive ears, but also to keep the entire herd in line, unless of course the horned cow was a member of his herd!

The "veteran" cow was still hyped up, and as always, just looking for some excitement so she chased after the wolf! Hans though, upon reaching the cow, gave her a solid wack across the behind while the wolf scurried away in a fright and flight. Finally getting the message, the cow stormed back down the bank, right through the light rapids along the shallower part of the river, and back to the camp site. Since the wolf was no longer visible, the combative cow no longer had a combatant, so it was easier to lead her in prideful triumph back across the river to safety with the rest of the herd.

Even though Hans' fellow campers were terrified out of their wits by the entire may-lay, everybody in the group was not only utterly entertained by the awing spectacle, but also blown away by just how vigilant and valiant Hans was in the presence of the wolves. Hans though, was not impressed by his bosses screaming out of their wits since it only encouraged the wolves, handing them a sense of confidence, superiority, and the belief that the people would offer no resistance. Hans' "bosses", the two older women, always screamed at the top of their lungs whenever the wolves reared their ugly heads, thinking that that would somehow scare them away. But quite contrary to the women's self-contrived conceptions, their screaming only brought the herd to disarray and into a state of panic, leaving the animals restless and over-alert and -stimulated. Such reactions alone merely left the wolves licking their chops. Well, only until Hans came to the rescue! Once the wolves left to seek out easier prey, the herd calmed down, ceasing its incessant baaing, snorting, and mooing. When Hans returned to the fire, he removed his soaking wet clothes and let them dry after swimming through the river. He then reproached his employers.

John Friesen

"Stop your screaming during the wolf attacks!! It incites the herd and provokes the wolves even more!!"

The 13-year-old and his parents, along with their dog stayed awake for the rest of the night keeping the fire going. They were too terrified to close their eyes, let alone fall asleep. They begged Hans,

"Please do not let us out of your sight!!"

For the rest of the night, Hans stayed close to them while vigilantly watching out for wolves, whose radiating eyes were easy to detect. But as Hans expected, the wolves didn't return that night. Wolves usually gave up after a single attempt at one location, in search of a more vulnerable targets. A shepherd of quality and his wages' worth must challenge a wolf, since wolves deem threats as an unnecessary risk. Wolves may appear cowardly on the surface at times, but they're simply calculating and clever. Unlike with humans, they don't let their emotions control them. And with good reason. Because if a wolf becomes injured, the pack simply leaves the lame wolf behind for dead.

When morning finally arrived, and the sun illuminated out from behind the darkness, everyone followed "the shepherd." While walking, the mother of the other boy asked Hans, *"Aren't you afraid??"* Hans replied,

"Of course, I'm afraid. But during those moments, you have to let go of your fear and do what's naturally necessary to protect the herd. Nature always leads my hand to protect the flock. My sense of fight, and not flight, fully kicks in! My grandma says that the Lord is my Shepherd."

By 7 am, they all reached town safe and sound. Everyone was finally relieved, at ease, and happy that they survived the night. The family that came along for the adventure never experienced such a frightening ordeal in their entire lives, and thought to themselves,

"Just who in their right mind would allow their kid to go pasturing, let alone be a full-time shepherd?!?!"

Whenever people told Grandmother, *"You're nuts for letting Hans pasture at night! Wolves will get him!"*, she replied in typical diplomatic Grandmother fashion, ironically, more likely stirring the person on.

"He'll be fine! There's nothing to worry about! Nothing will possibly happen to him. I know it."

Word of Hans' bravery and exploits spread throughout town rapidly. No kid offered to try their hand in a pasturing lesson ever again (with Hans), as they realized just how much effort was involved in keeping the wolves at bay and the herd in line and sound. Hans shepherded this herd for three summers until he almost turned twelve. He never lost a single animal over the course of those years during a time when other herdsmen incurred numerous losses, herdsmen who were sometimes equipped with shotguns. Hans even added a few to "his" herd and tally whenever a sheep happened to give birth in the summer. Hans himself would carry the babies along the way since the babies couldn't walk, and their mothers were unable to carry their offspring.

After pasturing and shepherding for the two women for three successive summers, Hans received an offer to pasture goats from another lady. During the spring of 1953, a stunning woman in her early 40's with black hair, approached Hans on the street and made him an offer that he couldn't refuse. However, his prior employers didn't take his decision and departure too lightly or with grace, threatening Hans,

"You're not allowed to quit!! You don't know the rules German boy!! We'll call the police on you!! If you do leave us, we'll hire someone to beat you to a pulp!! You won't know what hit you scrawny!!"

The women had tremendous tempers and trouble finding anyone else to pasture, or at least, at Hans' caliber, so they threatened him out of desperation. A man and his son ultimately overtook that herd from Hans during the "4th summer" of pasturing. But, they were not nearly as successful as Hans. They ended up losing a few calves to the wolves that summer, even while carrying a shotgun. The men were so petrified at the sight of the wolves that they were unable to even pull the trigger. Afterwards, the townspeople made them the laughing stock of Jug.

"Two grown adults couldn't do the job of a young boy. He had no problem warding off wolves barefoot with a stick."

But the backwards compliment in Hans' direction didn't help his cause though. On the contrary, it only created more animosity between the father and son, and Hans. They even went as far as threatening Hans, instructing him, *"Watch your back!!!"* Hans immediately told his new employer.

"People are threatening me. They might even go after you. I have no clue how far they'll go to make their point."

The lady casually responded, *"Don't worry about a thing! They'll have to deal with me first."*

The two stari "babushkas" ultimately had to give up on the pasturing profession a year later. They themselves resigned to the fact that they couldn't handle the task on their own, or at least without Hans. Unlike the two old women, Hans had a great (4th) summer of pasturing! Hans' offer from the lady with the goats was just too good to be true! She offered him twice the amount that he was getting from his prior employers, so how could he refuse. The goat lady even provided Hans with half a litre of milk, along with a piece of bread and a few potatoes a day. That wasn't the greatest incentive though. Solely pasturing goats and sheep could be carried out during the day. Unlike cows, goats and sheep weren't easily susceptible to the unforgiving pesky wasps and horseflies, so it wasn't a problem to take the goats and sheep grazing during the day, an actuality that Hans rejoiced in!

On his new job, Hans never even had to enter into the forested meadows situated over 5 km outside of town since the goats could leisurely graze on the short grass along the hillsides. To further Hans' pleasure, the lady actually paid Hans double what she originally promised, while giving him twice the food that they initially agreed upon. Hans was in love!

The woman in her 40's was pleasant, nice-looking, tall with long legs, but most importantly, she gave Hans his freedom and displayed immense appreciation. Hans desired to marry a woman just like her one day. This "goat" lady was not only extremely generous, but also couldn't comprehend just why the people were so mean to Hans since he never did them any harm. With motherly instincts, she told Hans,

"Just let me know if anyone threatens you again! I'll take care of it!"

Hans blushingly smiled back at her and thought,

"She certainly would! She's the opposite of my mother! Why couldn't I've been born to this goat lady!!"

Although Hans had a pleasant and rewarding summer of pasturing, he, nevertheless, still encountered a few altercations with his old buddies, the wolves. Even during the day, wolves occasionally attempted to get a hold of a goat or two. On one pristine and beautifully sunny July day, as Hans alertly, yet tranquilly sat on the hillside overlooking the herd below as a gentle breeze puffed out of the southwest, he all of a sudden noticed some movement in the corner of his eye coming out of the east. Turning to his left, Hans spotted a sneaky and sly grey wolf on the prowl moving westwards in the direction of the herd. This lone wolf, hunting without his trusty pack, had his sights on snatching a little white lamb that was staring northwards, standing about 5 metres from its mom. Ensnaring its prey from behind was a typical hunting maneuver of a lone wolf, since a lone wolf wasn't in any position to take any risks while hunting solo.

As this wolf slowly and calculatedly approached the lamb, Hans meticulously monitored the prowling wolf's movements. Goats and sheep normally grunted or snorted out in fear in the presence of looming danger before attempting to run away as a tight and well-knit pack; however, not one animal from the herd was alerted by the presence of this wolf, which was odd, considering that goats and sheep almost always picked up on their predators, meaning that this wolf was pretty slick.

Hans vigilantly looked around for other wolves, but didn't detect any in the near vicinity, which confirmed that this wolf was acting as an "Einzelgänger", lone wolf. Instead of confronting the wolf head on, Hans applied the wolves' sly tactic of sneaking up from behind by circling around from the other side so he'd go undetected, just like the wolf, silently crawling towards the wolf while it inconspicuously crept in the direction of the lamb. Every time that the wolf briefly stopped in order to prevent alerting the lambs, Hans picked up his pace and a little bit more ground on the wolf. The wolf was so completely focused on the lamb at hand that he didn't recognize that he too was being hunted. By the time that the wolf finally got within striking distance of the lamb, Hans steadfastly snuck up right behind the wolf and raised his trusty, long flexible stick, before wham!! With all of his might, Hans lashed the wolf right across the back! Out of complete and utter shock, bewilderment, and horrible agony, the wolf leapt high in the air, actually making a summersault before sprinting away right past Hans, yet not before leaving a trail of feces behind. The wolf seemingly didn't even know what hit him, let alone notice Hans standing there. As for Hans, he swore that he never saw that same wolf ever again.

Weeks later, on a mild day with a light drizzle, Hans found himself once again tranquilly sitting on a stump, with a stick and whip in hand, behind a bush at the edge of the forest, until suddenly a strong echoing of warning snorts and grunts emanated from the goats. Instantly going on high alert, Hans prepared for combat. As Hans guardedly rose, he cautiously glanced to his left into the bushes where he was greeted by nothing other than the face of a wolf staring right back at him! The wolf's breath swept across Hans' face and dirty blonde hair while their eyes interlocked! Before Hans could even begin to react, he noticed that the wolf was actually more startled than him. Slowly pulling back, the wolf clearly didn't want any part of Hans! Though, the same couldn't be said for Hans!

In a state of shock, the wolf's first instinct was to take a step backwards, and slowly retreat. But not Hans'! His first instinct was to spring to his feet and track after the wolf with whip and stick in hand! Hans was just itching at a chance to give the wolf a wack right across its back! Yet, in his pursuit, Hans shockingly spotted four other wolves surrounding him! This wolf was unexpectedly not alone! Hans was encircled, but he didn't require a split second to gain his composure. Instead of panicking, Hans aggressively swung himself and his stick around in a circle, catching a couple of wolves right across the nose along the way! With the wolves flustered, Hans diplomatically cracked his whip. Full of horse hair at its end, the whip cracked off like a rifle shot, which sent the wolves seeking cover! They instantaneously high-tailed it into the forest as if they were fired out of a canon.

Instead of heading after the wolves in full force, Hans sprinted in the direction of the herd to ensure that all of the goats and sheep were all still intact. Following a head count, he concluded that there were no losses or victims, just like always. As usual, Hans completed his summer of pasturing without any causalities; however, little did he know that that would be his final summer on the job. When winter came and went, spring arrived once again. Yet, this spring brought news that the fourth sewing shop was on the verge of closing down and relocating to the city of Perm, a city about 45 km north of Jug. Following the sewing shop's devastating closure, Grandmother had a lot more free time, which led her to reflect upon the past, and incidentally, worry about the future, since once again, they were surrounded by precarious uncertainty. During this time, Grandmother kept in touch with her ex-brother-in-law, the widower of Grandmother's deceased sister who was burned alive in a barn alongside Grandmother's very own son Gerhart during the concluding months of WWII. Grandmother informed Jacob that the 4th sewing shop was about to close down, leaving then with neither work, nor a place to stay. This "Uncle" Jacob (Friesen), of no blood relations to Hans and Grandmother, responded by letting Grandmother know that her and Hans were more than welcome to move in with his new family in Zajarsk, Irkutskaya Oblast (province).

This (ex-)brother-in-law of Grandmother was once sent to a Gulag labour camp in the heart, or rather, the hellhole of Russia a decade earlier. Right before his release, Grandmother sent him a letter informing him that his wife, Grandmother's sister, was burnt alive by Polish partisans during the concluding months of WWII. Learning of his wife's brutal death left Uncle Jacob utterly devastated and beyond repair. A bitter resentment remained within him till his death. His deplorable time in the Gulag only exasperated his agony. Jacob eventually re-married and had another child (and two more later on) together with his new wife. Despite ultimately having three children together with his new wife, his new kids couldn't replace the three children from his first marriage whose fate and whereabouts were still unknown. He always assumed that they too were murdered by the Russians or Polish partisans.

"Uncle" Jacob's offer tempted Grandmother, especially after being locked out of the building, and fully aware that a 5th sewing shop within Jug was not opening. None of the other workers from the sewing shop relocated to the site of the new location, so making a move to Perm to work at the new sewing shop was evidently not an option. On the other hand, Grandmother, along with Hans was still not so keen on relocating to Zajarsk (Zayarsk), and moving in with her (ex-) brother-in-law. Jacob lived about 1,000 km east of Novosibirsk on the Agara River, roughly 600 km north of Mongolia, where the climate was actually inconceivably much harsher than in Jug. Zajarsk was situated right in the heart of Siberia within a permafrost region that was known to be the coldest part of the world.

Therefore, Hans and Grandmother decided to stave it out in Jug, at least for the time being, yet not before Hans picked the lock at the closed down sewing shop in order to make it their place of residence once again. All of the windows in the sewing shop complex had been boarded up, but Hans installed hinges on one of the shutters so that Grandmother could watch the sun set.

People of the community knew that they were squatting in the closed down sewing shop, but in this instance, nobody felt like stirring the pot and getting them evicted. So, for the time being, Hans and Grandmother took up residence there without encountering any resistance from the local residents or authorities. Hans and Grandmother hoped that they could find a way to sustain themselves and survive. During this time, Hans received pay and food for his rendered services of pasturing horses at the lumber camp that belonged to the furniture factory. He actually stayed at the camp for about two months that summer while Grandmother lived all alone, merely living off of potatoes that she grew in "their" backyard garden after Hans and Grandmother planted seeds in the garden during Spring. When summer came, the fruits of their toil were harvested, providing Grandmother with a source of food and nutrition.

Hans continued to lumber away at the lumber camp, while Grandmother remained jobless. Luckily enough though, two broken sewing machines were left behind; one operated by hand, the other by foot. Before heading off to lumber camp, Hans was fortuitously able to repair both of the machines, which Grandmother used to sew for the townspeople in need of her services to earn a bit of money. Hans eventually returned back from the lumber camp at beginning of August when he got another job as an apprentice at the furniture factory.

During this juncture, Grandmother once again contemplated their future. And even though she still didn't desire to swap Jug for Zajarsk, especially because the climate in Jug was still quite favourable in relation the brutal conditions of Siberia, Grandmother, nevertheless began to re-consider Jacob's offer of letting them move in with him more and more with each passing day. She was fully aware that her and Hans' stay at the old sewing shop was only temporary since they were residing there illegally. Hence, it would only be a matter of time before they'd be evicted and sent packing. And since they were not making enough money to rent an apartment, they would be rendered homeless before they knew it if they didn't react, homeless amongst another unforgiving emerging autumn and winter in Jug. Just what to do......

CHAPTER 34

Trek of 1954

The only viable solution was to finally take Uncle Jacob up on his offer, and head off to live with him and his family in Zajarsk. Jacob helped to sell them on the idea by letting them know that if they were to come, *"Hans could definitely continue his schooling."* – something that Hans and Grandmother explicitly emphasized was very important to them. So, at this point, their next step was to find a way to save up enough money in order to buy a few train tickets for their southeast journey to Zajarsk, which was situated along the Angara River - the only river that flowed out of Lake Bajkal - the largest fresh water lake in the world in terms of volume. To fund their exodus east, Grandmother and Hans sold the two sewing machines that the manager at the sewing shop let them keep. There was also a large pile of firewood leftover that they managed to sell, generating a little extra cash in the process. In addition, Hans had saved up some rubles from pasturing horses and goats, as well as from his apprenticeship at the furniture factory. Even the manager at the furniture factory helped them out by being nice enough to give Hans defective material in order to make a trunk, which his co-workers caringly ended up making for him as a parting gift.

And even though the trunk was too big for their meagre and few effects and possessions, which basically only consisted of their blanket, some clothes, and a few pots that barely covered the bottom of the chest, the trunk would serve them well as a bench while they waited for hours upon hours on end for their trains to arrive during their vast voyage. They both wore the same clothes day in, day out, so "fortunately", they were able to re-locate without hauling a hoard of belongings. After finally gathering up enough money to pay for the train ride, Grandmother and Hans were ready to make the move to Zajarsk. They just had to wait for their ride, a furniture delivery truck, which Hans arranged through buddies at the furniture factory. The truck made deliveries to Perm every couple of days, so the employees at the factory agreed to drop Hans and Grandmother off at the Perm Train Station on their next delivery date.

Before departing for the train station, Grandmother went around saying good bye to all of her German friends with whom she kept in touch with later on by mail. After Hans bid farewell to all of his friends and past co-workers, the day came when they were off to Perm. From there, they would have to travel to Tayshet in order to hop on the Trans-Siberian Railway, a route that began in Moscow and traveled all the way to the Soviet east coast city of Vladivostok. As the employees of the furniture factory dropped Hans and Grandmother off at the Perm Train Station, they warned Grandmother and Hans,

"Be on high alert! That place is infested with thieves, derelicts, con artists, scammers, and drunks, the various forms of criminals that make up the bottom feeders of society."

Hans and Grandmother thanked the men and bid them farewell. Though as warned, within less than a minute of arriving outside of the train station, a few sketchy low-lifes were already preying upon Hans and Grandmother. Right at the high-rising steps of the entrance, a short guy short of teeth in his 30's in an oversized brown coat with a scruffy face containing more scares than Hans wished to count, approached Hans and Grandmother.

"You guys a'r hittin' the train? Ya gonna nee' some tix! Here! Tak'a'ook. Good price for ya! Only one ruble each! They tak'ya anywhere!"

As Hans apprehensively looked down upon the brown worn-out tickets that didn't necessary look fake, but beyond doubt the wrong kind of tickets, he noticed that it said "1 Ruble" on the ticket. Hans responded brashly to the vagrant.

"Is that so!! Oh, boy! These tickets that you're looking to peddle are only good for travelling within the city confines of Perm, assuming that they haven't already expired! What kind of fools do you take us for! Enough with your mumbo-jumbo!"

Two tickets to Tayshet cost 200 rubles a piece. Nevertheless, the guy kept on insisting that they needed to purchase that specific ticket in order to be able to buy, or at least use the 200-ruble tickets to reach Tayshet on the Trans-Siberian Railway. Brusquely brushing the peddler aside as if he had dealt with people like him for his entire life, Hans and Grandmother walked up the outside stone steps, hauling their chest, and entered the elegant, renaissance-style train station, which was quite the paradox to the sight of vagrants that Hans and Grandmother saw infesting the massive hall. As feared, it was only a matter of time before a few vagabonds approached Hans and Grandmother in an attempt to swindle away what little money that Hans and Grandmother had. Before Hans had any time to glance around the majestic and imposing train station for the ticket booth, a few others vagrants unsuccessfully tried to pick at their empty pockets and rob their near-empty trunk. Hans had their 500 rubles tucked away in his underwear. But they didn't deter other thieves one bit.

Moments later, after setting down their chest for a rest bite, a few men in their 40's with scruffy beards and a presence not worth absorbing picked up Hans' and Grandmother's trunk and gingerly scurried off with it in a blatant and shameless act of overt thievery, even though they acted as if they were doing Hans and Grandmother a favour. Hans immediately chased them down in his bare feet and jumped right on top of the trunk before yelling at the top of his lungs,

"Let it go, it's mine! Get lost! It's mine!! It's mine!!"

The crooks eventually dropped the chest, and scudded off like mice in search of a hole when they saw an employee of the train station, a heavy set, strong built, uniformed linebacker-type woman in her 30's with short black hair rushing towards them. She appeared like someone who you didn't want to tangle with, unless of course you were seeking a hopeless battle and some mindless havoc. Without any hesitation, she sternly, yet amicably asked Hans,

'Where are you heading young man?"

Hans replied with a proud look,

"My Grandmother and I are heading to Tayshet. We're moving to Zajarsk. But we need to buy our tickets."

The train station employee responded, *"Follow me, I can help you!"*, before she escorted them to a safer spot nestled in the corner of the train station closer to the ticket booth; a place where they couldn't be approached from behind. She instructed them,

"Just scream as loud as you can if anyone comes around you! The next train heading to Tayshet leaves tomorrow. My shift is almost over for the day, but I'll let my replacement know to keep an eye on both of you tonight! But be careful, and watch over all of your belongings at all times! Be vigilant, ok! And do not move anywhere from this spot!"

Before walking away, she told them, *"I'll be back tomorrow and I'll help you buy your tickets. Sleep tight!"*

Hans and Grandmother gratefully smiled and thanked her. Throughout the night, every now and then, the employee on the night shift checked up on Hans and Grandmother. But the two couldn't sleep. Hans constantly monitored the 6-foot diameter white clock face mounted on the 30-foot high gray marble wall, highly anticipating morning. When dawn finally arrived, and the glowing of sunlight penetrated through the 10-foot-high stained-glass windows along the east wing, the imposing, yet friendly train station employee returned.

"Morning! You survived! Good job! Your train will be leaving later on in the afternoon."

When noon finally arrived, she came by once again and instructed Hans,

"Come with me to the ticket counter and we'll finally get your tickets! Have your money ready."

Hans nodded appreciatively. He was looking forward to their journey as he had an insatiable appetite for adventures. But the crowd in the "queue" was also eager to leave Perm, leading them to aggressively and forcefully throng towards the ticket counters furnished with brass bar facings and jade countertops. Other travellers had absolutely no respect for neither each other nor any person of authority. To make matters worse, there was no properly organized line. Everybody was pushing and shoving each other aside as if it were a matter of life and death. Even the woman, an employee of the train station, had to muscle her way through to the ticket counter. The entire train station was chaotic and riotous. Yelling and screaming ricocheted off the gray, stone building walls and corridor of the monolithic train station. Nevertheless, the employee ultimately purchased two train tickets to Tayshet on Hans' and Grandmother's behalf before hollering to them over the chorus of chaotic clamor, barking, and bellowing inside of the station.

I'll let you know when your train arrives! Don't run anywhere in the meantime will ya!?! This place is a madhouse!"

The train station was a complete zoo, which was a contradiction to the neoclassical, yellow majestic, yet angelic exterior façade of the Perm I Railway Station, or as it read on the sign, *"завивка железнодорожная станция"*. Everyone was pushing each other aside in order to purchase tickets, because if the train were full, travellers would have to wait a whole day to catch the next train.

An hour later, Grandmother's and Hans' long-awaited train finally arrived. A cute, yet seemingly stern railway station attendant in her late 20's approached Hans and Grandmother.

"Please follow me to your train."

She could tell that they weren't frequent travellers by train, so she gave them a little extra special treatment. After helping them board the train, yet before departing, she warned them,

"Hang onto your tickets! Filthy derelicts will attempt to steal them from you! Then they'll try to re-sell them onto other travelers! That's how it works around here! They're worst than the capitalists! So, watch out for the filthy mutts and vermin that intoxicate the sewers that their own morass infests!"

Hans and Grandmother were quite amused by her sophisticated, geo-political philosophical tirade. Luckily, they had friendly and helpful train station employees to assist them through this ordeal. After hopping onto the train, they entered into a passenger car that contained narrow checkered seats along with small tables situated in between them that folded down to the level of the seats, converting seating places into beds. Grandmother ended up sleeping on such a contraption throughout the nights while Hans assumed his typical train journey "sleeping arrangement" by getting up and sleeping on his typical "bunk bed" above, which in reality, was just a shelf for baggage. This trip reminded Hans of his travels from Copenhagen to Jug about nine years earlier.

Hans and Grandmother travelled on the train from Perm, through the Ural Mountains and across a part of Siberia for two to three days, before arriving in Ust-kut. From there, they had to change trains before continuing on to Tayshet, a city situated on the Lena River, about 1,000 km from Irkutsk. However, upon arrival in Tayshet they discovered that their connecting train was located at an adjacent train station that was roughly 2 km from the main Tayshet station, so Grandmother and Hans had to find a way to reach it before they could board a train heading to Zajarsk. As they both remained standing outside of the train station, dumbfounded on a dirt road, they suddenly came across a man in his 50's with long white hair and a long slender nose in a beat-up, blue hillbilly pick-up truck. Seeing Hans and Grandmother stranded in distress, the man leaned across the passenger seat and yelped to Hans and Grandmother through the open window of his truck as dust trickled in.

"Where ya'tu head'in?" Hans responded apprehensively.

"We're heading to Zajarsk, but they said that we have to head to another train station and take a train from there."

The man responded, with an accent that Hans had never heard before.

"That's certainly troo' youn'man! And as it ju'so happens, I take people to that very treen station fer a fee of course, coz nothin's free, you know!"

Grandmother merrily injected as she walked towards the passenger door.

"That's good enough for me. Now Hans, please have him load our trunk into the back."

Hans then hopped into the back of the truck, along with their trunk. The road that they were forced to travel on was an unmanicured dirt road containing massive ruts. To prevent the truck from getting stuck in these trench-like potholes, the driver accelerated to feverously motor through these ruts. Although this ride was relatively short, it was, nonetheless, quite stressful and rigorous, but they took it in stride. Grandmother sat in the cab of the truck bouncing up and down, yelling the entire way,

"Yahoooo! Woooo-weeee!!!"

Grandmother made the best of whatever was thrown her way. She seemingly blindly accepted and never questioned every happening that God presented at her doorstep that tested her resolve while He resolutely sustained her. Hans, on the other hand, sat in the back bouncing up and down and sliding from side to side, simply just going with the flow of the motion of the truck while unacceptably questioning just why his parents abandoned him, wondering the whole time if he would ever see them again. His legs were left bruised from hammering against the sides of the pick-up truck along his way. Despite the memorable ride, they were both quite relieved when the driver hit the brakes and parked his truck at Tayshet's side "train station" in what appeared more like a potato field than a parking lot.

After paying the driver a few rubles, he unloaded their trunk from the truck, and subsequently pointed to the place in which they could buy their tickets. As they approached the building, it didn't take them long to figure out that the "ticket office" was nothing more than an old timber house that was converted into a general store. A railway station wasn't anywhere to be seen. Worry and wonder overcame Grandmother and Hans. Did the truck driver simply drop them off in the middle of nowhere for the profit of a few rubles? Not even a loading platform appeared amongst the vastness of the Tayshet countryside and darkness. An eerie feeling filled them both when they entered the old wooden general store that reeked of whiskey, slightly concealing the musky scent of decaying lumber. Behind an old, rotting wooden counter stood a woman in her 40's with long, straight black hair with a few strands of grey dangling above an expressionless face. Hans apprehensively enquired,

"Is this a train station?"

Not a word stimulated the entrenched impression on her face, yet her eyes became ignited with hyperbolic excitement as she replied, *"Sure is young man!"* Hans brashly responded,

"Appears a bit rustic in my eyes, but I guess that's the allure to leave. So, does a train to Zajarsk motor along these tracks?"

With a bit of shock shown amongst her smile lines as a result of Hans' sassy first line, the woman retorted,

"Sure does little boy! Ain't you a little young to be up so late? Your train heading to Zajarsk going through Bratsk, she'll be here tomorrow. You can just wait outside and relax. And don't worry about the man outside! He's harmless. Guy couldn't hurt a fly, let alone a prudent, young lad like yourself."

Hans handed her a few rubles in exchange for their tickets, but the shopkeeper didn't have any change to offer, so alternatively, she handed them ¾ of a bottle of vodka. With bewildered eyes, Hans speechlessly accepted the vodka as their change, even though neither he nor Grandmother drank. The woman behind the counter had the last word, facetiously stating,

"Enjoy your trip and try not to consume all that vodka tonight. You may require it tomorrow. But you'll definitely need it in Zajarsk!"

With a wink and a massive grin, she added, *"Always drink responsibly!"*

After rolling her eyes, Grandmother stuck the bottle into her bag that she herself made out of cloth. Grandmother made sure that the bottle was positioned upright since the opening was meagrely sealed with a rolled-up piece of paper. The neck of the bottle conspicuously stuck out of her bag the entire time. After exiting the general store in order to wait for the train, Grandmother and Hans gazed upon a flat area that was desolate and deserted, except for the general store, a bunch of trees and shrubs, a few houses puffing smoke out of brick chimneys in the distance, and a scruffy man aimlessly roaming around the vicinity. Hans' sense of complacency eventually metamorphosed into a feeling of calmness and serenity. The identical feeling that he cherished while he and Grandmother lived by the river in Jug penetrated within him, almost piercing his soul with peace. During that moment, he had no need to incessantly wonder just why his mother abandoned him, and what made him so inferior to the rest. Turning his head to the right, he heard the woman locking up the general store for the night. She then approached Hans and Grandmother with clattering keys, and bid them farewell.

"You shouldn't be afraid of the scruffy man. He's harmless. And if you want to have a fire, burn away. You just have to gather up some firewood. Just don't burn any tires. Too much CO_2 you know."

Winking again, she added, *"Maybe drunkie-scruffy can help you. Sleep tight!!"*

After the woman left, Hans and Grandmother sat back down on their trunk and camped out right under a tree in front of the store, just waiting for the train or to doze off – whatever came first. Hans, strangely enough, as if Grandmother could read thoughts, or sense vibrations and brain waves, heard her say, *"Don't worry. We'll find your parents."* They both managed to doze off and on throughout the entire night. When morning came and the sun crept into the horizon, breaching through thick, white clouds brushed with red as the sun's rays painted their pristine puffy facades, Hans and Grandmother saw the scruffy man lying on the ground, snoring away like a lion. Though, what was not visible to them was the empty bottle next to him. When the storekeeper came back to open up shop, she said,

"I see that you made a friend. So, did you offer him the entire bottle of vodka?"

Hans puzzledly replied, *"What do you mean?"* The woman pointed and said, *"How sober does he look?"*

"Drunkie-scruffy" was knocked out completely plastered. When Grandmother looked into her bag, she noticed that the bottle was missing. The shopkeeper smiled and strolled inside the general store for another day of service. Not long afterwards, their train, which turned out to be a freight train with one passenger car attached, finally arrived. It smelt like chicken feed.

CHAPTER 35

Zajarsk

After a day's travel, Grandmother and Hans finally arrived at the Zajarsk Train Station. Snow carpeted the lush, green grass, even though it was the end of August. Jacob Friesen awaited them at the train station with his horse and wagon. Jacob was in his 50's, but the strain and torment that inflicted his demeanour made him appear as if he had lived for 100's of years. His youthful skin, strangely enough though, somewhat concealed the façade that his eyes portrayed. After greeting them in German, without a welcome hug, he mentioned,

"It worked out quite well for you two, because if you would've missed your train to Bratsk, you would've had to wait another week for the next train travelling to Zajarsk to come. The train from Tayshet to Bratsk only runs once a week."

Eventually, they all climbed onto Jacob's wagon and made the 10-km journey to his homestead situated on the west end of town. His home, made out of logs, consisted of two rooms, but no running water. The house was heated by a wood stove and lit by a few lightbulbs; however, they couldn't be turned on by a switch because the electricity was activated by a city generator that went on at 6 a.m. and off at 9 pm. Country-wide electricity was one of the advancements that took shape in Russia following WWII. Despite obliterating much of Russia, WWII compelled the country to evolve further in order to defeat the German war machine. Such quantum technological advancements hadn't taken place in Russia since the time of Czar Alexander III, nearly a century earlier. Nevertheless, Russia still relied heavily upon dated German equipment, stunting its modernization process.

Uncle Jacob's house didn't possess any indoor plumbing, so they had to use a repulsive outhouse in the backyard when nature called. Almost the entire backyard was a vegetable garden that still had a few frozen potatoes laying on the ground. Near the back of the plot, there was a drafty, partially sealed shed where a cow, pig, and a few chickens resided. When Hans and Grandmother walked into Jacob's house for the first time, after their long and arduous train journey, they were greeted by Jacob's pregnant wife, their 3-year-old son, and Uncle Jacob's mother-in-law.

Jacob worked at a sawmill that was within walking distance of his home. When Hans first stepped off of the train, Uncle Jacob immediately sized up Hans' 13-year-old slim, yet muscular frame. Jacob figured that Hans could be of some use to him on the job at the sawmill. So, the next day, Uncle Jacob took Hans to work with him, where he forced Hans to cut logs into boards and beams. Only a day after their arrival, Jacob had already broken his promise to Grandmother about letting Hans go to school. Instead, Uncle Jacob forced Hans to come to work with him each and every day at a sawmill belonging to the MTS or, Machinery and Tractor Station, which worked in cooperation with the Kolkhoz. Although Hans was technically too young to work, he was given permission since his "legal guardian", Grandmother, was unable to earn a living in her condition. Hans ended-up earning just as much as Uncle Jacob at the mill, but ultimately, Hans rarely got to see a cent. But being remunerated was the least of Hans' problems.

After work one day, Hans was toiling away in the garden in the backyard of Uncle Jacob's domain, when all of sudden he felt a lash upon his back! Then another! A memory from a decade back of his mother whacking him with a branch entered Hans' senses. Though, when he looked back in the present moment, Hans didn't see the presence of his missing mother, but rather a whip in Uncle Jacob's hand! He caught Hans right across the shoulders! Yet, on his third attempt, Hans grabbed the whip from Jacob's hand and informed him,

"If you try that again, I'll whip you back! Got it!"

Before moving into Jacob's place, Grandmother wrote a letter explicitly stating that Hans intends to go to school, if they elect to move to Zajarsk. Jacob promised that Hans will be able to attend. However, when they arrived in Zajarsk and spoke of Hans going to school, Jacob flipped out and screamed,

"I can only feed so many mouths!! I'm gonna teach Hans how to work and earn his keep!! That boy will learn how to work!! Work!! Work!! Work!! And not become a worthless philosopher!!"

Hans' intentions, however, were never to become a freeloader and live there as a loafer. Such an option never existed in his entire life, so the idea never entered Hans' mind. He knew that school was only half-days, which meant that there was plenty of time for him to contribute to the family. In an attempt to prove his worth, dedication, and true intentions while making a good first impression with Uncle Jacob, Hans took a look at Jacob's open rotting "shed" one Sunday, and suggested,

"Uncle Jacob, I could build you a barn. We could easily get some left-over wood from the sawmill."

Uncle Jacob, somewhat sceptical, yet somewhat excited, mentioned,

"Well, I don't have any carpentry skills, so I'm unable to build a barn. But if you want to put one up, then go right ahead! Knock yourself out!"

Jacob's inability to build a barn only enthused Hans even more to prove just how more skilled he was than his brutal tyrant of a landlord. Bound to demonstrate his capabilities, Hans, the very next day, used Jacob's horse and wagon to transport a couple loads of wood, made up of discarded half-split logs and other pieces of wood that couldn't be used to manufacture furniture at the mill, to Jacob's home. But erecting a barn in this part of the world was no pleasant task. Hans had to wear a net over his face the entire time. Malicious and vicious black flies asserted their dominance in this region of the world. In town, the flies weren't too bad, but near the forest they were literally merciless and deadly! A boy once lost his way through the blackfly-plagued forest, just to never find his way out alive. Insects fed off of him until he became a lifeless corpse. Uncle Jacob's place was infested with black flies, but to nowhere near the degree within the woods, making the construction of the barn reasonably manageable.

First off, Hans started with the floor of the barn. Thereupon, he constructed the walls before assembling the roof. Hans designed double-panel walls that were filled in with saw dust that acted as insulation. For the roof, Hans used the same kind of half-log boards as for the floor, though for the roof he laid the curved-sides up. The rounded portion of the logs covered up the "joints", which prevented water from seeping into the barn. The slope of the roof helped the water to drain off. With having no nails at his disposal, Hans had to transform wire into spikes in order to hold everything in place. Inside of the barn, Hans partitioned spaces off so there were separate rooms for the cow, pig, and a closed off chicken coop on top in which Hans laid a live electrical wire leading from the house, which he attached to a light bulb. Besides the discarded window that Hans found at the mill, this light bulb was the only, yet by no means inadequate source of light within the barn. This bulb generated so much heat that it actually helped the hens lay eggs all winter long. Uncle Jacob sold these eggs, along with cow's milk at the town's market square to supplement his income.

A night after completing the barn and returning from the market with Uncle Jacob, Hans went to sleep and had a very peculiar and inexplicable dream. During that November night, he envisioned a new-born girl lying in a crib somewhere in Yugoslavia. Moments later, Hans awakened in a sweat, absolutely convinced that the vision was real. He was just as certain that the birth had taken place as he was that his dream wasn't merely a dream, but rather a vision of reality that left Hans with his head in the clouds and unable to sleep for the rest of the night. When Hans finally got up to have a boiled egg for breakfast at the kitchen table the next morning, he was still in a complete daze.

"Hans! Hans! Hans! What the hell is a matter with you!"

Hans suddenly felt a whack right across the back of his head! When Hans turned around startled, though still quite subdued, he looked into the eyes of no one other than Uncle Jacob. Jacob looked at him slant-eyed, yet utterly ecstatic at the same time.

"What kind of a trance are you in you dummkopf!! I called your name three times! But who cares about that! That barn of yours! It's exactly how I envisioned it, but even better! Where have you been my whole life you little brat!! I could've used you in the Gulags!"

Uncle Jacob started telling everyone about how talented his now 14-year-old "nephew" was, and what he was capable of creating. In Jacob's eyes, Hans was quite the "acquisition". Needless to say, Jacob didn't permit Hans to resume his schooling since Hans was much more valuable to him when he worked. Hans, on the other hand, was completely devastated. He enjoyed learning in school, and always had his sights set on pursuing higher education. Hans mentioned to Grandmother that he would still like to go to school, and requested that she appeal to Uncle Jacob. Her response though, was bluntly simple.

"Be quiet and thankful that Uncle Jacob took us in out of the bottom of his heart!"

Hans thought to himself, *"No, out of the bottom of his pocket book!"*

Hans constantly dreamt of continuing his schooling one day, in spite of Uncle Jacob's firm stance. Yet, notwithstanding all of Hans' hard work, contributions, visions, and aspirations, Hans' fate still remained in "Uncle" Jacob Friesen's hands. Despite sharing the same family name, there were no defined blood relations between Jacob and Hans, even though he was very controlling, domineering, temperamental, and at times, awfully rigid, just like Hans' mother. Everything had to be done his way. Presenting himself as the head of the family, only he, and no one else, besides perhaps his new wife could make the decisions. He controlled all of the finances, which included Hans' wages.

Before getting entangled with this Uncle Jacob, Hans was free to make all of his own decisions, so becoming mixed up with this sociopathic member of the family was extremely testing for Hans. Though, as long as Hans and Grandmother remained under Jacob's roof, Jacob had all of the say in his one kitchen, one room house – a room that was a bedroom, Grandmother's sewing area, and living area all in one. Hans, as usual, didn't end up with the best sleeping arrangement. He was left to sleep on a bench next to the door of the main entrance. The boards making up the door contained small cervices between each of them. To prevent air from seeping in between the gaps, old potato sacks were thrown over the door in order to seal the spaces. There was also a large gap underneath the door as well, so Hans shoved rags into the space to inhibit snow and wind from blowing in, something that left the family dog that slept underneath Hans' sleeping bench more than content, well, only until Hans occasionally rolled off of the 12-inch-wide pew and landed right on top of the poor dog! His landings below didn't necessarily wake Hans up, but the wail of the surprised and awakened dog did! But luckily enough for Hans, once he finished off building the new barn, the chickens no longer had to sleep inside the house next to him on frigid nights.

CHAPTER 36

Harvest

In July, it was tradition, regardless of profession, for many citizens of Zajarsk to travel roughly 50 km to a government-allocated field for the autumn harvest. All Machinery and Tractors Station's (MTS) manual labourers, along with their families were respectively coerced to cut grass for a weekend during the annual hay harvest. Professions working for the MTS, or *машинно-тракторная станция*, or rather Mashinno-traktornaya stantsiya, including doctors and vets also participated in the annual event. It was truly a collective, communist effort. Everyone was required in full force during the harvest since the window to reap the grass was very brief due to restrictive weather conditions. Winter came quite early in that region of Russia. Though, despite their gruelling toils, a lot of people immensely enjoyed the harvest time. Spending a few days outdoors afforded the people the opportunity to savour what nature had to offer.

Hans was obliged to partake in the annual harvest, but he was luckily enough paid for his work. He would be the first one to arrive by horse and wagon at the site, whereas others, along with the rest of the family would arrive by pick-up truck two weeks later. Hans, though, didn't quite totally share their need to relish in nature because the area had an apparent and serious infestation of poisonous "Gaduka Snakes" or "Vipera Berus". To compound Hans' concerns, he was apprehensive when it came to making the 50-km journey alone on a wagon, especially at dusk when he became easy prey for bandits. But when Hans expressed his apprehensions to Uncle Jacob before his departure, Jacob retorted,

"Just go! I'm gonna teach you how to work boy! Here, take this 20-calibre shotgun! If any bandits try anything, just blow their heads off! Make sure you get their names afterwards and we'll send their families a bill for the cost of the bullets."

The next morning, Hans hitched the horse to the wagon and headed off in the direction of the harvest grounds. Rejoicing in the freedom of being away from Uncle Jacob and the family, Hans glanced into the vista of fields amongst fields as if they ran right into the beautiful blue sky. A few hours later, dusk appeared on the horizon. Hans desperately hoped to reach the harvest site by nightfall. Eagerly continuing along his way down foreign dirt roads, Hans all of a sudden noticed the headlights of an old rusty truck approaching, momentarily blinding him. An obnoxious laugh, almost a loathsome cackle, originated from the truck as the four passengers suspiciously glared with crooked smiles right in Hans' direction as they crossed paths before Hans proceeded west into the sunset. Their presence left Hans with an eerie feeling, especially because he could see out of the corner of his eye that they were still looking back at him. Hans was certain that it would only be a matter of time before that truck would be on Hans' tail – he encountered that sort before – they were probably just looking for a place to make a 3-point-turn and pursue Hans and his slow-moving wagon.

Hans, though, had no intentions of learning about their motives, so he immediately veered off down a semi-concealed side path covered with 18-inch high grass, and eventually hid the wagon and horse in an open meadow behind a hillside where trees, bushes, and a stream were situated. Hans detached the horse from the wagon, just in case he had to make a daring and darting getaway. Hiding behind some bushes, 50 metres from the road, with the wagon and horse inconspicuously parked on the other side of the hill, Hans suddenly heard the sounds of a roaring truck motor in the distance. When the on-coming vehicle slowed down to nearly a standstill, Hans saw two guys in the cab, and three in the back, the same guys he crossed paths with him minutes earlier. As time seemingly stood still, Hans heard one of the passengers say,

"Where did he go? Do you see him? He couldn't have gone too far. Keep looking!"

Hans' first thought was, *"They wanna steal the horse and leave me for dead."*

Finding out what they had up their sleeves was not in Hans' plans, so he remained quiet until the coast was clear. Hans patiently waited about half an hour right in the middle of nowhere, after the truck and men disappeared in the opposite direction, before he reattached the horse to the wagon and progressed along on his way. Hans drove on unmolested for a few more kilometres until in the near distance he saw a series of walls that enclosed an out-of-commission work camp connected to a stone quarry that was functional while the government was building a railway line, years earlier. Uncle Jacob mentioned this complex when they discussed the exact location of the harvest field. Hans was relieved to reach his destination before nightfall. He couldn't have fathomed tracking around in the ominous darkness.

Entering a vast and desolate hay meadow amongst the shadows of dusk, Hans saw a tiny, abandoned, and deserted building that belonged to a commandant of the defunct work camp. Completely exhausted, Hans slowly opened the old wooden door of the musty quarters and walked inside where he glared down at a comfortable hay cot. Just before happily launching himself into the straw that awaited him, a 3-foot, checkered grey and white snake appeared out of the woodwork and golden hay! Both were absolutely as startled as the other! Hans instantaneously jumped back! From an S-shaped coil, the snake sprung up in Hans direction, darting through the air! Missing Hans by an inch, the snake landed on the floor next to him. Hans was completely beside himself! He could have never imagined in his wildest nightmares that a snake could perform such an acrobatic manoeuvre. In Jug, Hans saw the odd garter snake, but nothing like this. Desperate to remove the snake from his presence, Hans aggressively attempted to shoo the snake away with a stick that he found lying against the wall. But the snake showed no sign of urgency in its movements, almost as if it were purposely looking to provoke Hans. In an attempt to inform the snake that it was slithering too slowly for Hans' liking, Hans took the stick and liberty to smack the snake right over its back! The snake appeared incapacitated for about a minute before gaining its composure. But instead of obediently obeying Hans, the snake fully coiled up this time, right before propelling itself upwards into mid-air! This breed of Siberian snake had the ability to elevate themselves from the ground up with lightning speed, transforming themselves into one-metre-long, self-propelled ascending arrows.

This sight absolutely terrified Hans at first. Though, after observing the flight pattern, Hans realized that these snakes were unable to change direction in mid-air. After a little practice, Hans learned how to wack these snakes right over the back with a stick, at times while elevated, temporarily paralyzing the snakes in the process. Recognizing that the snakes were not as dangerous as they made themselves out to be, Hans desired to have a little more fun with them. So, in Hans' typical adventurous nature, he grabbed a long stick and used it to place a few of the temporarily incapacitated snakes from the cabin together into a jar, before sadistically watching them go at each other, instead of them attacking him.

Hans realized that these snakes were everywhere! All over the commandant's quarters! In cupboards! Even in the stove! In the field! Down by the river! In equipment! Absolutely everywhere! A few days after arriving at the harvest site, Hans, out of frustration and sadistic pleasure, started hammering dead snakes to fence posts for birds like the majestic White Siberian Crane to collect - and perhaps, even as a warning to other snakes that Hans too was a predator, a predator to reckon with.

But the snakes were not the only threat in Hans' vicinity. He also became more than acquainted with an imposing, Baikal brown bear that was marauding around the woods on the fields' perimeter, living off of blueberries, insects, and fish. This bear soon discovered that Hans' humour and pleasure wasn't only reserved for the snakes. In order to confuse and disorient this 700-lb bear, Hans hurled rocks into the woods. As the echoes of the stones colliding with trees cascaded and reverberated throughout the forest, the bear looked around to discover the origins of the sounds, thinking that someone, or something was prowling around in its vicinity. Yet, the bear saw nothing, except for perhaps Hans laughing away in the distance. The bear became so confused and frustrated that it eventually took off in search of tranquility. However, as with the snakes, Hans' act was not completely out of satirical amusement. If the bear were to sneak up, probably out of sheer curiosity, and spook Hans' horse, it could cause Hans' ride to storm off and leave not only Hans stranded, but also in severe trouble for losing a Kolkhoz horse.

At night time, the horse warned Hans of the bear's presence by neighing that rung along the desolate countryside. Before going to sleep every night, Hans cooked up potatoes, macaroni, and even fish that he caught down by the river, over an open fire. Relishing in the serene setting, Hans stared up at the stars and cherishing the fact that nobody, including Uncle Jacob, and even Hans' mother, was there to abuse him and leave him walking on eggshells. Soothed by the stillness of his surroundings, Hans savoured his nights feeling as if no one else existed, filling his senses with blissful space.

During the days, Hans cut grass with a reaper at his own pace; feasted on berries from the woods; and became refreshed by the water from the river during his breaks. But all that changed when the rest of the MTS team, including Uncle Jacob showed up by truck two weeks following Hans' arrival. At 5 a.m., they all regimentally woke up, had breakfast, and cut grass until 11 a.m., at which time it became much more difficult to slice through the grass after the morning dew dissipated. Everyone wore nets during reaping in order to protect themselves from the pesky and vicious mosquitoes and black flies. But the nets didn't put a halt to the endless buzzing of the maddening insects. Following their pre-noon lunch in which they devoured a few potatoes, along with some macaroni that were fried up in a cast iron pan smeared in lard cooked up in the commandant's kitchen, the men helped the women turn grass over for drying before taking a nap. Thereupon, later on in the afternoon, they all picked up their reapers and resumed cutting. Dusk's dew dampened the grass, brightening up their spirits since the moisture simplified the task. The MTS workers, along with family members reaped and turned grass until dark. Every evening, after the rest of the people arrived, Hans prepared the tools for the next morning by sharpening the "kosas", or reapers, prior to going to bed. At night, some went into the commandant's quarter for a good night's rest while others slept right in or under their wagons for the entire night with nothing besides a blanket. Yet, before falling asleep, everyone made sure that no snake had slithered into their hay sleeping bunks, or whatever they called their bed for the night.

One warm morning, Hans woke up early and dashed down to the river to wash his face in the fresh cold water. Sweat drizzled from his entire body the day before, so Hans welcomed a refresher. After sprinting through the field, he sprung off the river bank, landing right next to the water along the stoned and pebbled shore. Flowing in a pristine cascade in harmony with nature's melody, the river's water looked rejuvenating. Looking into the smoothly streaming water, Hans squatted down, and without any inhibitions dipped his hands into the river, grabbing two scoops of water. The touch of the cold spring soothed Hans' senses only until a snake suddenly appeared in front of Hans' face! The long reptile looked directly up at Hans with its black, beady eyes, and reciprocated the shock within Hans' eyes! But luckily enough, the coiled snake was still drowsy and groggy, or otherwise, it would've struck Hans right in the face! But instead, it simply uncoiled and gingerly slithered away rather disoriented. Hans was overwhelmingly relieved, but only until after breakfast.

Because if he weren't facing snakes, then he had to deal with Uncle Jacob, who made sure to make Hans' life a living hell as they toiled away. While slicing through the grass used for hay, Jacob remained right on Hans' heels, with kosa in hand, the entire time. To cut grass with a reaper, or "kosa", the worker required a good rhythm, stamina, torso-strength, and endurance. At first, this task was utterly taxing for Hans, who was about fifteen at the time. Despite being muscular, Han still had to contour to the conditions. It took some time for any beginner to acquire the necessary skills, specific muscles, and ability to reap with a kosa, assuming that he could manage and get the hang of it at all. The "activity" was so strenuous that the operator required extremely strong abdominal muscles in order to endure the side to side swinging motion because it put tremendous pressure on the core of the body.

Initially, Hans felt like his gut was going to burst! The pain was absolutely excruciating! But he couldn't slow down since Jacob was right on his heels cutting away with the sharp kosa without any regard for Hans' safety, seemingly just looking to catch him. And perhaps that's why Uncle Jacob warned Hans prior to reaping away,

"If you don't keep up with the pace, I'm gonna slash your ankles!! I'm gonna teach you how to work boy!!"

Little Hans wore two belts that acted as a harness that kept his abdomen in place. The brace provided Hans with enough security, just so it didn't constantly feel like his gut was going to explode. Though, ironically enough, by the end of the weekend, it was Uncle Jacob who couldn't keep up with Hans.

The kosa required sharpening every few minutes, since it became dull relatively quickly, so the worker kept a long sharpening stone in his pocket. The sharpening process only took a few seconds. Uncle Jacob and Hans shared the same stone until it eventually broke in two from wear and tear. After that, Jacob took the big piece with the handle attached for himself, and left Hans with the little piece. The next time that Hans sharpened his kosa, the stone slipped within his hand, causing the blade to slash his thumb. With no time to halt, Hans wrapped his bloody and slit thumb in a sweaty handkerchief before resuming to toil away. Uncle Jacob never showed Hans any mercy, which meant that Hans had to see the task through to the end. Uncle Jacob repeatedly reiterated,

"I'm gonna teach you how to work boy!"

Uncle Jacob carried the bitterness of losing his wife, kids, and house during WWII, which only exasperated after he was sent to Siberia to work in hard labour camps throughout the 1940's after being captured as a POW during WWII. While enduring through and surviving the work camps, Uncle Jacob believed that his entire family was dead. It was later revealed that only his wife was burned in a barn in Poland, and that in fact his three kids fled to Paraguay with Hans' grandfather, who was related to the kids only through marriage. After suffering these hardships, Jacob seemingly wanted to pass along all of his pain and misery onto Hans. Suffice to say, the end of the weekend harvest couldn't come soon enough for Hans, especially because Uncle Jacob would return to his regular job on Monday and be out of Hans' hair, whereas Hans, and a few other men planned to stay behind for a few days to pile up the haystacks.

CHAPTER 37

Poisoned

After harvest season, it didn't get any easier for Hans. Before going back to his regular tasks at the MTS, Hans stopped in at the local general store that was situated on the MTS complex grounds to buy a snack. Hans entered the old timbered building and asked,

"Some pickled anchovies, please."

Turning around, the female storekeeper, with bitter looking crevices in her cheeks instead of graceful smile lines, opened up a fresh, wooden barrel of pickled anchovies. The top layer was usually thrown away and discarded since these anchovies were not safe to eat; however, the woman, who knew of Hans' German descent, sinisterly skimmed off the usually spoiled and toxic top layer, and sold them to Hans without him even knowing it. Hans then left the store and went to work on the generator where he noticed the family cat roaming around the area. When Hans popped a few anchovies into his mouth, he found that they tasted a bit off, but instead of letting them go to waste, he kept devouring them, and even offered a few to the cat.

Though, when Hans went to bed that night, he discovered that that he made a grave mistake! Hans found himself in excruciating pain. It felt as if somebody were slicing into his stomach with a razor blade in every possible direction. Tossing and turning throughout the entire night, Hans dreamt of the pain swiftly fading. But when the following morning arrived, Hans wasn't feeling any better. He was unable to remain still and at ease, which left him constantly fidgeting in an attempt to quell his discomfort. Even the family dog became rather annoyed with Hans. The pooch doggedly kept glaring at Hans, as if he were questioning Hans about just why he was in constant jitters. In an attempt to dilute the poison infesting and plaguing his body, Hans consumed copious amounts of water, but it was of little consolation. When Hans finally stepped out of the door of the house on that very next morning, he noticed that his companion, the cat, was lying there motionless on her back with her paws up. Hans immediately thought to himself,

"Now, that's a strange way for the cat to nap."

Yet, when he called her name, there was neither movement nor a response, even after Hans affectionately rubbed the cat's belly. Her body was as stiff as a rock. Hans knew at that very moment,

"The cat must've become poisoned by the anchovies that the evil woman from the general store sold me! Hans became horrifically enraged! As his blood boiled, he screamed to himself,

"That stupid witch at the general store just killed my cat!!! I should kill her right now!!! She's earned it!! But why did I have to share those anchovies with the cat?!?! I knew they tasted off!!"

Even years following the 2nd World War, resentment towards ethnic Germans was quite high all across Russia. At times, people knew no limits when it came to succumbing to their bitterness and thirst to exact revenge in the cruelest possible of ways against the brethren of their much-hated enemy to the west, and in this case, the family cat. Hans remained in tremendous pain. He expected the same fate as the cat; he thought that it was only a matter of hours before his time was up. Certain that he wasn't going to see another day, Hans truly felt like killing the woman at the general store. But fortunately, or unfortunately, the unbearable pain only lasted for another horrific three days. During this time, Hans constantly threw up; experienced hot and cold spells; and consumed nothing besides water. He eventually pleaded with God,

"Please just give me the strength to endure and survive! I still gotta find my parents!"

In spite of being ravaged by the brutal illness, Hans went on with all of his daily chores and work. People rarely showed Hans any mercy, so he just persisted and performed the duties that were expected of him. The only one who seemed concerned about Hans' welfare was the dog who kept following Hans wherever he went. He simply wouldn't let Hans out of his sight, something out of character for the family dog. The pooch constantly kept giving Hans sad faces, almost as if he vicariously sensed Hans' pain. The mutt even mimicked groans of agony, making it seem like the dog was in even more pain than Hans. After the ordeal was finally over, and Hans regained full health, the dog reverted back to his normal behaviour.

Hans too returned to his normal self, which helped him catch the eye of the supervisor at the machine shop that was located within the same MTS compound where Hans worked at the sawmill. Besides the sawmill, there was also an open site repair shop where tractors, combines, trucks, plows, seeding machines, and other farming equipment were repaired. A blacksmith's shop and a house, along with horse stables and even a bull for breeding were situated on the premises. Lumber was delivered in by horse and wagon to the facility. The compound also contained a bunkhouse for 20-30 workers from nearby villages who worked at the Kolkhoz. The entire complex was surrounded by a fence made up of six-foot-tall wooden boards, with a gate situated at the entrance. A sizable guard in a bulky black coat stood on watch in front. Not far from the gate was the general store within the compound that was open to the general public. This complex also had its own piston steam driver generator that provided power and electricity for all of the equipment, structures, and buildings within the compound, along with surrounding houses. Excess steam was used for heating the machine shop buildings where the repairs were carried out.

It was the serious-looking manager from this machine shop building who approached Hans one day after Hans fixed a few cast-iron frames at the sawmill, and asked,

"How'bout you come work on the lathe, and grinding and boring machines at the machine shop young man? We're now one short, so we need someone for the grinders. What do'ya think boy? You seem quite sharp. I've heard really damn good things about ya! That uncle or whatever of yours never stops talking about that barn that you built for him and his animals."

Hans energetically replied, *"Sure thing! I'll gladly join your team, sir. But you just gotta do the paperwork."*

After Hans accepted the offer, the machine shop manager obtained permission from the director to hire him. Hans' first task was to work with the grinder used for grinding crankshafts, which was a delicate procedure that required extreme precision and accuracy. Setting up the grinder for different stokes and crankshafts was a fiddly task, so someone capable, articulate, and skilled was essential in order to properly carry out this procedure. Hans' new job also encompassed repairing cast iron cracks that were caused by vibrations generated during the production process. Nobody could fix them. Well, nobody until Hans suggested that they should simply design and place a bracket over the cast iron crack.

Hans eventually moved on to making bolts, nuts, and gears, and even started boring and grinding out cylinder engine blocks, before polishing them, as well as making shafts and cutting out grooves. In general, Hans was responsible for producing all possible parts for the equipment. He even made oil and pressure rings for the pistons, which was a lengthy procedure.

But if that weren't enough work, the man responsible for the horses and bull departed due to health issues, so the director approached Hans and asked him if he could even take over that position as well. The role entailed feeding and watering the horses in the morning, and then cleaning the stables in the evening. And although the bull used to inseminate and impregnate the cows from the community was usually abrasive and moody, he oddly enough loved Hans, making Hans a perfect fit for the job. Hans happily accepted this position, leaving him with two paying jobs before he turned the age of 15. His work day started off at 6 a.m., at the stables, which is when he fetched water for the horses. Hans then headed over to the machine shop where he started at 8 a.m. and worked till 5 p.m., before heading back to stables and working till 7 p.m. But then Hans discovered that that was seemingly not enough for him either when the MTS manager approached Hans once again and suggested that he look after the portable generator from 5 p.m. till 11 p.m. The portable generator provided light for the compound during these hours because the main generator was shut down at 5 p.m. This responsibility became Hans' third paying job.

Uncle Jacob was absolutely ecstatic over all of Hans' success since Jacob had unequivocally no problem taking his 100% cut of Hans' wages. As already mentioned, Jacob made it quite clear that he was the head of the household. As the lord of the manor, Uncle Jacob took it upon himself to be solely responsible for monitoring and "apportioning" all of the finances and income that were entering the family's coffers. Accordingly, he had no qualms when it came to collecting, or rather stealing all of Hans' wages. Uncle Jacob justified his actions by stating,

"You owe me bigtime boy!! I graciously opened up my arms and home to you two! Without me you'd both be dead! I balance the books here, not you!!! I sustain you!!!"

In Uncle Jacob's eyes at least, he was fairly entitled to everything that he could get his fingers on, even if a portion of that fairly belonged to Hans. Jacob eventually had two more kids, but with Hans bringing in the hefty brunt of the income, they were all well taken care of, especially with Grandmother also passing along the majority of her meagre proceeds earned from occasionally sewing items for the town's folk for a fee. Luckily enough though for Hans, Grandmother occasionally slipped Hans a few rubles from time to time, though she explicitly told him, *"But say nothing!"* Hans used the money to buy himself some food.

CHAPTER 38

Research Lab

Every spring, as a form of Zajarsk entertainment, crowds gathered by the fast flowing 50-foot-wide river and watched enormous pieces of ice, sometimes carrying cows, wolves, moose, bears, foxes, and even the odd person, float down the river through town. These sights to behold brought a great deal of excitement to the residents of the relatively gray town after a harsh winter. As the temperatures increased throughout spring, melting and thinning ice pushed the water level upwards. Such a phenomenon caused the surface ice to rise and break apart, sometimes in perfect circles, before sailing down the river. People and animals regularly used the ice's surface to travel on; yet, in spring, when the ice cracked and suddenly broke apart, occasionally animals, and even sometimes people aboard couldn't reach solid ground in time, leaving them caught on floating ice as it cruised down the Angara River, water that flowed from Lake Baikal into the Yenisei River. "Passengers" had to wait until the floating ice hopefully collided with the mainland, where it got stuck, giving the animals or people a chance to disembark. The water was absolutely freezing cold, so if you were to fall in, you had virtually no chance of surviving.

In the spring of 1956, Uncle Jacob sold his house and land, property that increased in value after Hans built the barn on the property, yet eventually became worthless years later when it was flooded in a dam construction project. Following the sale, the entire family moved into a house within the MTS compound that was offered to them rent-free. Yet, much to Uncle

Jacob's chagrin, the saw mill in which Uncle Jacob worked broke down beyond repair later on that year. Operations ceased. This saw mill was never replaced. Uncle Jacob was left to accept a job on the outskirts of town at the MTS veterinarian clinic that was located about 1 Km away from the MTS, situated across the street from a trade school for mechanics where students worked and studied. The clinic was a complex of office buildings and structures with labs and stables, where sick animals were housed.

Uncle Jacob tended to these sick animals along with performing various other tasks. The horses and bull from the MTS complex were transferred into this facility, a place where Hans eventually had to start going to in order to take care of the animals. Across the road from this veterinarian complex was another fenced off compound that had a yard along with a house, barn, and stables. It was surrounded by fields and a lush, emerald green forest covered with majestic fir trees, some reaching almost 250 feet into the air. When the firs were covered in snow, it was quite the sight to behold, especially amongst the pristine cloudless, blue and sunny sky on a minus 35-degree Celsius afternoon. Following massive snow falls, the reflection off the snow was at times blinding.

Half of the house across the street from the veterinarian complex was occupied by a husband and a wife, who were both scientists, while the other half of the building was converted into a research lab. Research experiments on animal skins were carried out at this facility by these scientists, who were both in their late 20's. Along with the house, they were also provided with a horse, sleigh, and a wagon for transportation. Whenever these research scientists from across the road saw a young boy (Hans) heading into the neighbouring complex to carry out laborious tasks, they curiously wondered to themselves,

"Just why isn't this boy in school during such hours??"

One day, they eventually crossed the snow-covered road and walked towards Hans as he was about enter the veterinarian complex.

"Hello young man. Do you have a second? We were just wondering why it is that you're working there when you should be attending school? Education is extremely important!"

Somewhat speechless by their approach, and surprised by their advice, Hans' first thought was,

"What a nice-looking couple." He then explained to them,

"I don't have any parents. My grandmother and I live with my "great uncle", who's forcing me to go to work in order to earn our keep. He steals, or rather "withholds" and garnishes all of our earnings. He constantly tells me, ""I'm gonna teach you how to work boy!" He's a tyrant. He makes Stalin look like Mother Teresa."

The couple from the research facility adamantly instructed Hans,

"Get your education! You need to get a degree if you ever expect to get anywhere in this life! You're not going to live in this god-forsaken Siberia all of your life are you!?!? We're here for three years only because we were told by the government authorities that we must stay here after finishing university."

Over time, they both got to know Hans even better, and eventually approached Hans again a week later.

"Never mind your cruel uncle! You should come work for us! You can go to school in the morning and carry out your chores here after lunch. We'd need you to fetch us some water from the well that's about half a kilometre away from the house. There's no running water in this hell-hole of Siberia!! Just think it all over and get back to us."

A few days later, they waited for Hans to arrive for work at the veterinarian clinic in the morning, before asking him,

"So, have you thought about our offer? Would you like to come work for us? Your duties would also include cutting wood that you'll fetch from the forest and bring back to the main building with the horse. You can ride, right?

You'd also be responsible for ploughing the land around the compound. You can plough, right? Of course, you can! It'll also be your job to look after our horse and cut grass for hay. You'll love Antoniov, our awesome horse! You can work a kosa, right?"

Enticing Hans further, they added,

"You'd even get to do a bit of lab work. You can plant, right? We're planting potatoes, cabbage, carrots, beans, tomatoes, and lots of other stuff. We've got a generous budget from the government. We can pay you more than you're earning now."

Hans replied excitedly,

"Of course!! I love horses of course! I can do anything! I learned a whole pile of trades while living in Jug!"

Hans was absolutely enthralled at the prospect of working for these hip and proactive scientists. But in doing so, he would have to quit his other jobs, which left him a bit apprehensive, especially because he could already picture Jacob's derisive reaction. Hans got used to Uncle Jacob's sinister ways and demeanour, but his mean-spirited, explosive and eruptive reactions sometimes still got the best of Hans. Filled with anxieties over confronting Jacob, Hans believed that perhaps remaining conformingly obsequious to Jacob's demands was his best solution. Yet, despite Hans' fear, he found the scientist's offer extremely tempting, or better said, too good to be true, especially considering that this job paid more than his other three jobs combined. With that sort of money, Hans could even get a place of his own for him and Grandmother, even though he knew that Grandmother wouldn't agree to it since she enjoyed having the company of Jacob's family. The next day, Hans apprehensively approached Jacob in the family kitchen furnished with a washing bin and brick wood stove equipped with a cast iron cooking plate, and confidently informed him,

"I'm quitting my jobs at the MTS! I'm done with all that mumbo-jumbo! I got a better offer at the research lab! I'm not wasting my time with the stinky MTS anymore!! But I'll still help you out with the animals at the vet clinic.

And I'm resuming my schooling! I'm gonna be smarter than you. People at the research centre said that I must go to school! It's been all agreed upon."

But such an arrangement didn't suit Uncle Jacob one bit! He didn't like any part of it, since he wouldn't have Hans at his complete beck and call. As expected, surrendering power over Hans left Jacob extremely furious and in an uproar! Bellowing for the whole household to hear. Jacob replied,

"We'll just see about that!! I'm gonna talk to those people about all this nonsense!! They, nor you can dictate my household, you ungrateful 16-year old skunk!!

The next day, Uncle Jacob stormed into the house of the research scientists and told them,

"Who do you think you are!?!? Stay out of our family matters! Who do you scientists take us for, you dobels!?!?! Stick to quarks and stay out of my family's business you quacks! Hans belongs to me! I'll get you sent to the Gulags!"

The wife of the other scientist, with short black hair and a soft round face orpedly retorted by instructing Jacob,

"Don't waste your or our time threating us! It's slavery what you're doing!! We're going to sick the authorities on you!"

Jacob's attitude though, didn't deter Hans from accepting the research station job and going back to school. Education was extremely important to Hans, despite the fact that Uncle Jacob didn't share his sediments. But Hans recognized that if living with Uncle Jacob were to become totally unbearable after his decision, he and Grandmother, or perhaps only he could still get a place of his (their) own, possibly even at the research facility. And Hans wasn't the only one to recognize this actuality. Jacob began to fathom that such a move could come to fruition, and this worried him since Hans was bringing in more money for the family than the apparent "breadwinner" Jacob himself. When the scientists found out that Uncle Jacob was taking all of Hans' money, they spoke to Jacob again and let him know,

John Friesen

"It isn't right and fair what you're doing with Vana's (Hans') money! We're paying him, not you! Vana should only be paying you for room and board! That's it!!"

After the scientists' discussion with Uncle Jacob, Hans was finally allowed to start saving some of his earnings. When he ultimately banked up enough money, Hans bought himself a calf that he named "Calfie", which he raised with the intent of selling it on after she grew up in order to earn a little extra money through a sweet capital gain. Hans was ambitious and wanted to get ahead in life, so he was extremely happy to be back in school, along with earning some extra cash on the side. Finally starting Grade 6, Hans learned a lot not only in school, where ironically enough he was taught how to write and read in German (and not just speak), but also at the research lab where he was testing animal skins for diseases. Seeing that Hans was a quick, curious, and diligent learner, the scientists also made him responsible for distilling; filtering, and labeling samples; and keeping not only records of changes, but also the house warm. All of the wood for the stove was cut by hand. Back then, only specific lumber camps had access to chainsaws. Moreover, Hans cut up skins and placed them in glass tubes filled with a solvent, and then left them extracting for hours. After the extraction was complete, Hans filtered the contents by pouring them through a funnel that was stuffed with cotton filters that captured the solids. The solution was then collected in a beaker, and analyzed by the scientists who compiled the results.

Hans continued away at this job for the ensuing two years, during which he had very little contact with Uncle Jacob, mainly because whenever Hans arrived home everyone including Jacob was already fast asleep. Hans didn't even have time to do his homework, and actually had to complete it during recess. In the vicinity of his school, there was gym where guys in their late teens, early 20's hung out and trained. They were an extremely arrogant and cocky bunch of guys. One day, while Hans worked away on his homework at recess, the guys from the gym hollered,

"Come on over Ivan! We need members."

Hans retorted, *"Ok, why not."*

As he walked in, he noticed that most of the guys had crooked, almost devious grins across their faces. Timidly walking into the gym, Hans saw a boxing ring surrounded by three slack ropes with a worn-out canvass for a floor. Before stepping into the ring, a sweaty muscular teen in a tank top with a blonde crewcut handed Hans a pair of tight red boxing gloves for sparring.

"Here, you'll need these so you don't hurt your hands."

As Hans started putting on the gloves, his opponent, standing directly across from him, out of nowhere feverously began punching Hans, smacking and bouncing Hans' head right up against the stone wall behind him! Despite being completely stunned and disoriented, Hans, without hesitation, instantaneously fought back. With one mighty swing of his right hand, the muscular Hans hammered his opponent right in the nose with a haymaker, knocking the boxer right out and to the ground! The group of guys from the gym instantly stormed to their comrade's side and defence, screaming,

"Look what you did!!! Look what you did Vana!! Get lost!! Don't ever come back, you German brute!!"

Hans also came across plenty of bullies in school as well. Just like in Jug. Hans was versed in defending himself against all sorts of brutes and then some. Hans possessed the mentality and wiliness of an experienced soldier – an intrinsic trait invisible to his foes. So, a few months after the boxing knock-out, during a break in school, Vsevolod, a massive boy in his late teens who reminded Hans of a gigantic version of Victor from Jug, thinking Hans' tiny frame and innocent demeanour made him easy prey, came up to Hans face-to-face in the hallway, and lifted him up into the air by clutching Hans in a suffocating bear hug! Vsevolod let Hans know,

"I don't like your stupid and ugly German face!! I'm gonna give ya a new head! You're not going to enjoy this nearly as much as me blondie!! I'll readjust your back while I'm at it! You're gonna look handsome in a wheelchair pretty boy!"

Staying true to his word, Vsevolod tried to body-slam Hans right into the ground on his spine while using Hans' body as a cushion to protect himself upon landing. Stuck in Vsevolod's clutches, Hans persistently wiggled and twisted his wiry, yet muscular frame, attempting a barrel roll maneuver. Struggling with Hans' "insolence" and shifty movements, Vsevolod shuttered and fell out of kilter until he completely lost his balance, leading him to fall right onto his back, smashing the back of his head up against the wooden floor! With Vsevolod on the ground in a strong daze and haze, the other kids around them broke out into laughter. In triumph, Hans stood up and theatrically glared down upon Vsevolod, remorselessly telling him,

"It serves you right Vsevolod! Nobody tries to break my back and smash in my head!! I always win!! Just go ask those stupid idiots at the boxing centre across the street!! I'm like Joe Louis to them!! Now look at you! Was it worth it!! You're a disgrace to Zajarsk!!"

Despite staving off the attack of the bully, Hans still found other dangers. If not at school, then at work. On one winter afternoon after school, Hans headed down to the river on his horse and sleigh to fetch a tank full of water for the veterinarian clinic. When Hans arrived, he picked up a metal 5L bucket and dipped it into the ice-cold water through a hole within the frozen river, before dumping the water into a 250-litre steel cistern tank attached to the sleigh. When Hans was done, he sat back down in the sleigh ready to grab the reins as he watched another man, along with his horse and sleigh, drive up the hill away from the river in the direction of the railroad tracks. But Hans wasn't the only one to notice them. Hans' horse, a retired racing thoroughbred, deemed that man's and horse's departure from along the river bank as nothing less than a challenge to a race!

Before Hans could barely get the reins wrapped around his hands, his horse had already bolted after the other man's wagon! Hans saw no problem with his horse's competitive spirit, and was quite amused, but only until a kilometre later when they were about to cross the railway tracks while a train approached in the near distance! With the train engineer's whistle blaring as he attempted to bring the slow locomotive to a halt, Hans' retired racehorse heard nothing since it only had one thing in his sights - the horse ahead of him in "the race!" Hans instantly thought,

"What's this wrangler trying to prove! He's already a champ to me!"

Hans yanked on the reins with all of his might, but it was no use! He simply couldn't corral his horse that was about to cross the tracks with the train only a few metres away! Before Hans knew it, he felt a colossal force uplift the sleigh from his left side! Water soared and splattered throughout the air while the ringing of the whistle entered Hans' ears as his head rang! Lying on the ground, Hans looked up and found the sleigh turned on its side! In complete awe at what had just transpired, the train engineer looked back out of the window of the moving locomotive to see Hans gingerly waving back at him, bringing a massive grim to the engineer's face while a complete look of bewilderment captured Hans' horse, perhaps merely as a result of him "losing the race."

CHAPTER 39

The Great Flood

In 1957, the entire town was notified that the government was building a dam in Bratsk, on the Angara River, 70 km downstream from Zajarsk. This meant that the entire area of Zajarsk below the hill line, including the MTS and research facility, lied right within the flood zone. All land along the river would ultimately be underwater, meaning that the majority of the people within the region would have to evacuate and relocate. At this time, Uncle Jacob's sister lived in Sverlovsk, across the Ural Mountains near Perm, but she was on the verge of making a move to a suburb of Frunze. Jacob decided that he too was going to join his sister's family by uprooting and heading in that direction. So, before Jacob's sister moved to the greater Frunze area, she purchased a home for not only herself, but also Uncle Jacob's family as well.

Uncle Jacob's sister-in-law and her family also intended to make a move in the direction of Frunze from Zajarsk, just so the entire family could stay together. Frunze (modern day Bishkek), was located in Kyrgyzstan, USSR, right next to the Kazakhstan border, roughly 200 km north of China. Grandmother discovered that a lot ethnic Germans from the Denmark to Jug train trek were living in Jambul (modern day Taraz), Kazakhstan, so she more than welcomed the move in that direction since there would be a lot of familiar German faces living within a few 100 kilometres of them. The move then became even more enticing after learning that there were much fewer ethnic Russians residing in that area, which meant fewer enemies for Hans to evade or fight.

CHAPTER 40

Parents Located

Uncle Jacob's brother-in-law was involved in a thorough search for missing family members, a search conducted in secrecy. If the KGB were to ever discover what he was partaking in, it would be deemed as a form of "espionage", a "subversive" illegal activity punishable by time in the Gulag or even worse. One day, Jacob's brother-in-law surprisingly approached Hans.

"Could you provide me with a little information about your parents? But this conversation never took place, so keep quiet about what I'm doing. Just tell me, but don't ask any questions!"

Completely sceptical, Hans' only thought was, *"Yeah, good luck finding them!"*

Yet, only until Hans received a letter a few months later! When Hans arrived home late from work as usual, Jacob, oddly cordial with Hans, handed him a mysterious white envelope with a Canadian stamp marked with a red maple leaf on it.

"This came for you today."

Touching the envelope led a billion of sensations run through Hans' body. A part of him desired to toss the envelop away, but the other part of him was led by a surging force that desired to have his life-long questions answered. Much to Grandmother's surprise, it appeared as if Hans' and her family was living in Canada of all places. But they wouldn't know for sure until Hans opened the envelop. So, after taking one long and deep breathe, Hans took a narrow-tipped knife from the kitchen and slid it into a gap in the paper until he sliced through the top of the envelop. Hans gulped as he unfolded the hand-written letter folded in three. Anxiously glaring at beautiful German calligraphy, Hans read the first letter followed by the second in his mind until he spelled off a word before he spoke aloud for the whole family to hear as they waited in splendid, yet nervous anticipation.

"Is this you Hans?

I really hope so. We were informed that you are now residing in Kyrgyzstan of all places. But just how can that be?"

Hans' skin instantly quivered. Through the correspondence, Hans discovered,

"You now have a brother as well, along with your sister Wanda."

Wanda was born in the same town as Hans in modern day Ukraine three years after Hans came into the world. In addition, they all learned,

"Hans, your paternal grandfather, the husband of your grandmother, now lives in Paraguay where he is raising Uncle Jacob's and your grandmother's sister's three children. He's raising them as if they were his own. His address is Waldstraße 15, Neufürstenwerder, Mariscal Estigarribia, Paraguay."

Uncle Jacob, along with his family became absolutely ecstatic after learning of the whereabouts of his children, who he assumed never even survived the war! The news brought Jacob's normally bitter eyes to tears while Grandmother's slightly creased eyes teared from bliss. Without even giving it a second to ponder, Grandmother immediately went to write her husband a letter.

Yet, how Hans' parents read about his possible whereabouts in the St. Catharines Standard, a local newspaper in the vicinity of Niagara

Falls, Canada remained a mystery to him. Apparently, it was all a part of a clandestine underground displaced German Mennonite and Jewish network functioning across the globe under the KGB's watchful eyes. However, everyone was quite shocked about just how far away Hans' parents and Grandmother's husband ultimately moved. No one ever imagined that they all would've have left Europe, assuming that they had survived, let alone head all the way to Canada and Paraguay after the war. Jacob thought aloud,

"But why the heck Paraguay of all countries? And South America?? Peru, and perhaps Uruguay, I can understand. But Paraguay??"

On the other hand, Hans' first thought to himself was,

"Perhaps this will change this miserable bugger for the better!"

Nevertheless, Uncle Jacob was amazingly relieved to know that his kids were still alive and in good hands, as their "uncle", (only through marriages), was taking care of and raising them. Hans' parents could seemingly also only rejoice in finding out about the whereabouts of their lost relatives, not to mention their very own son. The letter explained,

"Hans, your father was looking for you and the rest of the family right after the conclusion of the war."

Despite that explanation, Hans still had the odd doubt about the whole situation.

"Eventually, father discovered that you and your grandmother were both in Copenhagen, Denmark. However, Father was ultimately informed that you two were shipped back to the USSR, three days prior to him learning of your deportation. But the exact destination was unknown and never revealed to him."

Hans' parents, along with his sister Wanda, elected to move to Canada because Hans' father's uncle was already living in Beamsville, Ontario, Canada, after immigrating there in 1925. With relatives already in place there, Hans' parents believed that Canada would be a good country to gain a fresh start, although upon arrival they truly wondered why! Their living conditions were actually quite shabby in relation to what they experienced in Hanover, Germany, even right after the city was bombarded, where they lived between 1945 and 1948. Within the letter to Hans, Mother stated,

"I am already working on the visa applications to get you out of the USSR. I will forward them onto you when they're complete and finalized."

She also affectionately, yet not remorsefully wrote in her letters,

"We miss you so much! We can't wait to see you! You can come here and run our construction company! Your siblings have no interest in carrying on the family business, so you're the one! We can't wait to see you again. We don't know how we've survived so long without you!"

As soon as Hans located his parents, the whereabouts of the rest of the family came to light, bringing peace and closure to everybody while providing Hans with a sense of pride for being the one who was indirectly responsible for it all. But Hans had more than pride on his mind. After resigning himself to an oppressed and parentless life in Russia, he had hope of a life with something more – his family.

Mother's endearing letters made Hans feel like a genuine part of the family, and most importantly, loved by his parents – the wish of every child. Optimism filled his veins as thoughts of forgiveness entered his mind, even though Mother's letter made no mention of an apology for losing him. But that was now snow from yesterday. By this time, Hans was 17. As soon as he received the visa applications from his family in the mail months later, Hans headed off by train to Bratsk, a city located about 70 Km west of Zajarsk where the regional government's KBG office was situated. When Hans finally found the correct building, he peered up at an imposing five storey building located in the downtown area, a building that gave off an aura that spoke nothing of liberation and favour despite its angelic white façade. The building showcased 2-storey high Doric columns at the entrance and French windows for as long as the eye could see, which was quite the paradox to the drab concrete buildings lining the street. Before travelling to Bratsk, Hans hoped that he could possibly soak up some sights on this trip, but unfortunately, there were no sights worth savouring in the frigidly cold and grey mildly industrial city of Bratsk that the Communists fully left their mark on.

Hans was required to forward the papers and application received from Canada onto the KGB for processing, something he preferred to do in person. When Hans entered the sterile, baroque-style building housing the KGB offices, he saw how it had been tainted by hideous communist furniture, designs, and fixtures. But before he could find more flaws within the KGB offices to divert away from his nervousness, a grave looking watchman in his 40's and a blue uniform at reception brusquely barked out, almost as if to intimidate Hans,

"What's your business here?"

Without a word, Hans nervously handed the man his papers that possessed light traces of sweat.

"3rd Floor. Foreign Affairs."

The guard handed the papers back to Hans. After taking the wide marble staircase upwards, Hans nervously knocked on a closed thick wooden door. After fretfully waiting for what felt like hours, he heard,

"Come in!"

Hans entered a wide room, probably an old drawing room or study for Russian aristocracy from centuries past, before he approached an elegant marble table that was echelons beyond Communist taste. Too nervous to inspect the two people behind the counter who refused to greet him, Hans promptly explained to them, with tones of excitement, yet hues of apprehension,

"Good day. I have located my missing parents, so I wish to move to Ka-na-da to be reunited with them." The authorities, a miserable, stern looking man in his 50's along with his protégé, a younger woman with short black hair in a

John Friesen

brown wool sweater, both presenting expressionless demeanours, instantly told Hans in a male voice,

"Fair enough. You may leave Zajarsk, and head to "Ka-na-da" to be with your family."

Hans became absolutely filled with glee! He was utterly blown away with just how compliant and accommodating the government was reacting. Hans thought to himself,

"How could it be so easy?? Who would've known it! These KGB guys aren't so bad after all. Why would anyone ever insult the KGB?!? They're actually rather upstanding and outstanding gentlemen!"

However, things rapidly changed as soon as the two KGB authoritarians looked over the papers and realized that they were issued in English. The man then tersely enquired,

"Just why are these documents in English? Is this a joke?"

Hans wondered to himself, *"Should I tell them that "Ka-na-da" is on the North Pole?"*

The man and woman behind the counter then started looking for "Ka-na-da" on a map of the USSR. When they couldn't locate it, they brusquely inquired,

"Where is this Ka-na-da, and just why were these papers issued in English!?! Is this a joke, German joke-boy?"

As beads of sweat expelled from Hans' forehead, Hans hesitantly replied,

"It's in America, sir. Canada is in America."

Hans witnessed the utter shock and disgust in their faces! He knew right then just what kind of trouble he had got himself into. After hearing that, the man in his 50's with a shaved head, and his apprentice, a girl in her late

282

20's with gray eyes and an attractive tone of black in her eye wells, began consulting with each other to discuss the matter amongst themselves before the man concluded,

"Canada is in America!! America is our enemy!! Those capitalist bastards want to crush us! You want to join that!?!?! You desire to betray the Motherland do you!?!? You, my German, Soviet compatriot, you may not leave the USSR!!! That, young man is not permitted!!"

To make matters worse, they refused to return Hans' papers and became extremely arrogant, with the woman finally no longer remaining a silent spectator by stating,

"You will not see these English documents ever again!!"

Hans walked out of the office completely devastated! He then started off on his way back to the train station, or which ever way his broken heart led him. Still distressed by this turn of events, he headed off with his head down, face drooped. Feeling depressed, Hans could barely drag his legs. Though, when he entered a tranquil alley and heard the resonating of footsteps behind him, an eerie sensation overcame him. Life instantaneously came back to his legs as he thought to himself,

"Is that the KGB? Did those two clowns from the office notify them!?!? Are they gonna beat me up for attempting to commit treason? I've seen it before. They'll beat me to a pulp and leave me for dead!"

Hans increased the tempo of his footsteps to see if the four feet behind him would also accelerate. As anticipated, the pace of the echoing steps trailing behind him also stepped up a notch. Hans then knew it.

"KGB!!! Or at the very least, their auxiliary goons, who are much worse!"

When Hans glanced back a bit, after rounding a corner, he noticed that the two men had semi-concealed wooden clubs in their grasps.

"Definitely KGB!!"

Serious danger was lurking. Hans knew that he had to find a way to evade and lose these two young men looking to make a name for themselves in the KGB world before it was too late! Zigzagging through the streets and alleyways as nightfall fell upon Bratsk, Hans contemplated if he should take the night freight train to Zajarsk. But he knew that it was already too late, especially because the goons most certainly knew about that train as well. He would have to wait till morning for the next train to Zajarsk to arrive, assuming that he'd live to board it. Taking another quick glance over his shoulder, Hans saw that the two husky men in black winter coats were still right on his tail! Steadily rounding another corner, Hans suddenly discovered a loose board within a fence. Luckily enough, after taking a stick between the eyes years earlier in Jug, Hans learned to obsessively search out loose boards in fences in his attempts to avoid predators of all sorts. Hence, Hans could spot a loose fence board a mile away. Sprinting over to the fence, Hans slid the plank of wood to the side and snuck through the gap in the fence before re-setting the board to its proper position. When Hans turned around, he discovered a yard with a barn. Chickens quietly clucked in the near distance, but Hans didn't stir them up a bit. His presence hopefully went undetected. Silently hiding, Hans hoped that the two goons pursuing him would pass by and disappear forever.

Moments later, Hans heard footsteps. The clattering sound of two men walking by ricocheted off of two-story wooden and brick buildings throughout the still night until all fell silent once again. Hans hoped that they wouldn't return; however, minutes later, right before Hans intended to slide the fence board aside, sounds of reverberating footsteps recommenced! Grabbing a hold of the jarred fence board, Hans held it firmly in place as if he were holding on for his dear life. A harsh voice repeatedly bellowed out, *"Куда он делся?? Куда он делся?? (Where did he go?? Where did he go??)"*, adding,

"It's too dark to find his tracks."

The other man responded in a sharp and penetrating voice.

"Wait until we find him! We'll beat the crap out of that clown and teach him a lesson about going to America!"

Moments later, the silence of a brutally cold night resurfaced, almost deafening and deadly upon Hans' ears. Hans thought to himself,

"Are they truly gone? Or did they simply head to the train station to wait for me there? It's getting late. But how am I gonna get out of Russia? How will I ever get to "Ca-na-da" and see my family who can't wait to see me? Who want me to take over the family business! Wow, what an honour! I better just sleep in this barn for the night, and wait for the morning train."

Hans uncomfortably lied the night away on the closed off stinky barn floor on a -30 Celsius night, frequently dozing on and off here and there. A nightmare of being beaten to a pulp by the KGB awakened Hans every hour. Fear of his mother's reactions from a time far off woke him seemingly every half an hour. Then Hans woke in a freezing sweat to a little ruckus. Was it the goons? Groggily looking to his right, Hans saw a dog lying on the hay within the barn, looking back at him, but the black pooch didn't even let out a bark in Hans' presence. Sounds of drops dripping into a metal bucket completely startled Hans. It was morning. Scents of hay mixed in with Hans' groggy vision of a man milking a cow led Hans to realize that he was no longer dreaming. But the man with the cow suspected nothing. When he was done with gently tugging on the cow's nipples, the man vacated the barn, right before Hans crawled out of the barn and cautiously edged his way towards the loose board in the fence. As Hans inhaled the brisk, fresh, and crisp morning air under light rays of sun while he scurried through the knee-high snow that soaked his pant legs, he smelt the scent of animals embedded within his clothes as he savoured the sights of the morning mist. Peace overcame him after the thrill from the evening before, causing Hans to be instilled with a strong sense of confidence as he walked towards the train station; however, Hans strongly suspected that the goons would be there waiting for him upon the platform adjacent to a wooden ticket office, anticipating that Hans would board the morning train.

As expected, when Hans arrived at the Bratsk Main Station, he saw the two KGB goons from the night before eagerly pacing back and forth, waiting at the platform in aggressive anticipation. In an attempt to evade them, Hans inconspicuously walked further up the tracks in the direction of Zajarsk, away for the train station so that the two men wouldn't catch a glimpse of him. After crossing over a rusty metal bridge and reaching the other side of the tracks in order to remain out of the KGB henchmen's sights, Hans hid along a snowy, sloped bank, just waiting for a black locomotive-led freight train, with a passenger compartment attached to it to slowly roll by in his direction. When Hans heard the locomotive sluggishly depart the train station, and chug its way towards him, he prepared himself to leap into the passenger compartment while the train slugged along at a snail's pace. Moment's later, Hans found himself inside of the passenger compartment, where the train conductor smiled at him and said,

"They were waiting for you. They looked puzzled and disappointed. Damn KGB!"

Hans smiled back at him and said, *"It must be my lucky day."*

But at this point Hans felt hopelessly devastated after not receiving his clearance to head to Canada to reunite with his family. Conversely though, Hans was truly relieved that the KGB didn't bash in his skull. Even the train employee knew about the KGB's antics. Every Russian did. They were hated. If those goons would've gotten a hold of Hans, they most certainly would've left him for dead on that minus 30 Celsius day.

When Hans arrived back home in Zajarsk hours later, he explained to his family what happened, and elected to wait until he moved near Frunze, the current capital of Kyrgyzstan, before once again attempting to apply for a move to Canada. Upon arrival, Hans told his family, *"I have no intention of ever going back to Bratsk ever again! Never!! Never I say!!"*

Not long afterwards, Grandmother received a letter from her German friend in Jug, telling her that two 18-year-old German boys were beaten to death by Russians there. Her friends feared for their lives as they never knew when they would be next. Grandmother's friend from Jug mentioned that she desired a move to Jambul, present day Taraz, Kazakhstan, since the Kazakhstanis didn't have animosity towards the Germans, in contrary to many Russians, since the people in Kazakhstan and even Kyrgyzstan saw the Russians more as foes and conquerors than anything else. At the time, approximately one million ethnic Germans were already living in Kazakhstan.

As soon as you turned 16 years of age, you required a passport in order to move from city to city within the USSR. Since Hans had to prepare for his relocation to the suburbs of Frunze, he applied for a Soviet passport. Upon arriving at the passport bureau in Zajarsk, Hans was told,

"First, you must furnish a birth certificate before we can consider your application."

Since Hans didn't possess a birth certificate, he wrote to his parents in Canada and asked them to send him a copy of his Russian birth certificate. Hans and Grandmother lost all of their papers, belongings, and documents during the war. Hans only possessed a "German Citizenship Card", which was issued to him in Warthegau during WWII. But he wouldn't have dared to furnish the Soviet authorities with that piece of ID, especially considering the fact that it was issued with a swastika printed on the cover. Ultimately, Hans returned to the passport bureau to inform the authorities,

"I was unable to obtain a copy of my birth certificate. I asked my parents, but they don't have a copy either."

The man behind the counter responded,

"You should write to the authorities in your place of birth."

Much to Hans' chagrin, the authorities in Zaporozhe, the region in which Hans was born, sent Hans a letter informing him that the archives were burned during the war, so they were unable to provide Hans with any records relating to his birth. After notifying the local passport bureau of the situation, they nevertheless once again told Hans to contact the authorities in Zaporozhya. So again, Hans wrote to them, but the response remained the same.

CHAPTER 41

Off to Kyrgyzstan - 1958

Becoming pressed for time, the family became nervous. Hans had to leave for Frunze, Kyrgyzstan, USSR, in less than a week, since Jacob's sister had already purchased a house for them there. If it remained empty, it could become vandalised, and even possibly inhabited by squatters, making it imperative that someone reside there – that someone was Hans. The rest of the family was going to stick around in Zajarsk until the relocation deadline arrived, which meant that they still had three more months to sell whatever belongings that they couldn't or didn't desire to carry along with them to Kyrgyzstan.

Hans eventually went to the local passport bureau one more time with all of the rejection letters from the authorities in Zaporozhe in hand, and explained his situation. The official manager was not in at the time, so the secretary explained to Hans, *"All that I can provide you with is a 6-month temporary passport"*, which unknowingly to Hans at the time was usually only issued to criminals and political rivals of the state. After obtaining his temporary passport, the type of passport that Hans possessed for most of his Soviet life (occasionally making him appear like a criminal), Hans went home and packed his few belongings in a little suitcase before boarding a train to Frunze. But first, Hans had to travel to Bratsk, the city in which the KGB goons chased after him only a few months earlier, where he had to switch trains in order to embark on his journey south to Kyrgyzstan. Luckily enough though, the KGB wasn't expecting Hans in Bratsk. From there, another train transported Hans to Tayshet, where he boarded the Trans-Siberian Railway. From Tayshet, Hans travelled off to Novosibirsk, where he once again transferred to another train, that this time was heading in the direction of Alma-ata, Kazakhstan. Though, before Hans could arrive in Alma-ata, a railway bridge along the breathtaking vast and lush green Kyrgyz mountain range capped with snow-covered peaks had to be repaired following the spring thaw flooding.

The train sat along the track stagnant for the next four days. It was during this delay that Hans noticed a man continually meandering throughout the train. This peculiar character walked up and down the aisle, right by Hans on more than a few occasions, almost as if he wanted to communicate with or reveal something to Hans. The man eventually took a good, long hard look at Hans before finally glancing at the free seat next to him, before finally asking,

"May I sit here? Is someone sitting here? Is this place free?"

Hans responded, *"It's all yours!"*

The man in his 40's had darker hair and an olive complexion. Hans sensed a certain astounding aura surrounding him, yet before Hans could inspect his appearance any further, the fellow glared into Hans' bright blue eyes, seemingly not seeing an appearance at all as he curiously enquired,

"Where are you heading young man? I'm from the Caucasus region. In and around Georgia. Where Stalin, the man of steel was from. Where are you from boy?"

Hans happily told the comforting and pleasant man,

"I was born in Zaporozhe. But I'm now moving to Frunze. My entire family is moving there from Zajarsk. They're building a dam and are gonna flood that place. They'll drown us all if we stick around."

The man strangely enough reacted as if he already knew what Hans had just told him, or at the very least, as if Hans' answer was irrelevant and trivial. The man then asked,

"You don't mind if I read your palm, do you? Your left hand? Is that okay?"

Hans apprehensively nodded, sensing that this was the exact reason that the man took a seat right next to him. Lightly touching Hans' hand, the man from the Caucasus brought Hans' palm upward to face the heavens. A presence glided over Hans' hand, each touch feeling like a cloud was hovering over Hans' palm, or rather, like fog skimming over mountains. Brushing Hans' hand as if the man were lightly dusting sand off of a rock's facade, the man eventually spoke.

"Where you're going, you won't be there long. About two years or so. Then you'll be in another place again. Like a leaping frog in a pond going from stone to stone."

Goosebumps overcame Hans. He couldn't tell if his skin shrieked as a result of the man's words, touches, or simply because this man emitted the most peculiar of vibes.

"You'll have two serious injuries, but don't worry, you'll survive. They won't be that horrible. But then you'll have a long, long trip over the ocean. And your, father, oh! Oh. Sorry. He's gonna die at the age of 68. And you, you're gonna leave the USSR in '68. You'll end up rich, but lonely."

Hans wondered to himself,

"Can you also be lonely even when you're surrounded by family – feeling lonely with family around you, yet perhaps a family with its own distant thoughts and schemes that perpetually defy yours?"

Hans felt like he was in another dimension. He sensed feelings that had never touched him before, yet feelings that he knew all too well. The man then remarked,

"And your mother, hmmm.... Um, your mother..."

He kept brushing and searching the creases along Hans' palm.

"So, do you know your parents? Hmmm.., your mother. Ummm. I sense something. I sense something. Very strange."

Hans then thought to himself,

"It seems like he knows something about my mom, but doesn't want to share it with me. Is it bad? Would he withhold good info? A good prophecy? So, what isn't he telling me? What isn't he revealing? What's with the secrecy? Strange. Very strange."

Hans posed these questions to himself, but deep down he already truly knew his mother and what possessed her. He knew.... He simply knew.

The man then thanked Hans for his time and vanished into another train wagon, almost as if he never existed. He practically disappeared into thin air, leaving Hans in a haze and daze. After the train set-off once again, Hans eventually changed trains for the last time, this time in Alma-Ata, Kazakhstan, before arriving in Frunze eight days after departing Zajarsk. From the main station in Frunze, Hans hopped onto a bus that took him to Novopavlovka, a small suburb about 5 km west of the centre of Frunze. When Hans left Zajarsk, it was -30 degrees Celsius, which was a typical March temperature for that region of Siberia. However, after eight days of travelling, Hans was surprisingly greeted by mild weather and blooming flowers when he finally reached Frunze, and then Novopavlovka, Kyrgyzstan. Hans arrived all bundled up, seemingly ready for a blizzard on a sunny 15-degree Celsius day with a slight, yet refreshing breeze.

The people this region greeted Hans with an odd look, as if he had arrived from another planet. By the time Hans located Uncle Jacob's sister's place, he was completely exhausted. After apprehensively knocking on the thin wooden door of what was hopefully her white adobe home, Jacob's sister, who was in her late 40's with a child-like smile, happily and excitedly hugged Hans.

"I'm so happy you made it safe and sound Hans. Look at you! You're all grow up – strong and handsome. Let's go to your new home shall we! You must be exhausted!"

During their minute walk to his new house, Hans ceaselessly glanced at the exotic houses made out of mud and straw blocks that were as white-washed as the 6-foot-tall adobe walls surrounding the properties, which was the norm here as opposed to the protective wooden fences that Hans was so accustomed to seeing in Jug. The roofs in this area were made out of a thatched together indigenous species of bulrush-like weeds that Hans saw growing along the irrigation canals, rivers, and streams throughout the area. Hans felt like he had been sent to a paradise after spending a hell of a time in Zajarsk and Jug. After catching a glimpse of downtown Frunze from the train station, Hans could hardly wait to explore the metropolitan packed with romantic antiquated pedestrian squares nestled in amongst the spectacular snow-covered mountains and lush green hills of the region.

Upon entry into his new thatched roof home, Hans found the one room place with a kitchen completely bare and empty. In the front of the house sat a mud, adobe wall that surrounded a courtyard containing a deep stone well, an apple tree, and a sturdy wooden barn by the creek. Not far from Hans' new place was the facility and equipment used to produce the adobe bricks. Mud was dug out from the ground and mixed with straw before the block was placed in the sun to dry. Most of the well dug holes were never back-filled, leaving them filled with rain water that could never completely evaporate within the moist climate of the area. People came to these grounds with their own moulds, which were rectangular boxes with dividers from which four blocks could be made. The individual blocks were formed and levelled before being dumped out onto the ground in order to dry.

On Hans' first night, he slept on the wooden floor of the barren house, which surprisingly was actually a better sleeping arrangement than when the rest of the family arrived and Hans was relegated to sleeping in the open-walled attic amongst the elements on bags of grain with a burlap sack as a blanket. Yet, before Hans could vision the future arrival of

Jacob and the rest of the family, he abruptly awakened to the sounds of *"hee-haw! hee-haw! hee-haw!"* It was morning. The neighbour's donkey informed him so. With the sun starting to rise, Hans stood up and looked out of a wooden window frame with pealing paint. Hans heard a donkey, but oddly enough, he found himself staring at the neighbour's camel, leaving Hans wondering if this were all a dream. Still half asleep, Hans strolled outside where he discovered his new neighbour shirtless. The man appeared somewhat oriental, yet somewhat Persian, yet even somewhat Russian – simply rather exotic, though quite at peace based on his subtle movements and demeanour - a man who appreciated life and seemingly his new-found company as he happily approached Hans. This man in his 30's, who possessed the aura of a bright-eyed child, started chatting with Hans, eventually letting him know,

"My name iz Sergei. I'm a firefighter at a factory that produces agricultural equipment in Frunze."

Hans informed him, *"I'm looking for work. Are they looking?"*

The firefighter keenly replied,

"I'll take'r look to see if da factory iz hiring anyone and I'll get back to ya tonight. They're always lookin' fer newcomers."

Hans informed the man,

"I'm a machinist if that helps. But that's irrelevant. I'll do anything that needs to be done. I'd dearly appreciate it if you could help me out! I just wanna start working.

With a mischievous and devilish grin, Hans added, *"I'll even whip your camel for a fee if need be."*

That very evening, after work, that very same amicable neighbour knocked on Hans' door.

"Evening new neighbour! The tool and die department at da factory iz lookin' fer someone. I arranged an interview fr'ya' fer tomorrow. That works, doesn't it? You'll do fine. But how ya gonna arrive? Ya know what – take my bike. Or better yet – have'er! You can pay fer'er when some rubles start com'in'yer way!"

Hans nodded with excitement and said,

"Oh, wow! Of course! Thanks a lot!! Much obliged! Thank-you so much! Спасибо! Спасибо!"

Hans was speechlessly appreciative and ecstatic. After successfully completing the interview the following day, the factory offered Hans a position as a machinist, and not as a tool and die maker as anticipated; Hans started the job that very same week. After Hans' first day on the job, Sergei stepped into Hans' courtyard and enquired,

"So how goes yer first day mate?"

Hans responded with an appreciative grin, *"It was great! Thanks again for the opportunity."*

Sergei replied with a carefree smile,

"No problem. What'er neighbours for! So, are ya gonna live in yer' plac' here all alone, or ya waiting for company? We all need company don't we."

Enjoying his peace and freedom, Hans coyly, and a bit uneasily replied,

"Maybe. But sometimes you are the best company that you can find. When you're on your own, you're at nobody else's mercy, assuming of course you can show yourself mercy."

The rest of the family was expected to arrive in Kyrgyzstan in about three months. When the firefighter heard that, he mentioned,

John Friesen

"As ya can see and hear and smell, I own a donkey, a camel, a horse, and two wagons - one for small loads with the donkey, and one for large ones like furniture and stuff with the horse. I could go to the train station to pick up yer family if ya like. On the side, I use my animals and wagon fe'transporting items and chattels, and even people and stuff. Animals gotta be helpful, or what else are they good for? Am I right? But like I said, I pick up people from the city. It's good to earn a little extra cash on the side, no? I'll haul yer folks in if ya desire fer a fair neighbourly fare, neighbour."

Before giving Hans a friendly wink, Sergei headed home.

Hans, at the time, only had the blue, one-speed bicycle that he quickly paid Sergei for since Hans had plenty of money to spend with Jacob not around to siphon off his wages. Hans used this bike to travel 15 km to and from work each way to the machinist shop that operated with three 8-hour shifts per day. The bike and Hans became inseparable. They were putting on as much as 60 km on some days, depending on which rotating shift that Hans had to work. But Hans couldn't complain, because during his commute he appreciatively savoured Frunze's picturesque scenery amongst the mountainous, immensely green and lush backdrop. Even though Frunze was equipped with street cars and bus services, Hans still preferred travelling by bike. He absolutely loved having the freedom to freely go where he desired, without the limitations set by timetables, bus routes, and Uncle Jacob, while Hans cherished the workout and conjured up healthy sweat to go along with it within his new-found paradise.

The extremely verdant and blossoming region was irrigated by a network of well dug ditches and canals that ran through the fields, right into the city and surrounding towns. Many of the backyards possessed luscious gardens and orchards. When the blossoms bloomed, the air became filled with a wonderful herbal aroma, which was quite the contrary to the Siberian scent of pine that Hans became all too accustomed to while living in Zajarsk. The water required to sustain the lush vegetation was supplied by the breathtaking snow-covered mountains whose peaks were decorated year-round with white ice and snow. During the summer, the ice and snow perched upon the mountain peaks, some soaring 7,000 metres in the air, melted, inadvertently offering the citizens in and around Frunze a fresh and steady supply of water.

Winters in Frunze were extremely mild in comparison to the conditions of Jug and Zajarsk. So instead of marching through heavy snowfall like Hans was more than acquainted with in Russia, Hans spent his future winters in Frunze avoiding puddles resulting from the abundant rainfall and unmanicured dirt roads. Occasionally, flakes fell overnight, sometimes right on Hans while he slept within the exposed attic, under a thatched roof. But the snow, more times than not, melted away by the time the next morning appeared on the horizon. Yet, nothing lessened the surprise whenever Hans woke-up with a blanket of snow covering him from head-to-toe after a pile of flakes blew in on an angle all over his "bed" throughout the night.

Summers in Frunze were extremely hot and dry, some days reaching 40 degrees Celsius, leaving the skies offering a stunning, clear blue portrait to peer into and savour. Every morning, Hans went to the well and dumped a bucket of freezing water over his head before heading off to work. The nights were usually cloudless and pitch black, except for the enchanting illumination of stars that complimented the gentle and calming cool air that swept down from the Tian Shan mountains. The flowing air acted as a form of natural air conditioning, making Frunze's gorgeous summer nights quite comfortable. During the days, Hans delighted in the sight of the seas of red poppy seed fields, where opium was harvested for medical and medicinal purposes. Whenever Hans perched himself high above in the mountains, and looked into the distance, he bore witness to the desolate bareness of the desert. All of the settlements in the area were built right around the mountains, the source of water for all of the villages and cities in the region, so the desert remained barren and sparsely populated.

Staring directly downwards from the top of the mountains at the expansive city, Hans saw a green oasis that awaited him below. He had the entire summer-like spring to himself to experience what his new region had to offer. Sometimes, Hans ventured out into the mountains on his bike and watched the native Kyrgyz people, semi-nomadic Muslims who had

Hun, Tatar, Mongol, and Dingling roots, tending to their grazing sheep along the alpine pastures. Hans sometimes stopped and chatted with the Kyrgyz people if they spoke any Russian. The Kyrgyz were gracious and humble natives to the area who usually resided in the villages along the mountain slopes, but frequently made short exoduses with their herds along the hillsides. Occasionally, the herders offered Hans some "kumis", a fermented horse or camel milk concoction. The Kyrgyz stored the milk in bags; and although the milk didn't taste all that bad, it smelt rather pungent.

But the smell of some non-sour milk didn't prevent Hans from relishing in his peace and serenity during his first few months in Frunze, while Jacob and the rest of the family tied up loose ends in Zajarsk. During this juncture, there wasn't a soul around to push Hans to carry out additional work, just like there wasn't an animal to tend to and take care of. Whenever Hans lied on the lawn in the back courtyard of his home and gazed upwards at the dazzling stars, Hans whispered to himself,

"Why couldn't have I moved here from the start? But I guess Someone else had a better idea. But just why couldn't have my family been from here from the onset? I'm sure they didn't here a gunshot during the war in this part of the world. I wish this moment could never end."

Frunze was also home to a park containing a manmade lake where Hans went swimming. And unlike Jug and Zajarsk, Frunze was cultured by the arts, opera, and ballet, even though Hans was a bit of an unsophisticated, harmless brute. Nevertheless, when Hans wasn't working and savouring his nights, he had plenty of time to visit the theatres, where he took in productions of Swan Lake, Shakhrazade, and The Nutcracker, or headed to the cinemas, library, and museums. If Hans wasn't appreciating the arts, then he was devouring his favourite fruits and vegetables at the markets where he tasted a variety of exotic, sweet, and flavourful fresh fruit. Watermelons and honeydews were his fruits of choice. These bazaar vendors, at their wooden stands draped in light tarps cut up the fruit for sampling so everyone could taste the quality of their offerings. Hans was like a kid in a candy store. He couldn't even remember tasting a fruit prior to his arrival in Frunze. Even behind his new house, Hans had instant access to cherry, pear, peach, apple, apricot, and plum trees, and not to mention grapes growing on vines right and ripely within picking distance. Hans was absolutely in heaven in his new region of the USSR.

Hans absolutely adored his time immersed in freedom. He realized that's all that he ever needed – a need to be as free as bird – free from the tyrants of the world who only sought to rule him. And as expected, Hans' life regrettably changed when Uncle Jacob and his family arrived in Novopavlovka, a suburb of Frunze, three months later. Uncle Jacob was possessed by more power and starkly driven by control than ever, leading Jacob to constantly find more work for Hans to carry out. This normally entailed Uncle Jacob passing on a good portion of his own work to Hans after Jacob started his position at the Kolkhoz in Frunze. Uncle Jacob was the type of religious hypocrite who made a Pharisee appear genuine and righteous. Jacob refused to do any work on Sunday, not even feed the livestock, as according to him, it was a *"day of rest"*. But seemingly only for him. Jacob had absolutely no problem instructing Hans to perform "his" tasks and chores, which included making bricks from manure that were used for heating and cooking.

But once fall came, Hans started Grade 8, regardless of the fact that Uncle Jacob still didn't approve of him going to school one bit. And he wasn't the only one. Initially, the school didn't want to admit Hans since the faculty feared that his attendance would be sporadic at best, mainly due to his 15-km commute to and from school on his bike. It even took a while to convince the school board just to hear his pleas, but ultimately, it was no one other than a female Russian-Jewish math teacher who stood up for the Germanic Hans, and agreed that he shouldn't be denied an education. Though, there were stipulations surrounding his enrollment. She told Hans,

"We'll take you into our classes, but only under one condition – if you miss one class, you're out!"

Hans felt completely and unconditionally relieved and told her,

John Friesen

"I really appreciate what you're doing for me! You're an amazing woman! I won't let you down ma'am! I'll be at every class. You can count on me!"

It was Hans' only chance to go to school since classes were offered at night as well, after Hans' day shifts at the machine shop. This specific school that operated in cooperation with the factory where Hans was employed accommodated factory workers who wanted to further themselves by pursuing their high school diploma. Students' ages spanned from as young as 18, to as old as 50 years of age.

Luckily enough, the school offered classes throughout the day and evening. So, regardless of when the worker's shift took place, there wasn't an excuse to miss school. Hence, the Jewish teacher knew that Hans had no justification to forgo a class, besides as a result of illness or perhaps injury. She believed in Hans when no one else would, so she wanted to make sure that he kept to his side of the bargain. She ended up checking up on Hans almost every day to make sure that he stuck to his promise.

Although Hans received encouragement from people regarding his studies, Uncle Jacob still didn't like the idea of him continuing his education since it meant not only that Uncle Jacob didn't have full control over Hans, but also that Hans couldn't get a second or third or even fifth job on the side to fill Uncle Jacob's coffers in the process. Jacob was 100% convinced that Hans was wasting his time seeking an education, since in "Uncle's" eyes, Hans first *"had to learn how to work!"* Jacob also didn't fail to mention to Hans,

"Nobody is crazy enough as you to travel 30 km to get to school and back! It's ridiculous!"

Hans thought, but bit his tongue,

"I'd travel 15,000 miles to school if it got me away from you, you old kook!"

On top of his schooling commute, Hans also still had to travel 15 km on his bike to get to work. Depending upon his shift, Hans sometimes had to return home from work in order to carry out his chores before jumping

300

back onto his bike and repeating his 15 km, or 30-minute journey into the city in order to attend four hours of evening classes from 7 p.m. till 11 p.m. Hans swore that he could ride his bike while sleeping, which let him regenerate before work, his classes, and dealing with the antics of Uncle Jacob, whose very own sister who lived around the corner didn't agree with one bit. She let her brother Jacob know, *"Hans should only have to pay rent! You're taking advantage of him!"*

This comment brought a massive grin to Hans' face, but Uncle Jacob responded with his typical, tyrannical rhetoric.

"You can't spoil him! He'll become a lazy bum. The boy has gotta learn how to work!"

Despite Hans' loathing for his cruel uncle, he still attempted to make the best of the situation by trying to mollify and keep his uncle as content as possible. So, every Sunday, for his next two years, Hans, on Uncle Jacob's behalf, "volunteered" out of compulsion to transport milk with oxen from the Kolkhoz to the dairy at 5 in the morning, and then again in the evening. The task became even more daunting since the oxen were very stubborn and slow. Hans experienced a troubling time with hitching the oxen to the wagon every Sunday morning, oxen that had absolutely no interest in wakening from their slumber. In an attempt to motivate and stir them up, Hans pulled or twisted the oxen's tails, poked at them, wacked them, or even literally lit a fire under their bums. Hans' responsibilities included carrying milk cans out of the barn; stacking them in rows on the wagon that was used to transport the milk about 1.5 km to the pasteurizing facility that took over an hour to reach at an oxen's pace.

Hans, though, could fall asleep on the wagon during this stretch and rest assured that the oxen would pull right up to the loading ramp. The oxen amazingly actually knew their way to and from the dairy. Upon arrival at the processing plant, where cream and cheese were produced, Hans unloaded the tin milk cans before pouring the milk into enormous vats. After every milk tin was emptied, Hans returned the oxen and the two feet tall tin milk containers that he first had to rinse out to the Kolkhoz. And even though it was Uncle Jacob's responsibility to make these Sunday milk deliveries, Jacob forced Hans to carry-out these duties even though Jacob's sister incessantly nagged at him whenever she stopped by.

"You treat Hans horribly! It's an utter hypocrisy and completely unjust! You have neither a right to take all of Hans' earnings away from him, nor treat him like your own personal slave!"

Uncle Jacob responded with his typical counterargument.

"I don't want to spoil the boy! Hans has to learn how to work!! He doesn't have any parents to show him how to toil, so I'm doing that for them. Those clowns living in Ka-na-da owe me big time for raising their son! I'm gonna let'em know it when I fly over there one day!! I'm gonna be rich!"

Jacob's sister's pleas fell on deaf ears. He continued to take all of Hans' earnings, regardless of the fact that Uncle Jacob had a decent paying job at the government-run Kolkhoz farm that possessed luscious orchards, healthy dairy cows, perfect vineyards, wineries for cider, sugar beets, and watermelon fields. Along the roadside, the Kolkhoz set up wooden booths and sold half litre jugs of wine for 50 kopeks.

CHAPTER 42

Working Away in Frunze

Luckily enough, Hans had an excuse to get away from Uncle Jacob after he turned 18, an age in which every able-bodied man could be drafted into the Russian army. In the spring of 1959, Hans received a letter from the army drafting centre in Frunze, stating he that was required to report for duty. Upon arrival, they screened Hans for physical endurance and abilities by instructing him to participate in a test that consisted of performing swimming, running, and jumping exercises, as well as push-ups, chin-ups, and grenade throwing drills. Hans carried out all of the exercises and drills exceptionally well. There were also military workouts that tested his agility and ability to react quickly. Upon successful completion of all of these tests, the participants could decide whether they wanted to join the navy, air force, or army. If an applicant failed the tests, he was required to join the labour military contingent, which was a workforce deployed for digging ditches and trenches, and building structures. These workers usually had some sort of vision, learning, or physical disability, leaving them unsuitable for the army, unlike their serving brethren who relished in playing with their military toys and gadgets. On the contrary, their civilian comrades truly had to work, and hence got paid accordingly as ordinary civilians,

Hans ultimately elected to join the army, who sent him to be schooled to become a tank-truck driver. Such training was normally done prior to being officially drafted into the army. During this time, the cadet still lived at home and wasn't required to wear a uniform. While away "on duty", Hans' employers were obligated to pay him while he carried out his one month of "service" and schooling at the trade school. The military provided Hans with a meagre stipend of one ruble a day. After completing his training, Hans was ready to be drafted with a "chauffeur", or rather tank-truck license. However, once the drafting centre checked into Hans' family background and discovered that he only had a grandmother, who neither was working nor receiving a pension, the army decided not to draft Hans after all. They let him know, *"It's your responsibility to support your grandmother."* Little did they know that Hans was already helping to support Jacob's entire family.

So, Hans returned to work. While working for the Ministry of Agriculture (factory), Hans received a plaque that year stating that he was a "Working Superman" for his exemplary work and piece-work diligence and success as he worked away on the metal lay after he designed his own tools for the job in order to speed up his pace; yet, after not receiving additional monetary remuneration for his exceptional efforts, Hans became demotivated, so he ultimately slowed down his pace on the dangerous job that left some of his co-workers mangled or even dead on the night shift after dozing off on the equipment. Though, with intra-company ethnic rivalries, Hans wondered if the work on the equipment truly was the cause of their death. Hans knew enough to keep his head down during the night shift, even though it wasn't enough to prevent a pipe being swung at his head before he socked his Chechen assailant. Employee rivalries brought out the worst during the scarcely supervised night shift, leaving people always speculating whether the accidents were in fact uninvestigated murders. Hans didn't want to experience such a destiny, so he ultimately sought new work. After obtaining his new truck-tank license, Hans ultimately took a job at a trucking company where he started out as mechanic. But after giving his two weeks notice, yet before departing his job at the Ministry of Agriculture, Hans' superiors assigned him to the worst job imaginable - piling up 50 Kg conveyor belts used for the combines.

Once those two weeks were up, Hans worked for a few months at the trucking company as a mechanic, before eventually getting redeployed to the blacksmith department where Hans' valued expertise made him a perfect fit for the job. In spite of the hard, arduous, physical labour expected of him, which included pounding a sledge hammer for the entire day, Hans savoured toiling away, almost as an escape and release from his emotional agony. Even though Hans' heart was still broken after not being allowed to reunite with his family in Canada, his body gradually hardened up so much the liquid injected into him during a vaccination actually squirted right back into the nurse's face when she pulled the needle out. The vaccine could barely penetrate his solid muscles.

Regardless of Hans' harden-up physique, he also had a soft side as well. So, when the brother in-law to Uncle Jacob's new wife, a skilled and gifted rabbit breeder gifted Hans with a rabbit, Hans became so filled with glee that he immediately sprinted down to a desolate and abandoned portion of land near the railroad tracks to pick some grass for the rabbit. Focused on the task at hand, Hans didn't even notice the Kolkhoz's watchman responsible for overlooking the adjacent orchard derisively glaring at him. Once he saw Hans plucking away at the weed-like grass near the railway tracks, the watchman became jolted into asserting his authority by exercising a power trip. After tearing out enough grass to feed the rabbit, Hans began to casually rise from all fours until he turned his head and felt a double-barreled shotgun belonging to the grey-goateed late 40's-year-old watchman right in his face! The horse-backed watchman venomously uttered,

"I'm gonna blow your head off boy!"

Hans very causally countered, *"Go ahead! But imagine the mess you're gonna make!"*

The watchman snidely retorted, *"Who cares! Nobody would miss you anyway German boy!"*

Hans was frantically terrified on the inside, and even a bit sullenly hurt by that comment, but he showed no signs of trepidation, which led the horseman responsible for protecting the orchard's grapes and other fruit from pilferage to back down and ride away. But not before hollering,

"Don't le'me catch'a 'round here again boy!! Hear'tat boy!"

Hans concealed his fears, tears, and terror for the world not to see while he slowly crumbled on the inside as a rush of vicious anger ran through his veins. His fury penetrated so deep that Hans' nose began to run a bit after the incident; a part of him truly wanted to storm after the watchman and wack him right across the face with the barrel of that shotgun. But Hans knew better and exercised temperance. Nonetheless, Hans remained perturbed for days on end. Yearning to vent his frustration, Hans headed over to his school chum Yaroslav's place, who lived right next to the orchard. After Hans grieved to Yaroslav, he emphatically assured Hans,

"Don't worry! We're gonna fix him! That much I know!"

The next day, the boys, along with Yaroslav's younger brother Vladi, who like his brother had bushy black hair and a narrow nose with a light bump on it, sat on the family's back porch and engaged in cavalier conversation, casually waiting for the horseman to stroll by. When the watchman eventually entered into Yarolav's sights, he inconspicuously threw a tiny apple in the direction of the horse, catching it on the thigh while the watchman pompously sat on the horse's back. Absolutely spooked, the horse's two front legs soared into the air! Unable to hang on, the watchman was tossed to the ground! As he mindlessly glanced around in awe, the boys giggled away in silence. The dim-witted, village idiot of a watchman seemingly assumed that an apple had fallen from the tree. He never even suspected that the boys, who nonchalantly appeared as if they were locked in innocent, yet deep conversation the entire time carried out the deed. When the horseman was out of sight and earshot, the boys howled it up while they sat on the elevated porch at the back of Yaroslav's house that overlooked the orchard. After a few more "apple falling" incidents, the horseman eventually stopped entering the vicinity of Yaroslav's porch. He just couldn't grasp why his horse was "strangely" and constantly spooked whenever stepping in that area of the orchard. Hans' rift with the watchman seemed to be settled, but Hans always came across more enemies.

On his last night at the Ministry of Agriculture, Hans found himself riding his bike to the factory for the night shift. Amongst pitch black darkness and hollowed silence, Hans remained vigilantly focussed on the narrow dirt road to avoid ending up in the ditch. Then, suddenly out of nowhere, Hans heard the roar of a truck in the distance. Many that drove trucks travelled with attached hay trailers that contained tree stumps the size of half-sized telephone poles that were used to secure hay stacks being transported in the trailer. Some drivers though, also sought "entertainment" with these poles by laying these massive stumps vertically across the empty trailer floor, with one end protruding outwards along the shoulder of the road. The drivers' intent - to attempt to hammer a roadside bike rider right in the back of the head!

While Hans drove along the roadside on that very evening, he heard the truck approaching him from behind. Sounds of a sinister, cackling sort of laugh accompanied the roar of the accelerating engine. Hans knew that something was up, so he went on high alert, preparing for the most horrific of the worst. As the truck neared, Hans kept his head upwards and face forward, appearing as if he hadn't heard a peep. When the clamour of the motor and the yelping of inebriated yokels climaxed, Hans instantly ducked his head right in the nick of time! The 400-pound log soared over Hans' head, gently brushing his flowing and shaggy dirty blonde hair in the wind. Hans avoided the pole, though in many of these instances the bicyclists lost their heads. Some truck drivers didn't appreciate sharing "their" roads with bike riders. These perpetrators purposely laid their log beams horizontally within a hay-less trailer, just searching for carnage.

Though, it wasn't necessarily always done with malicious intent. Weeks later, on a bright afternoon, Hans saw a man in his 60's with a straw hat approaching a street corner. A huge truck with a hay-less wagon drove with a horizontally-positioned wooden beam. The massive log slightly protruded outside of the wagon as the truck innocently advanced through town in the direction of the street corner where the old man in the straw hat slowly tiptoed towards, seemingly oblivious to his surroundings, completely unaware of the nearing truck. As Hans lost vision of the man, he suddenly heard a loud screeching of tires! The driver attempted to brake by slamming his foot against the pedal with a tremendous thrust! But it was too late. Without even a turn of the head or a tuck of the neck, the old man in the straw hat didn't react one bit until his brains smashed right out of his skull! Hans' jawed instantly dropped in awe! His eyes couldn't believe what he had just witnessed as the victim placidly stepped in the way of the pole seconds earlier as the truck innocently approached the street crossing in broad daylight. In Hans' eyes', it appeared like a suicide mission that will haunt the driver until the day he dies, but no one will ever know the true intentions of the victim, and perhaps even the driver.

Usually the driver and truck passengers obnoxiously laughed before and after their atrocious nighttime heinous hit and runs while being drunk out their minds. Hans witnessed many bikers get mowed-down from behind and their brains spatter all over the road, so he was always ready to evade these wooden poles. One never forgets, but rather only becomes moulded by such acts of butchery. Hans survived, but he wasn't spared of being tainted, just like the driver on this occasion who clenched his head in his hands as he sobbed while the straw hat of the old man lied on the hood of the truck.

CHAPTER 43

Novosibirsk

Despite settling in within the delightful metropolis of Frunze, Hans and Grandmother were once again on the verge of another move. Though, this time it was on account of all people, Hans' father in Canada. At the time, Grandmother wasn't only communicating with her husband in Paraguay, her daughter in Canada, but also with Hans' father, Cornelius. One day, Grandmother received a letter from Father stating,

"I've discovered that my brother Jacob is now living in Novosibirsk. Go live with him. He's blood. He's Hans' real Uncle Jacob, unlike that other "Uncle" Jacob. That guy is a fraud! My son shouldn't be sleeping on the roof, especially in winter like some sort of rodent!"

Father arranged everything, and Grandmother ultimately elected to heed Cornelius' word, though with mixed emotions. Despite enjoying the pleasant weather and German community in Frunze, Grandmother believed that Hans belonged with his true family where he wouldn't have to sleep in an exposed attic on grain sacks. So, she too felt that it was in "their" best interests if they both went to live with Cornelius' brother and his family in Novosibirsk, a city of one million people, yet a city that only had one gas station at the time. Though, before the move could materialize, Hans' true Uncle Jacob had to not only secure a bigger apartment that could house all of them, but also help Hans obtain a position at the electrical company where Uncle Jacob worked.

Hans, in the meantime, continued to go to night school in Frunze, with the intent of completing Grade 9, while the paperwork for his move to Novosibirsk was being processed. Grade 10, Hans' final year of high school would have to be completed in Novosibirsk. Nevertheless, Hans still dreamt about getting to Canada and reuniting with his parents, so he reapplied for permission to leave the USSR; though this time around, he applied through the authorities in Frunze.

Months later, the "new" Uncle Jacob, who served in the German army as a translator at the age of 13 during WWII, ultimately obtained a new and much bigger apartment in the northern outskirts of Novosibirsk along Krasnyy Prospekt in the vicinity of a local airport and an industrial zone lined with factories. Their new apartment was big enough to house Hans and Grandmother, along with Uncle Jacob's entire family, where they all had the "luxury" of sharing an outhouse with 16 other families. So, Grandmother and Hans finally packed up their belongings in preparation of their departure from Novopavlovka and "Uncle" Jacob. After two years of living in the greater Frunze area, Hans and Grandmother found themselves off on the train once again. Hans knew little of this "new" Uncle Jacob. He only recalls being told that this Jacob once "kidnapped" him when Hans was only nine months old. But he did know that like the Jacob of Zajarsk and Frunze, this Jacob also served time in a brutal Russian hard labour mining camp. Jacob, Cornelius' brother, was sentenced to 12-years in a Gulag located in the vicinity of the Arctic Circle where he only ultimately served out 6 years for illegally "Ukrainainizing", or rather "de-Germanizing" his last name to "Friesenko". Though, after Stalin's death, Uncle Jacob was shown some leniency during the "Khrushchev Thaw", when Khrushchev had numerous "political" prisoners released from the Gulags, leading Jacob's sentence to be halved. Nevertheless, the effects of living and toiling in such confines were devastating; prisoners left as mental wrecks and in shambles. Emotionally, psychologically, and even physically crushed after their sentence and service in the Gulags, most inmates returned to society as a dark shadow of their former selves. Hans once met a distant uncle who turned into a complete drug addict after completing his "service" in the coal mines of a Gulag work camp.

Yet, before arriving in Novosibirsk, Hans and Grandmother first visited a few friends in Jambul (modern-day Taraz), Kazakhstan for three days. These people lived in Jug in the communal house with Hans and Grandmother, but they too re-located over the years. A lot of Hans' friends or child roommates from Jug were now already married with kids. Hans though, would be the only one from all of these kids to ultimately obtain a high school diploma. After leaving Jambul, Hans and Grandmother made a stop in Pavlodar, Kazakhstan to visit Grandmother's brother-in-law who was 84-years-old and living off a meagre pension of $5 per month. Hans, on the other hand, was in his early 20's, ambitious, full of hope, and ready to work and prove himself in the Siberian metropolis of Novosibirsk.

Upon arrival, Hans' first assignment at the electrical company, where he ended up working for four years, was to assist on a massive construction project. All of Hans' assignments were based in Novosibirsk, and in foreign cities until Hans completed his high school diploma through night school, which was when he was finally forced to take on projects in various cities throughout the province for about 3 to 6 months at a time, sometimes in absolutely freezing and deplorable conditions. Working such a trade only strengthened Hans' resolve to go to university and even Canada; but those aspirations had to be put on hold.

While attending night school in Novosibirsk, Hans became acquainted with a young man named Anatoly, who came from a relatively wealthy family. His father, who looked sophisticated, especially by sporting suavely slicked back salt and pepper hair, was a member of the Communist party; but Anatoly, his ruggedly handsome son with thick dark hair, auburn eyes, and a chiselled face was nothing less than a cavalier vigilante. In Anatoly's free time, he created cardboard bombs consisting of nails and explosives, bombs that he set off into public places. Yet, strangely enough, Anatoly was one of the nicest and pleasantest guy Hans ever met. He and his parents had the friendliest of demeanours. Occasionally, Anatoly's parents invited Hans to their place for supper, and even once to the family cottage, or "Dacha", a rural wooden cabin for the Soviet elite. Anatoly's father was a highly-ranked officer in the army during WWII, but luckily enough, wasn't purged by Stalin following the war. If a war veteran became popular in the public eye, his days were usually numbered within a Stalin regime that was driven by obsessive paranoia. But being a highly-regarded ex-army-officer had its perks. During their time at the Dacha, Anatoly's father, a man in his 60's with a gentle look, endearing mannerisms, but stern yet youthful eyes, said to Hans,

"Vana, you are of German roots, no? Look around at all of our nice stuff - these belongings and chattels. The Red Army looted it all from the Germans during and after the war! We love this stuff! War is an ugly mix of beauty and brutality, with a dash of plundering and pillaging that's perversely justified by cold, callous, and penetrating pontification and ideology."

Anatoly's family resided amongst the "Communist aristocracy" in the suburbs of Novosibirsk, where they drove an expensive Russian Volga car that cost ten years the salary of the average worker. Their residence even had a public garage and on-site mechanic. However, their son, Anatoly, enjoyed hanging out with a sort that was integrated with the riff-rats of bottom-feeders who infested the underworld of Novosibirsk's degenerate society. These types of proletarians took up residence within the confines, vaults, and attics of the main train station. Occasionally, the police carried out well-planned raids on this group, but the majority of the time, even they were too scared to interfere with these train station dweller's and squatters' wheeling's and dealings.

One time, a group of these thugs even left the muscular Hans shaking in his knees when they approached him near the train station entrance with the intent of mugging Hans and ruffling him up. Yet, his fear quickly subsided when Anatoly saw what was going on, and immediately interjected, hollering out *"не он!! (Not Him!)."* Anatoly clearly had a standing with this gang that eventually dispersed in search of other targets. Hans believed that perhaps the gangs knew of Anatoly's dad's status, and he simply left it that.

But despite these niceties that Anatoly portrayed to Hans, Anatoly was a teen constantly in search of a rush, and especially got a severe kick out of violent antics. It was like a drug to him. The fact that he never got punished for any of his deeds only fuelled his fire and sparked his imagination. When Hans learned of Anatoly's tomfoolery and "larks", Hans was absolutely appalled. Anatoly's parents, out of concern, approached Hans one day and asked,

"Can you talk with him." Hans replied, *"I'll see what I can do. I hope he'll listen to me."*

When Hans saw Anatoly at school a few nights later, he let Anatoly have a piece of his mind.

"You come from a wealthy family and you do stuff like this! You're nuts! I'm done with you! You're hurting people with your bloody package-bombs!"

Hans believes that his lecture may have worked, but he'll never truly know because they lost contact when night school concluded for the year. Staying in touch was difficult during this period in Russian history as most commoners didn't have phones, so Hans never got to learn the rest of Anatoly's story.......

CHAPTER 44

Canadian Embassy

Following the completion of his high school diploma, Hans was assigned to numerous distant work projects. On one assignment, Hans was sent to Krasnoyarsk, Russia's frigid and much more unforgiving version of the windy city of Chicago. Brutal outdoors temperatures amongst horrific blizzardy winter conditions occasionally took lives on such job sites. During this assignment in Krasnoyarsk, Hans was working within the protected confines of a massive equipment manufacturing facility where he found himself 25 feet off the ground, installing high-voltage hydro wires. At times, Hans and his co-workers were required to climb over 50 feet into the air – usually without any safety belts. Hans witnessed bodies soar to their immediate death on more than one occasion. Fatalities were more than an exception. Victims either splattered onto solid concrete, or were electrocuted while working on hydro towers. All tasks were risky, so the workers were required to carry out their duties with the upmost care and caution if they expected to survive. Though sometimes, safety had to be sacrificed to get the job done. Other times, the workers "sacrificed" themselves through on-site drunkenness and obscene recklessness.

While Hans was standing on a crane over 25 feet off the ground tightening metal joints on a massive stanchion, he removed his hand from the protective railing and grabbed a hold of the wrench with both hands; yet, before he knew it, Hans had applied too much force while twisting the wrench, and consequently, his feet slipped! Hans fell into an instant freefall! He instantaneously thought, *"This is the end of me!"*

Though, after a split-second, or a 15-foot drop, Hans felt his back hammer against a protective metal sheet covering a transformer. Instead of plummeting to his death, the 1/1000 scenario played out. Hans, in astonishment, landed on something other than concrete over 25 feet below! As Hans smashed down against a solid corrugated sheet of metal, he incidentally collided against a transformer below, causing it to short-circuit and explode, leaving a massive 6-foot hole in the metal panel! The explosion launched Hans into the air before he astonishingly landed onto the concrete floor 10 feet below, right on his two feet. He walked away completely unscathed, and in utter disbelief over what happened, but he wasn't the only one. His co-workers and supervisors refused to even listen to one word of his story, even though all of the lights in the building went out. Totally skeptical, Hans' boss snappishly responded,

"Oh, boy!! Yeah, sure! I have no time for such nonsense Ivan! I wasn't born yesterday! No one has access to the transistor area besides authorized engineers! Quit wasting my time with your fictitious and fallacious fairy tales Tolstoy!"

Weeks later, Hans received a letter stating that he had been drafted into the army and was required to report for a 35-day military exercise in Tomsk. At the time, Hans was infected with blood poisoning, which occurred on the job while he was welding. His elbow became so swelled up that he lived under tremendous pain. The illness was so debilitating that Hans eventually admitted himself into emergency. There were no doctors on duty at the time of his arrival, but luckily enough, the receptionist nurse, a beautiful and tall woman with blond hair in her 40's was able to offer her services. When she looked at Hans' infected elbow, she diagnosed,

"You have blood poisoning. So just how much pain can you endure?"

She was very blunt and self-assured, seemingly just like Hans, who very macho-like, yet coyly, with an ounce of apprehension, responded back, *"Let's find out."* Hans' arm was placed onto the counter by the nurse. Hans thought to himself,

"Nothing can be worse than the pain that I'm going through at this very moment."

However, Hans was proven wrong after the nurse disinfected the diseased area of his elbow and told him, *"Look away."* What she didn't want Hans to see was that she was holding a pair of long medical tweezers that she used to pinch off a piece of the infected skin, right before she forced her tweezers directly into his swollen and discoloured elbow. When she pulled out the tweezers, Hans could hear the fluid gushing out of elbow, dripping into a paper cup that the nurse was holding. Stuffing the wound full of cotton gauze, she hoped that the wound would heal from the inside out. Before leaving, the nurse made Hans a sling out of a cheese cloth and told him,

"Wear this under your arm until the wound heals up. Make sure that you keep the area clean and disinfected!"

Not necessarily following the nurse's order, Hans reported the next day to the military base in Novosibirsk. Upon arrival, the military personal completely ignored Hans' painful condition, and the fact that Hans' arm was in a sling. They instead instructed Hans,

"Go help load the trucks, tanks, and other equipment onto the train."

As soon as everything was loaded and ready to go, the group of recruits left for Tomsk, where the training exercises were carried out. The drills included target shooting and building a pontoon bridge over a river. Military officers also attempted to simulate a battle during a nuclear attack by filling the bottom of a drum with explosives, and setting off the TNT until the contents of the drum kaboomed, creating a mushroom cloud that resembled the sights of a miniature version of the Hiroshima nuclear attack.

After Hans' 35 days of service in Tomsk were complete, Hans went back to "exploring" the USSR by labouring on foreign assignments that sent him to cities like Irkutsk, Krasnoyarsk, and Iskitim (70 Km south-east of Novosibirsk), which is where Hans ended up working with a few German engineers from Leipzig. Unable to speak Russian, Hans conversed with

317

these German engineers in high German or "Hochdeutsch", a rather different form of German from the Mennonite dialect of "Plattdeutsch" that Hans was accustomed to speaking. These Germans from Leipzig arrived in Russia in order to supervise the installation of East German electrical equipment. Hans and his Uncle Jacob worked with this team from East Germany for an entire year until the project in Iskitim was complete.

Afterwards, Hans had a week of transitioning between assignments, so he decided to travelled to Moscow with his new German friends to do a little sight-seeing. They all visited art galleries, cafes, and the Kremlin together, but Hans had another reason for his trip. He desired to pay the Canadian Embassy a visit. Though, before heading into the city to try chances at the embassy, Hans bid farewell to his German co-workers by sharing a coffee with them in an international flights cafeteria at the airport while the East Germans awaited their flight back to Leipzig. As Hans waited with the Germans at the airport in Moscow, ready to wish them farewell, he actually momentarily contemplated the option of hopping onto a plane with them and escaping to East Germany. Though, what good would have that done. The Stasi, East Germany's version of the KGB, was known to be even more brutal and heartless than the KGB.

And besides, Hans didn't travel to Moscow to escape to Germany, but rather to go to the Canadian Embassy located in the downtown area. Or was their possibly another way to get to Canada? Because while engaged in entertaining conversation with the engineers from Leipzig, Hans felt a tap on his shoulder. When he turned around, he was instructed in Russian by an airport employee,

"Come! Come! You're going to miss your plane to Sweden!"

Hans was being offered the prospect of hopping onto a plane with a group of Swedish tourists who were heading to Stockholm. Hans then turned to his German friends with a smile across his face. A man from the Leipzig work crew said to Hans in German,

"Here's your chance. It may never come your way again."

318

Looking back at the airport employee, Hans remained speechless for a few seconds before silently waving the airport employee away. Turning to his German friends, Hans told them,

"No. I can't abandon Grandmother. But man, was that tempting! The only reason that I came to Moscow was to find a way out. But my way to Canada is with Grandmother. Only with Grandmother."

Hans declined the opportunity to go to Sweden, and instead, bid farewell to his German co-workers before heading over on a city bus towards the Canadian Embassy in order to enquire about obtaining a Canadian visa. Stepping off at the Sivtsev Vrazhek bus stop, Hans' boots touched down into puddle that slowly evaporated under the spring sun. After fives minutes of circling the block, Hans noticed a white and red flag with a maple leaf in the middle gentling blowing through in the wind. Hans was a street crossing away from the Canadian Embassy! As he eagerly marched across the empty street, Hans wondered to himself, *"Is this truly my ticket to Canada? To my family?"* As he hesitantly approached the Art Nouveau-looking yellow-stoned Canadian Embassy building with white trim around the windows, a building surrounded by thin street metal barriers along with a chain-link fence, a sense of nervousness consumed Hans.

"But do I really want to go live with a family who are like complete strangers? And do they really want to see me, or are they just being friendly because they know perfectly well that there's no way I'll escape the USSR? Or is there?"

Approaching the KGB manned black 8-foot high gate, Hans pulled out his passport and handed it to the stern-looking guard in his 30's with deep-set eyes in a bomber jacket. As the guard flipped through the pages, Hans suddenly felt a hand aggressively grasp his shoulder. When he turned around, Hans saw a few more Russian officials dressed in black jackets and hats converge upon him. As Hans thought to himself, *"Oh boy, what have I done. This was definitely not a good idea,"* the Russian officers asked Hans to follow them. They took Hans into custody before he even had a chance to step onto "Canadian soil". They placed Hans into a yellow Soviet police van where they all silently sat nearly 10 minutes until the van stopped in front of a majestic, mainly orange-façade, with a grey-stoned first floor 5-story building. Hans was being dropped off at the dreaded central KGB headquarters in Lubyanka Square, located less than a kilometre from the Kremlin, and even closer to Red Square.

The driver then opened the back door of the van. The two officers who apprehended Hans at the Canadian Embassy clutched Hans' arms and marched him inside the building and down a set of stairs. From a festive coffee and farewell with his German co-workers earlier, Hans found himself in the hands of KGB being treated like a criminal. In a state of fear, Hans' thoughts turned negative. He began to wonder if he could be sent to a Gulag or even worse. Hans had seen what happened to family members for seemingly even less severe "offences".

Before Hans knew it, he found himself sitting in a cold basement room on a grey metal chair, a chair as grey as the cold stone base of the building that he sat in. Eventually, a short man in his 30's with a stern face and dainty hands entered the room with a cigarette in his right hand. As his eyes spoke of power and fury, he demanded to know,

"Why were you rummaging around the Canadian Embassy!! Who do you think you are and what sort of activities are you partaking in?!?!"

Hans pleaded back, *"I just want to be re-united with my parents!"*

After further interrogation at the KGB headquarters, the man instructed Hans,

"Go directly back to Novosibirsk! You have no business at the Canadian Embassy! And you never will German-boy! Go home or we'll throw you in jail!"

As Hans was chauffeured back to his hotel by the police, Hans wondered to himself,

"Is this really all worth it?"

CHAPTER 45

Research Lab

Months later, Hans found himself on a local job assignment in Novosibirsk for the electrical company, which entailed installing high voltage cables at the Novosibirsk Science Research Institute of Energy. Surprisingly, almost miraculously, an opportunity to switch jobs came about for Hans on this assignment when a lab manager at the research institute, after seeing Hans in action, approached him.

"Would you like to come work directly for the institute?"

Hans became ecstatic over the wonderful job offer.

"Sure!! I'll first just have to give my two-weeks notice. Hopefully there shouldn't be any issues."

However, when Hans went into his manager's office and handed him his resignation letter, the manager laughed right in Hans' face while tearing the paper to pieces! The man is his 50's, with sagging cheeks and drooping eyelids as a result of an unhealthy diet of vodka, cigarettes, and sausage, went on to formally inform Hans in a very informal manner,

"You're not going anywhere! The electrical company needs you on this project! Now get out of my face boy!"

The next day, when Hans returned to the research institute and regrettably told the lab manager, *"My boss at the electrical company isn't permitting me to leave my current position."*, the lab manager unexpectedly wasn't concerned one bit. He instructed Hans,

"Go back and pick up your record of work booklet. It shows how long you were at your jobs; what your duties were; and when and why you quit. Just do that. Okay."

Back then in the USSR, every worker's career had to be documented and logged inside of such a book. The position that Hans was offered at the Science Research Institute of Energy would have been a lab job in which Hans would perform experiments relating to the transference of electricity over long distances. Such tasks excited Hans greatly, especially because he would work inside, and be shielded from the brutal Siberian weather; he also always desired to study electrical engineering, which would have been the icing on the opportunity. This position offered Hans the perfect chance to fulfill his aspirations, while capturing his curiosity. Hence, when Hans' resignation was rejected, he felt absolutely crushed.

"There goes all my dreams once again! I'm gonna be stuck working these rubbishy jobs for the rest of my bloody and wretched life! Life is pathetic, especially with these Russian bastards!"

After having his move to not only Canada, but also this new position blocked, Hans' animosity towards Russians only heightened, especially because Hans considered obtaining this position at the research institution to truly be a dream come true. Not only were the responsibilities of this job exciting, but also away from heat, cold, rain, snow, animals, insects… and not to mention, death-defying 25-foot drops onto concrete. Hans would even be able to wear a suit in this position, which made him feel dignified. Hans occasionally had a taste for vanity, and flaunting his superficial appearance, perhaps in an attempt to fill the void from being parentless and regularly degraded.

The Science Research Institute of Energy was affiliated with the local research university, so Hans' rejuvenating aspirations of attending university could have finally come to fruition. Though, after the rejection, Hans felt drained of all energy and hope, leaving him feeling completely humiliated and helpless; yet, he couldn't express his sediments, in fear of reprisals. Hans could've been sent to a Gulag for dissent, if he were to convey any qualms over his boss' decision. Hans felt like he'd be doomed and gloomed for the rest of his life after encountering such a blow and dead-end state once again.

For many years, it was law in Russia that you could never leave a job unless you were moving to a different city. However, the rule recently changed, prior to Hans' resignation request. The law only stated that you had to give two weeks notice prior to obtaining full clearance to transfer to a new position. Nevertheless, the electrical company stood firm on their stance. They were convinced, or least enforced the impression upon Hans that they still had the right to deny Hans permission to leave his current position, leaving Hans in ruins.

Well, at least for only a day, because as it just so happened, when Hans nervously approached his boss again the following morning regarding the Worker's Log, his current manager's attitude completely changed. Hans' boss, a tall imposing man with short brown hair, was not his typical arrogant self. He, oddly enough, came across as nervous and actually greeted Hans quite politely, addressing him as "Mr. Friesen". With a childish grin on his face, he went on to explain,

"The authorities at the research lab called to inform us that we must give you, Mr. Friesen, permission to leave your current duties in order for you to pursue your desired endeavour."

His boss then handed Hans a document with traces of sweat on the paper.

"Here are your transfer request clearance papers. I wish you all the best in the future Mr. Friesen. Thanks for all your great contributions! We've been through quite a bit together!"

He then gave Hans a big hug. The following morning was Hans' first day at the Science Research Institute of Energy as a lab worker. Hans was on cloud 9! To make matters even better, the team of engineers and technicians there were extremely welcoming and warm. Most of Hans' new coworkers were taking night courses at the university located across the river, which Hans also eventually enrolled in years later.

During Hans' first week on the job, he was required to head to the passport office in order to renew his 6-month passport, just like always. When Hans entered the office, he was unpleasantly greeted by a bitter looking war veteran in his 50's who was missing a leg. Hans apprehensively, yet confidently approached the man at the passport bureau's counter.

"Hello sir, I'd like to renew my passport please. It's going to expire soon."

The snarly, battle-hardened ex-soldier stared down at Hans' passport, and then looked up at Hans with a perturbed and condescending glance.

"This is a 6-month passport!! So, you're a brigand and felonious!! What kind of criminal are you, you derelict and vagrant?!?! Are you a German spy?!? You belong in jail, you German swine! Where did you serve your time??" Which crime did you commit?!? I'm gonna send you to jail, you filth!!"

Hans thought to himself,

"Man, did this guy wake up on the wrong side of the hay! All of this over a 6-month passport!"

But deep down, Hans was utterly petrified. Responding in his usual brash manner, Hans timidly, yet proudly responded to the man,

"I'm yet to commit a crime to this day, sir. Unless breathing is a felony. I've been using this passport for years. It's never been an issue."

The 50 + year old, disabled war veteran retorted viciously!

"This time is your last, you German pig!! Get out and never come back!! Go back to jail where you belong!"

Hans returned to work the next day and told his boss what transpired at the passport office. Hans' boss responded, *"I'll take care of it! Just go back again tomorrow."*

Hans returned to the passport office the following day. Upon nervously creeping into the old and rickety wooden building, though filled with a fresh scent, Hans looked directly at the debilitated and mentally anguished war veteran behind the counter, whose placated and pacified demeanour gave the impression that he'd just been castrated and experienced a lobotomy all in one. Hans noticed that he was strikingly different this time around. The man had a child-like exuberance about him, which even made him appear even a bit youthful. As Hans approached him, the war veteran's puppy-dog eyes gazed into Hans' as he affirmatively, yet empathetically expressed to Hans, at times in a playful manner, as if he were able to express his true personality that he had concealed for decades.

"Please come into my office Mr. Friesen. Please, please pull up a chair sir, you handsome devil. I'm sorry Mr. Friesen. There was a misunderstanding yesterday. I realize that you are a law-abiding citizen, and not a filthy and disgusting vagrant like lots of us. Here's a 5-year passport lad, you well-behaved man. Please accept my apology and say hello to your Grandmother for me."

Walking out with a massive grin from shoulder to shoulder, Hans was now able to travel to Alma Alta, Kazakhstan for two weeks for a research project. When Hans returned from Alma Alta, his duties at the research lab in Novosibirsk entailed experimenting with transformers and generators, while the engineers worked on the calculations. The lab tech performed the experiments. The real results were compared to engineers' hypothetical or anticipated outcomes, before Hans postulated the findings. The generators that Hans serviced and operated were situated in the basement of the building, whereas the transformer room was on the ground floor. Across the hall, there were instrument panels where experiments were monitored. Results were calculated within a large computer room situated on the second floor. Each experiment was carried out at least three times. The results were ultimately extrapolated and then once again hypothesized. The efficiency of the hydro generator and transformer were analyzed even further at the manufacturing facility, which was located across the river next to the university.

The science institute also had a hydro dam that was built along the river at its disposal. Engineers were responsible for measuring the efficiency of the generators and transformers relating to the dam. At the research institution, these results were applied in the designing, creating, and subsequently testing of models, tasks that Hans happily carried out. He was fascinated and challenged by his new work environment, though he felt as if he were playing with toys, in comparison to what he was accustomed to when he operated actual, real life-size equipment during his years in the field on outdoor assignments with the electrical company.

Not only did Hans' professional life completely change after taking the job at the research institute, but his social life also metamorphized. The university across the river was equipped with erosion monitoring stations and boats that the employees were allowed to use for recreational purposes, so Hans joined his coworkers in row boat excursions, travelling between monitoring stations and nearby islands where they all swam, snorkelled, fished, and camped together over an open fire. In the winter, they utilized these amenities in order to go ice fishing. But Hans' fun only begun. Attending birthday parties, New Year's Eve bashes, and outdoor events, such as skiing excursions, became a regular occurrence.

Yet, Hans realized that he still required to maintain a watchful eye. Continuously applying to leave the USSR placed him on the KGB radar, something he clearly learned during a company excursion organized through the Science Research Institute of Energy. Hans was so excited about going on this cross-country skiing trip with his co-workers that he could barely sleep the night before. The following brisk and sunny morning, the entire group arrived by train to the wooded countryside. Stepping off the train while locked in playful banter, a light wind swept across the face of Hans, who remained absolutely enthralled about going skiing; however, everyone was not necessarily totally thrilled to see Hans. With each application to leave the USSR, Hans sensed that he made a few more enemies each time, especially amongst the KGB circle whose tentacles had even infiltrated research institute. The KGB liked to stage "accidents" and "violations" whenever they dealt with possible traitors. After exiting the train station, the group of research institute employees passed through a resort for Communist Party members, territory that could be deemed as a "restricted area" by the authorities if need be. As the group, amongst hoards upon hordes of other groups from other companies and institutions slowly strolled by the Communist resort on their cross-country skis, "a member" from the research institution group inconspicuously stormed ahead of everyone in the direction of a Communist resort guard holding a shotgun. As the suspected KGB informant, whose face was concealed by a balaclava, stood next to the gunman, he instantly gestured in Hans' direction while tugging at his own coat. The armed guard, in a black toque and ankle length black winter coat, suddenly bolted in Hans' direction! Members from Hans' group saw this and immediately hollered,

"Run, Vana (Hans), Run!"

Clutching his poles, Hans skied away in his blue coat like never before! Amongst the throng of skiers, the security guard couldn't get Hans completely in his sights in his on-foot pursuit of Hans. Amongst the may-lay, numerous research institute employees desperately attempted to purposely impede the guard by getting in his way and blocking his path, acts that afforded Hans the chance to speed away and escape the "restricted area". The entire research institute group eventually caught up to the frenzied Hans in the woods where, despite the dampened mood, they all skied along the hillside for the day. On their way back, Hans swapped jackets with guy in a yellow coat from the research institution, and took a solo detour through the high snow, thereby completely bypassing and circumventing the Communist resort on his way back to the train station. The entire incident left Hans puzzled with regard to what truly spurred on the unpleasant episode, yet his life went on as usual for the time being.

The Science Research Institute of Energy also had their own volunteer, travelling performing group that visited desolate northern Siberian villages. Hans was up for anything and everything, especially after the latest KGB incident, so he happily joined – getting him out of Novosibirsk for a while was an ancillary benefit. The 10-person travelling performing group consisted of an accordion player, a ballet dancer, singer, and group of background singers that Hans happily belted out cords with. Over the years, Hans became a ski instructor, so he was made responsible for taking care of the ski equipment when they took their show on the road.

So, on a brisk and blustery January morning, the performing group flew into northern Siberia on a green, one engine swaying plane that glided along in the air so low that Hans could actually clearly see moose and wolves roaming throughout the woods below. After landing within the frozen snow-covered fields a few hours after take-off on the absolutely frigid winter "afternoon" that was black as night when they landed, the group gathered up all of their belongings and ski gear before cross-country skiing a kilometre to an adjoining village. The volunteer performing group hoped to thoroughly entertain the people who lived in the isolated oil-drilling villages based in northern Siberia that were only reachable by a bush plane mounted with skis for landing. Situated in the middle of swamp land that was completely frozen solid over during the winter, this region of Siberia was unreachable by any roads. When the land was completely iced-over throughout the colder months, bulldozers could transfer in drilling rigs in order to test for oil. In the spring, however, the ground thawed, forcing workers to move equipment to a higher elevation after the land became flooded.

Suffice to say, the lonely locals indigenous to this reclusive region openly welcomed their visitors from the research institute into their homes, providing them with room and board during the duration of the group's stay. In the evenings, the town's people were rewarded when they gathered inside of old multi-purpose halls, where they savoured two-hour performances that included singing, dancing, theatrical plays, and musical recitals with instruments such as an accordion and a balalaika, a triangular Russian, stringed instrument that resembles a guitar. Hans sang, and acted in the plays during these lively exhibitions. The local villagers deeply appreciated the performances, and usually became quite energetic during the shows. The elated spectators clapped for and cheered on the performers who brightened up their lives, at least for a night within their barren towns of darkness during the six-month northern Siberian winter.

The following mornings, the people in the village usually and graciously prepared the performers breakfast before the group moved on to the next village on skis. Most of the villages were separated by about 10 km, with some being further away than others. In one village, Hans attempted to display his toughness and idiocy by going outdoors to a well in -35-degree Celsius weather, where he took off his shirt in order to "wash up for dinner." One of his buddies, however, stole the show by dumping a bucket of freezing cold water over Hans' head from behind, right before Hans was able to reach the well. After the wet and chilling experience, Hans figured that he was "washed-up for dinner," so instead of dipping his torso into a barrel of bone-chilling water, he happily dried himself off by a warm fire. His original aim was to show the villagers that the city folk were just as tough, though perhaps a bit more backwards than the back-wood village dwellers and yokels. News of Hans' daring "feat", though somewhat thwarted by his friend's interjection, spread quickly throughout the neighbouring villages. They eventually humorously started asking Hans, *"Are you okay? Did you stave off illness after the attack?"*

Days later, the weather became even more inconceivable frigid, bitter, and windy. That morning, the locals sympathetically, and as a token of their appreciation, offered the group a ride to the next village in an old, blue Lada pick-up truck. Much obliged, the research institute group happily loaded themselves up into the truck, some taking their place in the open-aired back of the vehicle. Driving smoothly along, the group was making good time on that blistery and blizzardy morning until the truck suddenly got stuck in a snow drift! Revving the gas, the grooves below the tires dug deeper into the snow with each passing thrust against the gas pedal. Jumping out from the cab, a couple of the performers heaved the truck from behind, but the vehicle just wouldn't budge as snow soared through the air. Hans remained sitting still, along with others in the open back of the truck, in hope that the truck would regain its way. Minutes later, in an attempt to assist, Hans finally tried to stand up, but his limbs fell lifeless. Despite his further efforts, he could barely move. After stagnantly sitting for over 15 minutes in the back of the truck, it felt as if his blood flow had completely come to a halt. Hans instantaneously sensed memories of being frozen stuck in that train wagon along the journey from Copenhagen to Jug from 20 years earlier. Sensations suddenly drifted through his veins while he subconsciously suppressed past pain. Seemingly unthawed through his thoughts, Hans' blood circulation streamed enough through his veins to raise his legs and torso in order to gingerly exit the truck while the driver tracked back on foot to get a bulldozer to free the truck from the snow trench. In the meantime, the performance group high-tailed it on skis in the direction of the next village.

Hans regarded the truck becoming stuck in the snow as a blessing in disguise. He's certain that if the group of people in the back of the open flatbed truck remained there motionless for any longer, they would've eventually acquired frostbite and succumbed to the conditions. Their low blood flow, as a result of sitting motionless in blistering cold conditions could've spelled the end for them. As they skied onwards, their body temperature increased with each stride and swing of the pole. Ultimately, a bulldozer arrived in order to haul the truck out of the snow bank before the man drove the truck back to his village.

The group spent the last night of their 10-day voyage of performing and travelling with a family that actually brought their cow and her calf right into the house, where they all sleep in a one room wooden hut together. As Hans peered around that one-room house that evening, memories and sensations from the communal house in Jug flooded through him as if he were skimming through his own personal Akashic records. Filled with an overpowering sense of awareness, Hans instantly wondered about his parents, and the parents of the two boys who drowned almost twenty years ago. Rearing back into the past, Hans questioned just why God lets humans became so devastated with such hardships. People like him, people like Grandmother. Hans' eyes then instantaneously opened. Morning came for Hans on another day as another dream came and went, while his relatively speaking dream-life continued.

The group's fulfilling adventure had come to an end, even though the memories remained in the hearts of the locals, not to mention Hans' for a time to come. The villagers were as appreciative as they were warm-hearted and hospitable, something that definitely made the group's experience just that much more gratifying. When they arrived back at the research institute the next day in Novosibirsk, they felt not only at home, but also tighter than ever as chums after their adventures.

Hans felt bonded to his coworkers like never before, yet a reunion with his parents remained on his mind – with the intent of either embracing or scorning his parents – only Hans knew. Hans insatiably chased a ghost that constantly touched him while he diverted away from his thoughts while working away and enjoying life at the research institute where the workers were provided with a gym, tennis rackets, ping pong tables, chess boards, skis, and sleeping bags for excursions. During lunch, they all played chess or partook in a game of ping pong. Hans even volunteered to take care of the equipment and organize events. Utterly enthusiastic with the task at hand, Hans posted advertisements on the department bulletin boards in order to engage others to sign up for activities in an attempt to entice many more to get involved. Comradery in the department soared.

When the next winter came, the group wished to organize sometime special over the holidays, so they looked into renting a winter dacha in the woods. Therefore, one weekend, about a month or so before Christmas and New Years, Hans and a few co-workers scouted out cottages in a rural, wooded area, 30 Km north of Novosibirsk, where they could savour the holiday and snowy landscape. Cross-country skiing amongst the birch trees, rugged hills, and pristine white powder that glowed like heaven when the bright light shone down from high above made this area a magical wintertime paradise. As Hans and a few buddies meandered through the gorgeous snow-covered woods in search of accommodations, they suddenly stumbled across a cottage and the watchman in charge of overlooking the dachas in the area. Hans eagerly approached the overweight maintenance man in his 40's.

"Hello! We're looking to rent a cottage? How about this one? Could we rent this hut over the holidays?"

The man apprehensively, but friendlily, yet firmly replied,

"No, no! Your type is usually too rowdy and causes damages. But do you want to share a little vodka with me? I'm not in the mood to drink alone."

The man led Hans and his friends into the kitchen of the hut and grabbed a few small juice glasses from a rickety wooden cupboard. Suckling on vodka together, the man soberly mentioned,

"My still is broken. It broke down. The pipe broke. It really ticks me off! I love making my own vodka! It's cheaper and tastes much better!"

Hans, in his typical confident and brash manner told the man,

"We can fix it! I'll bring ya a new pipe and install it! I can get that thing working again. No problem for me whatsoever!"

With a weary skeptical grin across his face, the maintenance man let Hans know,

"If this could be done, I could reconsider you guys renting the place. People like me are happier and more accepting when we're drunk."

So, Hans and a friend came by the following weekend with their tools and some parts, and after a little toil, they ultimately fixed the "maintenance" man's liquor still. Seeing it functioning again after many "dry" days, sent the cottage maintenance man into heaven!

"You guys can use the cottage for the weekend! You're amazing! As far as I'm concerned, you can have the dacha! You saved my life! Life without drinking, is living without a life!! You guys are god-sent! Hallelujah!"

In all of their glory, Hans asked the man with the cabin, *"How much for the entire holiday week?"*

The plump man in undersized clothing with a childish grin responded,

"You made my still work again. You don't owe me a cent. I will be indebted to you for the rest of my life! Even an eternity! I'm born again!"

Hans became ecstatically filled with glee because the cabin was absolutely perfect! It was 2 km from the train station, and there was plenty of dead and dry wood in the surrounding forest for burning a glowing fire. Amongst the wilderness was a manmade lake. Numerous cottages, usually for government diplomats were in the vicinity. Inside of the cabin, there was a wood stove, which in essence, was nothing more than a steal drum with a smoke hood for ventilation; but nonetheless, the cabin made for a great cross-country skiing holiday get-a-way retreat. Gorgeous scenery. Trails and hills for skiing. Good company. What more could one ask for.

After impatiently waiting in exhilarating anticipation, the Christmas week finally arrived. A group of about ten met at the Novosibirsk Main Train Station on a chilly Friday morning and hopped onto a regional train that chugged into the woods. One member of the group, though, was overly friendly and amicable. Almost suspiciously. He was in his mid-30's, with a chiselled jaw, deep-set eyes, and cropped black hair. His name was Victor, and he desired to be the congenial life of the party, yet in a seemingly very artificially and contrived façade-like manner. After reaching the cottage, before even giving anyone time to settle in, Victor hollered out,

"Let's hit the trails! I'm pumped! There's apparently a gorgeous stretch that leads to a manmade lake. From there we can check out the tourist and diplomats' boats! Who's gonna join me! Let's go Ivan! Are you in? Of course you are, you adventure-adrenaline junkie!!"

His energy was contagious and endearing, even though many from the research institute believed that Victor was definitely a "snitch," or rather, an undercover KGB informant. Five from the group of ten grabbed their skis and before they knew it, they were storming down an untouched white path in the direction of the harbour. As they neared the boats nestled around a tiny wharf that appeared in the distance, their ring-leader, the suspected KGB agent Victor, was speedily gliding, opening up

John Friesen

a 100-metre gap between him and the pack. He was the first to reach the lake. When the others closed in on the anchored boats, they saw Victor in a deep discussion with a drastically overweight boat watchman who was in his 40's, wearing a blue winter parka that barely fit him. The watchman was standing on the deck of a cruise boat for excursions that was frozen right into the lake. Victor and the watchman were chatting and deviously glaring right in Hans' direction. Hans immediately thought to himself,

"Don't go near that boat!! That is a "restricted area". That guy must be KGB! Something is definitely up."

It was still daytime. Gleaming rays of sunlight reflected back off the white and crisp winter blanket. But luckily enough, the light shone back right in the watchman's eyes, partially blinding him, but not Hans, making it easier for him to spot the obese watchman suddenly pull out a shotgun from behind the boat's wooden railing! Feverously waddling off the boat like walrus trapped in an obese penguin's frame, the watchman stormed in Hans' direction! Like a flash of lightning, Hans bolted away on his skis! The gunman, on foot stepped into a foot of snow and pursued Hans, but he couldn't get Hans in his sights, especially with the sun directly in his eyes. After a minute of attempting to chase Hans down through the high snow amongst the Siberian forest, the gunman became too exhausted to hold his weapon, let alone fire his shotgun with an ounce of accuracy. The jumbo-sized guard then capsized into the untouched snow like a sinking battleship, completely out of breath.

Stepping onto government property could've been deemed to be a serious offence in the USSR, and that was allegedly Hans' crime and the guard's justification for chasing him off and seeking to blow his head off. One never knew if the KGB's henchmen truly desired to eliminate their targets, or if they merely wished to scare the living hell out of him to keep him on edge. But either way, Hans didn't want to find out while he sped away through the woods on his cross-country skis, swiftly making his way back to the cabin. He was fully aware that KGB agents and their goons or informants didn't need a legitimate reason to pursue a potential dissident, or anyone for that matter. The KGB savoured having power over others, and if they were afforded a carte blanche to inflict damages, then even better.

Back at the hut hours later, Hans asked the alleged KGB informant, Victor,

"What the hell was that? What was with that guy?"

Victor casually responded, *"It's his job to keep people away from the boat."*

Hans countered, *"But you were standing next to the boat right beside him! Tell me that much then will ya!?!"*

Victor didn't say a word back......

CHAPTER 46

Summer Fun

When summer arrived, the group went for weekend camping and fishing trips on research institute grounds and facilities equipped with row boats that they used to reach many of the beautiful sandy islands along a water reservoir connected to the dammed off Novosibirsk Voda Hramlishe river. The breeze and winds gusted through the intertwined islands carrying away the unpleasant and unbearable Siberian insects. Siberia was a breeding ground for black flies and mosquitos, especially within the forests where they congregated and literally hovered like looming black clouds. People were unable to enter these forests in the heart of summer without a mosquito net covering their faces. Flesh-biting flies and vicious mosquitos were merciless, and occasionally horrendously deadly. So, lucky enough, Hans and his friends were spared from insect infestation during these excursions, letting them have their fun, and occasionally even revenge by catching ¾ of a golf ball sized horseflies in their hands, before sticking a stick of hay right into the horseflies' butts. The extra weight severely restricted the horseflies' ability to fly, eventually leading to their death.

In the usually calm and tranquil evenings, the group happily sat by the camp fire and sang folk songs in peace deep into the dark night. Hans loved his job and responsibilities at the research institute just as much as having the opportunity to take part in these excursions and social events. Hans felt like a part of the greatest social network in Russia; he felt fully complete, at least for the time being. Intermingling with the group contributed substantially in all areas of his life, helping him to forget about not only the family that he strangely enough still so desired to re-unite with in Canada, but also his uncle's family that he, at times, had a strenuous relationship with in Novosibirsk. And even though Hans was perhaps temporarily evading suppressed and buried pain, he paradoxically, finally felt fulfilled and complete. Seemingly for the first time in his life, Hans didn't feel like a member of the outcast. Everything was going his way, as if all of the pieces had finally fallen into place in his broken life. Words just couldn't express how he felt. His research and contributions at work were valued by this very close-knit group who enjoyed each others' company while holding each other in high regard. Hans' life seemed more like a fairy tale than reality. For short glimpses of time, he even wondered about just what value re-uniting with his family would bring – perhaps not any value at all besides the upheaval of a distressing and damaging truth. But little did Hans know that destiny was pushing for the family reunion. Moreover, the idea was already embedded, an idea or rather fallacy of belonging to a normal functioning family subconsciously loomed large within Hans.

CHAPTER 47

Infection

The old lab, within the deteriorating current research building became too small so the employees started moving the lab equipment from the current building to the newly constructed Science Research Institute of Energy building across the way. Equipment and panels were being set up with relay switches; and wires and cables were being ran into the control room on the first floor of the new building. All employees assisted in the move. As Hans entered and looked around the basement room in which he grabbed some equipment from, he bore witness to a creepy, dungeon-like cellar that was accompanied by a musty odour. The room left Hans with shivers going down his spine. But those shivers immediately turned into a sharp pain in his elbow after he picked up a transmitter and accidently scraped himself on a piece of shelving. Hans' elbow stung for a bit, but he didn't think much of it since the scratch was so minor.

Yet, by the very next morning, Hans thought otherwise when he saw that his elbow had completely swollen up, despite the fact that he only picked up a tiny cut that barely bled under his long sleeve shirt the prior afternoon. The swelling though, increased substantially throughout the day. But Hans, nevertheless, still attempted ski on the weekend. However, the fun didn't last for long. His arm became heavy and gradually turned blue with each passing swipe of the pole. By the time Monday morning came along, the swelling had doubled in size. Hans had no other choice but to go into

John Friesen

the medical clinic at the research complex. Hans approached the attractive doctor with a slender frame in her 30's.

"Something happened during the move on Friday. Something is not quite right with my right elbow. Please take a look. See! Am I right?"

After further examining Hans' elbow, the stunning doctor with long and straight blond hair with a slight wave informed Hans,

"You have to go to the hospital immediately! Your elbow must be operated on! Why didn't you come to us immediately on Friday?!?!"

In typical Hans fashion, he didn't think much of it and wasn't overly concerned. He assumed that the healing was going to be as quick and "easy" as it was for him when he first acquired blood poisoning years earlier, so he couldn't comprehend just why she showed such concern. Heeding the doctor's directive, Hans headed over to the hospital. Upon arrival, the doctors meticulously inspected his elbow. Each touch and word spoken made Hans nervous. He didn't want anything to be wrong with him, which ironically enough led his occasional thought to turn to the worst. After running a few tests, a male doctor in his forties with longer black hair combed to the side and sideburns demanded to know,

"How did this happen?!?! Where were you?!? This is not good at all!! Not good whatsoever!! Are you a grave digger of some sort?? We'll have to operate on you tomorrow!! This is grave!"

Despite the doctor's dire pessimism, Grandmother's voice kept running through Hans' head.

"Nothing will happen to know. You'll be fine."

Grandmother had experienced every atrocious outcome possible, but she somehow only knew how to foresee positive conclusions. Nevertheless, the doctors were determined to figure out just where Hans could've possibly come into contact with such a deadly bacterium. They became extremely concerned. The medical team didn't want anybody else to become infected. Upon further investigation, it came to the light of day that the old equipment was stored in a building that had been converted into a temporary morgue during the WWII. Not only old research equipment, but also people with deadly gangrene were once thrown into this basement room. The bacteria evidently had survived for over 20 years!

Hans was quickly prepped for surgery the very next morning. During this time in Russia, ether was heavily used as the anaesthetic of choice. In applying the drug, the doctor doused a ball of cotton in ether till it vaporized. He then covered Hans' nose and mouth with the ether-draped cotton until the substance became inhaled, knocking Hans right out. Hans found this experience absolutely atrocious. Whenever he still thinks of it, his skin jitters. He can still taste the ether. His body completely rejected the pungent odour that was released by the substance. The anesthetic eventually knocked Hans out, but evidently not for long enough. Right in the middle of the procedure Hans groggily re-awakened, vaguely hearing,

"He's awake!! Knock him out again!! Get the ether!!"

Another dosage of the absolutely repulsively tasting drug had to be administered. When Hans woke up a bit later, he felt relieved as the pain was finally gone, which according to him, meant that the operation must have gone quite well. Opening his eyes, Hans looked around, noticing that not only was he in a room with twenty other patients, but also that his vision was quite blurry. He could barely make out a face hovering over him, which resembled his doctor from the clinic, the woman in her mid 30's with long blond hair and gorgeous blue eyes. Her disposition was extremely empathetic, something that was all too well depicted in her pleasant, angelic demeanor and attractive face. It was as if the beauty of her soul perfectly portrayed her stunning appearance. Even though Hans' mouth desired to water in her presence, his mouth was extremely dry after the ether applications, so the doctor wetted his lips with a cotton swab. She made sure to keep Hans' head raised so he couldn't possibly swallow his tongue. Moistening his lips was normally the nurses' duty; however, there were too many patients to tend and mend to, making it impossible for the nurses to take care of each and every patient's need. The clinic doctor showed true devotion to Hans and went well beyond her call of duty. She seemingly took it upon herself to make sure that Hans was provided with the best care possible.

Following the surgery, Hans was fed intravenously. He still felt extremely ill and had absolutely no interest in eating. The ether dosage was too high and excessive for his body. Hans was hooked up to an IV for 13 days. That liquid "formula" was his only source of nutrition during this time, a period in which he lost a considers amount of weight. The doctor eventually informed Hans,

"You're very fortunate that your immune system is working so well at controlling the infection! It's been contained to the arm, so it hasn't spread to any other part of the body. That's a great sign!"

Hans felt emotionally comforted by that message, yet nevertheless, still physically deteriorated. The medical team was trying different medications and concoctions, but nothing was helping Hans to fully recover. He gradually became gravely ill and completely exhausted from fighting. The doctors were losing complete hope of a recovery of any kind. However, one of the doctors still had an ounce of faith.

"Ask a friend to bring you a bottle of cognac! It might bring back your appetite! You look like a skeleton!"

A day later, Hans' friend from work, Kir, appeared with a nice-looking, colourful bottle of cognac (double the price of a standard bottle of vodka) and a shot glass. Kir pulled up a chair right next to Hans' bed. Too weak and listless to say much, Hans was relegated to only gracefully listening. Kir eventually pushed his chair up even closer to Hans' bed, ready to tell a story.

"I spoke with my aunt and she told me that during the 2nd World War, she had an illness and was operated on. She couldn't be saved and was declared dead. Since she was dead, they tossed her corpse amongst gangrene victims into a converted morgue within the same cellar where you scraped your arm and picked up your illness. She was dead, or at least according to scientific facts.

So, they chucked her body on top of a pile of dead people who were no more. Everyone thought that she was dead, but it didn't matter what the doctors believed, since all what mattered was what my aunt thought and felt when she suddenly awakened within the morgue, just to find herself lying on top of a mound of cold and naked dead bodies in the blackest of darkness where she could sense death all around her.

She didn't know what to think as she felt decay and perdition upon her skin. As a disgustingly cold sensation flowed through her, she finally realized that she had been left for dead inside of a morgue. Instantly, a bellowed yelp of terror ricocheted throughout the morgue for no one to hear as her shriek fell on deaf ears. Her hollers where done in vain. Nobody came to rescue her. Or perhaps they simply didn't hear her. Well, at the very least, until the paramedics coincidently entered the morgue in order to dispose of some more "dead" bodies. As they opened the door and entered the morgue to dump more corpses onto the pile, there was my aunt crawling around like a crab."

Kir then started howling with laughter before continuing.

"The morgue workers were so terrified that they simply dropped the bodies that they were dumping onto the pile and stormed out of the morgue like a bunch of chickens who had never seem an alive body before! Or maybe they just weren't that friendly. But since they seemingly had an anathema when it came to assisting my poor, innocent aunt, she simply exited through the open door with her own strength and headed to her home about a block away where she made herself dinner. Those guys didn't even bother re-closing the door! Evidently, the doctors thought that she died during the surgery. They were certain that she kicked the bucket. They declared her dead. But she had another idea."

Before Kir departed in kicks and giggles, he left the bottle of cognac behind and went home for the day. Hans then waited for mealtime to arrive. When the nurse strolled by with metal platters on her cart, Hans blurted out in a raspy and course voice with a grin on his face,

"I'm in for dinner this evening! Dinner for one please!"

Still in shock, the nurse handed Hans the meal tray and said.

John Friesen

"Bon Appetite!"

Hans poured himself a 50-ml glass of the cognac before downing the shot. He swore that he had just swallowed a fireball! A burning sensation engulfed his throat before roaring downwards into his stomach. A few moments later, Hans' appetite miraculously re-emerged! He felt a visceral physical feeling that he hadn't sensed for some time. Hope began to flow through his veins for the first time in a long while, but since he was sharing a hospital room with a bunch of alcoholics, he had to protect his "bottle of hope" under his pillow.

In Russia, there was a massive black market for vodka and other alcohol at the time. A customer knocked on a door of a "known house" and placed money in a slot. A bottle then came out through the slot in return. No person was ever seen. But Hans' roommates were in no condition to head to a "known house" – they could barely reach the washroom on their own, let alone venture out into the city. Besides, Hans' roommates preferred vodka over cognac. Nevertheless, if Hans expected to enjoy a meal ever again, he had to protect that bottle of cognac with his life, since his roommates knew no boundary when it came to getting their hands on some booze. Within the room, all of beds lied along side a wall, except for Hans'. His bed was front and centre, right in the middle of the room for all to see. His fellow roommates could easily catch a tempting glimpse of each and every one of his swigs. Hans downed shots before every meal that he absolutely savoured. When the doctor finally came back to check up on him, she told Hans,

"Alcohol is always a last resort. It might cure you or kill you. You are one of the lucky ones. Though, there was one case that still amazes me. A teenage boy came in one day with a massive lump on his elbow. The kid was frightened out of his wits so his parents brought him a bottle of vodka to calm him down. He drank the entire bottle and was completely knocked out! The next morning, we went to operate on his elbow, but we couldn't find the lump anywhere! It was mindboggling!"

Before leaving the room, the doctor added,

"You stayed calf and collected through this entire ordeal so the infection did not spread throughout the rest of your body. And you had great support from your work colleagues. Them coming to visit you on a daily basis definitely helped you remain positive and hopeful, which kept your spirits high. You concentrated on healing and the body did the rest."

Hans' co-workers from the research institute collected money in order to buy Hans cookies, sausages, and fruits, including lemons and oranges, which were quite exotic to Russia at the time. Hans had such immense cravings for sour foods that he actually ate entire lemons without peeling away their skins. His "spectators" laughed hysterically at such a sight. They simply couldn't believe that someone could humanly eat the skin off of a lemon. But Hans' coworkers weren't the only ones providing Hans with a helping hand. Hans' superiors somehow arranged for Hans to obtain a special medication that wasn't available through the hospital. Everybody at the research institute was quite concerned about Hans, so they were willing to do whatever it took to see him through to a successful recovery.

Hans was extremely fortunate to be surrounded by such caring people, especially his superiors, some of whom were members of the Communist Party. Official party members had access to resources that were usually unattainable by an "ordinary" citizen like Hans. Influential connections at work enabled Hans to acquire preferential treatment and inaccessible, exotic, and special medications and tinctures. These specific medications were under lock and key, only intended to be consumed by one person - Hans - and nobody else. The nurses joked,

"Oh, so you're the one with connections and special privileges. We have never seen these medications ever before. They must come from abroad."

Hans, though, had to bathe in a simple cast iron bathtub, just like the rest of the patients. Throughout his stay, Hans saw people come into the hospital completely frozen stiff who had to be bathed in cold water overnight in order to recalibrate their bodies to a normal temperature after getting completely inebriated on the streets in the heart of winter. Some "patients" were not only so frozen that their clothes couldn't be removed, but also so drunk that they couldn't even feel that they were frozen solid. During the summer, drunks found along the streets were stripped down and sprayed with a hose with cold water at the police station in an attempt to sober them up. The offender had to pay a fine and their employer was notified of their misdemeanour, but at least they avoided a stay in the hospital like their winter-offender counterparts.

Hans had different types of roommates enter and exit his 20+ bed communal hospital room. On one Sunday afternoon, an 18-year-old only child was brought in, alongside his parents, with a serious thigh infection. The teenager was absolutely terrified and in a furious panic. His parents appeared like they hadn't slept in weeks when they entered the room in a state of muted melancholy, as opposed to their son who was screaming at the top of his lungs.

"I don't want to die!! I don't want to die!!!"

Seeing him in such a state made Hans want to cut out the boy's infection himself. The hospital refused to operate on weekends since a meeting of physicians couldn't convene. When Monday morning arrived, the doctors finally reached a consensus, and intended to operate on the boy, but it was no longer necessary. It was too late. The boy was already dead. Days later, a 16-year-old was admitted into in Hans' room with a tremendously high fever. Nothing could help the poor kid recover. Eventually a nurse suggested,

"Vana, perhaps you should let the boy take one of your pills and see if it can reverse his fortunes."

Hans responded,

"I have no control over them. It's the hospital's medication. I have no qualms when it comes to helping someone else. I'm not selfish like my parents!"

Despite the jab of resentment directed at his parents who oddly enough Hans still desired to become re-united with, Hans was fully on board with the idea of sharing his medication. To make sure that it was permissible to administer "Han's" medication on the boy, the doctor personally approached Hans in order to get his expressed consent. Each and every single one of "his" under lock and key pills had to be signed out. Fortunately, at this point in Han's medical rollercoaster ride he was almost fully healed, though the 16-year-old boy was not, so a nurse provided him with one of Hans' pills; however, the teenager reacted negatively to the medication. Rashes overtook his body the very next day. And although neither Hans nor his pills could help the boy's cause, Hans' work colleagues definitely helped Hans' condition by always bringing beautifully written scrolls of well wishes to the hospital. Even while Hans wasn't out of the woods by any means, Hans' co-workers tried to minimize his illness with humour in an attempt to prove that laughter truly is the best medicine. One morning, a bunch of Hans' co-workers walked into his room and set up camp next to his bed.

"Vana, we've documented and logged every single one of your mistakes and mishaps that you've committed during your time at the research station."

One line in the log stated,

"When we went camping, Ivan forgot to bring the tea even though it was explicitly stated that it was his responsibility. However, in typical Ivan fashion, he refused to own up to doing something wrong. Instead of confessing to forgetting the tea, he attempted to be concealingly resourceful by grabbing some dried hay from a haystack. Ivan simply boiled these "herbs" in an attempt to pass off his concoction as "tea"."

During that camping excursion, ironically enough, everybody absolutely loved the tea! Everyone was just dying to find out where Hans acquired such a wonderfully brewed "tea". Initially, Hans told them,

"I bought it at a very exotic, but not erotic special herbal store that only sells this tea during Christmas."

Though, after persistently and insistently inquiring about what kind of tea it was, and where he got it, Hans caved in and confessed. *"I forgot the tea.*

John Friesen

You're drinking hay!" Despite his candidness, the group refused to accept Hans' "truth", so he retorted,

"If that's tea, then where's the packaging? Did anyone actually see me pull out any tea at all?"

They then all broke out laughing over Hans' little prank or charade, before one buddy bellowed out next to the open camp fire,

"That's our Ivan!"

CHAPTER 48

Recovery and Transformers

Back at the hospital, Hans was regaining strength with each passing day. After twenty days in the hospital, he was finally discharged. Over the course of the illness, Hans lost almost 20 pounds, dropping down to roughly only 120 pounds for his 5'8" frame. Nevertheless, Hans finally and happily returned back to work at the Science Research Institute of Energy. However, after only a couple of days, not only did the swelling, but also the discolouration in his arm return. His arm pigment once again turned blue. All of the contaminated tissue was undoubtedly not removed. Hans once again returned to the on-site clinic. The doctor then transferred Hans directly back to the hospital where the doctors operated on his arm once again. Luckily enough though, this time around he only spent a few days in the hospital before being discharged once again. Yet, it was only a matter of few days of working until the swelling and discolouration reared their ugly presence for a third time. Hans underwent a third operation. Over a period of three months, Hans' arm was operated on five times. On the fifth attempt, the doctor actually wanted to amputate Hans' arm. Hans, though, vehemently protested.

"You can pursue that option as a last resort. But for the time being, I still have hope. I still sense that my arm will fully heal."

The doctor didn't argue with Hans' positive outlook, but he nevertheless informed him,

"We must put your arm into a cast. So, you have two options – either, Option #1, have the cast set so that the arm remains straight down, or option #2, have the cast set so the arm is bent, which means that you can at least, theoretically, still write with your arm. But good luck with that!"

Ultimately, Hans elected for option #2. The next day, the doctors placed Hans' arm is a cast. In diligent, persistent, and somewhat recklessly-determined Hans fashion, he went back to work the following day. But it wasn't easy. With Hans' dominant, or "strong" arm being infected, he had to almost fully rely on his left arm, which at first was extremely awkward, especially considering the fact that the cast on his right side was quite heavy. Seemingly simple tasks like dressing, undressing, and showering felt extremely awkward and challenging. Shaving with a razor was flat out the most difficult test, leaving Hans testy, especially every time that his face bled when he nicked himself attempting to remove his stubble. And even though his right arm was positioned within the cast in a manner that left him able to write, Hans, nevertheless attempted to write with his left hand. Initially, his writing was rather illegible; however, his left hand quickly conditioned to the act of writing. In spite of the gradual progress of Hans' right arm, the doctors remained rather pessimistic, cautioning Hans,

"Your arm will have to remain in a sling for the rest of your life. That's the only way that it can "heal," or rather, prevent the swelling from returning. And do not try to move your arm! It'll be your own funeral!"

But as usual, Hans was stubborn. He deemed their advice unacceptable. Hans just couldn't imagine not being able to use both of his arms ever again. And as weeks passed, Hans' persistence paid off. He could actually feel his right arm beginning to heal up. Even the pain was slowly subsiding. In Hans' medical, spiritual, and physical opinion the arm felt like it was springing back to life! His prognosis prompted him to start bending his arm once again. At first, he only moved his arm within his cast to the point that it still felt comfortable. Yet, as time progressed, and his arm felt stronger, Hans began making even more "aggressive" and pronounced movements to the point that he eventually cleaved the cast at the elbow.

Hans made regular visits to the doctor. During Hans' latest check-up, the doctor saw the cracked cast and worryingly questioned,

"What happened!?! Why is the cast broken??"

Hans brashly explained,

"The cast is too weak, or perhaps my arm is too strong. So much for your remedial medical advice."

Hans, in detail, let the doctor know what he'd been doing with his arm, and what caused the breakage in the cast. Surprisingly enough, the doctor optimistically responded with excitement.

"That's a very good sign young man! Just keep on doing what you've been doing! Sometimes doctors' pessimism is off. But we must justify our existence! If everything is in order with your arm at our next appointment, I'll remove the remainder of the cast. But man, good thing that you were doing what you were doing and moving the darn thing! You're the exception!"

After three months of agony, the entire cast was finally removed. Hans though still had to go for therapy at the clinic for half an hour, every single day. His progress was monitored over the ensuing nine months. A year after the onset of the disease, Hans' arm not only regained 90% of its movement, but also reacquired basically all of its strength. During Hans' recovery, the research institute gave Hans tasks that he could carry out relatively easily with his left (other) arm. His right arm remained in a sling for those nine months after the cast came off. Nevertheless, Hans still helped out with experiments, and even went over electrical drawings. Sometimes, he even completed them himself. Every time an experiment was conducted, a drawing of the procedure had to be created. Yet, some were incomplete or even inaccurate, so it was Hans' responsibility to complete or correct them respectively and representatively.

The lab where Hans worked, which employed over 300 people, was responsible for designing hydro dams, generators, transformers, and lines intended to transfer hydro over distant destinations. Hans' main task, prior to his illness, was to assemble model transformers and generators; however, due to his arm injury and resulting time off, Hans fell behind on all of his projects. His colleagues attempted to carry out his role, but they lacked the necessary skills, know-how, patience, and experience to successfully assemble the transformers and generators, so the equipment was unable to function at its peak efficiency. Hans' former colleague, who was designated to carry out the same duties as Hans was sent to Leningrad (St. Petersburg) for three months of extensive training, but he quit upon return to Novosibirsk. To make matters worse, he left his replacements with only drawings, and nothing else. Castings were shipped in from Leningrad, but Hans still had to figure out how to create the transformer all on his own.

Prior to his illness, Hans was assigned to a project that consisted of designing and building a machine that could produce coils for the transformer for research purposes. This assignment was a priority task of the colossal project, as the entire undertaking depended upon the transformers. So, when Hans returned to work, he had a pile of pressure on him since this assignment was more or less shelved for three months during his bout with the illness. When Hans was back in full force, he worked overtime every day in order to catch up with all of the tasks. This talisman endeavour was in the works for a very long time, and actually entered its infancy stage long before Hans even came on board. Though, the results were always disappointing and left a lot to be desired. The Novosibirsk Research Institute of Energy was working in collaboration with the Electrical Institute of Leningrad, which was where the housing and rotors for the generators were made. For that reason, the engineer from Novosibirsk was sent to Leningrad in order to learn how to make the cores and assemble them for greater efficiency.

If the results couldn't be improved upon, the project would have to be scrapped. So, as a last resort, the job was handed to Hans as a result of his track record in terms of accuracy, precision, and patience. He was also the only one in the lab who had worked with life-size equipment, and not simply just models. His manager commented,

"Vana, nobody else has been able to succeed with the task before us. If you're unable to get it up and running smoothly, so help us God!"

To kickoff Hans' new challenge, he thoroughly examined the transformers. Upon further inspection, he noticed that the steel plates and core of the transformer were of poor quality. More specifically, the shearing of the plates and their baked-on coatings were sub-par at best, so Hans saw a lot of room for improvement. Since the manufacturing of the plates was not carried out by the research institute itself, Hans' team was in no position to be able to personally play a part in improving the manufacturing process, so better suppliers had to be vetted; yet, in the meantime, while they waited for the new plates to arrive, Hans worked on making the coils.

Hans designed a tool made with precise dimensions in order to be able to create coiled wires that would eventually be attached to the assembled transformer plates (cores). He started out with a flat ¼ inch by 1/16-inch-thick wire that was about 30 feet in length and covered by a spool of "sewing" thread for insulation. However, this thread was extremely finicky and flimsy, making it prone to displacement. Extreme care was required when working with this very sensitive form of insulation. If it were to become damaged, it would be permanently ruined and the coil would have to be scrapped. Past workers became utterly frustrated with this actuality. Hans started assembling the coil by winding half of the wire in one direction before flipping it over and winding the other half in the opposite direction. This daunting task tested the patience of even the calmest and most placid of blokes. Engineers who previously worked on assembling the transformers knew that it was imperative that all of the coils be of equivalent resistance, or otherwise the efficiency would be low. But they did not know how to achieve this desired optimal result. It required patience, dexterity, and being extremely particular and meticulous, traits very few have.

When Hans returned from the hospital, his boss, somewhat discouraged, yet somewhat strangely amused, pointed to a pile and said,

"This heap of discarded material perfectly portrays our frustration and lack of success surrounding this project. We're hoping you can help reverse our fortunes."

Attempting to transfer a million volts across an enormous distance like Siberia was a massively ambitious endeavour to say the least. When Hans initially started working on the project, he was quite surprised to see that even though all of the wires were of the same length and diameter, the resistance varied. After measuring the resistance, he noticed that it deviated depending on at which point the resistance was measured. Normally, the resistance was assessed at the ends, after the transformer was assembled and coiled. The resistance varied depending on where the short piece of the wire was hooked up at the contact point to straight four-inch pieces of wire that made up the electrical lines. Hans eventually observed that various square coils in the chain were wound up in opposing directions causing them to work against each other. Upon discover of this deficiency, Hans proudly called over his boss.

"See how all of these combined coils have been wound up in opposite directions – we thought that didn't matter, but it does! It's causing the wiring to work against each other, which is reducing the efficiency level to a meagre 60%."

Hans' boss, a pleasant man with a round face in his early 50's with not only a jump in his step, but also immense animosity towards the Communists for plundering his noble family's wealth during and after the Red Revolution, listened to Hans attentively until he eagerly asked, *"So, you can change the technique?"* With a proud, almost arrogant grin across his face, Hans confidently responded, *"Absolutely!"* After a few weeks of working diligently at modifying the configuration, which included altering the assembly process by welding with the same metal instead of soldering with lead like his predecessors, Hans assembled his first transformer and nervously awaited the "moment of truth". As Hans and the team ran the device and compiled the figures, they were ready for the results. Verifying the results, Hans' boss cried out,

"The transformer turned out an efficiency level of 97%! Way to go you son of a gun Vana!!" Such an operating performance left the rest of the team feeling ecstatic - the first dividend after a lot of time and toil on the project.

To help attain such a result, Hans used an ohmmeter, a device for measuring wire resistance, to determine that each wire had a different resistance, even though they were of the "same length". A minute and "immaterial" contrast in the lengths actually made a monumental difference. To attain identical lengths, Hans minimized the detriments of fatigue by working in 10-minute intervals since the work was not only very intense, but also required immaculate precision and concentration. Workers admitted that their vision went blurry when they laid the plates. Therefore, coffee breaks were mandatory. "Excess plates", which were usually discarded, as a result of imprecise assembly created gaps in between the plates. These "undetectable" micrometre gaps created the impression that "excess plates" still remained even though all of them were required to properly complete the assembly of the model. Hans also identified that all of the plates were not of the same thickness. New, optimal plates of higher quality and precision were eventually ordered.

The manner in which the new steel plates were precisely assembled played a crucial role in achieving the 97% efficiency level. To make sure that such a high efficiency level could be consistently attained, the scientists and engineers perpetually re-tested the transformer. Hans' manager and the rest of the crew were thrilled over the great result and the fact that the project was finished. The endeavour turned out to be a complete success! A second transformer was then assembled in an attempt to duplicate their success and they weren't disappointed. The second transformer reached a successful efficiency level of 96%! A third transformer was built, and it too generated an excellent efficiency result.

However, when Hans was busy with building generators, they passed on the task of assembling the transformers on to another engineer. After testing a "post-Hans era" transformer, a disappointingly low 60's (%) efficiency result was generated. Following this unacceptable outcome, Hans' boss approached him.

"Vana, we only reached 60%! What are we doing wrong?!? Can you take this transformer apart, and re-assemble it?"

When Hans completed the task at hand, the transformer reached a solid efficiency result of 98%! The research team realized that the difference between an efficient and inefficient transformer came down to the precision that was exercised while the transformer was being assembled. Five different engineers attempted to meticulously assemble a few transformers; yet, they only achieved sub-optimal results. Therefore, Hans was responsible for assembling the final transformers.

To top off Hans week, during his walk home down Krasnyy Prospekt on a late June day, he saw a motorcade procession of cars packed with Russian dignitaries and foreign diplomats. When Hans looked closer into a few of the cars, Hans caught a glimpse of Charles De Gaulle, Walter Ulbricht, and Khrushchev cruising by. His jaw instantly dropped in total shock. Hans comically thought to himself,

"I didn't even know that De Gaulle knew where Novosibirsk was! He must've made a wrong turn and ended up here. And who voluntarily spends time with Walter Ulbricht?!?!?"

CHAPTER 49

Over a Cliff

In the meantime, Hans persistently kept applying for permission to go to Canada in order to be re-united with his parents. Year after year, the Russian authorities denied Hans' request by rejecting his application, leaving Hans feeling dejected. To make matters worse, Hans' "treacherous" activities kept him on the radar of the dreaded KGB, making him a keener target of the "Committee for State Security" with every attempt to "abandon" the Motherland. In the eyes of the KGB, Hans was openly looking to "commit treason", even though the laws, which were set in cooperation with the British authorities at the end of WWII, stated that cases involving family reunification were an exception to the USSR's strict expatriation laws. Nonetheless, the KGB felt that Hans needed to learn a lesson in loyalty; resultantly, more "accidents" emerged in Hans' life.

On the way back from a camping trip in the summer 1967, Hans innocently stood, with a knapsack strapped onto his back, by the exit of a moving train wagon. As the train sluggishly chugged along, slowly approaching the main train station, Hans opened the exit door and leaned a bit outside to see just how far it was to his "stop". Hans' goal was to jump off the slow-moving train before arriving at the main train station, which was further from Hans' home. Yet, before Hans knew it, he felt a heaving shove from behind! Someone walking by had attempted to thrust Hans right out of the moving train! Luckily enough though, his left hand remained clutched to the railing, so Hans was able to hang on for dear life while the rest of his body swung outside of the train! With all of his might, and one foot still planted within the train wagon while Hans' other leg and torso swayed outside locked in a battle against the gusting wind and moving locomotive, Hans tried to pull himself back up inside of the train. Lunging with his dangling arm, he attempted to grab a hold of the railing inside with both hands, but to no prevail.

Hans knew that if couldn't get both of his hands on the railing, he could soon find himself underneath the moving train! Hans' heavy backpack impeded him from grasping a hold of the railing with his dangling hand. Hindered by the weight attached to his back, Hans attempted to relinquish his backpack, but to no avail. Yet, in a strange twist of events, Hans' deadweight, burdening backpack suddenly hammered against something, hurling him right back into the train! Propelled onto the floor of the train wagon, Hans peeked his head out and looked back where he saw the steel column that not only supported a streetcar bridge above, but also launched Hans back into the train, rescuing him in the process. Hans survived another day to experience another "accident".

Hans' uncle was aware that the KGB were targeting people who desired to make an exodus out of the country. Their goal was to murder or brutally mangle the applicants, and then make their deaths or injuries appear as if it were accidently so nobody would on catch to what the KGB was doing. Hiring "outside goons" or "auxiliary" KGB "members" was the organization's specialty in order to proclaim its innocence after such incidents. Hans' uncle vehemently warned Hans,

"You better watch your back! Take extra care and be super cautious at all times! Or otherwise, it'll be your neck! The KGB doesn't know anything about leniency! You ain't dealing with any Pioneers (boy scouts) These bastards mean business!! Just go to the Gulags and see for yourself!"

Before the incident on the train, Hans became accustomed to going around at ease, and believed that his years of being un-provokingly targeted by adolescent hateful kids and the KGB, like in Bratsk were far removed. However, he was sharply mistaken. The "accident" was an eye-opener, especially after a few sporadic skiing incidents in which he was accused of "trespassing". Hans' worries returned where he buried them. The episode on the train brought back horrible memories of his necessity to constantly be on high alert no matter the occasion. Nevertheless, Hans felt fortunate for the fact that his life was spared once again. He walked off the train with not only a few scratches, but also a renewed sense of vigilance that he once lived with during his time in Jug. His resolve to escape the USSR resultantly only strengthened.

Grandmother still kept in touch with people who she lived with in Zaporozhe before WWII torn the community apart, so she knew exactly the course that their lives had taken. Through their correspondence, Grandmother discovered that a woman who she befriended had moved to the other end of Novosibirsk. She began visiting her once in a while, but since Grandmother was not only too frail to get on the streetcar by herself, but also unable to figure out how to reach the woman's apartment on her own, Hans had to accompany her. So, one Sunday morning, Hans and Grandmother went to visit her friend. When they arrived, the lady's grandson just happened to be there. The chiselled, stone-face young man in his 20's with dirty blonde short hair greeted them with no greeting at all, besides a serious demeanour, before eventually approaching Hans in Russian.

"How about we go for a boat tour? It's a gorgeous day to hit the river. What do ya say friend?"

Hans instantly glanced into Grandmother's eyes. They radiated with waves of apprehension. Though, she remained silent. She simply didn't expect the woman's grandson to be at her apartment. Although Hans shared the same sediments and was hesitant, for some reason he couldn't refuse the invitation. Hans and the grandson then left the apartment and arrived at the port via the tram 30 minutes later to catch the next boat. After boarding and buying their tickets, Hans and his new friend went upstairs to the top, outdoor portion of the rather crammed two-tier white boat sizable enough for about 200 people. As their boat slowly travelled down the River Ob, Hans' light brown hair blew in the wind. To break the

John Friesen

uncomfortable silence, Hans said, *"What a gorgeous day."* But Hans' new friend didn't respond. He seemingly purposely avoided conversing with him. The guy seemed distant, as if his thoughts were elsewhere.

But Hans had no problem with that. He preferred to gaze off into the near distance, becoming hypnotized by the endless trees situated along the bank. Some were leaning or about to capsize right into the river as the flowing water slowly and gradually swept minute portions of the bank away. The boat cruised down the river for about an hour before temporarily docking at a conservation island that was partially covered by a young forest. At this point, Hans' new "friend" turned to him and said,

"This is our stop."

Hans exited the boat amongst a crowd, before the boat continued along on its way down stream. It would eventually return in a couple of hours to pick everyone up and take them back to the city. After everyone got off the boat at the stop, Hans looked around for his travelling companion, but he mysteriously disappeared. As they both stepped towards the exit of the boat "together", the guy seemingly just vanished into thin air as if he were a ghost. Hans didn't know what to make of, not only the situation, but also the guy's behaviour, besides the fact that everything seemed very strange. Instead of bothering to search for him, Hans just stayed behind in the vicinity of the port and walked around the grounds of the island. A burst rumbled through Hans' gut, so he headed over to a wooden food stand to buy a snack. Afterwards, Hans merely strolled along the relatively high, elevated river bank munching away at his little cardboard jug of sardines. Innocently watching the murky, yet fast flowing water, Hans entered into deep contemplation as thoughts as swift as the river's current streamed through his head.

People in the area were savouring the gorgeous sunny day, laying down on blankets along the shoreline, just chatting away, seemingly in unison with the soothing squawking of the seagulls. A few families picnicked under trees within a common grove where light bonfires quietly seethed. Yet, the guy who was "nice" enough to invite Hans on this excursion was nowhere

360

to be found, seen, or heard. Hans noticed a group of men randomly talking amongst each other in the near distance, not far from some bushes in Hans' vicinity, but he didn't think much of them as his thoughts went elsewhere. Staring into the steadily flowing river, Hans wondered, at times comically, just what his parents and siblings in Canada were doing at that very moment.

"Are they fighting polar bears? Or are they rebuilding their igloo after a walrus ran into it? Do people there actually ride moose to work, or is that all a crazy joke?"

A childish grin overcame Hans' face at the absurdity of his thoughts. Though, before Hans could either contemplate over just why his parents abandoned him, or take another look at the people frolicking in the beautiful day, Hans suddenly felt someone viciously shove him from behind! Before he could take a look to find out who had just heaved him off of a 10-foot cliff, Hans found himself within the murky water after falling in head first! Upon landing, he heard a crunching noise as he collided with the uneven shallow shoreline of the riverbank dispersedly covered with shrubs and trees nestled in amongst the water. Hans immediately sensed that something was wrong with his neck as his head bobbled in the water. When Hans' head came up to the surface after plunging face first into the water, he was unable to escape the river. The bank was too high and steep to scale. Overwhelmingly forceful current carried Hans down stream! Helplessly floating along, Hans searched for a spot where he could manageably climb to safety. In the near distance, Hans came across a bush with branches growing along the bank, hanging right over top of the flowing river.

Using all of his might to swim over to the branches, Hans grabbed a hold of a protruding limb. Hanging onto the sprawling bush for about 30 seconds, Hans caught his breathe and took a painful respite until he pulled himself out of the water and gingerly climbed up the relatively low and flatter portion of the dirt bank. When Hans finally found himself back onto solid ground, he inspected his surroundings, seeking out his perpetrators, but no one suspiciously stood out. The guys who "innocently" walked by the bushes a few seconds before Hans was thrusted down the bank were nowhere to be seen. Completely soaked, Hans headed over to a groups' bonfire where he took off his clothes and placed them on the ground to dry. A man sarcastically asked Hans, *"Isn't it too cold to swim?"*

Hans, now wearing nothing more than his boxers, was in no mood to offer a wittily dry reply. Quite the contrary. His splitting headache, sore spine, and throbbing neck, which was only compounded by utter irritation over what had transpired since he dropped off Grandmother left Hans completely bitter, boorish, and furious. Nonetheless, Hans still had a lot of time to kill before the boat returned to take him back to the mainland. When his clothes finally dried, Hans dressed himself and returned to the dock where he searched for the fellow who he barely even knew, yet who still invited Hans to go on the worst boat excursion of his life. At this point, Hans truly wondered just why that guy invited him on this little trip in the first place. Shortly before the arrival of the boat, people queued up, awaiting their return to Novosibirsk after a day of soaking up the sun in tranquility, free from the hustle and bustle of the city. Looking to his left, Hans spotted "his friend" and immediately approached him. The guy looked Hans up from down and simply said, *"You look like a mess."*

Hans, somewhat snipingly responded,

"Somebody pushed me off a cliff into the river, but you wouldn't know anything about that now would you."

The guy displayed absolutely no signs of concern or astonishment. After they boarded the boat and headed back towards the city, not a word was exchanged the entire time. Hans and the guy with a gaze of utter arrogance and a square-shaped head eventually stepped into a street car. When the two of them arrived back at Grandmother's friend's apartment, Grandmother immediately asked Hans in a state of shock, *"What happened to you??!"* Hans tersely told her, *"I fell in the water."* Shortly afterwards, Hans and Grandmother left the lady's place and headed in the direction of the streetcar stop. After stepping onto the tram, Hans opened up to Grandmother.

"The excursion was absolutely bizarre. When we got off the boat, that guy simply vanished. And then later on, someone pushed me off a cliff into a steep river bank. My neck is absolutely killing me."

Grandmother didn't appear totally surprised, right before she opened up to Hans about a delicate matter from their past.

"I need to tell you something Hans. That guy's grandmother, my friend, also had quite the difficult life. She too had to endure a few traumatic experiences herself. After giving birth to two daughters, her husband suddenly died. A few years later, she re-married a wealthy widower who also lost his spouse. During the revolution, a group of bandits arrived at their home one day and dragged her, along with her new husband and two daughters out of their house and lined them up against a wall in preparation to execute them all. Yet, right before the bandits were ready to shoot away, one of the bandits, who used to work for this woman's new husband, instructed his "associates" to only shoot the man. They spared her and her daughters. Perhaps he knew that they had just recently married, so maybe they weren't as "guilty" as the husband who they shot and left for dead."

"During the Red Revolution, the communists took everything that this woman's family had, except for her second husband's hidden treasure chest of golden rubles that was buried, allegedly at the house. Years later, the father of your dad became mayor and took up residence at that very same house. Luckily enough, the communists apparently never found that chest of golden rubles, but your dad allegedly did. Well, at least according to that woman's family's presumptions.

I dearly believe that my friend has nothing to do with her family's machinations and her daughters' claim that your father and Uncle Jacob stole their family's buried treasure and now deserve retribution."

And even though Hans played absolutely no role in his father's unproven theft, Grandmother added,

"Some people believe that an entire family must be held accountable, and even pay for one family member's actions. My friend's family is bitter and

full of resentment over what happened to them. The guy from the boat trip - the grandson, apparently has ties to the KGB, just like his mom and aunt. He doesn't even know who his father truly is since his own mother wasn't even certain. They were not raised in the best conditions and under the best circumstances. So, going forward, be vigilant! Just like in Jug!"

After hearing this story, Hans thought back to a previous visit to Grandmother's friend's place when the woman's daughter was present. Right when Hans walked into the apartment to pick up Grandmother, he heard her say to the women, *"Leave him (Hans) out of it! He had nothing to do with it!"* At the time, Hans asked Grandmother what they were talking about. Grandmother didn't want to say anything bad about Hans' parents, so she simply told him,

"Your father was accused of taking something that didn't belong to him.

Grandmother never visited that woman ever again. What happened to Hans during that boat excursion opened Grandmother's eyes and elevated her already overwhelming heap of guilt. Eventually, it came to light that not only were two of those women's grandsons on the KBG's payroll, but also the boys' mother. Evidently, she was spying on people, chiefly ethnic Germans, by monitoring and "conversing" with them with the intent of passing along her "findings" onto the KGB. Apparently, the mother of the boys, who had two sons from two different fathers, wanted to work herself up in the (KGB) world, initially as a mere pigeon informant, regardless of what conceivable harm she could have caused to others.

After learning about the history and manner in which the family of Grandmother's friend lived and who they associated with, Hans ultimately realized that all of the strange occurrences that took place on that Sunday were not mere coincidences, but rather completely contrived set-ups all a part of an ugly scheme. Facing occurrences with members of the ruthless KGB was nothing new to Hans. At the research institute facility, every employee knew of an informant in his late 30's with a grim, tapered face named Stanislav. He did almost nothing at the research institute throughout the day, so he was easily spotted and picked out by his "co-workers", who concluded without a doubt that Stanislav was a KGB informant. He had absolutely no clue how to perform any of the necessary tasks for "his job" as an electrical engineer, so he clearly didn't belong.

When people realized that you worked for the KGB, they saw you as a traitor and a hired goon. As an act of retribution, employees at the Novosibirsk Research Institute of Energy attempted to set up Stanislav with the intent of humiliating him. One day, a few scientists approached Stanislav and requested that he troubleshoot a transmitter, something he knew absolutely nothing about. Stanislav, nonetheless, was up for the challenge and elected to monkey around the transmitter, which only made matters worse. Unsuccessful at the task at hand, Stanislav made himself into the laughing stock of the employees. But that was the least of Stanislav's concerns. While working away at attempting, or pretending to troubleshoot the transmitter, Stanislav burned himself on the live wires of the panel! Feeling painfully shamed and mortified, he instantaneously erupted, screaming out to the surrounding workers,

"You set me up! You set me up!!"

Shortly there afterwards, Stanislav departed the research institute as his cover was blown. Russians absolutely despised KGB agents, pigeons, and auxiliary goons. Instead of merely propagating fear and suspicion, these agents ironically enough also had to live in constant paranoia since they too became targets of the people who sought to expose, set up, and possibly even cause serious harm to these surreptitious "government delegates". At the same time, everyone had to vigilantly watch what they said in Stanislav's presence, since such informants were constantly seeking out dirt and "seditious declarations" in order to justify their significance.

CHAPTER 50

Pain in the Neck

Although Hans' neck was in constant pain after falling into the river, he kept going to work and carrying on his daily activities as if nothing happened. The pain originated in his neck; however, before he knew it, the agonizing discomfort made its way down into his shoulders. On the following weekend, despite the soreness, Hans went camping with buddies from work. On the trip, Hans miraculously managed to swim, dive, and even play volleyball. Despite the constant agony, Hans elected to go along with his buddies on the subsequent weekend to that exact same location to partake in some diving. As usual, Hans was the first one to dive into the water to show off just what he was made of; yet this time around he leapt head first right into a thick and shallow layer of sand!! Even though Hans presumed that there was no harm in diving in from the low river bank, the river's sand around the diving area must have shifted in the course of the week amongst the murky water, making the new depth visibly unknown.

Hans' pain became his buddies' gain, as they laughed to death over the fact that not only did Hans dive into sand head first, but also that his legs were actually sticking straight up out of the water as if he were doing a perpetual headstand. Hans' friend Kir had no interest in facing the same ordeal as Hans.

"We don't want the same fate as you Vana! Let's go scout out a new area to do some diving!" Eventually, they stumbled across a deep and suitable point

along the river bank to plunge in from, and before they knew it, everyone including Hans was nose-diving into the water as if there weren't a care or pain in the world. And although Hans' physical torment persisted, he stubbornly went on with all of his normal and adventurous activities without getting checked out by a doctor. Hans convinced himself that the injury wasn't too serious, so instead of cautiously slowing down and taking a respite, Hans went camping the following weekend where everyone frolicked in the fun of swimming and diving together, along with playing soccer. The truth is always painful to confront, so Hans preferred to live the façade and pretence, acting as if nothing were wrong. Hans' pride, and perhaps belief of being indestructible ("nicht vernichtbar") that he developed as a kid never permitted him to display any signs of weaknesses.

However, all that would change on the following Monday, when Hans' pain was so horrific that he could neither turn his head nor look down anymore. His neck was as stiff as a nail; though, seemingly not unbendable enough to prevent him from going to work. During the lunch hour, Hans' buddy Nikita, a young joker in his late 20's, went to the movie theatre to buy a few tickets for "*The Magnificent Seven*", starring Steve McQueen, who Hans, according to friends, shared a striking resemblance with. When Nikita came back, he asked Hans,

"Do you wanna join us for a flick this evening? The Magnificent Seven. It's with that dude that looks like you, you ruggedly handsome movie-star-like hunk you, Ivan (Hans)!"

At the time, Nikita noticed not only that Hans was in more pain than usual, but also that he couldn't even turn his neck. Nikita suggested, a tiny bit tongue-in-cheekily,

"You really should pay a visit to the on-site clinic here at the research facility. You need a medical opinion from a doctor. Your opinion is skewed by your own pig-headedness, you reckless fool."

Hans was always quite mulish and stubborn. Though in this case, Hans acquiesced to his friend's suggestion, and eventually headed over to see the resident doctor, realizing that the stinging pain wasn't going to evaporate into thin air. As soon as the doctor felt Hans' neck, she somewhat anxiously instructed him to *"Sit down. I'll return in a few minutes."* She quickly walked out of the room and locked the door behind her. While Hans waited, he wondered to himself in a state of anxious paranoia,

"Is she alerting the KGB? Is she going to tell them that I wasn't finished off after the boat excursion accident?"

Hans waited for his destiny to play out with the least of ease. He felt like fainting as the angst consumed him. About half an hour later, he heard the door unlock and open. Fidgetily wondering who the doctor was bringing, Hans sprang to his feet in fear! When the door fully swung open, Hans saw the doctor march into the room, and much to his shocking chagrin, she brought two fellows with her! At that very moment, Hans knew that she had alerted the KGB!! He had never seen these two guys in his entire life! Yet, with good reason! The two men turned out to be paramedics who were there to take Hans to the "hospital". The doctor explained to Hans,

"You've broken your neck! It requires immediate attention! We must transport you to a hospital for further extensive treatment!"

Hans' misgivings about her intentions were false, but his paranoia still didn't let him fully trust her. So, in typical Hans fashion, he mentioned to the doctor,

"I don't have time for this right now. Could this wait till morning? My friend just bought tickets for a movie this evening and I'm dying to see it! It's with a hunk who resembles me! Steve McQueen!! What's the rush anyway? You worry too much doc! We're all gonna die anyway."

The doctor wittingly responded, *"Why do you think I locked the door?!"* She had already experienced Hans' behaviour when he had blood poisoning, so she knew exactly who she was dealing with and what he would attempt in order to prevent going to the hospital. She then enquired, *"So when did this happen?"* Hans responded, *"About a month ago."* The doctor flabbergasted, squealed out *"A month ago!!!!"* Hans tried to mollify her by declaring,

"I was hoping that it would all go away on its own. You weren't supposed to find out."

In the doctor's opinion, *"You've already waited way too long, just like with your blood poisoning!!"*

For just how long he had been living with such horrible, unbearable pain left her mind-boggled. The doctor was not only extremely curious about the extent of this injury, but also wanted to make sure that Hans didn't escape the ambulance, so she drove with him and the two paramedics to the hospital. After Hans was admitted, the doctor at the hospital took X-rays. With the results in her hands, she informed Hans,

"Your 5th vertebrate is broken, or better said, for all intensive purposes it's been crushed. Your vertebrate basically broke in half and slid out of place, but luckily enough, without touching the spinal cord. For that reason alone, you're still able to move!"

The doctor vehemently reiterated,

"You can count your lucky stars that you weren't paralyzed from the neck down! Ridiculously lucky!!"

Eventually, they took Hans to a room and placed him on a bed with a sheet of plywood mounted on top of the mattress. The slab of plywood was set on a 30-degree slant. The medical team attached a harness, in which a rope was fastened, to Hans' head before sliding the rope with a weight affixed to it over a pulley. The doctor explained to Hans, *"You'll have to stay like this for an entire month!"*

The room in which Hans resided contained 13 beds in total. All of the patients that he shared the room with also had spinal injuries; some of them had already been there for years on end. When Hans was originally brought into the room, the other patients were making bets that Hans would "expire" within two days, since the previous patient who slept in Hans' bed died two days after being hospitalized.

Since Hans was sleeping in the only bed equipped with a sheet of plywood, perhaps his fellow roommates took that as a bad omen, especially considering the fact that the last man in that bed was now dead. But Hans didn't take a swan dive off a bridge like the prior fellow, so hopefully Hans' fate would turn out a little brighter. But Hans' roommates were not convinced. They bet bottles of vodka that Hans wouldn't survive another two days. His fellow patients didn't have much in their lives to live for, so in a strange way, this was their only form of entertainment and means of finding pleasure in life; well, besides whenever their wives stopped by with bottles of vodka that these male patients ironically enjoyed putting on the line in an attempt to parley their bottles into even more bottles of vodka. Despite their pessimism, Hans was optimistic, leading him to brashly tell the men,

"I'll walk out of this hospital a healthy man before each and every single one of you. When I get out, I'm gonna be doing a lot of drinking after I cash in on those bets! I'm going to be getting a lot drunker than all of you, that's for sure! You won't be able to quit your day jobs!"

Hans assumed that they were going to lose their wagers since they all bet against Hans' life, though he had more interest in cashing in the empties than consuming the vodka. In an old Russian tale, there are two men, a poor epicurean man who savours his vodka while enjoying life, and a middle-class stoic man who doesn't drink and lives a more economical and healthy life. The poor drunk eventually cashes in all of his empty vodka bottles and buys, not merely everything that he needs, but simply everything that he'll ever need again, besides perhaps the sub-par fish and potatoes that all of the patients lived off of at the hospital. The stoic, on the other hand, struggles to enjoy life as his obsession with money, health, and self-righteousness consumes him alive.

If Hans were to perish at the hospital, he had nothing to lose on these bets, just like if he survived. If he were dead, his roommates would have nothing to collect from him; yet, if he won, Hans would be left with a few bottles to take home with him. Hans, however, was eventually moved to another room with less alcoholics after a nurse told him, *"You don't belong here."*

Hans was transferred into a room with 15 to 20 beds that had more "ordinary" patients, or at the very least, ones whose stay was intended to only be temporary. His prior room was full of "lifers," ones who in most cases were a derelict who wallowed in their own self pity because they had nothing else to their lives besides drinking. But honestly, you couldn't blame them. The majority of them were brutally injured, sometimes even mangled, usually in street car accidents. During this juncture in Novosibirsk, the street cars were frequently so jammed pack that many "passengers" alternatively rode on top of or along the outside of the trams, anywhere that they had something to grab onto. In one horrific case, eleven people died after being electrocuted while travelling on top of a street car. Many others got injured simply getting on and off of the tram whenever it was extremely icy around the entrance or exit points. And suing the Soviet government authorities was never an option.

News of Hans' most recent injury spread quickly at work. It was only a matter of time before work colleagues and friends started coming by to pay Hans a visit. Heart-felt sorrow filled them after discovering that Hans once again had to endure something so traumatic, especially within a relatively short period of time. The people in Hans' life were absolutely in awe at just how much he had to go through. To make matters worse, this time around, the situation was quite precarious. Being permanently paralyzed was still a strong possibility if his spinal cord couldn't shift back into place. Hans, however, had absolutely no doubts. Grandmother's spoken voice from decades earlier echoed through his mind.

"Nothing will happen to you."

He could sense that everything was going to end up perfectly fine, even though it was taxing for him to lie in bed for an entire month with weights attached to him, especially because he could barely feed himself, let alone move around. However, Hans, luckily enough, was able to unhook the weight from the harness around his neck and sneak off to the restroom, even if it were frowned upon by the nurses who desired that he go in a tray while lying in bed. Hans though, was always an uncompliant patient; yet, be as that may be, he continuously claimed that his "inner voice was guiding him." And the voice of the palm reader from a decade earlier declaring, *"You'll have two serious injuries, but don't worry, you'll survive. They won't be that horrible.",* reassured Hans that everything was going exactly according to plan.

The day after Hans was rushed to the hospital, the research institute sent two cute girls, named Svetlana and Irene, to break the news to Grandmother. Svetlana and Irene, both in their 20's, with long black hair and slim figures were afraid to go visit Grandmother as they didn't enjoy being the bearers of bad news; though, when they arrived at Grandmother's place, much to their surprise, Grandmother greeted them warmly even though she was fully aware that they were there to convey less than encouraging news. After going into the kitchen to make the girls a tea, Svetlana and Irene finally informed Grandmother, and Jacob's wife who helped out as an interpreter,

"We don't know how to break this to you, but Ivan (Hans) is in the hospital. It's quite severe. He must remain in the hospital for at least a month."

Instead of tears, the girls shockingly faced a dear, old grandmother who took the news calmly in stride. What they found utterly astonishing was just how optimistically and upliftingly Grandmother responded to them. *"Not to worry, he'll be just fine. God will see to that."* Needless to say, the girls unanticipatedly left Grandmother's place quite relieved, yet still somewhat taken away by the fact that everything went so smoothly. Grandmother tenderly hugged and thanked them for coming by. When Svetlana and Irene went to visit Hans in the hospital, they let him know,

"Your grandmother is something else! Her reaction was astonishing. Actually, her attitude in general is quite astonishing! She seemingly doesn't have a worry in the world, and doesn't seem like she needs one, like all humans. She remarkably has all the faith in God that you'll undoubtedly recover to your old form!"

Someone from work stopped by to visit Hans every day. Even the doctor from the clinic at the research institute was diligently dedicated to Hans. At first, she came by almost everyday to make sure that Hans was not only

John Friesen

being an obedient patient, but most importantly, receiving the best possible treatment. She simply didn't like the idea of Hans sharing a room with a bunch of drunks, so she was more than happy when he got transferred to another room. Since the hospital was packed to the gills, some patients were left to their beds in the hallways, so relatively speaking, Hans was lucky to at least have a proper room to sleep in, even if it were along with some interesting company at times. Before being moved to another room, Hans engaged in entertaining conversations with the drunks or enjoyed their antics in between the moments that he passed his time by watching the bedbugs and other insects climb the walls – a typical sight in Novosibirsk at the time - almost envious of their seemingly effortless movements.

Uncle Jacob's wife, Hans' aunt through marriage, worked at the same hospital so she occasionally came by to pay Hans a visit. However, Hans' Uncle Jacob never came by. All what he could say was,

"How stupid could he be to break his neck! What a knucklehead! That mule is milking it and just trying to get out of work! He still owes me rent!! He never wants to work!"

This was a far cry off from the same Uncle Jacob who kidnapped the nine-month-old Hans from little Hans' mother's house when Uncle Jacob was only thirteen. Uncle Jacob became miserable after his six-year sentence in an absolutely deplorable Gulag work camp. Grandmother also never came by to visit Hans, but she at last had a more than reasonable excuse. She was simply incapable of making the trip without assistance. Therefore, Hans' aunt kept her apprised of Hans' condition.

CHAPTER 51

Casted in Plaster

After a month, Hans' vertebrae fell back into place. His spine miraculously healed itself right on schedule. Yet, they still had to place a cast around Hans' neck and most of his torso in order to make sure that his vertebrae stayed stretched out. It was imperative to the healing process. The cast also limited the exertion on Hans' neck while preventing him from putting pressure on the vertebrate, which could've caused it to slide back out of place. The cast stretched Hans' neck out by about an inch in length. The goal was to keep it at this distance for the ensuing two months. It took the medical staff roughly four hours to sculpt the cast to Hans' body. He "sat" in a chair for the entire time, or rather ordeal, with a harness attached to a rope and a goose-neck shaped contraption that was connected to a winch that was used to elongate his neck out while they set his body into the cast. Hans' butt barely touched the seat the entire time since the harness strapped around his neck kept him hunched upright, a stance leaving him somewhat resembling Quasimodo. The exertion was almost incapacitating.

During the "cheese cloth style" cast application process, layers upon layers of moist clothes were dipped into a starchy liquid solution inside of a pan and placed upon Hans until the clothes dried up right onto his body. Applying the cast was an extremely taxing and exhausting procedure for the patient. To compound matters, there was a concern that Hans' circulation might have been cut off by the harness, which could've choked him to death. Worried that he might faint out of exhaustion during the cast-mounting process, the medical staff, resultantly, were unable to administer pain-killers for the agony out of concern that the drugs might knock Hans right out, leaving him incapacitated. So instead, the doctor and nurses gave Hans other more conservative options and "remedies" for the pain such as talking to him; checking his blood pressure; instructing him to breath while they monitored his pulse; and last but not least, observing his eye movements and dilations. Keeping Hans stimulated during the procedure was imperative to his survival.

The doctor and three nurses attempted to keep Hans calm and focused on the end goal, which somewhat strangely enough was done by making him strenuously concentrate on how they were treating him and applying the cast. Distracting Hans from his own tormenting pain was seemingly the only way to make sure that he never sensed the need to succumb to the pressure during the clothe application process. At times, Hans felt like he couldn't hold on any longer, but luckily enough, after four strenuous and enduring hours, he found himself encapsulated within a torso cast that was finally mounted onto his body. Hans was ready to be discharged from the hospital, which meant that he could happily, yet not comfortably head home.

Walking out of the hospital in a cast, Hans awaited a long and exhausting rehabilitation stretch. But that didn't deter him from happily returning to work the very next day; even though the cast was uncomfortable to say the least. His skin underneath the cast became extremely itchy. Hans had to use a clothes hanger in order to scratch his irritated skin under the cast. To compound his issues, Hans was unable to shave underneath his chin and jaw, causing that region of his face to become rather itchy. But if that weren't bad enough, the constant pressure upon Hans' neck led to bruising, gradually leading it to turn black and blue. Sleeping was also a less than relaxing chore for Hans, as he simply couldn't find a comfortable sleeping position. Seemingly "routine" tasks like dressing tested not only his patience, but also his own sanity. Eventually, a buildup of dead skin formed under the cast, skin that couldn't be bathed for months. During the procedure, the doctor and nurses jokingly told Hans while they were mounting the cast, *"Nothing has killed you so far, but living with a cast just may."* Hans finally learned the hard way, just exactly what they meant by such a comment.

CHAPTER 52

Clearance

The injuries and illnesses may have weakened Hans, but they definitely didn't dampen his resolve to continue to apply for a move to Canada. And the fact that Hans wasn't frightened away from going to the intimidating and sometimes horrifying KGB office in order to plead his case, even after being pushed off of a cliff, clearly proved that point, Expecting the typical rejection on his visit to the KGB office, Hans approached the woman handling his case who gave him shocking news!

"Your grandmother may leave first. Then, you can follow her in due course when your cast is removed and you're fully healed up. It wouldn't look good on the Soviet to send you to Canada looking disabled now would it."

And though, on the surface, Hans excitedly agreed with the woman, deep down and internally Hans rolled his eyes at her pathetic rhetoric. Because since when did the KGB care about looking like choir boys. Nonetheless, that didn't spoil Hans' spirits, even though he still couldn't grasp the fact that finally, after 11 years of attempting to leave the Soviet Union, not to mention 23 years of separation from his parents, and constantly hearing "No!", he finally heard a "Yes!"

But Hans' work was far from over. First off, he had the daunting task of convincing Grandmother to make the trip alone, or rather without him to Canada. As expected, when he proposed the idea to Grandmother, she emphatically flat out refused. *"No! I wouldn't hear of it!"* However, after

Hans informed Grandmother that this could be her final chance to see her daughter, Grandmother had a change of heart, and ultimately acquiesced to Hans' request. So, once the necessary paperwork was processed and Hans provided 300 rubles to purchase her plane ticket, Grandmother found herself on the way to Canada.

Pleasantly enough, the KGB actually arranged everything for Grandmother's departure, except for taking her to the airport in Novosibirsk. So, Hans rode with her on the train to the airport with mixed emotions. The parting was difficult and full of fear, trepidation and uncertainty. They hadn't been separated for more than a few months over the course of Hans' life – almost 27 years. They simply just couldn't believe what was transpiring. Grandmother was going to see her missing daughter and granddaughter for the first time in almost 25 years! And meet a grandson who she had yet to see! Grandmother's and Hans' final words to each other, almost as if they came out of one mouth while they embraced at the airport departures gate were,

"I'll see you in Ka-na-da! Our journey together will resume there."

From Novosibirsk, Grandmother was flown to Moscow where she stayed for a few days. After living 50 years under communist rule, Grandmother was on the verge of leaving the USSR! As she boarded the plane at the airport in Moscow, she just couldn't fathom it; yet it was so. But Grandmother wasn't quite yet off to Canada, but rather, first off to Brussels, Belgium where she touched down a few hours after departing Moscow. A Russian hockey team in Brussels awaited, not only their flight to Toronto, but also, somewhat comically, Grandmother as well. She was the only 'regular' passenger on the hockey team's charter flight to Canada. And even though she couldn't completely understand them, since she never fully refined her Russian language skills, she nevertheless had a great time with them on the flight. The players made her feel extremely welcome, simply just like one of the guys on the team, except for that they treated her with the upmost respect and dignity, making her first intercontinental flight an absolute delight! Fond memories of that flight and the Russian hockey team became engrained within her for the remainder of her life. In total, her voyage from Novosibirsk via Moscow and Brussels to Toronto took ten days. Grandmother took the entire adventure in stride while never finding a need to worry. She was clearly built for the journeys that she travelled, journeys that she acceptingly, yet painfully endured.

Many months after Grandmother arrived in Canada, Hans, oddly enough, received a letter from Uncle Jacob in Frunze, stating that Hans was actually granted permission to go to Canada years earlier. However, the authorities later informed Hans that because he was no longer living in the Frunze region, the KGB revoked his permission to leave the USSR, stating that he must re-apply through his new "jurisdiction", which Hans did in Novosibirsk years later. The KGB office in Frunze was not run by Russians, but rather by the Kyrgyz, who showed a lot more leniency and empathy, especially considering that they resented their Russian conquerors. When Hans finally obtained permission to leave from the authorities in Novosibirsk, he was regarded as a cripple no longer of any value to society. At that point, Hans became a burden to the system, so they were prepared to gladly unload him onto Canada. Though, Hans still couldn't believe that it was real, constantly thinking to himself,

"I actually have parents and I'm going to live with them."

Unable to comprehend what he was attempting to decipher, while absorbing foreign sensations stemming from the unpredictable situation left Hans feeling a bit unnerved and anxious. Yet, when Hans realized that the palm reader (on the train) from almost 10 years earlier predicted that he would embark on a major trip overseas in 1968, he felt at ease since he knew that everything was going according to plan. Hans realized that the pieces of his destiny were merely falling into place. And although this comforted Hans, the quote, *"rich, but lonely"*, expressed by the soothsaying palm reader from 10 years prior still echoed though Hans' mind, causing the agonizing pain of being abandoned to mildly brew within him.

When Grandmother ultimately arrived in Canada, Hans was already free his cast. Though, before and after it was removed, Hans put in a lot of overtime at work to make up for the lost time from being hospitalized.

John Friesen

Though, it was extremely tough for Hans to function with the cast. Hence, Hans blessed the day, almost two months after being discharged, when he returned to the hospital for an appointment. This was when, upon further inspection, the doctor informed Hans,

"Everything has healed up. The irritating and debilitating cast that has casted a black plague over your life for the last two months can be removed! You must be quite relieved! But you can forget about doing hard, manual labour ever again. Your days of toiling are over!"

In due course, the doctor and two nurses gathered up their tools in preparation of working on Hans' cast. Upon entry into their "laboratory", Hans bore witness to a slicing axe, carpenter saw, hammer, chisel, and even a prying crowbar. Such a sight brought beads of sweat to Hans' forehead on this brisk November afternoon. Apprehensively laying himself onto the table, Hans suddenly felt an axe hammer against his torso! Then again! Then again! The medical team cut and chopped away at the cast as Hans' body bounced around with every swing of the weapon, or rather "apparatus", while letting Hans know,

"Ivan (Hans), when it hurts, let us know!" They also didn't fail to mention,

"After the procedure, you might have a concussion, which could set you into a coma."

Hans was surprisingly upbeat.

"I don't care, just as long as you get rid of this nauseating cast! If I forget that this damn thing ever existed, even better!"

They then reiterated, *"Once the cast is removed, you'll never be able to do any physical labour again."* Hans stubbornly, yet optimistically didn't believe one word of it, but nonetheless mollified the medical team, quite tongue in cheek, by stating, *"Of course! Of course I won't."* While working around Hans' sensitive and delicate neck area, the doctors and nurses elected to use a chisel to remove that portion of the cast. When the back part of the cast was finally removed, the nurses turned Hans over and began scraping and

380

chopping away at the front side of the cast. Fortunately, it wasn't necessary to completely cut through the front end of the cast, like with the back side. Nevertheless, an additional nurse eventually had to be brought in to assist them with the strenuous task at hand. Upon arrival, she cut at the cast with scissors while the other two nurses tried to pull apart and tear off the cast respectively and respectfully. Before long, they requested that Hans sit up in a chair so that they could yank the cast off through the arms at the front. With a few mighty tugs by the nurses after hours of chopping, dicing, and chiselling, the cast finally came off! Moments afterwards, the doctor directed Hans to *Walk "right" towards the door"*, which at the time meant "left" to Hans.

When he stood up and walked in the direction of his "right", Hans honestly felt as if he were walking towards the door until he surprisingly walked "right" into the wall! The doctor, somewhat giggling, informed Hans *"The disorientation is a result of the constant pressure on your nerves."* Though, it was only a matter of few seconds before Hans' ephemeral vertigo vanished, and everything went back to normal, leaving him feeling relieved! Hans had his freedom of motion once again, even though Hans never had any doubts from the onset. And most importantly, he was finally in a condition to fly to Canada! At long last, after almost 23 years, Hans was going to be re-united with his long-lost parents in just over a year! However, his superiors at the research institute, unequivocally didn't want Hans to leave! They actually even offered him an honorary degree in Electrical Engineering at the university, and not to mention an apartment right downtown, a place that was generally almost impossible to obtain. People usually had to wait approximately 10 to 20 years for such a apartment, unless of course they had special connections. Hans wondered just why they were willing to make an exception with him. Hans then thought to himself,

"What am I going to do with a Soviet honorary degree?? Especially in Canada?? There must a catch!"

If Hans accepted their "tokens of appreciation", Hans believed that the KGB may have elected to rescind his permission to leave the USSR. That's how things functioned in Russia for Hans (and everyone) – there was seemingly always something sinister behind their largess. You never truly knew what the KGB was planning, and where you stood while they were or weren't preparing to devise a scheme subjected against you. Hence, Hans exercised extreme caution, despite the fact that the degree was utterly tempting, especially considering that he had been working towards it at the university, and on the verge of enrolling into his second year. To add to the allure, they even offered Hans a significant pay increase, even though he was already earning the equivalent to the engineers. Despite refusing the offer, his bosses remained totally empathetic, expressing their happiness for Hans for finally having the opportunity to re-unite with his parents, and now his grandmother(s).

Hans' bosses also felt bad because despite him accumulating more than three months worth of overtime, his bosses were not permitted to pay him out. The research institute's policy was that the employees could only take their overtime in time-in-lieu. Hans, however, was extremely grateful to the research institute. He graciously declared,

"Don't worry about the extra time and the money. Can't bring much with me anyway! I've had such a blast working here! You took a chance on me. I feel so indebted to you all. I absolutely loved my tasks and responsibilities while working here. You guys were so loving and devoted to me while I had blood poisoning and the broken neck. I've never felt such a connection to an employer in my entire life, and never will! You offered me an opportunity of a lifetime! It afforded me the chance to discover and instill confidence within myself. I've experienced the best time of my life here at the Research Institute. I love you guys! Much obliged!"

Science International actually wanted to put members of the research team in its magazine for the scientists' and engineers' endeavours relating to the project of efficiently transferring electricity over vast distances. Past attempts came along with high energy losses, which didn't make the project worth pursuing, well at least until Hans came on-board. All-in-all, it was utterly difficult for Hans to say farewell to all of the great people who he became attached to and grew to cherish. It was rather traumatic for Hans to leave what finally felt like home. Yet, venturing into new and foreign territory was by no means a new adventure for Hans, leaving him convinced that moving to Canada wouldn't be perhaps as difficult as imagined, even though this exodus would definitely be the most difficult from them all. Hans wondered,

"Just how will life be in a new country where they speak a foreign language? A life with a "new" family that I don't even know? So just what will my family be like now? The same that I experienced in the past?"

CHAPTER 53

Moscow 1968

Like with Grandmother, the KGB made all of the travel arrangements for Hans, which included booking a room at the Ostankino Hotel on 29 Botanicheskaya Street, right next to the famous *"Парк Останкино"*, Ostankino Park in Moscow. After all of his farewells to his relatives, co-workers, and friends, Hans flew out of the Novosibirsk Airport before arriving in Moscow around noon that same day. Yet, when he reached the north Moscow multi-story drab brown brick façade Ostankino Hotel, Hans discovered,

"There's no room available for you at the moment, Mr. Friesen. You will have to wait until a bed becomes free in the morning."

The unfriendly, unamicable, and stern, bald-headed 5-foot male receptionist then instructed Hans,

"Leave your suitcase in the storage room. It is located behind the reception concierge. If you require anything from your luggage, you should let us know and we'll give you access to the storage room. But you may not, under any circumstances bring your luggage into your room. And until you are an official guest of the Ostankino Hotel, you are not permitted to loiter in our lobby. Though, if you are not around when a bed becomes available, you will forfeit your chance of obtaining it, and will have to wait until another bed becomes available."

In minus 30-degree Celsius weather, Hans was left with no other choice but to wander the streets of Moscow till morning, when a bed would hopefully become available. In typical communist fashion, nothing was simple and accommodating. After attempting to check in, Hans left the hotel and grabbed a bite to eat at a meagre coffee shop where he ate a bowl of borscht and a plain glazed donut that he savoured with a black tea. At the time, it was January, frigid cold, grey, damp, and rather foggy, a fog that touched the frozen ground and penetrated through the pores of Hans' face, making it rather unpleasant to be outside, let alone meander throughout the city for ten hours at night. With plenty of time to kill, Hans headed over to a tiny and empty local barber shop in the vicinity of the hotel for a shave. While shaving Hans' face with a 20-inch switch-blade-like razor, the barber, a man in his 40's with thin skin and a lined face who resembled a stern Soviet drill sergeant but behaved like a Red Army interrogation specialist, started posing what Hans deemed to be rather personal and prying questions. Hans had absolutely no interest in truthfully answering the barber when he enquired throughout the conversion,

"So, where are you going?" "Where are you staying?" "What are you doing here?" "Who are you going to visit?"

His questions seemed innocent enough, yet it all felt very suspicious. Coyly retorting, Hans told the barber,

"I'm visiting close friends and my aunt."

The barber then casually paused for a second before nonchalantly mentioning,

"You, know, it only takes a split second to cut your throat."

Hans coolly retorted, *"Can you imagine the mess. All of that blood all over your immaculate floor."*

Truly wondering if he had walked into a trap again, Hans pondered,

"So, is this guy truly working for the KGB? Perhaps I ought to be more careful. Who knows what the KGB is trying to pull. Or does this barber just have a sketchy and shady sense of humour? So, am I becoming a paranoid wreck? Just completely losing it? Or is my sub-conscious and id trying to communicate something to me."

After getting up from the chair and paying the barber a few rubles, Hans walked the streets of Moscow for the entire night. As he glanced down at the beautifully draped, snow-covered sidewalks, before gazing up into the nighttime sky as light flakes drifted down upon him, Hans contemplated away since he had nothing else to do besides remain frigid on a freezing Moscow night.

"Do the KGB want me to catch frostbite? They must be trying to get into my head. They must want me to crack before I ever meet my parents. I hope that I don't disappoint them. I'm going to impress my parents by all means! I'll prove my existence at all costs!! I'll teach them how dumb they were for abandoning me!! I'll work harder than ever! Like a filthy mule if need be!! I'll show them!! They'll learn what I'm made of!!"

When faint traces of the sun finally peaked out amongst the thinly spattered morning fog, Hans returned to the hotel to enquire about a bed at reception. This time around Hans was greeted by a younger, black-haired woman behind the counter who possessed piercing brown and deep, but not necessarily comforting and calming eyes. She let Hans know, *"You must still wait sir. A bed is not available. But it shouldn't be long now."* Hans felt completely exhausted, irritated, and annoyed; but nevertheless, he retorted passively in an attempt to give off the impression that he was a nice guy, even though deep down he was disgusted with how he was being treated and resented this woman because of it.

"While I wait, may I get access to my suitcase? I need to get my toothbrush and shaving stuff out so I can shave and brush my teeth in the washroom. Is that okay with you ma'am?"

She politely replied, *"Of course sir! Get what you need, sir!"*

Though, when Hans got to the storage room, he shockingly saw that his suitcase was open! All of his belongings were in complete disarray, some even spread out on the floor! Hans immediately went back to the front desk to enquire with the receptionist about what had happened to his suitcase and belongings. The woman in her late 20's causally replied,

"It fell over and must've opened. That's why some of your contents spilled out onto our nicely polished floor."

Hans then thought to himself,

"Yet, if that were true, why's the lock missing!?! She's a damn liar! But she's gorgeous and has nice teeth!"

Hans knew perfectly well that KGB had gone through his belongings, so he didn't even bother checking if anything were missing. At that point, he simply couldn't care less. So, he just left it at that. His passport and papers were on him, and that's all what mattered to Hans. When he returned from the washroom where he brushed his teeth and shaved once again to kill some time, he slowly walked over to the window of the lobby and glared out for what seemed like hours at the breath-taking snow-covered park gleaming bright in the sunlight across the street. Hans saw pure beauty, yet his mind reverted back to dark moments from his past only until Hans suddenly heard, *"Mr. Friesen! Mr. Friesen! Please come!"*

Before introspectively visualizing Mother hit Grandmother when Hans was only a few years old, Hans walked back to reception where he was greeted by a new receptionist who smelt like cheap Russian cigarettes. She informed Hans,

"Mr. Friesen, a bed on the 4th floor has become available. The room number is 413. Here is your key. The washroom is down the hall from your room."

When Hans stepped off of the elevator onto the red polyester carpeting on the 4th floor, he searched out room "413", which luckily enough wasn't far from the elevator. After unlocking the door with an oversized brass key, Hans entered the room where he saw four single beds draped in drab green sheets, a tiny table, with two filled ashtrays on top, surrounded by three chairs next to the window. Hans was not alone. Three men silently sat on their beds looking through their papers or the newspaper. Before long, the man holding the newspaper placed it onto the table and looked over at Hans. The man had thick blonde hair and a round face, and must have been in his early 40's. When Hans made eye contact with him, he asked, *"So where're you heading?"* Hans replied, *"Ka-na-da."*

The man happily said,

Oh, like my wife! We're from the Ukraine. My wife is gonna visit her father in Canada.

But he then somberly added, *I wanna go too, but I'm not permitted to accompany her."*

Hans, expressing a childish, innocent-looking grin across his face, proudly let the man know, *"I'm gonna live with my parents there."*

The man curiously desired to hear more, asking Hans,

"Do you wanna grab a tea with me and my wife downstairs?" The lonely Hans said, *"Sure! Thanks!"*

People flying out of Russia had to be in Moscow roughly 10 days prior to their departure. All travellers were forced to run from agency to agency in order to get their papers processed, slowly becoming worn down by Soviet bureaucracy in the process. Hans and the Ukrainian man's wife were both happy to have someone else to scamper around from building to building with. Tackling the ordeal of communist administrative intimidation, interrogation, and harassment was less of an unbearable torment with a "compatriot" who shared in your misery. The Ukrainian man's wife felt comforted to know that someone else was enduring the same burden that she was. This woman's husband was also appreciative of the fact that she had someone to at least converse with at the airport before the long flight to Canada.

John Friesen

The Soviet Republic applied paranoia and power to prey upon its citizens. Delegates and dignitaries sought out control by exercising their power and might. Power enhanced their significance, which further fueled their drive for more power, so when Hans entered the Foreign Affairs Ministry, the panel of three middle-aged men in ordinary black suits aggressively demanded to know,

"Why are you going to your father!?! Your father should be coming here!?! He was born here! Why did he abandon us? Why did he betray the Red Army!?! Why did he feel the need to be disloyal to the Motherland!?! Like father, like son, like every treacherous bloody traitor and deserter!!!"

To the stern Soviet authorities, Hans' father's actions, along with Hans' were simply inexcusable; yet, Hans was not the one on trial. So, despite their vicious interrogation and innuendo, the Soviet authorities officially authorized Hans to leave to *"Ka-na-da"*.

When he returned back to his hotel room that evening, after a grueling day of bureaucratic proceedings and processing paperwork, Hans discovered a new group of "guests" staying in his room. This became a regular occurrence - like a merry-go-round of "travelers" who in all likelihood included a few KGB agents. Even the Ukrainian fellow was transferred to a different room. For the first few nights, Hans felt his body being searched by patting hands while he pretended to be fast asleep. Hans lied on his stomach the entire time, with his papers and passport tucked away in his underwear just so these suspicious men couldn't get to them without turning Hans over; something that they seemingly didn't want to attempt. Hans figured that the men were definitely KGB agents who were looking to either take his papers away, just so he wouldn't be able to leave the country, or more likely establish if he were seeking to extradite "sensitive materials" to Canada. At this point, Hans could hardly wait to be on that plane. On many nights leading up to the flight, Hans went to his room to sit down at the table of the empty room in order to double-check that all of his papers were in order. But suddenly, three young men in suits of 25-30 years of age would come barging into the room.

390

As soon as the men entered, Hans vacated the room and headed downstairs to sit in the lobby, something that he was finally permitted to do after officially becoming guest at the hotel. Hans then sat there for hours on end, amongst chatting guests, many of whom were smoking away in a tiny meagre-looking lobby with tacky multi-coloured furniture. Some of the people were perhaps speaking English, though Hans couldn't tell. Hans remained in the lobby until he could no longer physically keep his eyes open. At that point, he returned to his room. Switching on the lights, Hans discovered the room completely empty. That night, somebody as usual searched him. When the touches and pats of the hands probing his body halted, Hans heard a man whisper to someone else, *"He has nothing on him."*

Even when Hans showered, he brought all of his papers and passport with him. He placed them into a plastic bag so that they wouldn't get wet, and took them right into the shower with him. The KGB and Soviet authorities desired to wear Hans down and out, just in case he attempted to engage in any subversive activity, such as transporting confidential documents. Under such close surveillance, a perpetrator would most likely either slip up from weariness, or simply abort their "mission". KGB agents were bent not only on proving their value by uncovering "incriminating" evidence, but also savouring the luxury of having power over people – power driving people into states of fear and anxiety till they're trembling – the same type of fear that leaves people petrified, compliant and obsequious to the state.

CHAPTER 54

Kanada 1968

After surviving ten tenacious days of bureaucratic interrogation at the hands of the Soviet authorities in Moscow, Hans finally got all of his emigration papers processed. All travellers heading off to Canada were required to gather in the lobby of the Ostankina Hotel, before being loaded onto a black bus that headed for the airport on a shivery and snowy Thursday morning. But Hans possessed shivers for another reason. At the age of 27, he was moving to another continent to be reunited with parents who he hadn't seen in 23 years! Upon arrival at the airport, every passenger was thoroughly searched by military police prior to boarding the plane. Being back at Moscow's *Международный Аэропорт Шереме́тьево* (Sheremetyevo International Airport) brought back memories of a time years earlier when Hans had his chance to escape the USSR with that Swedish travel group. Though, before Hans could conjure up another thought, a member of the military police instructed him, *"Take off your coat and empty your pockets!"*

Hans was thoroughly searched. He was not permitted to take more than the allowable $100 US dollars with him to Canada, so Hans converted all of the rubles to his name into US dollars at the airport before clearing customs. As he walked towards the boarding zone inside of the airport, Hans saw a woman in her 50's, who was covered in expensive jewelry containing gold, rubies, and diamonds, being searched by airport security and military police prior to boarding her flight. Multiple rings covered each of her fingers. A military border control officer eventually informed the woman,

"There's no need to travel to Canada with such expensive jewelry. When you return from your vacation we'll return it all to you."

As Hans looked into her sullen brown eyes, he could sense that she never intended to return to the USSR, or at least that was in all likelihood her original intent from the onset before being stripped of all of her priceless and precious jewelry; though, perhaps her initial plan never changed. After the police team gathered up all of her prized jewelry, the woman walked towards the plane muttering to a few of the other passengers, *"They're targeting me because I'm Jewish! Typical! No wonder I'm leaving this place!"*

After everyone was fully searched by the military police, Hans, along with the rest of the passengers were escorted outside along the black tarmac. Gently blowing snow dusted the runway as an amicable, yet stern-looking soldier in his 30's equipped with an automated AKA47 Kalashnikov machine gun led the travellers towards an entirely red-painted Tu-134A plane with a transparent glass nose. As flakes of snow came down from heaven, Hans looked into the magical white sky and inhaled his last breath of Russian air that smelt of the diesel fumes being expelled by the airport equipment in the vicinity.

After walking up twenty steps and boarding the plane, Hans fully realized, not only that there were only thirty-six other passengers on his flight, but also that after over 11 years of trying he was finally off to Canada to be re-united with his family! With his heart mildly papillating and excitement flowing through him, a petrifying sense of fear momentarily consumed Hans, creating a perfect case of cognitive dissonance. Glaring around the plane's modern-looking interior, Hans soaked up the atmosphere and the moment, but his mind was completely elsewhere as it fleetingly raced a mile a minute while Hans wondered to himself,

"Will my mom be the same miserable witch that she was when we separated? Or did time (in Canada) and being distanced from the war happily change her? Well, I've changed, so, so has she! It was wartime back then. How could

you blame her? But I don't even know my parents. And now I'm going live with them and work for the family business! Yet, with complete strangers?! Either way, my fortunes have definitely turned! They must be filled with guilt for what happened to me, even if it were all probably an accident. Not even this perpetual separation can deny the fact that I'm their son."

Though, before Hans could summon up another, possibly asinine thought, a Russian stewardess approached Hans. *"So where is your final destination sir?"* Hans replied, with a crescent grin across his face that grew with each passing word. *"Toronto and then Beamsville, Kanada, where I'll live with my parents."* Oddly enough, a look of disconcertment overtook the face of the beautiful stewardess, whose straight black hair was pulled back in a tight pony tail. She retorted,

"You're gonna have a rough time in Canada. You're gonna have to work really hard there."

As she walked away, Hans was absolutely dumbfounded and blindsided by her comment. He pondered, quite contrary to his prior thoughts,

"Just what kind of statement is that? "Rough time"? "Work really hard"? Who says that? Especially about life in Canada? Shouldn't life be easier in these so-called Western democracies? Or was she right? Was all the communist propaganda correct? People and their filthy and greedy companies just want to capitalize on and exploit everything, just to make a bloody buck? The end always justifies the means, just as long as the economy is strong and running well? Though, the communists are brutal and even they say Canada is "The Land of Milk and Honey". So, Canada must be a beautiful place. Why else would my family move there?"

Yet, Hans remembered once hearing,

"Europeans work to live, whereas Americans live to work. "So, was the stewardess right then? Is communism purely about power, whereas capitalism is solely about money and work, and to hell with the rest? Money equals happiness? It's simply that simple over there in America?"

Another thought entered Hans' head.

"A Russian will walk up to your face and pull the trigger while he looks you in the eyes. So, does that imply that a Canadian is someone who gains your trust right before she stabs you in the back?"

Following hours in mid-air, an announcement over the plane's intercom interrupted Hans' train of thought. The pilot informed the passengers over the loud speaker,

"Due to snowy weather conditions, we are unable to reach our intended destination of Montreal. Our plane is being re-routed to Gander, Newfoundland."

Hans then heard the passenger in his early 20's in the seat next to him say aloud in English with a smirk across his face, *"What's good for the goose, is good for the gander."* This parable, strangely enough left Hans feeling calm and comforted, even thought he didn't understand one word of it. Twelve hours after departing, their plane landed, seemingly in the middle of nowhere, not far off from the decaying, yet snowy rocky island shores at the Gander International Airport. From there, all of the passengers were transported in a bus to a quaint little hotel with a view overlooking a few majestic ice bergs where the passengers stayed for the night. As Hans sat in the lobby of the hotel drinking a late-night camomile tea, his excitement only mounted.

The following morning, the travellers hopped onto a smaller Canadian plane for a five-hour flight to Montreal, Quebec. As soon as Hans exited the airplane and entered the hallways of the Aéroport international Dorval de Montréal, he was greeted in Russian by a thin French man in his late 20's with long and thick sideburns. The man explained to Hans in Russian,

"I'm here to help you get onto the correct plane to Toronto. Do you know your parents' phone number?"

Hans nervously answered, *"Da. 1-416-563-8778"*

After dialling the number for Hans on a black phone situated at a check-in counter, the man handed Hans the receiver handset so Hans could speak to someone from his immediate family for the first time in over 23 years! Hans felt like jumping out of his skin! As his chest slightly tightened up, his throat burned dry. On the fourth ring, a male voice, who Hans assumed to be his father, answered saying, *"Hello!"* Hans responded in German.

"It's your son, Hans. I'm in Mon-tre-al."

Father reacted extremely surprised and surprisingly, very coldly. Hans uneasily informed Father,

"Mein Flug A-C-8-5-8 landet um 14:20 in Toronto von Montreal."

Hans let Father know that he was going to be arriving in Toronto from Montreal, and told him the flight number and expected time of arrival. Father abruptly responded, *"Wir werden Dich abholen! (We'll pick you up then)"*, and then brusquely hung up.

At that very moment, a very strong, eerie feeling overcame Hans, telling him that he shouldn't go to his parents' house. Father instilled Hans with a very enigmatic, almost unwelcoming feeling. His gruffness and complete lack of uplifting emotion was bewildering. Hans also found it extremely odd that Father seemingly wasn't even aware that he was arriving in Canada that day. All in all, something just felt really off. Hans wondered to himself,

"Was father just pretending that he wanted me in Canada because he thought I'd never be allowed out of Russia?"

An awful and consuming sense of nervousness overwhelmed Hans. He just wanted to remain in Montreal. If only he could. When Hans expressed his wishes, along with his reservations and apprehensions to the Quebecois man who was assisting him, the man replied,

"You're not permitted to stay in Montreal. Your family vouched for you. You must stay with them."

John Friesen

Hans had no other choice but to head to Toronto and "greet" his family. He immediately thought back to what the palm reader from that train ride said back in 1958.

"You'll take a long trip over the ocean in '68." "Your father will die at 68." "You will be wealthy, but lonely.""

So, what did that and this all mean? What was Hans getting himself into? He just lived out the best years of his life in Novosibirsk. Hans' hands and feet sweated profusely during the entire flight, right up until the plane touched down on the white, salt-stained runway at the Toronto International Airport in Malton, Mississauga. At this point, Hans felt like swallowing his tongue. Looking around at all of the signs and advertisements within and outside of the airport, Hans realized that he could barely read one word, confirming to him that he was definitely no longer in the Soviet Union. Hans only recognized the numbers and the odd word that resembled German.

After clearing customs and collecting his belongings at luggage claim, Hans nervously lugged his brown leather suitcase out of the baggage claim hall while his upper lip and right brow lightly quivered. Eventually, he entered the Arrivals foyer. When Hans anxiously glared into the crowd, he initially couldn't spot the family. Right before he could wonder to himself if they weren't going to show up, Hans saw Father, Mother, and his sister joyously waving in his direction, yet to differing degrees. Hans immediately recognized them from photos that Mother sent him while he was still living in Russia. Apprehensively approaching his family like a timid four-year-old child, Hans felt like he was starting off where he had left off. Yet, much to his astonishment, Father instantly embraced Hans in a heartfelt bearhug with more emotion and love than ever expected!

However, Mother hadn't changed much in the 23 years since she "lost" Hans, when they mysteriously and "accidentally" separated during their wagon exodus through Nazi Germany. Mother was quite cold to Hans in this instance, exhibiting the same demeanour that she displayed towards him while Hans was still a young child. She only offered Hans a heartless hug, a type of hug usually reserved for distant acquaintances and strangers. Feeling uneasy in her presence was nothing new for Hans; though, much to his astonishment, his sister Wanda, who couldn't even converse with him since she never learned much German, or at least gave off that impression, seemed more than thrilled to finally see her older brother for the first time in decades! The last time that they saw each other, Wanda was a one-year old. She was now 24, quite pretty with cute round cheeks and curly light brown hair draped with shades of blonde hair. She was living in Toronto at the time, working as a teacher.

After packing themselves into the family Oldsmobile, the Friesens bustled down the QEW highway in the direction of Hans' parents' house in Beamsville, a town located about an hour away from Toronto, and 30 minutes removed from Niagara Falls. Wanda followed them in a separate vehicle on her own. During the drive, in between the moments that Hans gazed into the distance at the snow-covered escarpment as the sun slowly set on a white, late afternoon in January, Hans and Father conversed with each other, though both not necessarily always certain about what the other was talking about. Yet, one thing was for sure – Mother remained quiet, cold, and distant.

Hans still felt completely overwhelmed. Following 23 years of physical separation, and a decade of searching - it finally happened – the wait was over. Hans though, couldn't help but wonder how it was all going to play out, and just what his family and destiny had in store for him. Father's welcome was warm, but Mother's aura gave Hans such a troubled, unnerving feeling that he wished that he had never laid eyes on her. In her presence, he felt like a distant stranger, merely *"the stupid guy from Russia."* A part of him finally felt "complete", yet another part sensed that something was not right. Nonetheless, Hans was tremendously excited to finally reunite with Grandmother after nearly three hundred days of separation.

When the metallic coloured Friesen family Oldsmobile drove into the mildly-sloped black tar driveway of Hans' new home, Hans saw Grandmother anxiously standing in the doorway of their partially brown brick, partially red brick house with a 2-car garage on the north end facing east, impatiently awaiting Hans' arrival. Grandmother spent 23 years raising Hans, which was more time than she spent with her very own daughter, causing her to feel closer to Hans than anyone else in the world. They were a team. So, as soon as Grandmother saw the car door swing open, she dashed out like a kid into the snow, letting the screen door slam behind her. Glee radiated from her eyes that were filled with tears of joy. She was not only elated, but also relieved that Hans successfully escaped the Soviet Union and was next to her once again. When Grandmother arrived in Canada, she constantly nervously wondered if the KGB would change their minds and prevent Hans from leaving. As her and Hans embraced in the snow-sprinkled driveway, Grandmother whispered into Hans' ear,

"My mission is finally complete. You are re-united with your parents. I can now die in peace."

An enormous burden weighed upon the thin and frail Grandmother during those 23 years that Hans was parentless. Her guilt over the "fact" that she gave in too easily after a brief, yet aggressive struggle with her daughter in which she accepted Hans into her arms, out of Hans' mother's hands, onto her wagon plagued Grandmother till her death. She always believed that if she had never taken Hans into her arms, he would've been by his mother's side for his entire life. Though, what kind of a life would've that been – that's a question that she feared to ponder, even though it was now all seemingly snow from yesterday. Hans was re-united with his mother and immediate family, and that's all what mattered. Grandmother knew that her prayers had finally been answered. However, in a strange twist of events, while hugging Hans with all of her might, Grandmother whispered an untimely and unforeseen message into his ear. *"Run away from this place. It is an evil home."* Hans was absolutely stunned! He immediately thought to himself,

"After being reunited with her very own daughter, my mother, after all of these years, and this comes out of her mouth?!?!? Just how could that come out of her mouth! Especially considering that she had no problem staying with a

man in Zajarsk who whipped me right across my back?!?! Someone who had
no problem stealing all of my money!?!? Just how could she say this me?!? Now
of all moments?!?!"

Grandmother validated her statement by stating,

"Your mother (Grandmother's daughter) is evil! She has all the wealth in the
world and everything someone needs, but she's (still) completely nuts. It's crazy!
But your father is OK."

Grandmother added,

"She is not my daughter! I can't understand what happened to her! She
mentally and physically abuses me! She pushes, hits, and constantly yells at me!"

All of this was unloaded onto Hans, even before he took his first step into
his parent's house. Grandmother went on to mention,

"Even with all of the hardships I had to endure in Russia, nobody ever treated
me like this! If I could go back to Russia, I would go back! That's for sure!"

Hans remembered how grateful he was to all of the people at the research
institute. They showed so much concern and love towards him. It was as if
Hans belonged to the most beautifully working and functioning "family"
in the world. Hans then pondered to himself,

"I left Russia for this?? What have I gotten myself into!! I traded in wonderful
people in Russia for people who behave like this!!! Is this all just a horrible
nightmare?? Or did I simply get brain damage when I fell off that cliff?"

From that time forward, Grandmother stayed glued to Han's side. Stepping
foot into his parents' house for the first time was a toxically intoxicating
moment for Hans. Father seemed somewhat spaced out while Mother
quietly fumed in the corner on her favourite green sofa. After witnessing
such bleakness, Hans knew at that very moment,

"All of my dreams are shattered! Once again! I'm now stuck with them, working construction for the rest of my life! The palm reader was correct! "Wealthy, but lonely", yet with family around?!?!"

When they all eventually sat down in the spacious family room that had a wide window overlooking Ontario Street, the main road leading into Beamsville from the freeway, Hans' parents and sister didn't even want to learn of Hans' tribulations, hardships, and life in Russia. They simply wouldn't hear of it. The parents were only interested in speaking about themselves. Father went on about how,

"Life was really tough for me in Russia, and then in Germany. So, we had no other choice but to head to Canada. Simply no choice. You have no clue just how much we had to endure."

Hans listened to a man who wasn't apologetic one bit for losing his son, but rather someone coming up with excuses while justifying his actions as he searched for sympathy. Not daring to interrupt Father as he pompously spoke away in German, Hans could only roll his eyes at Father's rhetoric as he went on.

"I, your mother, your sister, and my mom, we all immigrated here from Germany in '48. My dad was hauled away by the KGB, just to never return decades earlier. That was before you were born Johannes (Hans). I chose this part of Canada because my uncle lived here in Beamsville with his family. He sponsored us. My uncle's family came over from Russia, along with other Mennonites not long after WWI. There are lots of Mennonites in this region. Lots of us. This small town is a part of what is called the Niagara Region."

The migration policy pertaining to many new immigrants at that time was that they had to work on a farm for one year upon their arrival in Canada. The government was responsible for finding newcomers not only farms to work on, but also their living accommodations as well. Hans' family was initially placed on a farm on Victoria Avenue in Vineland, a small, partially rural township along the Niagara escarpment, a hamlet over from Beamsville.

After taking a sip from a shot glass of whiskey, perhaps to quell his guilt, Father continued, giving Hans no time to pose questions. Hans learned later on that Father never liked questions or being questioned – he only wanted you to hear what he wanted to let you know. Father refused to hear a thing about what his lost son had to endure in the USSR. Instead of listening, Father continued to ramble on, almost purposely preventing Hans from enquiring about why he was left behind when the rest of the family left for Canada.

"You wouldn't be able to imagine the old log house that we were forced to live in when we arrived here. You look around this house and see all this, but trust me, it wasn't always like this. We first lived in a hut built by early Mennonite pioneers. It belonged to the farmer that hired me. That relic of a place was our home for an entire year! One whole year! Nowadays huts like that are being showcased as preserved historical artifacts at some Mennonite Heritage Museum place. That primitive shack had nothing to do with "modern" society! That place didn't even have electricity! No running water! We had to use a stinky outhouse! You have absolutely no clue how we had to live! It was an enormous shock for us!!

Before arriving in Canada, we were city dwellers in Hannover, Germany between '45 and '48. Then these Canadians stuck us in that rustic hut here! We enjoyed many modern comforts over there, even though those limey Brits and Yanks bombed Hannover to hell and smithereens."

Even while residing in modern-day Ukraine in the 1930's, the Friesens had relatively lavish homes for their times, even in comparison to modern North American homes – and definitely much more lavish than their Vineland farm hut where they once resided. As Mother looked on agreeably, yet disinterestedly, the overweight Corny poured another shot of whiskey and puffed on his cigarette that he inhaled through a tiny white filter as he roared on with a mild sense of fury.

"When we got to Vineland it was horrible! We thought we made a wrong turn when we arrived! Your mother and I despised our new lives! Especially your Mother! She couldn't stop complaining! She wanted to go back to Germany!

We couldn't comprehend how Canada could be called "The Land of Milk and Honey", as people talked of it back then! When we moved into that god-forsaken hut, your mother was expecting Rudi. You'll meet him later. He's off at university."

As Father looked at Mother, seemingly almost with an ounce of derision, Father spoke on with animated, yet rigid arm movements full of tension.

"Needless to say, Maria (Hans' mother) found life here difficult enough with one child, so she had no interest in raising two children in such archaic conditions. But she did it. But she never wanted to leave Germany. But we had to go. We had no choice. Though, she desperately longed for a return to Germany, where life, according to her, was actually more "civil".

And when we got here we couldn't speak a damn word of English! We didn't know what that limey or Dutch farmer was saying to us! Didn't know what he wanted most the time! You mother was ready to pack her bags! She found the language barrier a tiring nuisance. I always heard (expressed in an irritated woman's voice), "Corny, let's get out of this place!" But she survived. After working a year on that farm, I got a job at GM in St. Catharines. A bigger town a few villages over."

Though, it didn't take Corny long to become disenchanted and weary with his position at General Motors, or rather, simply his position and standing in life in general. Father, or "Corny", as his associates called him, liked being in charge as "The Boss". For the most part, Corny wasn't used to, or at least didn't enjoy being controlled, especially by a capitalistic company not owned by himself. Father preferred to dictate. He didn't appreciate taking directions from anyone else, or to be more precise, he highly favoured giving orders to everyone else. Corny envisioned himself as a wheeling and dealing businessman, a bigshot. Corny saw no other way to live. In Hannover, he was known as a resourceful man of means. Relatives, who eventually also moved to Canada recalled their time back in Germany after the war, telling Hans,

"If you asked Corny, he'd get you anything that you needed. Just don't ask how he got it."

Right after WWII, Corny became acquainted with a Canadian-Mennonite German named Abrams, a Canadian soldier who belonged to a military unit that occupied Hannover after the German surrender. The German-speaking Abrams actually came from Beamsville of all places, and even went on to work alongside Corny in construction through Abrams' roofing business a decade after WWII concluded. As an Allied soldier, Abrams had access to provisions through a supply depot within the devastated, depleted, and destroyed city of Hannover. So whenever Corny pulled up to the Canadian barracks and provision warehouse in his German military-issued truck, a truck that Corny kept for himself after the Germans surrendered, Abrams provided Corny with whatever he needed for a palm-greasing fee. Cigarettes, clothing, nylons, food, and whatever else Abrams could get his hands on. Corny then sold these goods and items onto the German black market.

A businessman through and through, Corny knew that he was wasting his time simply working in a factory at GM. So one day, Corny decided that he was going to start his own construction company. During the 1950's, Beamsville was still in its infancy stage of growth, which meant that there were plenty of opportunities for a developer to capitalize on while the poker was still hot. Corny was afforded with not only a businessman's acumen, but also plenty of prospects from which to profit from, even if it literally required him to toil away in the trenches for his newly-founded construction company. Following Hans arrival in Canada, it didn't take long for him to hear Corny constantly complain and proclaim,

"You have no clue just how hard I had to work for all this! Absolutely no clue you damn fool!!"

Mother, on the other hand had a few jobs here and there, but seemingly nothing too strenuous. She "enjoyed" living as a kept woman. Hans though, could only wonder the entire time just how his parents could possibly complain and believe that they had it so rough. Or perhaps they merely moaned about their tumultuous times because they couldn't bear to listen to any of Hans' stories of harsh hardships.

John Friesen

During Hans' first few weeks in Canada, he consistently attempted to speak about his "adventurous" and arduous life in the USSR, but the parents always quickly cut him off, and alternatively spoke about their own "sufferings". It was as if they couldn't bear to listen to Hans' "tales", and learn about the pain that they inadvertently, or perhaps purposely perpetrated. Weeks after arriving, Hans already began wondering,

"Just how self-centred and disgustingly selfish could they possibly be!?! Though they're fully convinced that they're always the victim. They can't see it any other way! So, are they ever going to bring up how they lost me!?! Are they ever going to at least apologize!?! Or do they blame me for it all!?! So, was it truly all my fault?"

CHAPTER 55

Family Business

Hans didn't have much time to absorb everything that was transpiring in his life, simply because by his third day in Beamsville, Father, without giving it a second thought, sent Hans off to work despite the fact that he was still recovering from a broken neck. Corny justified this decision by stating,

"I have two parasites and I can't afford a third! I'm almost bankrupt, so I can't afford to pay you anything right now. You'll get your money at year's end! I'm in debt and the construction business has been in the red for the last three years and I can't get out of this bloody mess! I'm gonna teach you how to work son!"

Even though the doctors informed Hans that he'll never be able to do any physical labour again, Father offered Hans an alternative "medical opinion" by prescribing Hans another form of "medicine" quite contrary to the doctors' advice. From the start, Corny was looking for control, whilst Hans was looking to prove his worth and show just why he not only was worthy of their love, but also should have never been abandoned. Resultantly, Corny happily discovered a lost boy eagerly seeking his parents' approval, love, and most evidently, a reason to be deemed significant. So, it didn't take long for Hans' bully of a father to quickly realize that the possibility of acquiring control over one of his children was more than conceivable. Corny could sense during their first few discussions that Hans desperately yearned for Corny's acceptance. In order to fully secure his dominance and supremacy over Hans, Father steered Hans away from notions of fortunes and a life of leisure by revealing their dire situation.

"It may appear that we're wealthy; however, we could lose everything very easily! The forty apartment units are only three years old, but they're heavily mortgaged and already falling apart. We're basically broke. So, without your help, we'll lose everything! I need your help or otherwise we'll end up in ruins."

Hans read between the lines, and realized that he would be responsible for not only saving the company, but also all of the maintenance work required on the apartments whenever he wasn't occupied with construction projects. Hans, though, loved the idea of playing hero and family saviour, and Father knew that perfectly well! Corny was calculating and sly enough to know exactly how to motivate Hans' type. Hans was a visionary, leaving himself convinced that he could save the day and play the abandoned hero by helping to reverse the family's financial problems and turn their fortunes around – an aim that inadvertently made Hans obsequious and subservient in the process – something that Corny happily exploited and used to his advantage. Hans was glorified for his efforts at the research institute in Russia, and he desired to resurrect that status and the resulting praise that he was accustomed to acquiring through his skills, work ethic, and savoir-faire. Feeling that this would be a great opportunity to prove his worth, and show his family that they should've abandoned his two siblings before him, Hans knew that it was time to show his ingenuity and ability to work by impressing at all costs.

Following one of Corny's "fatherly rants, Hans scornfully and resentfully thought to himself,

"I'll teach them why they should've never tossed me aside! I'll show that Father of mine that I'm the most valuable from them all! They'll learn that they should've never tossed me to the wolves in Russia in that god-forsaken land!"

In addition to making his mark on the family business, Hans also had a few other ambitious personal aims implanted within his head. He had a burning desire to go to school during the days and learn English. At the time, there was a program in Canada for immigrants that offered them the chance to attend English classes and get paid for it. But Hans' determinations didn't stop there. He also desired to go to university in his pursuit of an Electrical Engineering degree, something Hans commenced while living in Novosibirsk. Yet, when Hans mentioned his ideas to Father, big Corny, who slightly resembled a shorter, wider-headed version of Boss Hog from the Dukes of Hazard with a comb-over, erupted.

"I already have two parasitic professors!! Those "Fressers" ("consuming pigs", in German) are a couple of parasites! I don't need a third tapeworm for a child!!!"

Hans' siblings, Wanda, and his younger brother Rudi both went to university and were highly intelligent, but in Corny's eyes, they were more of a financial burden than anything. Corny wasn't going to have a third "academic child", so he immediately sent Hans to work on a construction site in the heart of frigid January, making Hans think,

"I have definitely taken a considerable step backwards in my life! These may have been the sort of conditions I was accustomed to before I started at the research institute where I was a somebody! Now I'm back to being a bloody nothing! Just like when I arrived in Novosibirsk! Just a work mule for a drunk of a dad and a bitch of a mother!!"

All what Father saw in Hans was a hardened-up operative, or rather, a workhorse from the heart of Siberia who could endure anything and everything. And much to Father's satisfaction, his newly found son never let him down. Hans was much more skilled, learned, and armed with good old-fashioned gumption than ever imagined. But for Hans, he was once again at the mercy of a bully of a dictator who simply utilized Hans' work ethic and ability as a means to pay the bills and profit through dirt-cheap labour.

During Hans' first week in Canada, Father showed Hans the apartment buildings that he himself helped build. Leaky toilets and taps had to be repaired. Rotting floors had to be replaced. Unmaintained furnaces weren't functioning properly. Sewer lines required a massive overhaul. Laundry sinks were backed-up. But that wasn't everything. Father also showed Hans, not only the ceramic tiles that had to be replaced around the bathtubs after many had already fallen off, but also the ceilings that came down as a result of seepages. All-in-all, the apartments were a complete and disgusting mess! Hans' first thought was,

"What a bunch of poorly and cheaply built lemons! And they say we're backwards peasants in Russia! Arrogant fools! This is the best country in the world?? What a joke! And now I work for a tyrant in a "democracy" who doesn't have clue about building anything! And he's trying to lead me! I was a somebody in Russia! They truly valued me! Russians pay more attention to details, whereas Canadians simply focus on what's "up to code"."

Hans, though, then wondered, *"What code?"* To make matters worse, the water lines froze up and burst during the winters since the walls were not insulated. Every time this occurred, washrooms became flooded, which gradually led the ceiling of the highly-trafficked back door entrance to collapse. Pieces of the ceiling occasionally even came crashing down upon residents who threatened to counter with legal action. In addition, the townhouse apartments had a 2-foot overhang on the second floor in which all of the plumbing for the upstairs washrooms were situated. The bathtubs positioned right up against this outside wall resultantly created a lot of condensation on the second floor, causing the wood to rot and the re-applied ceramic tiles around the bathtub to peel away or pop right off the wall. Corny couldn't afford to buy new tiles, so he attempted to re-apply tiles that had already fallen off. Compounding the issues was the fact that the plaster was pealing off of the ceiling that buckled from contact with water. All of these repairs had to be attended to right away during the bitterly cold winter days and evenings, or otherwise the whole building could have fallen into complete decay. Or perhaps, Corny just wanted to utilize Hans around the clock so that he wouldn't be able to become comfortable at home after 9 to 5 days.

Hans became responsible for fixing ruptured pieces of pipe and replacing them with new ones, something carried out by soldering new pipes to adequate existing ones. Gloves couldn't be worn during the entire process, so conducting the daunting task in sub-zero conditions was more than unbearable. Even the pipes from the laundry tubs and kitchen sinks had to be replaced. And the condition of the parents' home wasn't much better. So, on one windy, blustery cold January evening, Hans arrived home from work and decided to help out, in an attempt to impress the family, by going up onto the snowy roof to patch up a leak next to the chimney with tar. The radiating full moon reflecting off of the snowy roof, along with rays of light originating from the street lights offered Hans sufficient lighting to work away into the frigid night. After brushing the snow encircling the chimney with a broom, Hans applied some of the hot tar that he heated up in the family's furnace room.

After about an hour, Hans finished the job and was ready to come down. Though as he stood up, a mighty gust of wind swept across Hans' face, causing his eyes to water. Then, all of a sudden, as Hans side-stepped down the snow-covered roof, another strong gust of wind howled through the night right before Hans heard a slamming thud! Looking over to his right, Hans saw that the ladder had fallen onto the solid, frozen snowy ground. At that very moment, Hans realized that he was stranded on top of the roof! Nobody was around to help him out. Out of despair, Hans defeatedly sat down in the snow upon the black shingles, and simply hoped that somebody would come along and rescue him. In the meantime, Hans wondered to himself,

"Just what the hell did I get myself into! Why did I come to this god-forsaken country to live with this horrific family?!? I'm here working, while that fat blimp stuffs and drinks himself out of his own personal misery for having a bitch for a wife and the most selfish kids ever!! So, when the hell is Corny gonna come out and check on me!!!"

During these moments, Father, Mother, and Hans' grandmothers ate away inside the warm confines of the Friesen home. The vision of Corny suckling away on his customary shot, or rather bottle of Whiskey left a bitter taste in Hans' mouth. After being stranded on the roof for nearly an hour, a lady in her 40's in a blue dress spotted Hans from her kitchen window. She immediately came out and crossed the street in an attempt to rescue Hans, but to no avail; she just couldn't lift the ladder out of the snow. Eventually, she hollered up to Hans, *"I'll go get your dad!"* Hans' first thought was, *"Oh, great! Now I'm gonna hear it from that lazy, fat blimp!!!"*

Minutes later, big Corny marched out of the house. As soon as Father arrived on scene, he snarled,

"Just how stupid could you be to put the ladder up in such a shabby way that it could come down so easily!?!?"

Hans thought, *"Oh boy! He sounds just like his bitter brother (Jacob in Novosibirsk)!!"*

The woman who came to Hans' rescue was absolutely appalled by Corny's vicious behaviour and vile tone of voice and told him so even though she couldn't understand one word of Corny's German rant.

"Why do you yell at him like that?!?! That's your son!!!"

Absolutely numb and frozen to the bones from the cold and gusting wind that took the ladder tumbling to the frozen, snowy, and icy ground, Hans could barely make his way down the ladder that Father placed up against the eavesdrop of the roof. Working an entire day on a cold construction site prior to going up on the roof didn't help Hans' cause. No one even bothered to check-up on Hans, after it was Father's incessant whining about the roof not being properly repaired by the contractors that prompted Hans to make an attempt at fixing the area around the chimney himself in the first place.

The following day, Hans had to attend to the uninsulated and leaking basement walls of the home. Suffice to say, the brutal task of not only digging around the walls, but also cleaning, pargeting, tarring, and applying water proofing, before backfilling the soil in sub-zero conditions brought Hans to dismay. However, that wasn't enough - another project mercilessly awaited him. The main sewer of the house was improperly laid, so whenever leaves, plastic, or snow covered the drain, the basement flooded – the exact basement in which Hans' parents made Hans sleep, a basement in which water ran down the walls. The accompanying moisture made Hans' room musty and damp, a room that was not as warm as the cozy conditions upstairs. And even though there was a comfortable bed and room on the main floor where Hans could've comfortably slept, that room was reserved for only one person – Hans' younger brother, Rudi - who no longer resided at home. Hans, on the other hand, was around and responsible to bring the home up to snub, as well as fixing chimneys at the apartments that were also leaking, causing not only fumes to enter homes, but also Hans to fume to himself.

"Your own blood, with silver spoons in their mouths, and now they want to draw gold from my sweat."

Hans carried out all of these tasks in the evenings, and even on weekends since during the day, he had to earn his keep and money by carrying out construction work. To add insult to injury, Hans was never compensated for all of the extra hours that he put into repairing the apartments and home, since to his newly-found father, Hans was "just" earning his keep. Big Corny shared the same sentiments and visions for Hans as all of Hans' "father figures" from his past. Hans seemingly had a knack for finding people who desired to take full advantage of him, while Hans' pride alone prevented him from defending himself and taking control of the situation by confronting his demons. God was seemingly trying to teach Hans a lesson by providing him with the same circumstances, though through different situations and protagonists, yet Hans refused to learn. Guilty of ignoring numerous signs and warnings, Hans was left to prove himself to horrific humans throughout his entire life, which meant working like a dog, usually on behalf of someone else.

A certain Uncle Henry, a manual labourer and bookkeeper for the construction company, once told Hans while on the work site,

"Your father quit after you arrived and set up his "office" at the local coffee shop. Corny traded in his coveralls for a suit and tie. I wish I could do the same."

Before Hans arrived, Father did, or at least attempted to carry out almost every single task pertaining to the construction business. Though, all that changed when Hans arrived from the Soviet Union and Corny discovered his workhorse. But if it were any consolation to Hans, he proved the doctors wrong. They informed him, *"You're no longer capable of carrying out any kind of strenuous labour, such as construction."* The Russians believed that after all of Hans' injuries, he was no longer useful to the country, leading the Soviet authorities to finally permit Hans to leave the USSR. But just like always, Hans proved the doctors wrong, though in this case, at his own expense. There was seemingly no stopping Hans when he was driven to impress anyone and everyone – or in this case - to appease his devious and inhumane parents. But it came at a cost. Hans experienced a strong lingering throbbing originating from his broken neck during his first two years in Canada. Past injuries and surgeries plagued Hans. Unnerving sensations traveled down from Hans' neck right into his shoulders, before reverberating through his arms. Hans' right arm eventually went completely numb; he couldn't even turn his head sideways. But as usual, Mother and Hans' old man showed absolutely no empathy. They assumed that Hans was pretending and faking his torment. Avoiding work at any cost was a typical ploy of their other two kids. And even though Father had to sign a document stating that he agreed to take care of and support Hans for life after Hans' horrific medical history was disclosed to the Canadian authorities when Hans' parents applied on his behalf to immigrate from the USSR, the parents showed Hans absolutely no compassion following his recently broken neck and not so distant multiple surgeries on his arm as a result of blood poisoning. Father made sure that the family profited from Hans' arrival, and not the other way around, by forcing Hans to help support them.

Corny simply knew no boundaries, unlike Hans' Russian compatriots. In Russia, Hans was shown sympathy by his employer while recovering from his illness and injuries, leaving Hans learning the hard way that the Russians showed him more mercy than his very own parents who compelled Hans to push a burdensome wheelbarrow around; shovel heavy gravel and dirt; use a pick; work with concrete; and in addition, frame houses. Such work induced a lot of pain within Hans' arm that was operated on five times. The throbbing aching was sometimes so horrific at night time that it kept Hans awake until the sun rose the following morning, when he had to go back to work. One day, Hans informed his parents, *"I'm experiencing excruciating pain."*, but his pleas fell on deaf ears. Father growled back in a tirade,

"You just don't want to work!! I don't need another suck! I already have two of them! You just don't want to work!! I'm gonna teach you how to work!"

Hans felt as if Father was afraid that Hans would turn into a loafing "moocher" if he wasn't pushed. Every time that Corny spoke to or about Hans, Father seemingly refused to regard Hans as if he were his child. He constantly addressed Hans in an authoritative manner as if Hans were merely an employee of Corny's and nothing more. Mother, on the other hand, who spent most of her time alone in her room whenever Hans was around, simply ignored Hans, along with his complaints, exactly like when Hans was a little child. Her solution was rather simple, something she repeatedly stated to Corny, though in English.

"Just get rid of that stupid guy from Russia!"

That phrase became engrained and echoed in Hans' mind for an eternity, even though he didn't fully understand the "phrase" at the time. Yet, eventually Hans fully caught on to all of their derisive declarations when he finally furthered his English skills years later. Mother's heartless statements were a far cry from her expressions of love declared through her more than amicable letters to Hans that he received while still living in the USSR.

"We want you here! We miss you so much! Come here and work. You can carry on the family business."

After reading those letters, Hans felt wanted, desired, and even loved - like a true member of the family. Though, the only truthful word in those letters was "work", resultantly, leading Hans to think,

"The Communists had much bigger hearts than Father and these beasts!"

But Corny's insults went even deeper when he found out that a chain for the backhoe went missing. Upon discovery, he approached Hans, viciously demanding to know,

"Where's the chain from the backhoe?!??!?! Hofmann says that you stole it!!"

Hans, absolutely beside himself after hearing such an absurd accusation, retorted appropriately with an absurdity of his own.

"Yeah, it's under my pillow. I sleep with it every night!"

Hans saw the humour in his response, but Corny certainly did not, especially after he actually checked underneath Hans' pillow. Not even after they both learned two weeks later that Hofmann had traded in the chain for a few bottles of wine did Corny offer Hans an apology following the preposterous accusation. Corny's behaviour more times than not left Hans in awe. Hans though, wrote all of Corny's antics off to post-war traumatic stress disorder, the same disorder that led Hans to be shot at in Russia by that madman on a horse decades earlier.

CHAPTER 56

The Siblings

In Hans' conquest to justify his existence, he sought to prove that he was just as valuable as, if not more so than his siblings Rudi and Wanda. Therefore, instead of rebelling against his parents, Hans worked harder than ever to please them in an attempt to acquire their approval. So, when spring arrived on the horizon, Hans, in his "free time", began mowing not only his parent's back yard, but also the expansive and neglected lawn that had grown to two feet in height at the apartment complexes. And much to Hans' satisfaction, their self-propelled push lawnmower designed for grooming golf course greens, though rather heavy and immobile, groomed quite elegantly once Hans repaired it. While Hans was down on all fours tending to the mower on a mildly pleasant sunny Sunday morning, with his hands covered in grease, Father, the "Old Man", approached Hans in the near distance. Witnessing his workhorse in action, Corny wished to motivate Hans even further by declaring,

"One day, this will all be yours. The others already got their share. I've raised 'em; paid for their education; and provided them with a good life. But you never got yours."

That made sense to Hans. It seemed only logical since Hans never received anything from Father throughout his entire life. However, time would only tell if the "Old Man" was sincere and honourable in his intentions. Corny though, sounded so convincing with his rhetoric.

"I've already done so much for the other two (kids), and I get nothing in return! They always want everything, and then even more and more and more!! Zwei Fressers!! They expect everything, yet appreciate nothing!"

Hans sensed Father's pain and disappointment deriving from the actions of Wanda and Rudi, which generated significant friction amongst the family. Mother spoiled Wanda and Rudi, incidentally aiding in her cause to occasionally turn them against their own father. Accordingly, Father felt compelled to strive for Rudi's and Wanda's appreciation, "love", and approval. Nevertheless, Wanda didn't feel favoured, and constantly reiterated, *"You spoil Rudi!"*

Mother helped pit each and every one of them against each other until vile rivalries became established. Unreserved, yet concealed animosity was the name of their game that was played within a rancorous and repulsive circle. While necessitating a shoulder to cry on, Father, sincerely, or perhaps insincerely, placated Hans with calculated diplomacy.

"You never ask for anything unlike your brother and sister, who always ask for material items and money as if that's suppose to make them feel any less miserable! We've done so much for those two, but they're still never happy and satisfied! Insatiable gluttons and "Fressers"! But you – you're a working machine! If we would've only got you out of Russia when you were 16, we'd be long time millionaires!"

Hans, at least on the surface, was usually happy with what he had - just as long as he got treated and paid fairly as well as deservedly recognized for his contributions; though, that was a rarity when it came to his family, leaving Hans infuriated. Behind Hans' "innocent" and docile demeanour resided a fury of resentment and an inferiority complex that ate at him while fuelling his madness as it consumed his heart. Hans tenaciously strived in an attempt to not be regarded as a "burden." But his drive only proliferated his own personal morass. The harder Hans pushed to prove his existence and be treated as a child by his parents, the wider the gap of injustice enlarged, which only split the cleft between him and his family further, a family in which each individual member saw himself or herself as their own division and entity.

Resenting the parents who never raised him, yet who sought to squeeze out as much sweat as possible left their newly discovered working mule, Hans, feeling like an ass in the presence of family whose conduct replicated the habits of parasitic tapeworms. Almost as a poetic paradox, Father and Mother doggedly offered Hans' siblings everything, while only providing Hans with their consequential resentment. Hans' own sense of deprival compelled him to intensely labour even further for his parents' acceptance, yet to no avail. Mother remained unceasingly protective of only her "Canadian" children, so they never learned proper ways, except to always get their way. Ironically enough though, it would be Wanda who occasionally blurted out, *"If it were up to Mother, she would've never had any kids! Not one I tell ya!"*

A few months following Hans' arrival in Canada, Wanda was set to marry a chap of British descent serving with the US army. This tall and strapping lad was born and raised in Beamsville; but since his parents couldn't afford to pay for his university tuition, he enlisted in the US army in order to get a free university education. Wanda and Rudi had resentment for their German roots, something rather common amongst children of first generation ethnic Germans in Canada at the time, leaving Wanda more than proud to take on a British name, something even Rudi sought to do by taking on his future's wife name "Herrington." Though, after Corny threatened to disinherit Rudi if he were ever to do so, Rudi had a change of heart.

When Wanda's wedding day eventually arrived, Hans' brother Rudi finally made his much-awaited appearance from Kingston, where he was studying math at the prestigious Queen's University. The festive occasion afforded Hans his first opportunity to meet his thin, tall, lanky, and dirty blonde-haired eight years younger brother who Hans had already heard a lot about. Rudi was quite the gifted student, and actually skipped a grade in elementary school. With his lofty intelligence, Rudi knew how to cruise his way through life by his smarts alone.

When Rudi entered the Friesen family home on the evening before Wanda's wedding day, Father formally introduced Hans to Rudi; yet, when Hans offered his brother his hand that Rudi seemingly reluctantly grasped, Rudi gave off the impression that Hans' existence was nearly irrelevant to him. Hans figured that perhaps the language barrier discouraged Rudi from conversing with Hans, so he just left their odd brotherly introduction at that. Following the wedding, Wanda and Hans' new brother-in-law Gary left for Europe where Gary was deployed by the US Army as a Lieutenant, or at least that's what Wanda claimed. He was going to be stationed at a military base in Germany for about two years prior to being recalled back to the USA where he would carry out the rest of his service, duty, and stint in the US Army. Savouring the fruits of his 2-year tour of service in Germany, Gary eventually enrolled in his US military-funded free education at Michigan University in Ann Arbor.

Gary should have been on cloud nine, after his not-so-death-defying feat in the US Army that afforded him free education and an experience abroad. But Hans could sense, even during the early stages of his arrival in Canada, animosity and arrogance originating from Gary, and eventually even from Hans' very own sister Wanda directed towards him. Prior to moving to Michigan, Wanda and Gary stopped by Hans' parents' house in order to gather up their belongings. Purchasing a new car wasn't necessary following their return to Canada, since Gary and Wanda were in possession of a VW Bug that Gary brought back with him from Germany. They only intended to use the vehicle to cruise around town, Europe, and the Autobahn while living in Germany; however, since the military covered the shipping costs to transport the vehicle back to Canada, Wanda and Gary happily brought the VW Bug home with them, even though the car wasn't functioning properly for some time. And by the time that they collected all of their belongings from the parents' house, and were ready to head off to Michigan, their Volkswagen Bug completely conked out. In a state of panic, Wanda and Gary immediately asked Hans, *"Could we "borrow" your car?"*

Hans responded graciously to their request, and off went Gary and Wanda to Ann Arbor in Hans' Ford Cougar. Yet, after returning from Michigan two weeks later, the two of them decided, *"We want to keep your car John (Hans)!"* To add insult to their shocking demand, Gary, who enjoyed poking at the poor-English speaking and understanding Hans blurted out,

"You don't even know how to maintain your car! And since you're living at home, you don't even need the Cougar! You've got the company pick-up truck."

Mother completely agreed.

"Go ahead. You two can keep John's car for as long as you want. I don't see a problem with that whatsoever."

But Father definitely did! He became absolutely livid! For once, Father stood up for Hans' cause by interjecting! Corny instantly bellowed out,

"That's John's car!! He paid for it himself! They're not taking it! They have no right to it!"

Hans didn't completely understand what was said, since it was all communicated in English, which he was still gradually learning at the time. However, Hans could certainty sense a lot of hostility from his sister and Gary after it was all said and done. They treated Hans as if he were an oblivious moron, deeming him as just the "stupid guy from Russia." Hans had very few opportunities to enrich his English language skills in Canada, especially after not learning a single word while living in the USSR. Either way, Hans knew enough though to know that his name had became anglicized to "John" from "Hans" after metamorphosing into "Ivan" in Russia, just as much as he was certain that Wanda and Gary were using condescending terms to characterize and address him. Yet, at the end of the day, it would be Wanda and Gary who turned out looking "stupid!" when it was discovered that their VW Bug's carburetor was simply in need of a good scrubbing. After a solid carburetor cleansing, the car was more drivable than ever. So, Gary and Wanda ultimately drove their Bug back to Michigan, instead of Hans' Cougar. In poetic fashion, and contrary to what Gary and Wanda claimed, it was they who could not maintain their car.

But that was of little consolation to Hans. He was left with such a strange feeling after each encounter with his sister and new husband. In this case, they actually made him feel as if he had taken something from Wanda and Gary, even though that was the furthest thing from the truth. But that was irrelevant. Hans merely saw himself as a member of the outcast within his new belittling surroundings. It was an extremely bitter and shocking "conclusion" after intensively striving to become re-united with his "family". Feeling utterly unwelcomed and out of place, Hans struggled with· agonising emotional pain and a perpetual sense of inferiority. To make matters worse, Hans' relationship with his brother Rudi wasn't any better. Yet, it was apparently solid enough for Rudi to ask Hans at the end of the summer, a year after Wanda's wedding,

"Can I take your car to Queen's University in Kingston big brother? It's the start of the fall semester and I need to transport a few belongings up there. What do ya say? Maybe you can come visit me up there."

Rudi's request, oddly enough finally made Hans feel somewhat like a true and accepted member of the family, even though Hans, deep down, knew that he was just being taken advantage of as usual through a means of calculating brotherly manipulation. Hans answered Rudi in broken English.

"You may take car. But bring back soon!"

Rudi responded, *"Sure thing big brother! Whatever you say! No problem!"*

Rudi usually returned to university by either going up with the train, or having his parents drive him up. But since he had numerous belongings to carry this time around, and not to mention access to Hans' car, Rudi wanted to travel and transport his effects in style, and what better way to arrive back at university than in his "new" brother's Ford Cougar, leaving Hans with the family business' blue Ford pick-up truck to drive around. Eight months later, Rudi returned the car at the end of the school year. He didn't even bother to come home for Christmas that year. To fuel Hans' grief, Rudi brought Hans' car back in such rough shape that some of the door handles were completely broken off. The Ford Cougar was so beaten up that the hood couldn't even properly close. Hans furiously erupted at the sight of his vehicle, especially considering that he provided Rudi with a vehicle that appeared virtually brand-new, but now looked like a 30-year-old car. Rudi, though, didn't feel bad about it one bit.

"That car was a piece of garbage and a pile of junk anyways!"

Hans immediately brought the car to the dealer a day later, since it was still under warranty; however, the dealer let Hans know,

"There's no warranty under such conditions! This vehicle has been completely abused! You've been reckless!"

Father too, wasn't impressed one bit either, but all what he could say was,

"The more you educate them, the dumber they become!"

Hans paid for new handles out of his own pocket, and even replaced them himself, along with adjusting the hood so that it could properly close once again. But the dents couldn't be remedied, remaining a constant visible reminder of just how horribly Hans was being treated by his atrocious family of monsters and misfits; yet, a family who he remained loyal to – loyalty, perhaps stemming from greed and hopes that one day Father would leave him everything as promised - a day when the "Old Man" would retire from being a wheeling and dealing businessman and hand the reins to Hans. Such brainwashing began in Russia, when Mother wrote,

"Father can hardly wait until you come over and take over the family business, Your brother and sister have no interest in it."

Hans wasn't too thrilled that the family business was in construction, but their invitation showed him that they were going to accept him as a member of their family, a family that he finally belonged to after decades of yearning for such, a yearning that constantly led Hans to attempt to please them. And so perhaps greed wasn't a driving factor behind Hans' motives whatsoever.

In the USSR, Hans knew that he had a family somewhere out there, but he didn't know just who was alive and who wasn't, leaving Hans living in suspense. So, when Hans arrived in Canada, he felt relieved to see his family intact, a family that he finally became a physical part of; yet, his state of relief was all too short-lived, especially after seeing that the interior of his Ford Cougar was also a complete mess, almost as if Rudi desired to hurt Hans on purpose. Rudi, as it just so happened, was using Hans' car to go drinking to Montreal with his university buddies over the weekends. Further unhidden signs of unruliness included the sight of tires that were so worn out from reckless driving that they too had to be replaced. Rudi's adolescent and insolent behaviour ruined the car, but Hans was footed with the bill. Hans' parents tried to minimize the damages.

"Rudi knew neither how to treat nor operate frozen locks, nor check the oil."

Following Rudi's year at university, the parents vehemently attempted to convince him to work for the family construction company over the summer. Though, Rudi wouldn't hear a word of it. Ultimately, yet reluctantly, the parents gave Rudi "permission" to use "his" savings from the parents-funded bank account to travel throughout Europe for the entire summer, almost seemingly and sadistically as a reward for Rudi's "exemplary" behaviour, instead of working with Hans for the family business like Father desired. Despite Corny's pleas, Rudi pompously proclaimed and explained, right in front of Hans' face,

"I don't want to work in construction with Hans because construction is only for dummies! Only stupid people work construction! I'm getting a university education! I am too smart for that!"

Not long after Rudi departed for Europe, a certain Uncle Henry, a distant family member, revealed to Hans while on the construction site during a break,

"That flunky Rudi failed a bunch of classes in university last year."

Rudi was the parents' favourite and golden boy, so they wouldn't have dared to inform Hans of Rudi's failing ways. It would've been a major disgrace if such information ever entered the air in the presence of their "inferior", slow-speaking, dim-witted sounding son in his non-native tongue, Hans. It was during Rudi's travels that Father and Mother became aware, and consequentially, utterly infuriated over the fact that Rudi had a sub-par year at Queen's University. And before they knew it, the word spread amongst the relatives, who surprisingly, and somewhat callously and mockingly basked in hearing of the demise of the "future Treasury Minister of Canada", yet deservingly so. Hans' parents constantly hoisted Rudi up onto pedestal, in front of and at the expense of other relatives and family friends, by minimizing and degrading the abilities of these same relatives' and family friends' kids with the upmost pleasure. News of Rudi's failures left his parents completely ashamed and furious, especially while he lived it up in Europe; however, in a strange twist of events, the parents actually placed the blame on no one other than Hans. *It's your fault that Rudi failed classes!! You let him have your car you Dummkopf!!"*

The fact that Rudi kept the Cougar without Hans' permission was irrelevant. Hans retorted,

"Ja. I was willing to lend Rudi the car to aid in his move to Kingston. And he could've taken the train, but you adamantly insisted that he take my car to Kingston! Not me! You! So, look in the mirror!!"

After somewhat reluctantly sharing Hans' sediments, the parents searched out new scapegoats, so they shifted the blame onto the other students from Beamsville who Rudi was studying with at Queen's University. Apparently, Rudi's fellow students were the culprits at fault, since they "clearly" instructed Rudi to keep the car. In the parents', at times delusional minds, their truth as they twisted it, probably sounded something like:

"Since you're the only one with a car, you keep it Rudi boy!! You keep it!! To hell with that invalid, Russian, Communist brother of yours!! You keep it Rudi boy so we can go party it up in Montreal every weekend!!"

But Rudi's lack of discretion went beyond these transgressions. Months later, after returning from Europe, Rudi took Hans' car to his girlfriend's parents' place in Peterborough after Hans was dumb enough to lend his

John Friesen

Ford Cougar out to Rudi once again. When Rudi returned from his trip up north, Hans' car came back fully covered in tar! Rudi absurdly took the Cougar through a freshly tarred side road without even bothering to wash Hans' car immediately afterwards, causing the tar to dry right onto the vehicle's body! Unable to remove the tar with a cloth upon the car's return, Hans temperamentally enquired with Rudi,

"Just why didn't you clean the car afterwards? So, are you gonna clean it now?!?!?"

Rudi simply and derogatorily laughed right in Hans' face, basically implying, *"What the hell are you talking about?!?"* Hans ultimately used gasoline to remove the tar from his car. Rudi believed that all physical labour was beneath him because he was bequeathed with the ability to be a math god. Hans' parents had extremely high hopes for Rudi who they regarded as a genius. They constantly reiterated,

"He's gonna be the Canadian Minister of Finance and Wanda is gonna be the Minister of Education!"

Following high school, Rudi got accepted into the illustrious Queen's University, leaving Hans' parents prouder than ever of their dear Rudi. Father felt like a king and the Kaiser all in one. However, their bragging exploits about Rudi's feats and aptitude had its downside. Upon learning of Rudi's failing ways, everyone whose kids were degraded by Rudi's parents started saying,

"Just how does Rudi go from being a whiz kid to a flunky!?!?!?! Ah, hahahahaha!"

It was an enormous blow to Corny's and Mother's massive egos. Conversely, both "Tante Mia", and her husband "Onkel Henry", a relative originally from Berlin and an accountant by trade prior to finding himself fighting on the front lines in the Battle of Stalingrad for the German Wehrmacht, could only rejoice in Rudi's downfall. Rudi's parents constantly minimized Uncle Henry's son, so Henry and his wife Mia smugly exulted in seeing the Friesens crash down to reality. To them, Rudi's demise looked really good on the big-mouth Friesens, especially because their egos were temporarily crushed and humiliated in the process. But Mia and Henry, both proud Germans, were also not immune and free from their egos, leading them, or at least only Mia to not think much of the "Russian" Hans. Though, all that changed at a family gathering, after Hans showed his smarts by figuring out how to use a nut-cracking device that no one else in the house could operate. Mia, who self-admittedly said she had no filter when she spoke, immediately "thanked" Hans, with a back-handed compliment.

"You're from Russia. You're supposed to be stupid."

It was such reciprocating mentalities that forced the entire Friesen clan, including Hans to be bent on proving just how important and seemingly "superior" they were while strikingly feeling inferior the entire time that they tried. The Friesens just had to prove their worth to the world, more times than not, by condemning and mocking the "onlookers". And perhaps that explains why they all possessed tempers that knew nothing of temperance.

Yet, nothing seemingly ever affected Rudi. He was immune to all reprimands. Even when his parents tightened the strings on his financing, Rudi easily circumvented the circumstances by somehow acquiring a student loan, despite the fact that his parents were paying for his entire education. The loan was used to fund his travels all over New York State throughout the summer holidays with his girlfriend, Mary. Father, once again, desired that Rudi work construction during the university summer break so that he could contribute to his own education. But Rudi wouldn't hear of it. He doggedly refused to heed Father's word, even if his actions left Father enraged and disappointed. Rudi's disobedience apparently struck Mother quite hard as well, but instead of facing Rudi's unruliness head on, she sought out a scapegoat, which more times than not was Hans. During Rudi's latest episode of antics, Mother vented her fury in the direction of Hans. She became colder towards him than ever. The silent tension could be cut with a chainsaw. Her amassed animosity especially erupted whenever other people mentioned,

John Friesen

"What a nice guy John (Hans) is! He's so hard-working and respectful to his parents even though they didn't even raise him."

Hans, however, in reality, had bitter and disdain loathing towards his parents for treating him despicably, especially after abandoning him as a child. Hans was leading a charade for the outside world to witness while he crumbled and withered on the inside, amassing a vicious bout of abhorrence. His façade and pretence plagued him internally, while his need for acceptance drove him to impress in his struggle for much yearned for affection, acceptance, and love from his parents – a fallacy that denied him reality while he invented a fictional fairy tale in his mind. Hans vehemently hoped that his parents would at least hold true to their promise, and ultimately leave him the entire company, or at the very least, Hans' fair (1/3) share of their estate. Receiving his fair share would not only confirm that they considered Hans as an equal to his siblings, but also act as an indication of remorse for losing him, even though the event surrounding his disappearance was NEVER brought up.

However, Hans was battling a force that he didn't understand, yet one that he knew all too well. Mother's antagonistic onslaught ultimately prevailed, resultantly dictating Hans, and to a certain degree Corny, to obsequiously obey Mother's semi-concealed directive. Hans' ego desired to show just how much he could contribute with his exemplary knowledge and skill to show that he wasn't merely the "stupid guy from Russia." Nevertheless, Rudi clearly remained Mother's favourite, vexing Hans in the process. After Rudi got a teaching job in Niagara Falls, after completing university, Mother rubbed salt in Hans' wounds.

"Look at how nicely dressed Rudi is! Rudi wears a suit! And look at you (Hans)! You're always filthy! You're a filthy, construction-working slob!"

Hans considered Rudi to be a defiant loafer and a fraud, whereas Hans always tried to do right by his parents, making himself a fraud in the process. The very next day, Hans epitomized and embodied his distorted reality by putting on a suit and sitting around the house elegantly dressed in an attempt to deride Mother, though inadvertently, becoming a reactionary marionette to his parents through his own actions.

Yet, despite "only" working construction, Hans eventually saved up enough money to purchase a brand-new Ford Mustang, rather than use the money to move into a place of his own, something that flabbergasted the nicely dressed Rudi, and even his now wife Mary. When they caught a glimpse of Hans' new car, jealousy and envy consumed them. Mary became so insatiably covetous that she blurted out,

"We want your Mustang John!"

Hans brashly responded, *"Look, I bought this car, you go buy your own!"*

But Rudi didn't stop there. He was persistent and relentless. He belligerently retorted,

"Why don't you go buy your own!! We all know that Father bought that car for you! I want it!"

Hans wouldn't back down either though, so it was only a matter of time before Mother approached Father and barked out, *"Corny, go buy Rudi a Mustang!"* Father, perturbed and non-obliging, vehemently reiterated, *"No! I bought Rudi a Nova!"*

But Hans sought more than a nice car. Witnessing Father's property development feats and the construction company flourish led Hans to desire a share in the success. Though, Hans sought it not by asking for a fair share of ownership in the company, but rather, by seeking the funds to purchase a parcel of land from the Town of Lincoln. The town ultimately provided Hans with the loan to purchase the land where he erected an industrial commercial building on Union Road in Beamsville (Lincoln) for himself in 1972, four years after Hans' arrival in Canada. And even though Father had to co-sign on the bank agreement to secure the mortgage to build the building, it was Hans alone who acquired enough cement building blocks from the local cement factory, which it sold to him as "seconds" since these blocks contained a few chips. Hans was resourceful, diligent, and industrious, traits that afforded him the means to excavate the foundations and lay the initial blocks for the base of the building on his own. When the foundations were finally finished, Hans hired a few trades people to lay the blocks and raise the roof to complete the building. To save money, Hans used unwanted gravel from people's driveways to fill in the inside and outside of the building. When people had their driveways paved with concrete, the gravel had to be removed, and Hans happily took it away for his own benefit.

One day, while on another job, as Hans rectified a major sewer installation problem relating to a new block of homes, Bezel, Corny's land speculation and construction associate and also a man of Russian origins, mentioned to Corny,

"John saved the day by correcting this sewer job! He's a miracle worker on that backhoe. Let's sell him some property below the asking price so he can share in the spoils by flipping the lands to make a return!"

Corny agreed. Hans ultimately sold the parcels of property that he acquired at a bargain basement price, landing himself a healthy profit. He then used those proceeds to cover a down payment and other building costs surrounding the construction of the shop.

Profiting from his business ventures, Hans became enticed to purchase another piece of property after a regular customer named Roy Cooke, a man in his 50's who made a fortune by buying cheaper, usually run-down homes before renovating them himself just to subsequently sell them off for a significant gain, approached Hans with a tempting proposition. Cooke, who occasionally helped Hans on the job site, sometimes even in a suit and tie, was a diligent worker, leading him to appreciate Hans' work ethic, even though Cooke didn't care much for Corny. Valuing all of Hans' back wrenching help, Cooke offered Hans some property right next to Hans' building for a good price. Following Cooke's proposal, Hans, with some savings from flipping properties and rental income, immediately approached Father about helping him obtain some immediate additional financing from the bank for the land purchase. Working long days made it impossible for Hans to head over to the bank since it closed at 5 pm on that Friday, and was completely closed on the Saturday. Father immediately and inquisitively enquired, *"What's this loan for?"* Hans answered Corny, *"It's for property for a second shop."* Father paused for a second, simply murmuring *"hmmmm"*, before telling Hans, *"Okay, I'll take care of it! I'll secure a loan."*

Hans' link to his family did in fact provide him with opportunities that others couldn't obtain, but inadvertently, left him remaining over-dependent upon them, especially if he expected to acquire the financing for a second property. Yet, when Hans approached Cooke and inquired about the property the following week, Cooke responded somewhat timidly and surprised.

"Oh, I sold it to your Father. He bought it for Rudi. Corny secured the mortgage. I assumed you knew all about it and were okay with it. I could've maybe got you a mortgage if I knew otherwise."

Hans, in shock and a state of fury, let Cooke know,

"I could've obtained the financing! You should've approached me first before selling it off to big Corny. My dad is a sleaze-ball! I'm the one who told Father about the land being up for sale in the first place!"

Hans was certain that Mother was behind all this! She surely must have intervened, leading Father to incidentally go behind Hans' back and buy the property, and ultimately construct the building for Rudi instead. Mother was the true boss behind closed doors. She controlled Father. The brutal tyrant Corny became a toadying puppy dog in Mother's presence, leading him to pass on his shame by dominating Hans, making him Corny's punching bag. Rudi necessitated the building because his teaching career wasn't going as planned. After a year of working as a high school teacher, Rudi, as told by relatives, had a nervous breakdown and couldn't continue, leading him to state,

"I want to work with John! I have to eat my words! Construction isn't only for dumb people."

Hans mockingly responded, *"Are you sure that you wanna work for a stupid guy?"*

Father was skeptical, but encouraging, while insulting Hans in the process. He informed Rudi, right in front of Hans, *"If John can do it, you can do it ten times better."*

But Rudi turned out to be more of a working loafer than a gofer in every way, which included capitalizing on having access to the construction company's gas tank to fill his personal car, something that Father desired Rudi to conceal from Hans. So, when Hans drove by the shop one evening while Rudi was pumping some gas into his car, Rudi drove off in a jiffy, leaving his company keys behind in the process. When Corny went to pump gas the next day at the shop and discovered a pair of keys just sitting in the pump, he stormed home in Hans' direction and let him have it!

"How stupid could you be you idiot to leave your keys in the pump!"

As Hans calmly looked into Corny's eyes, Hans casually stuck his hands into his pocket and pulled out his set of keys before retorting, *"My keys are right here. Whose keys do you have?"* Corny's tone immediately changed, but Hans' situation in his miserable family only continued to worsen. As for Rudi, he barely lasted a year in construction before citing *"issues with noise and dust"* as a reason to quit and elect to pursue a clerkship at an accounting firm, a position that Corny helped him obtain.

CHAPTER 57

Linguistic Assistance

Witnessing such a complete lack of gratitude and empathy only fuelled Hans' fire to distance himself from the family. But first, he had to properly learn the language by going to school if he ever expected to succeed on his own, despite the fact that his parents were totally against it. They kept reiterating,

"When we came to Canada, we didn't go to school and we've done quite well for ourselves! I don't need another educated bum!"

But Hans, perhaps for the first time, didn't care what Corny thought. On the contrary. Father's devious and demeaning behaviour only furthered Hans' desire to develop a stronger command of the language, something of a necessity in his aim to severe ties from the family business, and even distance himself from his ruthless family altogether if need be. Despite living in Canada for over four years at this time, Hans didn't pick up English as quickly as he would've liked as a result of the fact that Hans was well immersed in German - at home with his parents and grandmothers, and on the work site where he worked with Germans who only communicated in German. Hans even stumbled across Russian speakers like Bezel the odd time. Hence, if Hans expected to further his English language aptitude, he had to start going to school. Hans carried out the maintenance tasks for the forty apartment units that Father owned, compelling Hans to communicate with the tenants in order to learn what they required. During conversations with these people, Hans constantly thought to himself,

"How can I properly solve their problems if I don't even know what they're requesting half the time! It makes me feel like an idiot! But I'm not an idiot! I just don't know the language very well! And how could Rudi and Wanda hold that against me! I didn't grow up here! They just want to make a fool of me!"

Yet, luckily enough for Hans, an English teacher actually lived in one of Corny's apartments, a man who was encouraging Hans to go to school in order to expedite his English learnings and competence by becoming more ensconced in the language, as opposed to solely, slowly, and gradually learning the language through day-to-day interactions such as conversing at a store, or by watching TV, something that Hans had little time for. When the English teacher in the apartments, a man in his 50's of east Asian descent named Mr. Minks, informed Hans, *"I teach English as a second language in the evenings at Beamsville District Secondary School. I can get you in!"*, Hans immediately enrolled in the class. But the parents were not pleased about this one bit. They fully opposed it.

"There's too much to do for the company and around the house! You're just wasting your time going to school, you Dummkopf!"

Yet, since the classes were after dark and working hours, Hans knew perfectly well that his parents just wanted to prevent him from furthering and enjoying himself simply because they were miserable control-mongers. Father and Mother always made Hans feel that because he was living under their roof, and not paying any room and board, he was totally indebted to them, especially after helping him escape the USSR. Therefore, in their eyes, it was Hans' responsibility to carry out all of the chores on their behalf. The parents were utterly convinced that he simply owed it, and everything for that matter to them, inadvertently leading them to own Hans, their once, and perhaps still discarded son.

CHAPTER 58

Work and Strife

Hans tolerated all of the uncompromising demands that were forced upon him by his parents. Fearing rejection and being thrown onto the streets within a foreign country drove Hans into a state of compromising compliance. Thoughts of being sent back to Russia constantly loomed over Hans' head. Before obtaining Canadian citizenship, Hans required a sponsor in order to enter and live in the country. As a result of this actuality, Hans' parents carried a legitimate threat over Hans, making him feel guilty because of it. Hans, rather forcibly, became obliged to Corny, who constantly threatened Hans.

"I vouched and signed the papers for you to live here after you arrived disabled! I'm responsible for taking care of you so you don't become a burden to Canada's social system. But I can have you sent back! That much I promise you!"

Hans had to wait five years after his arrival before he could become eligible to apply for Canadian citizenship. But by that time, he fell into a lull of comfort of being taken care of, while believing in myths of fortunes bestowed by his family. The turmoil of residing with and being at the mercy of his parents left Hans more determined than ever to learn English. He was certain that he could land a job elsewhere as an electrician or machinist. Hans, without a doubt, carried the qualifications and know-how to perform such duties. Hans' body, as a result of past surgeries, still found construction too arduous and strenuous, which only added to his

John Friesen

motivation to find a new line of work. Though, whenever he let Father know that he desired to look for another job elsewhere, Father responded accordingly, by threatening Hans.

"If you dare to "abandon" the family and business, I'll have you sent back to Russia in a heartbeat!!"

Corny constantly fuelled the fire and Hans' desire to depart the family, and even Canada by saying,

"I don't need another parasite since I already raised two of them! Someone needs to work now!"

Hans wasn't sure if those were mere threats or promises. Though, he possessed mixed feelings when it came to returning to Russia. His newly found family was still relatively, or rather superficially important to Hans, or at the very least their acceptance, and perhaps even inheritance. And Hans also wasn't sure just what kind of future awaited him back in Russia if he were to return, leading Hans to wonder to himself,

"Would I be going back to a great job, or a horrible disaster? But at least I got a regular paycheque in Russia! Though, what about Grandmother? How could I abandon her in Canada after all what she has done for me? Especially because I'm the only one here to protect her from Mother's violent attacks."

Despite the fact that Hans' life in Russia was much better prior to immigrating to Canada, Hans, "the tenant", remained blindly and dutifully "loyal" to his parents till the end, even through all of these nasty lessons suffered at the hands of his "landlords". Hans though felt challenged, challenged into becoming a obsequious servant with dreams of a substantial final payoff, through submissively heeding Father's words, provocations, threats – which were limitless. Corny's thirst for complete and heartless dominance over Hans fuelled his motives, means, and ends. Nevertheless, Hans, still defiantly went to night school a couple of evenings a week in order to develop a stronger command of the English language.

Thoughts of moving out and becoming totally independent always entered Hans' head, but in the end, he never acted upon them. Not in Zajarsk. Not in Novosibirsk. Not in Frunze. Not in Beamsville. Hans liked being taken care of, regardless of the cost. Accepting condemnation seemed like the price of riding someone else's coattails. Even when Hans could've taken his chances by totally distancing himself from the family after obtaining Canadian citizenship after five years in Canada, Hans forwent such an opportunity in the hope that his family would come to their senses and make him a major partner in the prosperous family business. Hans worked extremely hard, long, and productive days for the construction company, becoming a vital money-generating apparatus and contributing element to the company, especially considering that he worked relatively for peanuts. For all intensive purposes, Hans became the company – a one-man show. If he were to disappear, so would the company. Hans acquired immense know-how during his time in Russia. His abilities were, at times, completely irreplaceable. But Hans was too much of a coward to ever exercise the leverage that he possessed, even though in Mother's eyes, Hans was nothing more than a liability and a constant reminder of her loathing for her very own life.

Regardless of Hans' contributions, Mother's abominating derision for Hans mounted over the years. But Father had other sediments. On one occasion, after Mother and Wanda accused Hans of stealing rent money while Hans was sitting in another room but still in earshot, Corny countered his controlling and dominant wife's demand, *"Just get rid of that stupid guy from Russia!"*

"But I need him! I need somebody to work! Your other two (kids) and her freeloading, lazy spouse (Gary) just want to milk us dry! Hans at least contributes! And I know that daughter of yours in skimming from our rent stash! And it was her who bought lawn furniture at the hardware store by using our construction supplies account! John knows nothing of those purchases! He doesn't even know about the account and Penner Hardware Store for that matter! And stop accusing him of stealing! He wouldn't take the money if you handed it to him! You're both just a bunch of stupid bitches!!"

Mother brutishly responded, *"The stupid guy from Russia stole that money. Don't blame Wanda!!"*

Weeks later, Hans enquired with Father, *"So, did you find the money?"* Father growled back,

"Ahhh! What are you talking! Wanda has been taking money from there all the time!"

Wanda ultimately worked for a couple of years before getting married, but nevertheless, still milked the parents till the end. Hans, on the other hand, earned a pay cheque through an honest living. Corny rather simply deposited a lump-sum payment into Hans' "bank account" at the end of the year, an account in which Hans obligingly signed blank cheques out of for his rental building expenses and God knows what else "on behalf of" Corny. And how Hans' remuneration was calculated – nobody knows. Hans never even saw the bank balance, let alone bank book of his very own account. And if Hans, god-forbid, were to ever question the basis for his salary or ask to see his own bank book, he was immediately retorted with threats.

"We got you out of Russia! Never forget that!! We can always send you back!! Why don't you trust me!! What kind of ungrateful son are you!?! I'm doing all this for you! You son of a gun!!"

CHAPTER 59

Prophesized Love

Luckily enough, Hans got to escape his family, if only for a few hours at a time be it, whenever he attended night school to advance his English skills. His anticipation to head off to his English classes at Niagara College in St. Catharines only strengthened after spotting and eventually becoming acquainted with a Slavic girl much younger than him. When Hans first laid eyes on her flowing brown hair and beautiful fair skin and blue eyes, his heart instantly melted. A voice inside of Hans' head, who he named "Gazoo", instantaneously told Hans, *"That's the girl that you're gonna marry!"*, despite the fact that he had yet to be introduced to her.

But all that changed, when their "acquaintanceship", which basically only consisted of Hans stalkily glaring in her direction during breaks, deepened when a teacher approached Hans and asked,

"Hey John. You're driving past Jordan right? Do you mind giving Darinka a lift home?"

Hans boyishly responded, *"Wow, your name is Darinka. Sure thing! Anytime!"*

As Hans drove Darinka home like a stud in his Mustang, Hans timidly, yet with excitement asked Darinka, *"So where are you from? And how old are you exactly?"*

Darinka told Hans in a sweet and delicate voice, with a Slavic accent,

"I'm from Yugoslavia. Slovenia to be exact. I moved to Canada with my mother to live with my older brother. I'm now sixteen. My dad died when I was five."

Hans' mind immediately reverted back to dream from about 16 years back in Zajarsk when Hans envisioned a new-born baby rocking in a crib in Yugoslavia. Hans met numerous ladies from Yugoslavia, but this was the first one that made "Gazoo" inform him, *"That's the girl that you're gonna marry!"*

Ten minutes later they arrived at Darinka's home, a small red brick bungalow with acres of vineyards along a country road highway. Before opening the car door, Darinka turned to Hans and said, *"Thanks a lot for the ride."*

Darinka was astonishingly 15 years Hans' junior, but his knees nevertheless shook in her presence as she walked away from his Ford Mustang in the direction of her home. Hans felt like a bit of a pervert for having an interest in a girl that age, but he couldn't control his engulfing infatuation with this prized beauty, almost as if an irrepressible innate force was driving him towards her. Needless to say, Hans was left totally mystified and speechless, especially as he recalled that premonition that he had in 1955 in which a baby girl was born in Yugoslavia – a dream in Zajarsk in which a voice within informed Hans, *"You're going to marry a girl from Yugoslavia. That very baby."*

Hans had driven other girls originating from Yugoslavia home, but he never felt the feelings that Darinka conjured up within him. It was as if he were living amidst a utopia in her presence. Hans, at the age of 31, had seemingly and finally met his guardian angel and woman of his dreams even though he looked old to the fifteen years younger Darinka. Though, in very non-dream like fashion, their acquaintanceship didn't develop smoothly after Hans, in his typical nervous and insecure fashion, blurted out to Darinka, while in the hallway at school a week later during a break, *"You've been here for a year! Your English isn't very good!"*

Hans overtly revealed his own insecurities through his insensitive insult, insults that he suffered at the hands of his very own siblings and family. Becoming utterly self-conscious about his English after being subjected to a horde of insults that he bore from the likes of his family circle who called him a "stupid Russian" right in front of his face left Hans judging and dissecting others' language skills in an attempt to make himself feel less inferior. Darinka, though, found his remark explicitly inexcusable. When she arrived home that night, she immediately told her mother,

"I never want to see that stupid Russian guy again! What a jerk!"

So much for Hans' dream......................

CHAPTER 60

Blood Test & Tough Love

One evening during a night of drinking in the Friesen family basement, one of Corny's business partners, a Russian man in his 50's named Bezel who also fought in the Soviet Red Army during WWII, began talking, somewhat facetiously, yet provokingly, in the presence of Father. Bezel, who Corny tried to embezzle money from years later, just randomly blurted out, after talking a bit with Hans as he walked by heading to his room,

"John is not your son! His Russian is too good! Your other kids can't speak anything besides English."

Bezel's comments definitely struck a cord with Corny. Gradually, Bezel's talk penetrated so deeply into Father's mind that he actually began questioning Hans' paternity. Corny became set on proving once and for all that Hans truly was from his flesh and blood. But first, Corny needed to obtain Hans' blood type in order to be able to determine if he truly were Hans' father. And Corny felt that the best way of doing this, without arousing any suspicions, was to instruct Hans,

"Go donate some blood. Be a good patron saint to your new nation! The hospitals need blood. I'm going to benevolently donate as well! So, let's go donate for a "good cause" together son! I love you so much boy!"

Despite being shocked by Corny's bizarre showcase of fatherly affection, Hans went to the hospital with Father to carry out a "good deed." Then, a few weeks afterwards, a card was sent to Hans and Father declaring Hans' blood type. Hans' blood matched Father's! When Corny saw the "results", joy filled his eyes! He immediately approached Hans and proclaimed,

"You are my son!! You truly are my son!! Your blood type is the same as mine! That mother of yours may not be the complete, game-playing bitch like I once presumed."

Hans was puzzled and mystified by Corny's ridiculously peculiar outburst, but he just left it at that, and didn't enquire any further into the root of Father's uncharacteristic display of immense bliss and love. It was the first time that Corny actually truly treated Hans as if he were his cherished son of his flesh and blood. But to Hans, the results were irrelevant. Grandmother raised him. Not Father. So, for all intents and purposes, it was more or less irrelevant who Hans' father truly was, even though he was always certain - Corny truly was his dad - despite innuendo circulating amongst the family circle claiming otherwise. Clearly, Corny didn't have much faith in his wife, or perhaps merely common law partner, as records of a marriage remained in question.

But the love towards Hans only lasted till Corny got completely plastered on vodka a few weeks later and decided to pay a visit to the construction site in a suit and state of inebriated fury, right in the heart of winter. Upon arrival, in typical Corny style, he began barking out ludicrous instructions. Hans' first thought was, *"Oh boy! What does this fat blob want now?!?"* Hans eventually stepped off of the yellow Ford backhoe equipped with a front loader that he was operating, and went to confront Father. And before Hans knew it, Corny was right up in Hans' face screaming,

"The backhoe is not level! The backhoe is not level! You're doing it all wrong!! I'm the boss!! Do it my way or you're fired! I'm the boss!! Right or wrong, I'm the boss!!!!!"

Recognizing that his old man had absolutely no clue about what he was talking about, Hans simply rolled his eyes at Corny, before wham!!! The old man kicked Hans right in the genitals!! In agonizing pain, Hans dropped directly down onto the frozen, snow-covered dirt in a jiffy. Father came by in a drunken rage just looking to cause havoc, and that's exactly what he brought, got, and delivered! Hans eventually stood up again, though within a day he had to head to the hospital after being unable to urinate. Upon admittance, Father told Hans to lie to the doctor, so Hans claimed, *"I slipped and fell on the backhoe."*

The doctor skeptically answered,

"Well, whatever happened, you've ruptured a vein. It's quite bad. We'll have to syphon out your urine every night till we operate."

Father, though, had a "different" medical opinion, announcing to Hans,

"It'll heal on its own! You don't need an operation! You need to work!"

But Corny's diagnosis didn't align with the doctors'. Hans went in for surgery a few weeks later, before eventually finally becoming healed. But that operation didn't bring an end to his misery. Father saw to that one night, a few months after the surgery when he and Hans found themselves engaged in a lengthy, seemingly civil discussion in the basement of their family home while Father became inebriated on his other liquor of choice, whiskey. A direct correlation between Father's level of drunkenness and his intensity of belligerent aggressiveness fully captured his states and actions. After hours of listening to Corny into the night, Hans got up saying, *"I'm going to bed. I gotta get up in a couple of hours to go to work."*

Father had been drinking heavily for hours throughout the evening, so he was completely plastered when Hans innocently desired to call it a night. As soon as Hans stood up and headed out of the room, Corny had other ideas. In a drunken stupor, Father ordered,

"Siit!! Siitt!!! Sitttt! Siiiittttt!!!! Sittttttiiittttt!"

Hans didn't take Father seriously, especially because he knew that emptying his bladder took first precedence. Or did it? Because all of a sudden - wham!! As if a sludge hammer had slammed right up against the back of his head, Hans was knocked out cold! A few seconds later,

Hans partially regained consciousness after taking a rectangular Seagrams 5-star Canadian, Rye Whiskey bottle right to the back of the head! Father instantly stormed over to Hans' side, bending down over him! Seemingly instantaneously sobering up, Corny was actually attempting to pick up Hans. In a state of paralysis, while in a complete daze, Hans could faintly hear Corny bellowing out,

"Wake up John!! Wake up son!! Don't die on me!! Don't die on me son!!!"

Corny then hollered upstairs to Hans' mother,

"Maria, I think I killed him!! I think I killed our son!!"

But Mother didn't react one bit as she sat on her favourite sofa mindlessly watched TV upstairs, just like always. Hans woke up the next morning in excruciating pain with a pounding headache. Corny then called Uncle Henry and had him drive Hans to a private house-clinic for a shot of cortisone. When the doctor enquired about what happened, Hans answered,

"We were framing and a 2 X 4 fell on my head."

The doctor wasn't convinced, but nevertheless, the tiles of Father's floor had to be replaced as a result of the glass bottle, along with Hans' head smashing down against the basement floor. Being a soldier in the Soviet Red Army during the Second World War deeply affected Corny's mental composition. At times, he simply just reacted without knowing of his ways. During his drunken, usually arrogant, anger-filled stupors, outbursts, and rants, Corny even told people, *"I chauffeured for Hitler in Germany!!"*

Though, it was all a complete lie. Father ended his time in the war driving trucks for the Germans in Germany after being captured as a Russian soldier, at which point he was instructed to switch sides once the German army learned of Father's Germanic roots. Nonetheless, Corny's nickname amongst his business and construction associates became "Hitler", for various, not necessarily flattering reasons. And like Hitler, Corny didn't shy away from entering the trenches whenever he toiled away. Even after

Hans arrived, Father occasionally hopped onto and operated the backhoe, usually completely plastered in an attempt to impress the on-lookers by carrying out some digging and shovelling maneuvers. One associate named Sentauer, a man in his 50's with rotting teeth who spent time England as a German POW turned Church painter, occasionally commented to Corny on his backhoe operating technique and ability.

"Corny, you're like a concert pianist on that thing!"

Uncle Henry, though, would beg to differ. Before Hans arrived in Canada, Father always got his hands dirty by working fulltime on the construction sites, which included hopping onto the backhoe. Lacking elegance, Corny, from time-to-time, let that piece of equipment recklessly swing and spin around like a free-wheeling top. In the process, Corny actually once caught Uncle Henry in the chest, cracking his ribs. In typical Corny fashion, he defended his "working mannerisms" by informing Uncle Henry, *"You were too close. It was all your fault!"* On Hans' first day on the job, while Corny attempted to *"show you how it's done"* on the backhoe, Uncle Henry warned Hans, *"Run away or he'll kill you with that thing! He doesn't know what he's doing!"*

Perhaps Hans should've taken that advice from the start and never looked back......

CHAPTER 61

Stabbing

Hans' misery with his family was more than balanced out whenever he headed to Niagara College for English class, where he eventually began talking civilly and salaciously flirting with Darinka. And even though she still possessed a distain dislike for Hans' provocative insulting ways, Darinka, oddly enough, was attracted to Hans' sense of humour, and not to mention felt sympathy for him after learning of his tumultuous life. She felt an obligation to rescue Hans, leading her to eventually agree to start going out with him. Yet on dates, Darinka learned of a less than comical side to Hans. Much to her astonishment, Hans didn't waste any time letting her know about his utter revulsion for his family, especially after witnessing how brutally Mother was treating his dear grandmother. Yet, somewhat hypocritically, not even Hans was immune to enduring unbearable, inhumane abuse and being able to walk away unscathed.

Though, despite what Hans revealed about his nasty family, Darinka was surprised at just how calm the family all behaved and spoke with each other when she was invited to a Friesen family gathering at Hans' home. As she looked around the room watching the Friesen family and friends seemingly locked in pleasant and merry discussions, Darinka's first thought was,

John Friesen

"Wow! What a civil and mild-mannered family. There's no screaming or yelling. It's quite the nice change from my family who seemingly sees yelling as some sort of necessary hobby."

But it didn't take long for Darinka to learn that perhaps nice façades are merely presented to conceal what shouldn't be repulsively expressed and revealed. Darinka's family showed no veneers, so you saw and heard exactly what everyone was about. They lived without pretence, quite contrary to Hans' family who was almost always locked in calculating chess-matches with different faces for different situations. Yet, like all facades, it's only a matter of time before they crack, and in some cases, brutally crumble.

After a few weeks of dating, Hans' parents went out to play cards, so Hans and Darinka agreed to take care of the grandmothers for the evening. Hans, however, was so wound-up by his parents that he harmed Grandmother more than he cared for her. Every time that she approached Hans, Darinka bore witness to the bitterness that lied deep within Hans' heart. He was abrupt and cold to the very same Grandmother who raised him. Darinka was left speechless. Hans' face of disgust and ugly reactions, normally accompanied by terse hand gestures directed towards Grandmother captured his encompassing pain and sorrow inside. Behind Hans innocent demeanour lied a narcissist who inflicted pain as easily as he endured and "accepted" it – he had become a combination of the people who he had encountered in his life. Hans' torment stripped him of his innocence while he stole Darinka's. She just couldn't believe how Hans could occasionally transform into a miserable and unbearable monster. At the same time, whenever he incessantly whined about how deplorable his family treated him, a part of Darinka felt sorry for Hans and believed that she could sooth his sorrow. The fact that her home life wasn't any better only reinforced her resolve and empathy.

So, despite seeing a darker side to Hans, Darinka agreed to go out with Hans one night, along with a few of his friends to a dance at Club Heidelberg in St. Catharines. A pleasant night of chatting, laughing, drinking, and dancing ensued until a group of young, rather drunk and disorderly men of Italian descent entered the hall. After Hans, Darinka, and their friends merrily returned to their table following a slow dance, they discovered that this group of men had taken their seats at the table. Hans, without hesitation, told the man sitting in one of the chairs, *"That's my friend's seat. You gotta move."* The extremely arrogant looking, six-foot tall black-haired man in his 20's with bulging eyes and a pudgy nose "diplomatically" responded with, *"Say please!"*

But the 5'8" Hans refused. A heated discussion broke out, and before Hans knew it, a sucker punch caught him right in the face! As his eye swelled up, a group of security guards escorted the aggressive Italian-Canadians out of the hall. Then, before Hans knew it, his nose started to bleed. To prevent making a mess inside, Hans stepped outside through a double-glass door onto the parking lot tarmac. Hans thought that the coast was clear when he stepped outside of the hall and inhaled the fresh and crisp air on the mild spring evening. But instead, Hans quickly discovered that the man who had sucker-punched him had pulled out a 5-inch knife and had already slashed a Heidelberg's employee's stomach! Tensions intensified and spilled out outdoors amongst the parking lot, causing the incident to erupt into a vicious may-lay! With one man already down with a stab wound to the belly, the knife-wheeling madman, who had already clocked Hans earlier on, was in search of more blood! The scuffle between the Italian men and security guards enflamed to the point that an off-duty cop had entered the fray and sights of the young Italian with a knife in hand, who eventually stormed in the direction of this tall policeman in pedestrian attire! Right before catching the law enforcer in a polyester shirt with the 5-inch blade, the off-duty cop twisted his torso sideways, mostly evading the knife-wheeling maniac whose blade struck the top of his belt while slightly cutting into his flesh!

Hans remained a mere spectator this whole time only until the momentum of the stammering man brandishing a knife thrusted him right into Hans! In shock, Hans' kneejerk reaction was to kick the assailant right in the family jewels, but it was too late! The blade penetrated right into Hans' ribs, barely missing his heart! In a state of disbelief, and not necessarily pain, Hans didn't know what hit him! A gash sliced through his skin right into his ribs, three inches below the mark of Hans' heart! Luckily enough, the blade only penetrated an inch deep into his body, avoiding any organs. Nevertheless, blood soaked his nice violet, button down polyester shirt after a heavy, penetrating feeling fell upon his rib cage!

When Darinka stepped outside looking for Hans, she found him sitting on the asphalt parking lot with his back up against the hall wall. Seeing his pristine shirt now covered in blood, Darinka felt an uncontrollable surge of fear frenzy over her as she screamed out,

"John!! (Hans!!)"

Hans leisurely looked up to her and calmly muttered out,

"I think I've been stabbed."

In shock, yet still composed, Darinka stormed back inside the building as Hans thought to himself,

"My nice shirt is ruined."

When Darinka entered through the glass-door side entrance of Club Heidelberg in search of help, she hollered out, *"I need a phone! I need a phone!"*

A voice behind the bar said, *"There's a pay phone down the hall."*

When Darinka located a payphone in the narrow corridor leading to the washrooms, she realized, immediately yelling aloud, *"I need 10 cents to make a phone call!!"*

A Slovenian man of all people rushed over to her side, and stuck a dime into the pay phone's slot before Darinka picked up the receiver and dialled the number for emergencies.

Hans was eventually rushed to the hospital at the same pace that the knife-wheeling lunatic chucked his bloody weapon aside and stormed away. Hours later, Hans received five stiches, whereas his assailant was picked up by cops after taking refuge in a coffee shop in the near vicinity. Hans never saw the man again, but allegedly, he whined like a baby in police custody. Refuted for having links to the mafia, the man got off with a slap on the wrist. In defence of his lunacy and wielding a knife, the man cited watching a violent movie, family issues, along with having $100 in his pocket at the time of his attacks.

Regardless of the scare and stitches, Corny forced Hans to go to work the very next day, causing Hans' unhealed stab wound to become infected after becoming contaminated by dust and dirt. Hans had to return to the hospital that night. The doctor, originally from Germany, told Hans in German,

"Du bist verrückt! (You're nuts) for going back to work so soon! You need at least two weeks off so the deep cut can properly heal!"

Hans sarcastically responded,

"You can tell that to my boss! Not that he'll listen. That's what happens when you work for your father! You get tough love!"

In shock, the doctor retorted, *"That guy is worse than the Gestapo! Absolutely no mercy!"*

Hans comically said, *"He's pro-Nazi, or at least fought for them! Stalin too! So, he learned from the best!"*

The wound was cleaned again and the stitches were re-threaded, but Father remained firm on his stance.

"You're not getting any time off! How stupid could you be to go dancing and get stabbed! It's your fault!"

Hans returned to work the very next day. But if it were any consolation, Hans ultimately received $900 in a court settlement, but he never saw a cent of it. But Corny certainly did.........

CHAPTER 62

Hans becomes a Father

After a couple of years of dating, Darinka discovered that she was pregnant. While returning home from English class, Darinka informed Hans in such a state of panic that she felt like jumping out of the car! Conversely, Hans became filled with such joyous excitement and glee that he calmed Darinka down by subtly stating, *"Don't worry, we'll get married!"*

Hans thought to himself,

"Through all of my ugly experiences here in Canada, Darinka is my only bright spot! Like a radiating star, her presence makes it all worth it and then some! She's the angel who has brought me to heaven! She's the only one who can get me out of this mess!"

By spring, they were married and had moved into one of Father's Drake Street apartments, 1 Km removed from Hans' parents' home, where in August, they returned from the hospital with their new-born, blond-haired daughter Irene. When Grandmother laid eyes on little Irene, in typical Grandmother fashion, she said, *"Woo-hoo! What a cute body!"*

Four years later, their second child, ""little", little Hans", or rather Johnny came into the world. But Grandmother wasn't around to witness his sight. Prior to Grandmother being admitted into the hospital, Hans saw her peacefully sitting outside on the porch of his parent's home while he drove by one afternoon. An uncomfortable feeling overwhelmed Hans, leading him to strangely enough think to himself, *"I should go talk to her. It may be my last chance."*

When Hans spoke with Grandmother, she was her typical cheery, positive self, and at peace. Not many words were exchanged, but rather mainly sediments and auras. The following day, she was rushed to the hospital where she ultimately died of a stroke. Hans was left absolutely heartbroken. The woman who raised him, the only one who was ever a mother to him, wouldn't get to see his kids grow up. An insurmountable emotional charge overtook Hans as he thought back to what they both endured together in Russia. Grandmother was his guardian angel, but now he had Darinka.

But Grandmother wasn't the only one to pass away. Father's mother, Grandmother Tzitzer (later Friesen), who came from an extremely wealthy upbringing with servants, also lived in the family home in Beamsville, but Hans never felt quite connected to her, especially after she was placed into a retirement home where she ultimately passed away. Despite being a good companion to Grandmother, Hans' wife Darinka also didn't necessarily possess pleasant memories of Corny's mom, Grandmother Tzitzer because she treated Darinka as if she never even existed. But perhaps that had something to do with Grandmother Tzitzer's upbringing, or simply due to the fact that she lived in chronic pain when Darinka met her. Grandmother Tzitzer was the type of lady who walked back and forth in the garage, since she deemed *"walking outside in public is only for peasants!"* But her attitudes possibly changed after Father accidently hit her with his car, accidentally knocking her over while she leisurely strolled within the confines of the Friesen's two-car garage. She eventually recovered before moving into a retirement home.

Following the deaths of Hans' grandmothers, Hans and his wife built a home of their own on Queen Street, about a 1 km removed from the parents' house. A decade earlier, Hans purchased an inexpensive parcel of marshland from Mother for about $1,800, after no one else desired to buy the property since it was merely a 10-foot-deep gully with a creek running through it that possessed no hydro, gas line, and water services.

Merely an unwanted ditch. Mother was ecstatic when she finally sold that undesirable piece of land that Corny purchased for speculation for her for almost nothing. After buying the land from Mother, Hans spent almost ten years gradually filling in the gulley with surplus soil that he got from various construction sites until the land was suitable enough to develop and build on once Hans completely enclosed the creek in 5-X 8-foot culverts spanning over 120 feet. With the soil settled, Hans constructed a driveway along with a house that Corny insidiously and sinisterly looked to modify by altering the specifications and design behind Hans' back. Corny got unwantedly involved in everything, more times than not, for no conceivable reason.

Yet, a fancy, white-bricked facade home with columns couldn't quell or conceal the many strains and much tensions within Hans' marriage, mainly resulting from him arrogantly and selfishly serving his parents' interests at the expense of his own immediate family of four, whose concerns constantly played second-fiddle to Corny's and Mother's wishes. And even though Hans married the Yugoslavian (Slovenian) girl of his dreams, he continuously encountered problems with his parents as they continued to control everything, including all of Hans' and Darinka's bank accounts and lives, leading Hans to approach Father one day and say,

"Give me what's mine! You don't even let me see my bank books. When I went to cash in the unemployment cheque, the banker told me, "You can't cash it in. We don't know you.""

In response, Father blew up ranting,

"You son of a gun!! After all what I did for you! Getting you out of Russia! And this is how you thank me! Why?!? Why don't you trust me?!? I'm your father, how can't you trust me?!?"

When Hans got married, he thought that Father would finally give him his independence, or at the very least, release his bank accounts. But Hans couldn't have been more wrong. Father dictatorially refused to acquiescence to all of Hans' requests, still leaving Hans completely at Father's mercy. Corny even monitored all of Hans' and Darinka's mail, since it all went, unopposed by Hans, directly into Father's mailbox. Despite being displeased with the situation, Hans absolutely feared always hearing from Corny,

"What, you don't trust me! You ungrateful bastard! That's what I get for getting you out of Russia! I'm the one who found you!"

Such a response constantly left Hans feeling guilty, not to mention speechless, but not speechless enough to inform Darinka that Corny should keep receiving their mail and controlling their bank accounts. The feisty and fair Darinka though, was not only not afraid of Corny, but also not too impressed with Corny's domineering ways, even though a part of Darinka believed that Corny simply wanted an excuse to stop by their place to see Corny's cherished grandkids whenever he dropped off the mail. The fact that Corny savoured some great home-cooking for lunch or dinner, or both at Hans' house on practically a daily basis, since his own wife rarely cooked for him only enticed Corny even more to fully meddle in Hans' and Darinka's lives. By going to their home every night, Corny could incidentally keep an eye on Hans' family and their intentions. Not even Darinka's mom was impressed. Corny's antics severely irritated her, especially when she had to feed the sizable and stout Corny at lunch. She couldn't even converse with Corny since Darinka's mom could only speak Slovenian. Being at the end of her rope, she complained to Darinka.

"Why am I feeding this guy lunch all the time! I'm old (mid-70's), and I have to take care of Irene and Johnny and my son-in-law. His wife is much younger than me! Why isn't she cooking for him!!"

And even though Corny usually merrily stopped by to visit his only grandchildren, in some instances, he stepped inside Hans' home in a miserable mood. His face displayed fury, while his mouth was vile – regardless of how trivial the "issue" presented before him seemed. On such occasions, Hans and Darinka knew exactly that the "siblings" were in town paying a visit. Mounting tensions in all Friesen households only intensified. But Father didn't need an excuse to escape the wife who he couldn't stand. And the fact that Darinka and her mom were both amazing cooks didn't discourage Corny one bit from stopping by Hans' home for a delicious meal. But Darinka and even her mother became more than disenchanted with Corny's parasitic ways and unbecoming behaviour.

Corny's snarly moods and actions brought Darinka to wit's end. She incessantly pleaded with Hans to severe ties with his family; yet all that she learned was that the apple didn't fall far from the tree - Hans vehemently refused, offering Darinka a few choice words in the same style that Corny belittled Hans. A friend of Hans eventually came by to beseech him to make his immediate family his priority, and to abandon his parents just like how they abandoned him. The family friend, a woman in her late 40's and of German descent, though born in modern-day Serbia, quoted *Genesis 2:24*, stating,

"A man shall leave his father and his mother and hold fast to his wife, and they shall become one flesh."

Hans' response was cowardly to say the least. *"But they're my parents."*

But what kind of parents were they if they wouldn't even provide Hans with a little time off to go on a family vacation. They justified their behaviour by reiterating to Hans that work and money truly are the only things in life that matter. Father and Mother fortified within Hans that life wasn't about enjoyment, but rather about amassing as much wealth as possible – regardless of if you ever intended to spend it. Hans attempted to engrain this same notion within Darinka, in part to forcibly dissuade her from asking for anything from Father or Hans. He reiterated that they should just put up with his parents' antics, since in the end it would all be worth it. Hans was optimistic, and believed that his parents would come to their senses and rectify their harm, leading Hans to burden Darinka with a lot of guilt for believing that she had any right to complain, let alone go on family vacations; but Darinka refused to remain silent.

"What are you doing?!? You're signing blank cheques! Why would I follow someone who does something so irresponsibly idiotic!?! You can kill me, but I'm going after that old man of yours! The house isn't even officially signed over to

us yet! They could take everything from us if they wanted to! Your priority is us – me and your kids! Not your parents!"

Hans knew that Darinka was his redeeming love and saviour who knew how to manage the finances, unlike Hans, but he nevertheless still arrogantly wanted everything done his way, even though he refused to do anything to alleviate their issues surrounding financial matters. Hans seemingly could live in a massive rut of a status quo and not react. But Darinka couldn't! She saw other families taking nice vacations, and going out for leisurely dinners and coffees, while Hans seemingly didn't have a cent or second to spare, staying obliged and loyal to only Corny's demands. During this time, while waiting for the parents to come to their senses, life with them became even more unbearable. Father's abuse and necessity to exploit Hans only got worse as Father became increasingly reassured that Hans would never defy him, fully aware that Hans was too deeply dependent upon Corny. Hans got so used to people having such ugly control over him, that even though he hated it, he felt "at home" with it. However, Hans' incessant complaining to Darinka everyday stirred her on to continuously plea with Hans to break ties from his family, letting him know that they could survive perfectly well without them, which in turn left Hans infuriated. Loud fights and shrill quarrels, mostly surrounding Hans' family and their full control over their lives erupted between Hans and Darinka to the point that she was ready to leave him. Even Hans' loyalty to his friends was stronger than to his family's, leading him to arrive home in the late hours of the night after helping a friend with his furniture business. This friend, clearly witnessing Hans' actions, summed up Hans' behaviour saying to Darinka,

"When I have a family, I'm not going to be like John. My family will come first!"

At this point, Darinka was at the end of her rope and had completely lost all hope and patience. She knew that she had no other choice but to react or the family would completely fall apart, which meant that she had to approach "The Boss", and creator of a majority of their disputes – Corny. Darinka decided to finally confront Corny when he came by for dinner on a Saturday evening, while Hans was still at work. Anxious over the inevitable forthcoming confrontation with Corny, Darinka drank wine throughout the day to build courage by numbing her nerves. She was suffering an unbearable anguish as a result of how Corny bullied and controlled her family as Hans sat aside spinelessly letting him.

So, when Corny let himself into the home through the garage entrance on that Saturday evening, and walked up the stairs towards the kitchen, Darinka politely approached him, sparing any formalities.

"You must start paying John on a regular basis, and not simply whenever you feel like it! And that money must enter a bank account controlled by John and I, and not an account controlled by you like it's always been done between you and John!

Felling liberated by her emancipating tirade, Darinka added a coup de grâce dagger slice by telling Corny,

"And you didn't lose John when he was four, you just left him behind (in Germany) on purpose!

Corny attentively listened quietly the entire time, letting Darinka speak freely. And even though Darinka's last comment penetrated Corny (and later on even Mother) deeply, his only response to her outburst was,

"I still love you."

Eventually, Father caved in and furnished Hans with a small cheque that was insultingly insufficient for his hard work, a payment Hans deposited into a bank account opened by Darinka. After over a decade in Canada, Hans was finally able to control a portion of his money! Moreover, Corny also agreed to officially sign over the property and home under Hans' and Darinka's names, following numerous years of delaying to do so. But regardless of Corny's goodwill gesture, family tensions continued to mount. Darinka's comment surrounding, *"you didn't lose Hans, you left him behind"*, struck a cord with Mother after Corny informed her of Darinka's accusation. In accordance with Mother's vindictive fashion, she sought retribution. So, at the next family gathering during Christmas Eve at Corny's family home, Mother got her revenge on Darinka by overtly refusing to serve her coffee as she poured cups for the rest of her guests. Mother's deed set off a fuse in the, at times, volatile Darinka. Feeling abused, mistreated, and completely broken, Darinka stormed out of the house and started walking back home believing that Hans would support her by leaving the party and eventually pick her up as she walked home. Yet, Hans never drove by. His loyalties remained to Corny, along with his family. Darinka became inconsolable. Hans' behaviour led Darinka to dismay, leaving her more furiously depleted and disenchanted than ever. Darinka felt disoriented as she walked through the pristine white snow that fell from the heavens as Darinka fell into her own personal abyss. Playing out all of Hans' selfish deeds within her head, Darinka didn't even notice an oncoming car as she crossed the street. When Darinka entered the present once again, she was alerted by the screeching of tires squealing down upon her! When she looked into the eyes of an irritated driver, she realized that she had almost been hit by an oncoming car! But Darinka wasn't phased one bit as her head remained elsewhere while she walked home completely beside herself.

Over the ensuing months, conflict only intensified as Corny's level of guilt soared while Darinka demanded more autonomy over her family. Feeling compromised, Corny responded to her with threats of his own.

"I got you your job as a chemist at Chipman (Darinka's employer)! If you don't behave, I can get you fired! And why are you constantly praising Chipman, but not Friesen Construction, my company! It bothers me!!

And never forgot, you finished your schooling at Niagara College and got your diploma (before Darinka obtained a University of Waterloo degree in Science) because I drove you there after your car broke down!! Never forget that!!"

Eventually, when Darinka gathered enough courage, she confronted Corny once again, making her wishes known that she desired complete control over Hans' shop, along with the incoming cheques that Corny was still shamelessly collecting.

"You're no longer collecting the rent cheques from John's building. That's his building! It has nothing to do with you! You have no right to that rent!"

Corny felt like a cornered dog in Darinka presence, and provocatively blurted out,

"Go back to Slovenia. We'll raise the kids! And you know what - if John's siblings would've never agreed to let him come over, we would've never allowed it, so be grateful to them! He's lucky that we got him out. He was just a Russian when I summoned for him!"

After the horrible experience of the prior Christmas, Darinka desired to spend the Christmas holidays away, and decided that she wanted to show the kids Florida. Yet, before driving down, they had to purchase a new vehicle for the trip. Hans, who unlike Darinka wasn't required to drive the kids around for their daily activities, nevertheless pompously insisted that they purchase the vehicle of his choice, a white, clumsy-looking, box-like Volkswagen Vanogan, a vehicle that Darinka found rather hideous to say the least. But with Corny-like control and revolting sternness, Hans told Darinka,

"If we don't buy this Vanogan, we're not going to Florida (for Christmas)!"

Darinka found Hans' miserable demeanour and arrogant insistence repulsive, but for the sake of avoiding the typical ugly quarrel, she let Hans have his way, if it meant that they could spend the Christmas holidays in Florida, and away from Hans' family. And despite a great Christmas adventure in Florida in the Vanagon, Hans' decision, as usual, only created hardships. The Vanogan turned out to be a severely troubled lemon, almost like Hans' and Darinka's marriage.

But Darinka wasn't the only one with Christmas-family grief. The ensuing Christmas, Hans, Darinka, and the kids once again spent Christmas Eve at the Corny Friesen household, during which Wanda and Gary were vacationing in Florida. On this occasion, Darinka found herself helping out Mother in the kitchen. As they worked away together at washing the dishes, Darinka saw a troubled look on Mother's face. Out of concern, Darinka, innocently enough, asked Mother, *"Is something wrong? Is something upsetting you?"* Attempting to hold back her tears, Mother blurted out, *"I don't want to live past 70."* Darinka was a bit shocked by her comment, but thought that she was, in all likelihood, just upset by the fact that Wanda wasn't around for the holidays. Yet, what Mother blurted out next left Darinka completely speechless.

"My husband beat me up after he found out that I lost John (Hans)!"

Darinka couldn't make any sense out of what she was hearing, or what exactly brought it on. Though, like a lot of things in the Friesen household, it remained a mystery hidden away for an eternity......

CHAPTER 63

The Odd Vision

Despite the tension within the family, Darinka remained sympathetic to Mother, who was terrified to sleep at home alone. She lived with such fear that she actually watched TV with a knife in the cushions of her sofa. Or at least that's what people said. To alleviate her concerns while she was left at home all alone during Corny's visit to Germany, Darinka sent Johnny and Irene, who both went somewhat reluctantly, to sleep over at Mother's place. Irene and Johnny always found their grandparents' home a bit creepy, especially alone with a grandmother who showed them plenty of unpleasant, almost indifferent emotions that were buried under her mound of bitterness. Resultantly, Irene always felt a big sisterly need to protect her little brother while sleeping at the grandparents', so she always made sure that her and her four years younger brother slept in the same bed while they unnervingly awaited the morning sun to rise.

The kids, though, were not the only ones who had trouble sleeping. Around that same night, Hans himself had an eerie dream. He envisioned little Johnny standing on a well. Immediately after awakening from his slumber on that very night, Hans found himself in a cold sweat. Consumed by bone-chilling tenseness, Hans emphatically explained his vision to Darinka. She had never seen Hans in such a state. His extreme trepidation seized Darinka, especially because Hans never told her about any of his dreams, simply because he told her that he never dreamt! But in this case, Hans adamantly and ardently let Darinka know with wild arms gestures,

John Friesen

"It was unbelievably real! I mean, it is real! it's really real!! It's going to happen! I envisioned clover, a white fence, two long planks covering a square well, and Johnny! Johnny was standing on two rotting planks covering the well!!"

Darinka responded,

"Ok. Okay. Calm down. There's no such well in the area. And we're not going anywhere. Sonny will be okay. It was only a dream. Johnny is fine."

But Hans wasn't, proclaiming,

"The vision was too real not to be true! It's prophetic! It's a dream to heed, not forget!"

Hans immediately rushed outside and sought out a well inside of their undeveloped backyard; but his search came up empty. Hans discovered nothing at all from his prophecy in his vicinity. There were a few drainage pipes along with a grate within their backyard, but neither wooden planks nor a well to be seen. An hour after searching through his rather rustic and partially grassless backyard, Hans slightly calmed down, right before their neighbour Wayne from across the street came over and surprisingly suggested,

"Hey John, let's go for an ice cream with all the kids. A few other neighbours are coming as well. Do you know that Avondale ice cream place in St. Catharines on the other side of the Welland Canal?"

Hans responded, *"I sure do! Sounds good! The kids will have fun! See you then Wayne!"*

As the adults enjoyed their ice cream on a wooden picnic table while the kids frolicked in the setting sun, Hans peered around, but couldn't spot little Johnny anywhere! Immediately glaring to his right, in the direction of the ice cream shop, Hans saw the kids playing, but none of them were Johnny; yet, when he peered to his left, Hans saw a white wooden fence in front of a field full of high clover in the near distance! And there amongst that landscape, Hans saw Johnny's blond curly locks through the clover! Immediately recognizing the white fence surrounding a field full of clover from his dream, Hans knew exactly what Johnny was standing on! Instantly turning to Darinka, Hans pointed into the distance and calmly said,

"That's the field, fence, and well from my dream. And there's Johnny. Stay calm! I'll go get him!"

Springing up to his feet, Hans unassumingly, yet with purpose walked in the direction of the clover field. Even though Hans strutted casually in order to prevent rousing Johnny, immerse fear flowed through his veins. And with good reason! After hopping over the fence, Hans bore witness to his only son quietly looking down into a square well as Johnny stood on a couple of old, rotting planks seemingly ready to collapse. In a state of panic on the inside, Hans' first instinct was to sprint over and grab Johnny, but instead, he calmly and slowly approached Johnny with composure not to spook him. Seconds later, Hans scooped up Johnny by his waist just in the nick of time! Staring down into the well, Hans saw murky water that was three feet below the wooden planks, but could've been 10 to 20 feet deep. It was like déjà vu for Hans! The sight of that well mirrored the exact vision that appeared in Hans' premonition that was clearly much more than a dream…

But that wasn't his only dream. On numerous nights, Hans dreamt about the aftermath of his father's death. He visualised ensuing heartless legal battles that followed. But then again, these were only dreams… Dreams of being regarded as an equal to his siblings… Dreams of inheriting his fair share…

CHAPTER 64

Father Approaches 68

Years later, Uncle Jacob from Zajarsk of all people came to Canada to pay the Friesens a quick visit while he was on vacation with his family who were visiting relatives in the States. When he arrived at Father's house, he informed Corny,

"You and Hans owe me an additional $17,000 in "gratitude money". I practically raised your son! You should be grateful and show some gratitude for what I did for him and his grandmother! We're not even family! So, pay up big guy!"

Father was completely blindsided by Uncle Jacob's comment, and probed Hans afterwards, enquiring if what Jacob were saying was true. Hans feverously retorted,

"I worked since the day I came to live with him till the day that I left. I even build him a nice barn! That monster already stole all of my money in Zajarsk and Frunze! He robbed me blind! He probably owes me money! He's just trying to seize an opportunity to steal some more! That guy is a crook!"

Yet, when Uncle Jacob then went to visit Hans, Darinka, and the kids, he diplomatically didn't mention a cent. Darinka actually found Jacob to be quite serene, almost a bit charming in an introverted kind of way. She simply couldn't sense an ounce of hostility from this on the surface, sensible, soft-spoken and -featured man who Hans painted out to be

469

nothing short of a monster. So much for first impressions… Or perhaps, it was all about nice impressions when Hans' wife and kids were around. Either way, Darinka couldn't help but thinking,

"John, probably provoked this guy, just like how he provokes me with his arrogant and self-important manner! A man "wise" in his own conceit!"

Not long after Uncle Jacob of Zajarsk headed back to Chicago, Mother was admitted into the hospital to undergo an open-heart bypass surgery. Following the operation, Hans and Darinka, along with their kids came by to pay her a visit. When they entered the room, Hans experienced a lustrous warmth from Mother that he had never sensed from her before. He felt like her son for the first time in his life! As Hans approached Mother, he became more drawn and hypnotized by the heartfelt loving energy that she emitted with his each passing step towards her hospital bed. Hans sensed with all of his might that she desired to communicate something to him. So, was she finally going to apologize for abandoning him when Hans was only four? Mother's words and aura were glowingly radiant – almost as if she had transformed into an angelic soul stemming from a profound epiphany. It was as if a major revelation were about to transpire - as if Mother wished to reveal something to Hans from the deepest depths of her soul – yet, only until out of nowhere Wanda, seemingly out of complete jealousy and resentment for seeing Hans and Mother bonding, interjected by somewhat forcefully leading Hans, Darinka, and their kids out of room.

"Mom is tired! She needs her rest! It's the best that you leave her alone! You're upsetting her!" As Hans saw Wanda behave so heartlessly selfish, a memory of Tante Mia saying, *"can't you see that your siblings are jealous of you!"*, floated through Hans' mind.

Many believe that when the body and flesh weaken, one becomes more selfless, and perhaps that's exactly what Mother experienced, exactly what Wanda feared; but despite Mother's seemingly re-birth-like transformation, Hans never learned what exactly Mother desired to express to him in the hospital on that very day. When Mother's health improved she reverted back to her same miserable self; however, the same couldn't be said for

Corny. His health condition suddenly worsened following another trip to Germany. But that wasn't the only change within him. Corny suddenly began to act oddly. Days before being admitted into the hospital, Father stopped by Hans' home on a cold winter day for a coffee, even though Hans and Darinka were not home. Only Irene and Johnny were around since their Oma had moved out by this time. After stepping inside Hans' home, Corny started loading the wood stove out of worry that his grandchildren were too cold. This was quite out of character for Corny, a man who showed little concern for others and their welfare. When Irene eventually made her grandfather a coffee, he perplexingly drank it on the stairs, almost as if he were not worthy of sitting at the family table. Corny behaved very differently, very humbly. He acted as though he had done them an inexcusable injustice, and owed something to them. The change was overtly obvious to Hans' family. After that very evening, Corny virtually stopped coming by for dinner. And if he did come over, he sat on the stairs in the basement and ate, as if he were seemingly not worthy of eating with the family. It were as if Father sensed something, perhaps sensed that his time was almost up.

A few days later, Corny stopped by Hans' shop and requested that Hans drive him to the hospital the very next day for a prostate surgery. But Hans found it all very odd. Corny looked down at him while Hans stood in the pit fixing the backhoe, but Hans felt like Corny was talking to a ghost. Corny's lips appeared as if they weren't even moving, leading Hans to actually look around to see who was truly speaking; still, Hans didn't see anyone else around. Goose bumps flooded Hans' skin. He just couldn't grasp what he was sensing, let alone know what was transpiring. While beginning to tremble, Father blurted out,

"I cheated, mistreated, and abused you. I'm sorry for that. I hope I have time straighten everything out. And don't trust your brother Rudi! Nor your mother. She's a bitch!"

Father became so choked up that he was left speechless, though not before strangely enough adding, *"Keep on digging away. I found my treasure by digging. And I still have to show you where the money is."* Hans' mind immediately went back to the story that Grandmother told him years ago, about how Corny and his brother Uncle Jacob allegedly dug up a buried treasure of golden rubles hidden under a massive oak tree in the backyard of the family house. Their dad was the mayor of Fürstenwerder at the time, before ultimately being taken away by the Communists, just to never be seen again. This same supposedly stolen buried treasure was allegedly the indirect reason for why Hans got pushed off of a cliff. So then, was that story of buried treasure not simply a myth, but something more? Was there actually some credence to that tale? Hans never truly found out. All he knew of was Father's golden ruble stashes from Corny's mother's dowry, money that Corny hid away in some of his apartments, specifically away from his wife and Hans' siblings who Father never trusted. But did Corny possess golden rubles from another source? Only history knows......

As Corny and Hans drove to the hospital the next day, Corny seemed somber, dampened, yet introspective. A surreal energy and demeanour overtook him as he remained silent during the entire drive. Hans saw a side to Father that he had never experienced before. Upon admittance into the hospital, Corny's health gradually worsened, especially following the surgery. Doctors gave him a month, maybe two to live. The family instantly anticipated the worst. Immediately after Corny had a stroke in the hospital, Rudi shockingly mentioned to Darinka over the phone,

"I went to see the lawyer and accountant today."

Darinka became quite upset. It appeared not only as if Corny's family were already writing him off, but also appallingly as if Rudi was more than indifferent when it came to Father's dying. Darinka's first thought was, *"Why is he already doing this? Why isn't he concentrating on his father getting well?"*

It was almost as if the siblings happily awaited Father's imminent passing as if it were merely a means to profit and nothing more. It was as if vultures were circling. Odd occurrences then began to transpire. The next day, Hans as usual went to pick up the mail for his parents; yet, when he attempted to open the mail box, he noticed that the locks had been changed. Hans found it strange, but left it at that and headed off to work. However, when Hans stopped in at the local co-op to fill up the construction equipment, Hans was notified, *"Only Mrs. Friesen can fill up her vehicle here."* "Mrs. Friesen" couldn't even drive. The co-op employees were fully well aware of this, and found news of these new restrictions as comical as Hans did. But it didn't stop there.

Following dinner that evening, Hans received a call from Mother informing him to come pick-up some weeds for disposal. After walking into the family garage and picking up a bushel, Hans headed back towards his truck, though only until he noticed that the key to the home that was always tucked away at the side entrance of the garage had mysteriously disappeared. Suspiciously surprised, Hans knocked on the home door. When Mother eventually answered, Hans informed her, *"The key is missing."* With eyes almost ready to pop out of their sockets, Mother viciously responded. *"We're gonna put the key in a new spot! When I find a new spot, I'll let you know!*

Hans knew where this was going, and casually retorted,

"Don't bother. And don't bother calling me to pick up the weeds ever again!"

Hans' reaction left Mother livid and fuming. He sensed that she felt uncomfortable, almost as if it weren't totally her idea to lock him out, leaving Hans certain that all of these strange occurrences had his siblings' names all over them. Around this time, Father attempted to call Hans and Martina one night, but he couldn't reach them. In a panic, Corny immediately called relatives from the Regier family, beseeching them to talk to Hans about a matter. Regrettably, Mr. Regier refused to hear of it, informing Corny,

"I can't tell him that! That's family business, so I won't get involved."

Corny suffered his first stroke the ensuing day. This tragic event spurred on even more disturbing family transgressions. While neither able to speak, nor utilise the left side of his body, Father awoke days after the stroke, just to discover Mother in the corner of his hospital room, sitting by the door peering in his direction. With his right hand, Corny signaled to his wife that he desired her bedside presence. Once Mother walked over and lowered her ear towards Corny's mouth, Corny clutched his wife by the neck with his right hand, prepared to strangle her to death! Freeing herself from Corny's grasp, Mother shamelessly (or protectively) went into the closet, right in front of Hans and Darinka who were visiting Corny, and took Father's wallet away before exiting the room. Hans and Darinka couldn't believe what they had just witnessed! Darinka felt completely ashamed for Hans' mother following the utterly embarrassing scene.

The events of that day sent Hans to bed early that night, where he dreamt about a continuous vision that regularly looped through his mind over the past six months prior to this disturbing occurrence with Mother. Hans once again saw signs of the future, witnessing what was going to become of his family. When Hans woke up the next morning, he realized that the recurring dream was truly a prophetic epiphany, just like the one with Johnny at the well. Darinka believed that the dream about Johnny was a warning, so when she heard of the visions Hans was having, she paid attention to them. Firstly, Hans envisioned the family Oldsmobile car and blue Ford pick-up truck being sold on the exact same day. Secondly, Hans saw an economic recession emerge, causing numerous soup kitchens to open and poverty to spread, while the interest rates dropped to almost 0%. Thirdly, Hans dreamt of himself reacquiring a contract with the local trailer park owner who vowed to never do business with Friesen Construction ever again. The owner of the trailer park detested the old man, Corny, so it would have taken Father's death to regain the contract of maintaining the trailer park. Hans' even had dreams about a lawsuit and a settlement sum. All of these visions ultimately materialized years later. A few mornings later, a phone call awakened Hans. Wanda of all people was on the other end. Without even greeting Hans with a hello, she demanded to know,

"Where's the money?!? Where did Father keep the money?!!? Where did he hide it?!?"

Tensions between Hans, Mother, and the siblings were mounting as Father lied on his death bed, seemingly just waiting to be free from the misery that he himself helped create. After another stroke, the doctor spoke to Mother, with Darinka in the vicinity, telling her,

"Your husband is getting to the point where we may have to put him on life support. You have to make a decision at that point if you want to put him on life support or let him die naturally."

Darinka immediately said, *"I'm going to the chapel. Does anyone want to join me?"*

Much to Darinka's surprise, Mother followed her. As they prayed away on their knees in the chapel, Mother, out of nowhere, said to Darinka,

"John has worked too hard already. He should give up working construction and focus on maintaining the apartments."

Darinka, a bit puzzled by Mother's comment said,

"Let's not focus on that. Let's concentrate on a healthy recovery."

Was Mother once again revealing her heart to Darinka, or was she systematically and calculatingly preparing herself for the inevitable since she knew exactly what was stated in Corny's will? Only time would reveal if she truly possessed an honest heart inside of her.....

CHAPTER 65

Father Dies

Darinka's and Mother's prayers were futilely done in vain. Exactly as the palm reader from that train in Russia foretold over 25 years earlier to Hans, Father died, on his hospital bed, at the age of 68. As months proceeded following Corny's death, Wanda and her husband Gary made frequent stays in the family home with Mother before ultimately selling their place in Toronto, quitting their jobs, and taking up full residence at Mother's. Mother now funded them. With everything in their grasps, they attempted to dissolve and liquidate the company, "CC Friesen Construction". As VP of the business, Hans could have prevented the company's closure after the local bank manager froze a majority of the company's assets and bank accounts, insisting that Hans was the only one with the authority to sign checks. Everything was tied up in Hans' name, but only until he was outwitted by Mother, Wanda, Rudi, and their lawyers, who directed Hans to sign a form of consent under the pretence that Hans would remain company Vice President. Unknowingly to Hans at the time, with his signature he incidentally gave Mother and the siblings permission to winddown the company and pillage and plunder the company's assets. It was all a ploy. The sequence of events leading up to the closure of the company epitomized the moments leading up to Corny's death.

Months later, Darinka and Hans stepped into the bank to ask for some information. During this visit, they learned that a company bank account had become frozen by the Royal Bank manager after Mother and Rudi informed the bank manager that Rudi was granted power of attorney to act on behalf of Mother with regard to company matters. The bank manager responded by telling them,

"John is the VP, therefore, until I hear from him, I will freeze all of the assets."

It was this occurrence, unknown to Hans and Darinka at that time months earlier, that led the Friesen family to dupe Hans via their scheming lawyers by having him sign over control of the company assets to them. But their greed and scheming didn't stop there. As soon as Father died, Hans' livelihood became a precarious uncertainty. Nobody was willing to communicate with him to indicate where he stood at that point. For the entire time leading up to his death, Corny was telling Hans, amongst others, that *"The company will all be yours (John's) one day!"*

However, after Father's death, Hans didn't know for sure if that were the truth. The fact that the family wasn't willing whatsoever to disclose any information to him only drove Hans' anxiety to intensify, leading him to head over to the family home to discuss the situation with Mother, Wanda, and Rudi; but none of them said a word. Upon his arrival, Mother immediately stormed away to her room, whereas Rudi and Wanda acted as if they didn't know a thing, even though they had already made a move to purge all of the assets from the construction company while they awaited their windfall from Mother deriving from Father's will. They had no interest in the company. Just the money. At this point, Hans felt completely hapless and helpless, so he contacted his/their lawyer, Roger Lewandowski, asking him when exactly the reading of the will would take place. Roger then informed Hans,

"There is nothing in the will for you."

Hans' next course of action was to contact the family's accountant, who simply advised Hans to get a lawyer. The ugliness was about to truly commence. Silence can only last for so long, especially when an amicable and fair resolution is irrelevant. Because why would Hans' mom and siblings seek an amicable conclusion – they already had access to everything. The lawyers only fuelled the fire by sending numerous trivial correspondences, containing every unpleasantry that was uttered back and forth between the family, seemingly just looking to exasperate a vicious circle that they sought to heavily profit from through billable hours. Eventually Hans' lawyer proclaimed, *"I got you one-third of the company."* Though, when Hans enquired about just how much that was worth, the lawyer responded with silence. Hans then fired that lawyer, and sought alternative legal consul based on recommendations from others; yet in the end, all of these lawyers were in one way or another involved with Corny and/or the Friesen family lawyer at one point or another, so they all seemingly had no interest in faithfully representing Hans' interests, leading Hans into dismay. Numerous futile outcomes with various lawyers, none of whom were ultimately retained, ensued. The fact that one lawyer "upliftingly" remarked, *"Is your mother sane?"*, was of little consolation to Hans. Though, instead of giving up, Hans and Darinka turned to a lawyer who was recommended by the Upper Canada Law Society named Daniel. During their first consultation, Daniel pompously boasted,

"When Roger (Mother's lawyer) hears that I'm on the case, he's going to be filled with fear."

But his bark was much louder than his bite, because as usual, this lawyer, like all the rest, didn't ultimately work on Hans' behalf, leading Darinka to tell Daniel,

"I'm done with all this! Just let'em have the money, or donate it to build a new hockey arena for the kids!"

Eventually, Daniel stated that no lawyer at his firm wished to represent them. At wits end, Darinka and Hans were ready to concede defeat, but first Darinka approached Corny's ex-associate, Bezel, seeing if he could recommend a lawyer worth her salt. When Darinka phoned Bezel, he informed her,

"I had a great lawyer from a firm in Toronto in my case against John's old man. He also had this feisty attorney named Jane aside him. She was also suburb!"

The lawyer that represented Bezel had retired, but Hans and Darinka were able to contact this Jane, an imposing woman in her 30's who they eventually successfully aligned with going forward in their search for justice and retribution. During their first discussion, Jane informed Hans and Darinka,

"Hmmm. Interesting. All those lawyers you went to, including Daniel, were involved in my case versus John's father and Roger. Very interesting..."

During this time, just like after Father's first stroke, Hans received various phone calls from Wanda, Rudi, and even Mother, who all demanded to know,

"Where's the money?!?!"

Hans, quite mockingly, before hanging up each time, told them,

You haven't found the money yet? Keep on looking! Even if I knew where, I wouldn't tell you!!"

They ultimately couldn't find anything. Well, at least to Hans' knowledge. After the reading of Father's will, it was declared that Mother shall receive everything, and following her death, the estate shall be split into three; however, such wishes never actually came to fruition. Mother, as she was legally entitled to do, divided up her windfall as she saw fit. First off, she gifted Wanda the "Drake Street apartments", while received Rudi some valuable land from Corny's plentiful estate. Wanda and Gary used CC Friesen Construction money to purchase a penthouse apartment in Naples, Florida. Hans was eventually "bestowed" with the right to buy the construction equipment from the family, yet, only after Mother, Rudi, and Wanda couldn't find any other suitable offers from other potential, more "suitable" suitors. But regardless of the lack of demand for the backhoe, bulldozer, and dump trunk, Mother and Hans' siblings initially refused to even sell the equipment to Hans; yet, since all the equipment was stored in Hans' building, the family couldn't obtain access to it until the rent was paid, rent that the real estate agent calculated to be in the amount of over $170,000 after she saw all of the paperwork. As expected, Hans demanded that this rent for storing the construction equipment in his shop for over a decade be paid since CC Friesen Construction never paid Hans a cent.

Even though the lawyers eventually, on behalf of Mother and the siblings, ultimately reluctantly accepted Hans' bid for the bulldozer, dump trunk, and backhoe at a dealership's assessed value, Hans, nonetheless, never saw a cent for rent that was owed to him. But this was only the tip of the iceberg. Later on, after Corny's death, Darinka calculated that on top of the $170K in unpaid rent, Corny collected an additional $80,000 in rent from Hans' tenants "on behalf of Hans", which Corny withheld for himself. Father justified his refusal to pay rent by constantly reiterating,

"I'm not paying you anything because in the end the company will be yours anyways."

This was all a lie – Hans only possessed 15% of the company – before and after his death. To add insult to injury, months later, after Hans went to Mother's house to discuss the family situation once again, she informed him in a state of rage,

"I consulted with a lawyer! You're disinherited, but you have to look after the apartments for free because you're my son!"

Hans countered, *"I was disinherited the day I was born!"*

There was a recent court ruling at the time in which a mother sued her son and won, forcing him to take care of her. So, Mother concluded that Hans was legally obliged to look after her since he was her oldest child. Yet, what Mother failed to recognize, was that she was in possession of hordes of cash and properties, meaning that she had the means to acquire aid for herself and properties without any assistance from Hans, which would've made Mother's claim absolutely preposterous in the eyes of the courts if her claim ever saw the light of day. Her mental state was so blurred and distorted that she didn't have the wherewithal to recognize that she had enough wealth to take up residence in a lavish retirement home, making her demand ludicrous, especially after she had just disinherited Hans.

This heated discussion between Hans and Mother erupted further right in front of "Tante" Mia and Darinka. Eventually, Mother stood up and screamed,

John Friesen

"I'm gonna get three lawyers to destroy you!"

Hans, in response, only fuelled Mother's fire by saying,

"You've been trying to destroy me for my entire life! You didn't succeed! What did I ever do to you? Why do you hate me so much? Do you really have a reason?"

As he looked deep into her creased eyes, Hans only saw the hatred of a lost soul as she furiously responded with a curt *"No!"* Darinka then interjected, proclaiming to Mother,

"You'll destroy the one who matters the most to you."

Mother, searing with rage was ready to attack Hans. Mia, seeing "her friend" in a fuming state of lunacy told Hans and Darinka,

"Get out before she has a heart attack!"

All this was a far cry from a time when Corny would take Irene, and then Johnny around town to show them "what's going on." On these drives, Corny pointed at all of the properties that he owned and told them, which a certain "Uncle Nick" attested to from his conversations with Corny,

"All of this will be yours one day!"

But when the will was read, Irene's and Johnny's names weren't mentioned once, as if they never even existed. Everyone found that strange. Well, everyone, not surprisingly, besides Wanda and Rudi. An appearance of a tampered will, along with Wanda's and Rudi's cunning will helped them usurp everything from the estate that they could. Or perhaps Corny didn't mean one word of what he said to his grandchildren, meaning that Rudi and Wanda fairly got what they deserved. As with many Friesen family secrets, this one too will probably never be told......

CHAPTER 66

Shareholders' Meeting & Lawsuit

During the first and final **CC** Friesen Construction shareholder meeting, it was established that Hans would personally purchase the company equipment and start a new construction company so he could continue on with his livelihood. Hans eventually restarted the company under the name "**JC** Friesen Construction". As the **CC** Friesen Construction company shareholder meeting proceeded, in which only Hans, Rudi, Mother, and the corresponding attorneys and accountant were intended to attend, Wanda, who had no business being at the meeting, much less putting out any demands, surprisingly entered the room! Despite not owning a single share in the company, Wanda inappropriately made her wishes known, screaming out amongst the lawyers, accountant, and family,

"Mother, don't let him use the Friesen name! Don't let him use the name!!"

The accountant surprisingly interceded.

"He can use his name." (Hans changed the "**CC**" to "**JC**")

But Wanda was only getting started. She in no way wanted this to end harmoniously, so she went on.

"You're overpaid, low-skilled labour!! You deserve nothing!! You should be grateful that we got you out of Russia!!! You must have a big fat chequing account! I know Father stashed your account!"

John Friesen

Wanda appeared jealous of Hans' and Father's business and "personal" relationship, and paranoidly assumed that Corny rewarded him heavily, an insinuation that was quite far from the truth, causing her behaviour to only aid in rubbing salt in Hans' wounds. Infuriated by her comment, Hans, nevertheless, responded with calm composure and a touch of irony.

"What have you done for the family in the last 21 years? Where were you? And where were you born Wanda? In the same place as me."

Wanda and Rudi were left speechless. Well, at least until Wanda senselessly blurted out,

"You're not entitled to anything because you didn't grow up with us! Do you know that while we were growing up Mother threw in our face the fact that you were starving in Russia, so we had no right to be so demanding and unappreciative! How do you think that made us feel!?!!?!"

After the meeting, Hans' lawyer, a piously devote religious man in his 40's, enquired,

"Who was that bitch?"

Hans, with a sarcastic grin across his face, responded, *"You've had the pleasure of meeting my sister."*

Hans then thought back to the moment when Wanda greeted him at the airport in Toronto two decades earlier and realized,

"Her greetings are always warm and bubbly, but that's just a theatrical pretence for the hate that's buried and burning inside of her. My family always tried to portray themselves as noble and classy, but today they revealed to the public who they've truly always been."

Before Hans contemplated even deeper into peoples' fake facades and their deceptive intentions, Mother's attorney, a man called Roger, who allegedly helped Corny embezzle money from his business partner Bezel, approached Hans. After Wanda, Rudi, and Mother left the building, Roger, who at one point also represented Hans, let Hans know,

"They want to bleed you dry! They even want your family house. Your mother believes that since the land value on "her property" has appreciated, she's entitled to more. Her estate is already worth $7.5 million."

Hans casually retorted with a rhetorical question.

"Why do you think her neighbour said that she has a "heart of ice"?"

"And we paid 'em $20K for it! They took our money! Now that old bag wants blood! I then paid them more for that property and home! And that plot was only a ravine until I personally filled it in and developed it for ten years! It only became worth something after I built that nice home on it with my sweat. I got the blocks and concrete for the foundation all by myself!!

*The land **was** in Mother's name, so she thinks she still owns it and is entitled to more! It's legally in my name! The home was registered under the company. I paid the company, but they put the money directly into their pockets! Either way, I was the company! I build the home! They may have helped a bit, but I paid more than my fair share! They just want to milk me dry!!"*

But in the end, Hans and Darinka saw some retribution years later after filing a lawsuit in which they successfully proved, with the help of their lawyer Jane, that Corny crookedly levied a $100,000 mortgage upon Hans' personal industrial building behind Hans' back in order to pay back Bezel. He told Darinka about that lawsuit in confidence.

"Corny and that crooked lawyer of his attempted to swindle money from me on property! The were caught attempting to fraud me! The courts fined that lawyer $80K! Corny had to pay me hundreds of thousands!!"

Corny was ruthless enough to foot Hans and his family with the bill after he was sued, and never paid it back before passing away. Ultimately, the courts ruled that Corny's estate had to pay the $100,000 back to Hans; however, he didn't receive a cent for the hefty interest amount that Hans and Darinka had pay on Corny's $100K mortgage amount. Furthermore, in this lawsuit that pinned Hans right up against his very own mother and siblings, Hans was also rewarded proceeds on the sale of lands linked to property and estates that Hans possessed shares in and was legally entitled to, but sums that Mother and his siblings attempted to withhold from Hans. Nonetheless, these settlement sums were a minute fraction of the remuneration and inheritance that the other two siblings were granted. But that was the price Hans paid for being left behind in Russia, the evident price of not being a "true" member of the Friesen "family".

When Hans learned of the unofficial finalized settlement amount, Hans enquired with the lawyer, *"Is that all?"* Days later she came back with another amount, an amount that matched the value in his dreams from years past. Once again, destiny proved to Hans that dreams are not merely dreams, but rather representations of a prewritten present....

CHAPTER 67

Father's Brother Visits Ka-na-da

When Uncle Jacob of Novosibirsk, Corny's brother, along with his family arrived in Canada one winter, his eyes were also set on a million-dollar windfall. Jacob desired his fair share of his older brother's estate. Upon entry into Mother's house, he immediately scoured everywhere, apparently in search of his mother's rubles that Corny apparently still possessed after immigrating from Germany. Hans knew nothing of Jacob's family trip to Canada, only until he shockingly saw Jacob's family casually strolling by the post office in Beamsville one afternoon as Hans drove home. Following a brief conversation, Hans said that he would pay them a visit. That evening, believing that Mother would be civil in their presence, Hans and his family stopped by Mother's home in order to politely pay the relatives a visit, something that seemed innocent enough. Yet, how wrong could have they been. When Hans, Darinka, Johnny, and Irene arrived, Mother was completely shocked and silently incensed. But rather than cause a scene and tarnish her "spotless" reputation in front her guests from Germany, Mother let Hans' family enter her home for the occasion in order to save face and offer a sense of normalcy in front of her guests from Germany. Though, it didn't take long for a heated discussion relating to the state of affairs following Father's death to erupt, ultimately leading Mother to snap and start screaming at Hans' family.

"Get out!! Get out of my house!!!"

Before everyone knew it, Mother was pushing Hans' family right out of the door! As Mother laid both of her hands on Darinka, she diplomatically responded to Mother,

"We just wanted to say hello to the relatives!"

Darinka's attempt to mollify Mother was deemed as nothing less than a declaration of war, and accordingly, Mother slapped Darinka right across the face! In response, while still in a state of astonishment, Darinka somewhat sarcastically enquired, "Well, *do you feel better now?!?!"* Fuelled with more fury than ever, Mother immediately stormed to her bedroom and locked the door behind her. Darinka followed her behind as a far as the bedroom door where Darinka pleaded with Mother.

"Please tell us why you are doing this to us! We have done nothing to you! We've only showed you respect! If it's the money you want, have it all! Just please tell us why you are doing this to us so we can make some sort of peace in our minds!"

Mother remained silent till the next morning when she unlocked the door to her room and stepped out to tend to her guests. Uncle Jacob's wife was completely blown away by Mother's temperament and this twisted turn of events. When Hans went on to tell her how he was treated before and after Father's untimely death, she couldn't believe it! Uncle Jacob's wife read all of the letters that Mother wrote to Hans while they all lived in Novosibirsk. Mother's words were pleasant, kind, and even loving. Mother expressed her desire to reunite with Hans.

"We want you here!" "We miss you so much!" "Come here and work!" "You can carry on the family business." "We can hardly wait to finally see you again!!"

What Uncle Jacob's wife learned and witnessed with her very own eyes was a far cry from what she had read in those letters prior to Hans' arrival in Canada. She then too began to wonder if Hans leaving the USSR was a blessing or a big disaster no longer in disguise. Yet, when she bore witness to Hans' wonderful wife, kids, and home when her family stopped by for dinner, she could see how blessed Hans truly was. If only he could see that as well.......

CHAPTER 68

Mother Dies

Hans has a vision. Swinging by a rope under a fire that blazes on a dry river bank, Mother cuts the rope with a knife, setting Hans free. Following his release, Hans leaps into the river, avoiding the flames. As he scales the bank to escape the river, Rudi, Wanda, and Gary appear, poking at him with sticks in an attempt to see him drown. Flowing with the current, Hans reaches a lower part of the bank and climbs to solid ground. Hans then awakens. It was only dream. Hans sits up in bed in a sweat, completely blind-sighted by the sight of Mother actually showing him remorse and compassion; still, not surprised by his siblings' desire to push for his demise and death, seemingly seeking revenge. Though, exacting revenge for what will always remain a mystery to Hans.

Days later, Hans receives a phone call from Germany. It's Uncle Jacob (from Novosibirsk) informing Hans that Mother is dead. He's uncharacteristically friendly, and enquires,

"Who exactly is collecting the rent from the apartments over there?

Uncle Jacob then declares,

"I have a million dollars in Canada. It's mine!!! And that mother of yours promised to buy me a car!"

Hans, not totally sure what he means by that comment, casually responds,

John Friesen

"But why are you telling me? I didn't get a cent! "Meiner Mutter war einem Grosse Schwein!" (My mother was a big pig!)"

Hans and his family never attended the funeral. To this day, Hans harbours resentment towards not only his now deceased parents, who both left Hans out of their wills, but also his two conniving siblings who he has broken complete ties with after they attempted to render him and his family homeless while they savoured their lives living lavishly throughout the world.

After Mother's funeral, a 20-cubic yard dumpster suddenly appeared in front of Mother's house one morning. The house was being gutted. Were Wanda and Rudi having the place torn apart in search of "the money" and apparent, hidden Russian golden rubles that Father secretly concealed from the rest of the world? Hans will never know. Only they know. Only they will ever know what drove them to such acts.

On one hand, Hans, let himself savour the little things since he didn't possess these humble luxuries for a large portion of his life. Yet, on the other hand, Hans still carries many burdening thoughts of bitterness and animosity towards his controlling and demeaning family, even though he now has the freedom to live the way he chooses, something he rarely had throughout his life. Consequently, harboured bitter hate silently eats Hans alive on the inside, or occasionally erupts within him for his family to see, leaving him *"rich, but lonely"* – perhaps rich, but lonely until Hans finally forgives his family and himself for subjecting his immediate family to such ugliness while acknowledging that disparaging words should never be heeded and contemplated over. Maybe only then will he be set free, free from feeling lonely with his own suffocating thoughts and shackling resentment for a family and siblings who got everything, even after all their malicious deeds and behaviour, behaviour from a family who made Hans feel like he never belonged, yet behaviour that seemingly got rewarded. Behaviour that stills haunts Hans between the moments that he carries the same cheerful, youthful spirit and blind optimism that helped him persevere through all his trials and tribulations in life.

Despite amassing his own wealth through his and Darinka's perseverance, Hans learns the exact meaning of *"rich, but lonely"* by resenting the ones who deemed riches as a replacement, ones who too live *"rich, but lonely."* But at least now Hans has a story to tell. Perhaps a story is all what we need, all what we have to tell in the end and nothing more. Maybe life is only about having a story to tell.......

Printed in the United States
By Bookmasters